The Muses' Library

★

PLAYS AND POEMS
OF
THOMAS LOVELL BEDDOES

THOMAS LOVELL BEDDOES

Photograph at Pembroke College, Oxford,
after the portrait by Nathan C. Branwhite, painted 1824

PLAYS AND POEMS
OF
THOMAS LOVELL
BEDDOES

edited
with an introduction
by

H. W. DONNER

Like the red outline of beginning Adam

HARVARD UNIVERSITY PRESS
CAMBRIDGE, MASSACHUSETTS

CONTENTS

PREFATORY NOTE

THE present collection of the Plays and Poems of Beddoes is far from complete, yet more than a Selection. It contains two comparative novelties. The early version of *Death's Jest-Book* is here for the first time printed *in toto*, so that it is now possible to read it exactly as Beddoes had intended it to be printed in 1829, whereas all later revisions are presented as Fragments. The second edition of the Anti-Strauss Greeting, also, containing additional notes, is now reprinted for the first time since its publication, the text included in the Oxford edition being in fact the first version, although erroneously described as the second in the Bibliography. It is always gratifying to acknowledge one's errors, and I am glad of this opportunity of correcting another mistake. A manuscript acquired by Colonel Wilkinson, containing the fragmentary *New-Born Star* ('An earth is born') and the *Tree of Life*, shows that these poems should both be given to the Southampton period or the previous year, as indicated by the watermark 1822. Neither is included in the present edition, the publication in one volume necessitating some excisions. Other omissions comprise the whole of the *Juvenilia*. For the rest some of the earlier and feebler attempts at lyrical poetry and fragments consisting of only one or two lines have been omitted. None of these excisions seem to call for an apology. Regrettable, however, is the inevitable omission of later fragments.

With the exceptions mentioned, the text is that of the Oxford edition throughout, and the numbers of the Dramatic Fragments assigned to them in that edition have been retained, except, for obvious reasons, where *Death's Jest-Book* is concerned, the Fragments of which are presented in an arrangement reflecting the action of the play. Where the titles given by Kelsall differ from Beddoes' own, the poet's have been preferred, but to facilitate reference those of Kelsall's edition may be identified in the Index. The arrangement of the texts is consistently chronological, so that both poems and dramatic fragments composed during the same period appear in juxtaposed sequence. Exceptions are unavoidably made within the different groups and this applies most particularly to the Fragments of *Death's Jest-Book*. I have abstained from all documentation of facts in the Introduction, the references being accessible in the present editor's *T. L. Beddoes*; *the Making of a Poet*, Blackwells, 1935, *The Works of T. L. Beddoes* and *The Browning Box*, both published by the Oxford University Press, 1935.

I beg to express my sincere thanks to Professor C. A. Weber who has supplied me with photostats of the *Anti-Straussianischer Graus-Gruss* in Tübingen University Library. I wish to thank also Mr. John Woodward who has been kind enough to read the manuscript of my Introduction. I am greatly indebted to the Oxford University Press for permission to use the Oxford text and equally to Messrs. Blackwell, who have kindly allowed me to quote from my biography of Beddoes. For kind permission to use other copyright material I beg to thank Sir John Murray for the passage from Browning's letter to Kelsall, Messrs. Chatto and Windus for the extract from Lytton Strachey's *Books and Characters*, and Mr. Edmund Blunden for the quotation from *Votive Tablets*. Finally I beg to offer my thanks to the Master, Fellows and Scholars of Pembroke College for permission to reproduce the photograph of the portrait.

H. W. D.

Oxford
  June 1948

INTRODUCTION

INTRODUCTION

ON 26 January 1849, at 9.30 in the evening, died at Basle in Switzerland, aged forty-five, Thomas Lovell Beddoes, 'de Bristol'—'Gentilhomme Anglais, Rentier'—in his lifetime one of the most obscure but after his death slowly recognized as one of the most remarkable of English poets; in the late Lytton Strachey's phrase, 'the last Elizabethan', but equally, in an age of Romantic exhaustion, the first of the moderns. The official records gave the cause of death as 'apoplexy', and not until forty years later were the real circumstances publicly disclosed as suicide, his death being the result of a poison he had taken, found in his possession. Nor was this the first attempt. A little more than six months earlier Beddoes had been received at the Basle Hospital out of the Cigogne Hotel, where, as the official records affirm, 'he had cut open an artery in his [left] leg'. The story was told in Basle how he kept tearing off the bandages in his determined effort to end a physical existence which had by then become a burden and a hindrance to his spiritual growth and aspirations. Little less than twenty years earlier, on 24 August 1829, the Pro-Rector of Göttingen University had recommended to his colleagues on the University Court that the sentence of relegation, pronounced on Beddoes, should take the most lenient form and be communicated to him as gently as possible, because he had learned from several sources that Beddoes had lately shown a tendency to spleen and even tried to commit suicide. From about this time dates his beautiful philosophy, which teaches that there is one source of all spiritual existence, the soul of the universe itself, and that the thirst for knowledge (so ardently sought by Beddoes all his life) is nothing but the desire of the individual to return to the home of his birth. The search for truth is thus identical with the wish to die, and the greater is the spiritual part within us, the more intense must be our wish to be reunited with that spring of spiritual power from which our lives flow like sparkling rivulets.

Beddoes is above all others the poet of death. Nobody has arrayed her (for Death had been revealed to him as a warm and tender mother) in such alluring beauty, nobody has clad physical corruption in such unspeakable horror, nobody spoken with such nostalgic longing of the death he was himself to seek so persistently. Out of their security the Victorians regarded his preoccupation as morbid, but we are gradually learning, in the school of devastating world wars, that

> *Life's a single pilgrim,*
> *Fighting unarmed amongst a thousand soldiers.*

And the throbbing presence of facts spiritual in his verse forbids any facile condemnation. Exactly because Beddoes viewed the death of the body in such lurid light, a firmer conviction of the immortality of the spirit forced itself upon him, and he became a prophet of a richer life in death. There is an almost threatening note in his latest fragments, as if he meant to say: Beware, the spirit will yet get the better of you. His self-inflicted death, whatever momentary misery may have been the direct cause, was the triumphant close of a career devoted to the discovery of proofs physical and spiritual of man's survival in another sphere. His suicide was an act of faith. For metaphysic as he was in a Germany of the early nineteenth century, dominated by the thought of Schelling, in the Middle Ages he would have been a devout whose visionary powers would have received direction towards the inner sources of religion and whose faith might have stood the test of martyrdom, although it is most likely that he would have been burned as a heretic and one not easily submitting to authority.

He knew death early, for he was only five and a half years old, when his father, 'the celebrated Dr. Beddoes', died on Christmas eve 1808. His death drew from Coleridge some of the most deep-felt utterances of grief recorded in his letters, and Southey said that from Dr. Beddoes he had 'hoped for more good to the human race than any other individual'. Both had been his patients, as well as Wordsworth; and Coleridge had wished to become his biographer. John George Lambton, Earl of Durham, lived as an orphan under his roof, and the Doctor was the promoter also of Sir Humphrey Davy, for he was, in the latter's words, 'good, great and generous'. James Watt was his early collaborator, and he left his children under the guardianship of Sir Davies Gilbert, M.P., P.R.S., scientist and antiquary. His wife, Anna, was the sister of Maria Edgeworth, daughters among twenty children of another remarkable man, Richard Lovell Edgeworth, educationalist, inventor, and practical philosopher. Nothing short of genius could have earned for Dr. Beddoes such a galaxy of friends and associates. And genius he undoubtedly possessed, universal, though erratic and inconstant.

His university career as Reader in chemistry at Oxford was interrupted from too ardent a zeal for the French revolution and open opposition to the government, but in the five years of his readership he had become known as a stimulating teacher and a pioneer of German learning and philosophy. His experiments had been bold and ingenious though inconclusive. He now turned his energies to the translation of learned foreign works and to authorship in verse and prose.

His poem on *Alexander's Expedition down the Hydaspes and the Indus to the Indian Ocean,* with copious learned notes, is one on the strangest books in English. His prose served an educational purpose. *The History of Isaac Jenkins, and Sarah his wife, and their three children,* to whose literary merits Mr. E. H. W. Meyerstein has drawn attention,[1] was designed to prevent drunkenness by instruction and so improve the physical and mental health of the people. His *Hygeia; or Essays moral and medical, on the causes affecting the personal state of our middling and affluent classes,* in three volumes, was part of his work for the propagation of the knowledge of the elements of medicine among the public, intended to effect the results of modern preventive medicine. In spite of the strangeness of his cures he enjoyed the highest reputation as practitioner, but his services to science were chiefly connected with the Pneumatic Institution which he erected at Bristol Hotwells for novel experiments with 'facticious airs'. Both Coleridge and Southey were among the first to sniff out of the green bag the nitrous oxide now known as 'laughing gas', whose properties, then unexplored, 'converted', says Cottle, the publisher, 'the laboratory into the region of hilarity and relaxation'.

Education interested the Doctor not only as a means of improving the health of the adult population. He was the instigator of the chapter on toys in his father-in-law's book on *Practical Education* and himself took the initiative of a subscription for rational toys. He believed also that instruction on sexual matters should be 'gravely, decently and early imparted to children of a tender age.' It was to start with natural history and the anatomy of animals and proceed through the dissection of pregnant frogs and hens to the witnessing of 'the labour-pains of a domestic quadruped'. As the

[1] *English,* III, 13, 1940, pp. 8–15.

loving father he was, 'he never secluded himself for
the purposes of study', says his biographer, Dr. Stock,
but 'it was uniformly his wish that his wife and
children should be in the same apartment'. There is no
telling what sights fed the observant eyes of the little
boy who was later to be 'for ever haunted' by the
problem and presence of death.

The Doctor was not universally popular, for he
was above all independent and possessed of a proud
reserve and coldness of manner when confronted with
strangers, but in the society of intimate friends he
could, says Richard Warner, the historian of Bath,
'exercise those powers of conversation, with which he
was highly endowed, but which he seldom displayed,
in general society'. 'Nothing', however, says Sir Humphry Davy, 'could be a stronger contrast to his apparent coldness in discussion, than his wild and active
imagination, which was as poetical as Darwin's.'

From his father, it seems, the poet inherited his
sense of independence and justice, his passion for truth
and universal thirst for knowledge, his keen interest in
languages and science, principally medicine; and it
seems no accident that it was in comparative anatomy
that he 'narrowly escaped becoming professor' at
Zürich. From his father also he seems to have derived
his visionary cast of mind, combined, however, with
his lack of method and sustained effort. His revolutionary pathos and benevolence towards political
refugees seem equally part and parcel of his paternal
inheritance. But the Doctor's eminent gift for literary
composition and poetical pastiche may well have been
reinforced by the Edgeworth strain in his son. For,
according to Sir Humphry Davy, the poet's mother
'possessed a fancy almost *poetical* in the highest sense
of the word, great warmth of affection, and dis-
interestedness of feeling, and, under favourable circumstances she would have been, even in talents, a

rival of Maria'. These gentler traits the poet shared, though, unhappily, the strong reserve, inherited from his father, seems to have disabled him from bringing them to bear on human relationships.[1]

According to the Church Registers the poet was born on 30 June 1803, at 3 Rodney Place, Clifton, and there he spent his childhood until he was eight years old, when his mother with the elder sister, himself, and a younger brother and sister went to live for three years at Great Malvern. In 1814 the family removed to Bath, and the boys entered the Grammar School. Occasional visits to Edgeworth-Town in Ireland should not be forgotten, because their aunt Maria then entertained the children with theatricals and old Edgeworth probably read, as was his habit, 'from the Arabian Tales to Shakespeare, Milton, Homer and the Greek Tragedians'. What appears to have become annual visits to Cheney Longville, the family seat in Shropshire, commenced in 1816, and in the correspondence of his guardian the poet soon emerges in a strong physical likeness to his father.

At Charterhouse School, where he entered in June 1817, he gained at once a high standing in the fifth form and, before he left, was the second boy of the school, having obtained at least three prizes for Latin and Greek compositions. His school-fellows remembered him too and contributed their impressions to Kelsall's Memoir of the poet more than thirty years later. One of them, Charles Dacres Bevan, had been his fag and thought he was something of a tyrant, but this impression was emphatically contradicted by friends who had known him for many years of his later life as always 'considerate, kind, benevolent, just' in his treatment of others. To the pensioners of the

---

[1] The best contribution on the subject of the poet's parents has come from the pen of Professor C. C. Abbot, *Durham University Journal*, 34, 1941–2, pp. 159–75.

Charterhouse, however, he was a terror, and Bevan gives an amusing description of his fights with 'Cod Sine-Breech', who used to hire a drummer of the guards as reinforcement. And when a truce was called, it was habitually celebrated with lobsters, oysters, porter and gin, and young Beddoes entertained his ex-enemies and his compulsory ally Bevan with singing and dancing and parodies of the famous actors he had seen on the stage, particularly, we are told, of Kean and Macready.

Beddoes, who was as little interested in games as his father had been before him at Bridgenorth, had a passion for the theatre and was both a good actor himself and a good judge of it. He performed many old English plays, and Bevan enjoyed them, in spite of being forced into them and having to submit to Beddoes' kicks or caresses, as the part required. He knew Shakespeare well when he came to the Charterhouse, and while he was there made himself familiar with the whole range of British drama. Sometimes he performed little scenes of his own invention. A locksmith, who had overcharged him for a bad lock, was made to regret it when he next came to work and Beddoes staged an interlude 'representing his last moments, disturbed by horror and remorse for his sins in the matter of the lock, his death, and funeral procession, which was interrupted by fiends who bore the body off to accompany the soul to eternal torments'.

No less spectacular was his appearance in defence of the threatened liberties of his fellows. Hockey, that had been played in the cloisters since time out of mind, was suddenly forbidden, and although he had never been seen with a hockey stick in his hand, Beddoes promptly decided to captain one of the teams and turned up looking 'ferociously grave' with feathers in his cap and a cardboard shield with a doubled fist for device and inscribed with the proud motto of the republican martyr Algernon Sidney, 'Manus haec inimica tyrannis'. The laughter of the masters ensured the continuance of the traditional game.

Bevan records more practical jokes contrived by Beddoes. He was usually forgiven, partly because his stern judges could not help laughing, partly for the perfect order he kept as prefect of his house. But even more remarkable was the ascendancy he acquired over his fellows. The nicknames he assigned to the 'Cods' were not the only ones he invented, and they stuck like leeches. He invented also a kind of slang which continued being spoken at Charterhouse for years after he had left, not out of love for its author, but from a conviction of its aptness. In the same way he was later to create a domain particularly his own in the realm of English poetry.

It appears to have been quite a fashion with schoolboys at that particular time to write tales of terror, and one by Beddoes has survived called *Scaroni, or The Mysterious Cave. A Romantic Fiction*, probably written before he was fifteen. Bevan records another title, *Cynthio and Bugboo*, and there is no reason to believe that Beddoes did not write more than one story while still at school. He certainly published a poem in the *Morning Post* in 1819 on the subject of a *Comet* then seen over London. He probably wrote the greater part of *Leopold*, the least mature of the fyttes of *The Improvisatore*, and perhaps *Alfarabi*. He may even have written a complete tragedy at Charterhouse, as Bevan asserts, but it could not have been *The Brides' Tragedy*, which was certainly not begun before his second year at Oxford. Mere fragments of his dramatic writings during his school days have survived.

In late April 1820 Sir Davies Gilbert accompanied his ward to Oxford, where Beddoes immediately went into residence at Pembroke, his father's college as well as his guardian's, not to mention Dr. Johnson. While still a freshman he published, in March 1821, a volume of verse, *The Improvisatore, In three fyttes, With Other Poems*. It is a volume now exceedingly rare, for growing ashamed of his youthful extravaganzas in later years he destroyed every copy on which he could lay his hands, visiting the bookshelves of his friends and cutting out the pages, leaving the binding intact but robbed of its contents. There seem to be no more than six or seven copies extant to-day. The verse tales are as full of death and horror as ever *Scaroni*, but also of a beauty of imagery and loveliness of fancy, a poetical richness, that in a poet not yet eighteen necessarily foreshadowed better things to come. His feeling for nature is conspicuous, and many passages of great beauty evince his familiarity with the evening sky. His descriptive power was better developed than the narrative, and the lyrical poems at the end of the volume are full of happy conceits, woven into arabesque patterns.

His next publication, *The Brides' Tragedy*, which appeared on the last of November 1822, shares in the same qualities, combined, however, with a visionary boldness of the imagination and a marked love for Elizabethan patterns of diction and phrasing. The dramatic blank verse is almost incredibly good for such a young man, and excited the whole-hearted admiration of his contemporaries. He was lauded by practically all the periodicals of the day, and George Darley in the *London Magazine* hailed him as 'a scion worthy of the stock from which Shakespeare and Marlow sprung'. The private correspondence of literary men echoed his name, and John Forster was to tell us nearly thirty years later that 'it became for a time the town-talk to speak of him'. A successful poetical career seemed to be cut out for him, but apart from *The*

Romance of the Lily in the following year Beddoes published next to nothing for the rest of his life.

Bevan, who followed the poet to Oxford in 1824, tells us of his rebellion against the college authorities, and how he brought his attendance at his tutor's classes to an end by going there with the pages of his book uncut, and when told to open them, disappearing only to get 'the largest butcher's knife he could buy, with which he begun to cut the leaves'. But Bevan had the story from Beddoes himself, and it may have been slightly exaggerated. Bevan also received the impression that he kept aloof from all society, but, if I am right in thinking that another contemporary and college friend, J. G. H. Bourne, has given his impressions of the poet under a fictitious name in one of his novels, this tells a different story. Meeting him in later years, says the author, he was much surprised at his change of manner:

'Now he appeared quiet, thoughtful, and retiring; at that time he had been the gayest of the gay, idle, and apparently thoughtless; yet he had obtained a character for singular talents, both with his tutors and his associates. The former considered that he must learn everything by a species of intuition, as they could never hear of his reading, and yet found him always prepared with his lectures; and the latter never saw him flinch from his glass or from any scheme of mischief; but, on the contrary, always prepared to enter into fresh frolics and fresh excesses. The truth was, that Derwent had a method in his madness. The exuberance of his animal spirits prevented his retiring from that society where he ever found himself so welcome an addition, and the applause that his jokes and his songs, which were always allowed to have more point and wit than those of any other, never failed to obtain, held him fast by those 'adamantine' bonds of vanity, which have such a spell over children of riper years. But, when the last echo of mirth had died away, and the last merry companion had staggered from his room, he would retreat from the scene of debauch to the quiet recess of his study, bind a wet towel round his burning temples, and with that head-dress sit down to

Unsphere the spirit of Plato,

or pursue the subtle distinctions of the Stagyrite. Nor did he confine his studies to the routine of tutorial guidance, or expect them to lead him to the prize of academical distinction. Such a prize, if worth any thing, he considered merely as the means of introduction, and a testimonial of recommendation. His real aim was to qualify himself for his appearance on the grand stage of life, the theatre of the world.'

The flavour, not even yet quite stale, of his college jokes seems to survive in his *Masque in the Moon.*

His lightheartedness in term-time, however, made it necessary for him to work in vacation, and so he went to spend the summer of 1823 at Southampton to read for his degree, wisely provided with an introduction from one of his kindly reviewers, the poet B. W. Procter, alias Barry Cornwall, to a lawyer's apprentice, Thomas Forbes Kelsall, who was to become the guardian of his manuscripts and literary fame, his future editor and biographer. From the first moment of their acquaintance Kelsall received the strongest possible impression of Beddoes' genius, and to him we owe a characterization of the poet as he was then and appeared later, invaluable to the student of his life and art.

What struck Kelsall most forcibly was Beddoes' 'manly, uncompromising independence' both of bearing and judgement. Looking back many years later to the beginnings of their friendship his admiration could not but increase for the precocious maturity of Beddoes' literary and scholastic achievements, for the inexhaustible power and originality of his creative genius, and for the unassailable integrity of his character. He loved literature with the whole ardour of his youthful being, but his aim was of the highest, as that of the young will be, and although he admired Wordsworth and Keats he gave his ungrudging allegiance to Shelley alone among his immediate predecessors and his inmost heart was with Shakespeare and the Elizabethans. With the merely pretty and sentimental, favoured by his contemporaries, he had little patience, and he asserted his views with a downrightness almost shocking even to his admirers. The purely intellectual never lost its fascination for him, and intellect and imagination were to remain to him nothing but different instruments used for the same end, different ways towards the same goal—the discovery of truth. In the combination of intellect and poetry in the Elizabethan dramatists he could see his own aims achieved, and Kelsall was anxious to emphasize that, whatever affinity might be discerned between them, Beddoes was not an imitator of the founders of the British stage but a congenial mind working on living material, not on models 'taken from the marble of the tomb'.

Nobody could be a better companion than Beddoes at this early age, and even if he liked to talk of literature more than anything he would brighten any subject with glimpses of poetic learning or grotesque humour. He adored discussion and would not seldom exaggerate his own views for the sake of argument. Through Kelsall's long-winded lawyer's prose we can hear the 'squeaks' of 'the Fool himself' as he appeared, to Bourne at Pembroke and to Kelsall at Southampton or tasting with congenial companions the 'joys of Joy' at the Grand Hotel in Covent Garden. His good temper remained unruffled throughout his life and his dislikes never deteriorated into hatreds, but that he could be often provocative in his younger days and that his cold and reserved manner in after life was not invariably winning, of this Kelsall makes no secret. 'To the sordid vices he was altogether a stranger', and Kelsall makes a special point of the fact that Beddoes never bothered to try and increase the modest fortune that had come down to him from his father, being contented 'to pass through life with a very moderate, almost philosophic competence'. Apart from taking dutiful advantage of his guardian's privilege as an M.P. of free postage during his minority, he never sought to use family connexions for his own ends or his own promotion. Ambition he had none, unless it were that of one day becoming worthy of the praise bestowed on his early production, or, objectively, of enriching the domains of poetry and reviving British drama. His modesty was a model to all, and he never willingly spoke either of himself or of his works or projects.

Not without reason Kelsall was alarmed at the complete indifference with which Beddoes treated his manuscripts, destroying such as did not serve his immediate purpose, and so Kelsall determined to become his keeper and the guardian of his literary output. When going to Germany, two years later, as he thought for a short stay, the poet was to leave his early notebooks and other manuscripts in a trunk in London. Winter coming on, he needed his woolies and requested Kelsall to send them. From the manuscripts he asked to be excused, leaving it to Kelsall's discretion what was to be done with them, 'recommending them however to the dispensation of fire and sword'. Kelsall did no such thing. Poems addressed to Procter or Bourne also during Beddoes' long years of exile he obtained and copied. Every letter to himself he preserved. Whatever Beddoes wrote Kelsall's heart was in it. However embarrassing in life such devotion received its due in death. It was to Kelsall that Beddoes was to bequeath his manuscripts, and never did a literary executor tackle his task with more tactful enthusiasm. Devoting all his time to it, within a year of the poet's death Kelsall was to bring out *Death's Jest-Book*, overcoming the scruples of the Beddoes family by publishing anonymously and omitting all that might give offence to 'ears polite'. His discretion was rewarded, and in the following year he was able to issue the *Poems by the Late Thomas Lovell Beddoes ... With a Memoir*. Yet he was not to rest until the safety of the manuscripts seemed provided for. He had not been able to publish everything. The prose passages of *Death's Jest-Book* had been largely suppressed; the tales of *The Ivory Gate* were unprinted; poems and fragments remained in manuscript. Some scraps he had given away to admirers of the poet. The bulk he was to bequeath to Robert Browning whose enthusiasm for Beddoes had led Kelsall to believe that his great friend might rise to fame on the shoulders of the Victorian colossus. But between the decision and the deed was to come the discovery of the suicide. Browning deputed the task to Gosse, and Gosse was to do much for Beddoes. He wrote brilliantly about him; he added to the printed works; he made him loved as far, perhaps, as a poet of Beddoes' 'macabre' genius will ever be loved. But he shied off the labours of editing, and his notorious inaccuracy seems to have for ever endangered the recognition of the truth about Beddoes' life. His superficial inspection ended, the manuscripts were to disappear, never to be traced. Yet Beddoes' spirit of contradiction was to assert itself even in death and Kelsall's faith prove justified. For although Browning had relied on Gosse to edit *Death's Jest-Book* and the other poems as they stood in Beddoes' manuscripts, he had not withheld them from earnest inquirers like Dykes Campbell, who with an industry equalled only by Kelsall and with impeccable accuracy had taken copies *quasi facsimile* of Beddoes' holographs and of all the papers bearing on his biography in the 'Browning Box', assembled by Kelsall, so that, triumphing over time, they could be given to the world. In view of after-events the friendship formed with Kelsall in the summer of 1823 thus acquires an importance far in excess of what can have been apparent to either of them on their green rambles along the shores of the Solent.

In Kelsall's Memoir we get as near to the man Beddoes as we are likely ever to do. What incidents from his later life can be adduced in illustration of his character, only serve to complete the picture and to show how deep Kelsall had seen into his friend's nature. The lights and shades will always vary in the portraits of the same model by different artists, but in Kelsall's characterization, I have little doubt, is the essential Beddoes. It is perhaps significant that of the inner struggles, which must have been the lot of Beddoes no less than that of other highly imaginative people, artists and poets, more than other humans, even this devoted friend knew nothing. Even Bourne, the most congenial, I believe, of Beddoes' friends, could say no more in explanation of his erratic genius than the bare statement that 'Derwent' was 'made up of odd notions and wild principles'; again provided that my identification of Derwent with the poet is not mistaken.

The summer of 1823 and the following year or two were the most prolific in Beddoes' authorship. 'His poetic composition', says Kelsall, 'was then exceedingly facile:

'more than once or twice has he taken home with him at night some unfinished act of a drama, in which the editor had found much to admire, and, at the next meeting, has produced a new one, similar in design, but filled with other thoughts and fancies, which his teeming imagination had projected, in its sheer abundance, and not from any feeling, right or fastidious, of unworthiness in its predecessor. Of several of these very striking fragments, large and grand in their aspect as they each started into form,

Like the red outline of beginning Adam,

and not unworthy indeed to be associated with that Sistine creation of Michael Angelo, the only trace remaining is literally the impression thus deeply cut into their one observer's mind. The fine verse just quoted is the sole remnant, indelibly stamped on the editor's memory, of one of these extinct creations.'

We must share Kelsall's regret at the loss of so much of the easy production of those years, for the time was to come when writing became laborious to a poet estranged from his own language during decades of foreign residence. But Kelsall was right in his high appreciation of Beddoes' early work. There is that rare richness in it of poetic imagery, flowing with the abundance of a soul steeped in poetry, such as Shakespeare had, and Spenser, Marlowe, Shelley. There is imaginative power of the first order, a power to give life to objects dead to ordinary people, a visualization of the abstract, a spiritualization of the concrete, entirely out of the common reach even of poets. He can see 'a pale soul Fluttering in rocky hell' with such vividness that the image goes to illustrate the less immaterial but perhaps more exotic sight of a trochilus picking the teeth of a crocodile. He can compress the universe in a living image, seeing new-born stars bouncing like 'light deer Down a hill',

And the interstellar vale,
Through which some aged patient globe
(Whose gaunt sides no summers robe),
Like a prisoner through his grate,
Shivering in despair doth wait
For sunbeams broken, old, and pale.

On the other hand, he can give immensity to the aspirations of man, and describe the feelings of frustration, felt by

Man's ghost immortal,
Whom the corpse's earthen fences
From his vast existence bar.

There is already that quality in his verse of a fluttering bird beating its wings against the mirror of eternity.

Of the plays which occupied him during this period only fragments survive out of his notebooks. The finished parts of *The Last Man* and *Love's Arrow Poisoned* he took away with him to Germany, and what was not destroyed went into the making of *Death's Jest-Book*. Nowhere is his power more obvious than in these fragments, nowhere the imagery bolder or loftier. But what he lacked in dramatic composition was the faculty of sustained creation, the ability to concentrate on essentials in unfolding the story, of making characters credible in a natural situation, and of making them speak like human beings. They are all too Beddoesian, skating as it were on the thinnest of ice, 'that glassy interval 'twixt us and nothing', to use his own phrase, adopted with such satisfaction by Mr. Walter de la Mare.[1] And the plots are crowded with incident until the outlines become confused, each detail being worked out with all the intensity and passion at the command of this singularly gifted poet, but the whole broken irreparably to bits by the very

---

[1] *Behold, This Dreamer*, Faber and Faber, 1939.

strength of the single scenes. To that intensity of feeling we owe one of his finest achievements, *Torrismond*, written probably in the autumn of 1824, in which all the poet's pent-up passion had to vent itself in the first act, and he was unable to continue. We may say it was a mercy that the fragment was brought to a close before the whole parade of banquets and masques, conjuring and incest, murder and suicide was unrolled, but such was not Beddoes' intention. In *The Second Brother*, written apparently during the following winter, the full riot is let loose. There is plenty of grand rhetoric, poetry of the most exalted brand, a nervous energy almost unique, plenty of what used to be called 'tragic passion', but of human feeling not an inkling. Neither brother has one word of regret, much less of sorrow, for the death of his own brother; the succession to a petty throne is all that matters. But Beddoes himself knew full well the futility of thrones and was striving after something very much more important. Hence one after the other of his elaborately artificial plots was discarded and abandoned. Nothing but the perfect would satisfy him, and in his constant grappling with the stubborn material of his plots, he did achieve perfection in the creation of a dramatic blank verse, unequalled since the days of Shakespeare. Hence he could sacrifice without regret the unsuccessful plots which had served his apprenticeship. That a great mass of irrecoverable poetry was thrown on the fire at the same time he did not give one thought, for he was looking forward to pour his whole soul into a play of a power sufficient to regenerate the British stage, and he felt himself step by step accumulating that power.

It seems to me most probable that something happened which was to turn his thoughts in a special direction. In order to understand what it was, however, it is necessary to look again to his life of which we must not lose sight in analysing his mind. It would seem as if he applied himself fairly regularly to his academic studies even during the days and nights crowded with poetic visions at Southampton; and of his capacity for work there is ample proof. He could thus afford to stay away from Oxford, where during his first two years he had been in the habit of spending his Christmas and Easter vacations, perhaps because his family had become more inaccessible, living first in Jersey, then in northern France on account of the elder daughter's health. One such visit away from Oxford must have been to the Vicar of Great Malvern, Henry Card, either during the summer of 1822 or the following Michaelmas Term when he played truant to Oxford, probably while helping his friend, the clergyman, antiquary and playwright, in defining the different conceptions of the character of Caractacus in British drama. After the fruitful summer at Southampton in 1823 he went to Bristol in the New Year 1824 to stay with his aunt Emmeline King, *née* Edgeworth, and her husband, John King, olim König, Swiss by birth, but naturalized British and acclimatized Bristolian, formerly a student of theology, later surgeon, assistant to the poet's father, and a gifted amateur artist. And here again we get a glimpse of the living Beddoes, for Zoë King, his first cousin, was to tell Kelsall in later years that he was deeply attached to his 'godmother' and enjoyed her company. His own letters bear witness to his admiration and respect for his Clifton 'demi-uncle'. With him he frequently discussed literature and art, with his wife he often indulged in verbal contest for fun and in great friendliness, one of the subjects especially remembered by Zoë King being the merits of Pope's poetry, which her mother most particularly admired. Apparently she had a gift of bringing out all that was best in him, and he could give up 'his own strong *Beddoes* dislikes' in order to please her, and even submitted to going to evening parties and paying morning calls on his father's friends, although he did not like them himself. She also prevailed upon him to sit for his portrait, and so he was immortalized by the Bristol artist Nathan Branwhite in March 1824 in the 'shorn condition' consequent upon a severe illness which necessitated the cutting of his hair. The visit was to be repeated twelve months later, and in after-years it would seem as if Beddoes looked back occasionally with regret to the happy home-life he had shared with the Kings at Clifton.

On 6 May Beddoes commenced the examination for his degree at Oxford, but had to interrupt it on the 9th, on an urgent summons from his mother's death-bed at Florence. She had actually died four days earlier, although the news did not reach London till the 21st. Beddoes travelled a good deal slower and does not seem to have arrived at Florence much before the middle of June. All he could now do was to escort his sisters back to England, and he may even have accompanied them to Edgeworth-Town. On the way out he had seen opera and ballet in Paris and Milan and made acute comment on the performances in his letters. In Florence he called on Landor to whom he brought a letter of introduction, but now as ever, wherever he wandered in his vagrant life, he found his best recommendation in his father's name and reputation.

I think his mother must have meant much to him, not least because for some years he had been almost entirely separated from her. To her in filial pride he had dedicated *The Improvisatore*. Her poetical nature, charm and liveliness can hardly have failed to make her an object of his youthful adoration, and as far as his feminine characters are drawn from life, and not as was more frequently the case from literature, they seem to reflect a filial relationship rather than amorous. However that may be, his mother's death seems to have cut deep into his being. A change seems to come suddenly over his world of thought and feeling, as if a thick cloud had obscured the sun and turned noon into midnight. This change is especially noticeable in his attitude to death, which from now on comes to constitute a problem where before there was none.

It is true that in all his early poems there are corpses and charnelhouses, and even more characteristically loving embraces bestowed on the bodies of the dead. Literary fashion encouraged scenes of horror, and they need be taken no more seriously than Beddoes seems to have taken them himself, except perhaps that the particular incident, so often repeated in his youthful work, of a child literally poking death in the eye may have had something to do with his father's dissections of animals for the highly laudable purpose of familiarizing his children with natural phenomena and the zoological process of generation. It would seem as if Beddoes had become a little too familiar with such scenes. But there is nothing but enjoyment of them in his early verse, and from a different aspect he had viewed delightedly the dead bodies

Turning to daisies gently in the grave.

But, if it is not too hazardous to draw conclusions from a correspondence only fragmentarily preserved, the mere thought of the possibility of his mother's death seems to have produced in him an unbearable feeling of loneliness and fear. Once she was dead a horror of death comes over him, and in the forceful *Lines Written at Geneva* on the homeward journey his childish visions and, perhaps, his childish games in his father's zoological laboratory return in the awful aspect of the newly dead beholding

Their weary flesh, like an used mansion, sold
Unto a stranger, and see enter it
The earthquake winds and waters of the pit,
Or children's spirits in its holes to play.

If it stood alone this passage would count for little. It does not. The image returns in the shape of a nightmare *Dream of Dying* and is immediately followed in the same note-book by an even more awe-inspiring rendering of the same vision in *Leonigild's Apprehension*, apparently written in the following autumn. Nor did it cease haunting until years later.

Now literary fashion may account for much and may certainly explain why contemporaries like Beddoes and Poe should both employ the apparatus of the novel of terror, but even the vogue for Gothic romance during their formative years cannot supply the key to Beddoes' utter horror for many years to come of the physical fact of death and corruption or to that agonizing fear of himself of Poe's which gives to his spook fantasies the reality of life. Hence I believe that Beddoes, whose intimate contact with nature made him, St. Francis-like, recognize a fellow in all God's creatures, had indeed in his first and tenderest childhood become familiar with impressions from which the majority are mercifully spared. From the moment he realized what it all meant he withdrew within himself, contact with others became increasingly difficult, and his mind was forcibly turned in the one direction of the problem of death and its solution.

Fortunately this is a problem of two aspects, the physical and the spiritual. Beddoes would not have been a Romantic, born in the first years of the nineteenth century, unless he had shared in the contemporary belief in a spirit of man all powerful and even more potent than reason, which in the preceding ages had made man lord of creation. This is the theme which principally occupied him in the plays and poems now to be written. We need but scratch the surface of his verse to find beneath it the palpitations of his heart, the longings of his spirit to transcend merely physical limitations, the utter loneliness and the yearnings of humanity for love and friendship

> *In this December world, with men of ice,*
> *Cold sirs and madams.*

We can see the raw flesh bleeding in a way we could not, if the poet had succeeded in endowing his dramatic characters with an existence of their own, independent and objective. But he was too self-involved to make them speak any other language than his own, and so every line becomes, however imaginary the situation, a revelation of his own striving self.

The discarding of so many partly worked-out plots and unfinished plays is in itself a sign of his development. Most of the early stories he invented are sufficiently alike to justify one in regarding them as little more than variations on a single theme. We see it outlined in the draft for *Love's Arrow Poisoned*, the complications and double-crossings, misunderstandings and retributions, a complexity of weft beyond the power of any but the most consummate stage-hand to unravel and under any circumstances too involved for any audience to grasp, culminating, in true Elizabethan fashion, in a scene of weird melodrama, the return of the departed, mummery and carnage. The one among the old dramatists who, after Shakespeare and Marlowe, had fascinated Beddoes more than others, was Marston, the intellectual, self-torturing satirist. And so, in Marstonic fashion, he must end with a grand masque in which the hero must act the part of his own murdered self, until the moment of retribution arrives and he can plant his dagger in the usurper's breast. But Beddoes' is no mere historical review, like Marston's. In Romantic fashion it is preceded by an incantation, the purpose of which is to make the spectre discover where his treasures are hidden. In Romantic fashion, again, the conjuring is a fake, and instead of a ghost the real man appears, for while believed to have fallen to his death, he has actually been miraculously saved halfway down the precipice, just like Marston's Altofronto. The scene was sufficiently melodramatic not to be easily forgone by its youthful contriver, and so it appears again and again in various modifications. This, I feel convinced, is how *Torrismond* was planned to end; this was to be the end of *The Second Brother* also. It is not difficult to see that when Valeria is led to the Campo Santo at midnight in the last scene to be completed, she is there going to be made to act the part of her own ghost in order to prove Marcello's power over life and death, and thus help him gain the dominion over men's souls after which he strove. For while Beddoes was grappling with the technical problem of plot-construction, his mind was at the same time occupied with a totally different problem of a spiritual nature, the relationship of mind and matter, a question which, as far as I can understand, he had already tackled in *The Last Man*, although he had found his powers so far insufficient to provide a solution. The temptation must have been strong to unite the theme of his imagination with the plot of his fancy, and in *The Second Brother* we can see him at work.

This is the moment when he wrote to Kelsall, in January 1825, from his Clifton 'demi-uncle's':

'I am convinced the man who is to awaken the drama must be a bold trampling fellow—no creeper into worm-holes—no reviser even—however good.... With the greatest reverence for the antiquities of the drama, I still think we had better beget than revive—

attempt to give the literature of this age an idiosyn-
crasy and spirit of its own, and only raise a ghost to
gaze on, not to live with.'

In accordance with this theory Marcello tries to spread
his conquests, not like Tamburlane to the farthest
corners of the earth, but like a modern Faustus into
the inmost crannies of men's minds. The resurrection
of Valeria was to prove to Orazio Marcello's divine
power and throw him on the mercy of his tyrannical
brother. But since Valeria had never been dead, the
conjuring must remain a fake, and the real problem of
the power of the spirit over lifeless matter must remain
unsolved. Yet before completing *The Second Brother*
he had actually succeeded in an artistic treatment of
this mystery in his beautiful poem *Pygmalion*. Such is
the power of man's mind that it can endow the cold
marble with the divine spark of life, even if only at the
cost of its own extinction.

Pygmalion was written about the middle of May
1825, and on 8 June Beddoes wrote to Kelsall: 'I do
not intend to finish that 2nd Brother...but am thinking of a very Gothic-styled tragedy for w^h I have a
jewel of a name—DEATH'S JESTBOOK.' The death of
The Second Brother was the birth of *Death's Jest-Book*,
for Beddoes had come to realize that a mere stage-
trick, employed for the temporary advancement and
final overthrow of a diabolical design, could furnish
no adequate illustration of his most cherished notions;
and as soon as this became clear to him he abandoned
his play in the middle of the fourth act. There was to
be conjuring in *Death's Jest-Book* also, but no faked
resurrection this time. It was to be a raising into real
life of one truly dead, and the play was to prove
beyond any shadow of a doubt the immortality of the
soul and the power of the mind over matter. Undeniable proof of his thesis thus became an artistic

as well as a psychological necessity to a poet who was to confess himself 'haunted for ever' by the problem of death. If he really felt himself plagued by the early memories of unwitting desecration of its majesty, then he must also feel compelled to seek for proof spiritual and material that death is no more than an illusion and that in spite of it 'life remains triumphant'. And so while still at work on *The Second Brother* he had reached the decision to take up the study of medicine. While there must have been a strong element of heredity in his choice—and we do not know how seriously he had ever considered becoming a lawyer— the decision was nevertheless intimately connected with his dramatic authorship, and it is difficult to doubt that it was, at that particular moment, dictated by his determination to find scientific proof of the theory of which his play was to supply imaginative illustration. And so it was in full confidence of success and in the highest of spirits that Beddoes launched himself in a new career.

It was Dr. King who influenced him in the choice of Göttingen rather than Edinburgh as the scene of his medical first steps. He had been staying at Clifton since November 1824 and did not return to London till late in February or early March 1825. In April he went to Oxford where he received an ordinary B.A. degree on 5 May. Here he attended anatomical lectures, translated the *Philosophische Briefe* of Schiller for an under-graduate magazine, and wrote some fine poetry like *Pygmalion*, Here he drank the full draughts of an English spring, walking along the river in that intimacy with nature which is reflected in his verse-letter to Procter. He seems to have been thoroughly happy and poetic creation was easy again in the consciousness of a new power alive within him. In this mood he set out for Germany about the middle of July.

At Göttingen he worked hard, usually getting up,

according to his own account, at 5 and working with little relaxation and the shortest possible time set apart for meals until 10 at night, when he took out *Death's Jest-Book* and wrote a little, thus out-labouring 'the laborious Sauerkrauts'. He soon got to like the honesty and seriousness of the Germans and new spheres opened to him in their literature, philosophy and science. His letters are as high-spirited as ever, giving entertaining accounts of university professors and undergraduates. His highly developed sense of fun responded with its usual quickness to the absurdities of the Germans, and while he laughed at them he got to like them even better. For a time all went well. He made progress in his studies—Professor Blumenbach, the Nestor of German medical science, was to say that Beddoes was the best pupil he had had during the fifty years of his professorship—and *Death's Jest-Book* was nearing completion. Then there was a hitch. He could not get on with his play. All his high hopes of finding with the aid of medicine the proof positive of man's survival seemed frustrated. The organ of immortality, which I think it must have been his ambition to discover, still eluded him. What I have called elsewhere the 'skeleton complex' seized him. He sought 'with avidity for every shadow of a proof or probability of an after-existence, both in the material and immaterial nature of man'. Still he found nothing. An ordinary man might have despaired; the world of Beddoes' imagination tottered to its fall, the lofty edifice came crashing down. Although this was not to dawn on the poet until a little later, *Death's Jest-Book* was in the process of becoming *The Fool's Tragedy*.

For a time Beddoes seems to have lost his creative power while the blows of disillusion were raining over him. He sought refuge in cynicism but remained unsatisfied. He had lost his faith, and there was no help for him in the world. But he was young, between twenty-three and twenty-four, and gradually under soothing influences his spirits rallied. He had never taken his own person very seriously—his modesty and self-irony are the most endearing traits of that admirable correspondence which Swinburne lauded, like so many other critics after him. So, getting to know the plays and stories of Tieck, Beddoes responded readily to the German poet's theory of 'Romantic irony', and could set to work on his tragedy again in a flippant mood which contrasts sharply against the gruesomeness of what had gone before. He received help from another source as well. A new-found friend of Jewish origin could tell him details of ancient Hebrew belief in an organ of immortality, the bone Luz which 'withstands dissolution after death, out of which the body will be developed at the resurrection'. This served Beddoes' dramatic purpose even if it failed to convince the scientist in him. 'Luz is an excellent joke,' he was to write to Kelsall when the finished play was ultimately dispatched to England.

The new-formed friendship with Bernard Reich cannot have failed to mean something for Beddoes. Silent and unexpressed as I am afraid it remained, yet his affection for his penniless friend brought him a happiness apparently new to him. For one year the two friends shared lodgings, first in a curious octagonal house near the Teich, then during the warm season in a small summer-house. After that they parted company, but the friendship survived, and together they were to perform the migration to Würzburg in the autumn of 1829. Beddoes, who had never anticipated such a long, uninterrupted stay abroad, in the meanwhile paid a visit to England, staying with the Kings once more at Clifton and receiving his M.A. degree at Oxford on 16 April 1828. In London he met Kelsall and Bourne. On the return journey to Göttingen he visited Amsterdam, where in the autumn he stayed again for some weeks after another hurried visit to London, where, however, he did not see his English friends, except possibly Revell Phillips, a lawyer of the Middle Temple who managed his affairs for him during his foreign residence. Returned to Göttingen, he finished the preface to his play, copied the whole out clean, and then, it seems, immediately transcribed it for the press with no more alterations than would naturally suggest themselves in the process of copying it again. Before the end of February he dispatched the packet containing his precious manuscript book to England, the result of nearly four years' work, the mirror of his dreams and high aspirations, of doubt and failure and despair, of accepted disillusion, recovery and renewed hope. For such, if it is possible to compress the complexities of life in a bare formula, I believe to have been the course of Beddoes' spiritual development during those years.

There can be no doubt about it that Beddoes expected his play to cause a sensation in the literary world, and he even expressed his regret that 'so much absurdity in reviews' was likely to escape him where he was. Even in his deepest fits of despondency he cannot have imagined for one moment that it would not reach the press at all and that his best friends, wont to encourage him in his immaturity, would now become instrumental in suppressing his finest effort. On this one gigantic throw now rested all his hopes in the world. He can hardly himself have realized to what extent his work differed from the watered-down Romanticism of his contemporaries, except in his conviction of its superior merits. He was right. Some thirty years later Landor was to say: 'Nearly two centuries have elapsed since a work of the same wealth of genius as *Death's Jest-Book* was given to the world.' Conscious of powers that were to provoke such enthusiasm he cannot very well have made it clear to himself that a public that so far had refused to take Shelley and Keats to their bosom and among whom Blake had worked for so long unknown except to a small circle, would reject Beddoes also. And so Procter and Bourne decided against immediate publication, requesting the author in the meanwhile for substantial revision. Only Kelsall, with better knowledge of Beddoes' retiring pride, wanted to see the play published at once, although even he could not withhold his disappointment in the weakness of the character-drawing.

In a sense the critics were right also, from their point of view. *Death's Jest-Book* was not what they had a right to expect from the literary progeny whose début more than six years before had been proclaimed superior to that of Chatterton and Keats. And Procter at any rate must have felt some responsibility for his protégé. The faults of Beddoes' performance were glaring enough. The plot was as complicated and confused as ever. The dialogue as impossible. All the characters seem to declaim into the void, and none answer the others. There is no individualization, and this was the reason why Beddoes had been able seemingly without effort to incorporate parts of older plays. It was all his own drama, his own wrestling with the problems of the spirit, problems unsolved. For Beddoes himself had not noticed that his idea remained at cross-purposes with the action of the play, his elaborate Elizabethan plot at war with the central theme. He had failed to find, in Mr. Eliot's phrase, 'the objective correlative' of his thought. Nor can the 'Romantic irony' borrowed from the Germans have recommended itself to his English critics. It provided no solution, but on the contrary went to spoil one of his finest creations, the resurrected Wolfram; for what might have been appropriate to Mandrake, entertaining as it is, could not serve the spirit of retribution in the execution of an awe-inspiring task. It is undeniable that Beddoes' sense of fun, too, fed on queer food sometimes and is not even yet always recognized by critics except under the name of the grotesque, for from his earliest infancy his mind had so familiarized itself with skulls and crossbones that he derived infinite amusement from tossing them about like custard pies in a slap-stick comedy. His daring naturalism of language, entirely modern in its unavoidance of the homely and vigorous, was in complete contrast with his age. And to the faults apparent to his contemporaries we might add yet another. Although set in a defined historical milieu the whole spirit of the play is a product of its period and so essentially anachronistic. The ruined cathedral and churchyard were as inappropriate to the thirteenth century as they were congenial to Romanticism or acceptable to the Elizabethans. The same applies to the details. But the play had merits also surpassing anything produced by his contemporaries.

The very plot has a primitive directness commonly avoided in Romantic drama. Whereas contemporary practice ruled that murder could only be committed in a fit of sudden lunacy, a dislocation in the brain—and Beddoes had fallen into this error himself in his more youthful compositions—in *Death's Jest-Book* there is no shirking of the issue. But the plot and all its action is of course only a pretext for the poetry, yet a necessary pretext. In the dialogue arising out of the artificially contrived situations Beddoes could express that drama of the spirit to which the plot had failed to accommodate itself. In the songs sung by the dramatic characters their inmost essence is expressed. In others an epitome of the action and situation is given. In the blank verse of his play he had found the true objective correlative of his thought, and the poetical dialogue embodies the struggles of his mind, oscillating between life and death, time and eternity. It is Beddoes' very self.

Although he submitted to the verdict of his friends with model modesty and self-effacement, he could not withhold some groans at the thought of having to attempt the rewriting of what seemed the greater part of his play. Even so it never seems to have occurred to him that it would not be published in the following autumn. It was only when the work of revision got him into worse knots than ever, that he seems to have despaired of his play and of himself. Although no details are available this must have been the period of his depression at Göttingen when he tried to take his life. His exodus in fact became less grandiose though hardly less conspicuous.

On 12 August 1829 he seems to have decided to get completely and thoroughly drunk. Needless to say he succeeded, perhaps even beyond expectation, and certainly brought about consequences which he can hardly have foreseen. How he got there we do not know, but by 11.30 in the evening he had made himself such a thorough nuisance at Professor Himly's house and proved himself so intractable that a posse of university police was urgently summoned. Three 'bullers' turned up to remove the delinquent, no name having been mentioned in the S O S. On the way they could see a broken window, indicating which way the offender had taken, and another student obligingly informed them that he was still in the professor's house, as he had heard a loud noise inside. The three policemen entered and on the third landing were confronted with the professor's coachman and gardener leading between them a thoroughly soused student whom they immediately recognized as Beddoes. To remove him was not easy, for he defended himself valiantly and kicked them (on the shins, I suspect). So the student they had met outside was called in to help and repeatedly lent them a hand. With the assistance of an additional patrol of police they finally succeeded in taking Beddoes home to his lodgings in Weender-strasse. There he was carried upstairs, but it proved impossible to put him to bed. In fact he hit round with his stick so ferociously that he even cut off the neck of a bottle and sent it crashing through the window-pane into the street. However, they ultimately managed to place him on a sofa where he seemed to calm down, and when he appeared to be dozing off the policemen left. But within half an hour a new call arrived at the police headquarters from his landlord, saying Beddoes was making an awful noise in the house. When the reinforced patrol arrived, however, he was quiet and made no more noise that night. His landlord, nevertheless, could show them his trunk and writing-table and other belongings in the courtyard where he had thrown them out of the window. In so doing he had moreover fatally injured a turkey, so that the owner had been forced to destroy it. On the following morning Beddoes emerged and in the company of a few friends consumed eight bottles of wine in celebration of his deeds.

The next day he was forbidden to leave his lodgings between eight in the evening and six in the morning. Three days later he made his first appearance before the university court. He denied all knowledge of the offences charged against him, because he had been drunk and did not remember what had happened. He did recollect being at Professor Himly's, but could think of no reason why. He also recalled trying to open his trunk and throwing it out of the window when he could not find the key. The court adjourned, and the same evening Beddoes appeared between ten and eleven at a popular open-air restaurant and obstreperously demanded wine, which was refused. At the next meeting of the university court he was necessarily charged with this new offence, sufficiently grave to merit public relegation. Beddoes' excuse was that he had believed the period of his 'gating' to be over once the court had met a week before, and until then he had not transgressed.

It was now rumoured in Göttingen that Beddoes had intended leaving the university at Michaelmas and so wanted to have a gay time and plenty of ragging before going down, but this looks to me like a ruse intended to make his exit appear voluntary. The university authorities, however, could not close their eyes to the fact that drunkenness was on the increase among the undergraduates—this was only a year or two before Bismarck made his appearance there—and Beddoes' case had become so widely notorious that something had to be done. On the other hand, Beddoes had an excellent record, never having suffered other punishment than four days' imprisonment for the ragging of a university bedel, whereas his work had won him the respect of his teachers. Hence the charge was reduced to one of deliberate intoxication; it was agreed that in view of Beddoes' known tendency towards spleen even a short term of imprisonment was inadvisable lest greater harm should ensue, and it was decided that he should be sent down without further punishment, the sentence, however, to be conveyed to him with the utmost possible leniency and the stress placed on the fact that the sentence had been dictated not by the offence alone but also by consideration for his own good in the belief that a change of scene would be beneficial to him. On 24 August Beddoes was told to leave Göttingen within twenty-four hours. It was plainly impossible for him to settle all accounts in that brief space, and so he was sought at Weende where he was lingering, presumably while making up his mind where to go, by the landlord of the König von Preussen and made to sign an acknowledgement for a substantial sum owing to that innkeeper for wine consumed in his restaurant. Although he had given his barber a cherished skeleton in part payment of his bill, the duns may have speeded his departure, and before long he matriculated in the university of Würzburg. His friend Reich was accepted on 22 September, whereas Beddoes did not become a member of the university until 13 October, but I think they must have travelled together, although Beddoes had probably failed to provide himself with the ex-matriculation papers necessary for membership in another university and so had to write to Göttingen for them. His debts in the meanwhile remained unsettled until more than three years later the university took matters into its own hands, declared Beddoes publicly relegated for failure to honour his obligations, sold over 700 books belonging to him which had remained at his landlord's, paid his bills with the proceeds, and probably bagged the balance.

The Beddoes who made his appearance in Würzburg was a very different person from Robert Browning's 'capital skeleton-undergraduate' who had left England more than four years earlier. The Göttingen period had been one of intense struggle, rich experience, acute disappointment, and mortal agony, but Beddoes must have emerged from it a sobered and a more harmonious being, free from the self-torturing ambition of the very young, the skeleton-complex gone that had pursued him long but was now never again to appear in his verse; something of the fire extinguished, but a rich experience gained, and a deep fund of human emotion now at his command. The possibility of losing his younger sister who was dangerously ill at Florence the same autumn may have added to the new seriousness in his outlook. Moreover, after only one term's residence at Würzburg his friend Bernard Reich disappears from our records. His fate is unknown. If the 'loved longlost boy' of the *Dream Pedlary* is to be identified with him, it seems that he must have died. Beddoes certainly henceforth did 'consecrate [his] being'

> *To that divinest hope, which none can know of*
> *Who have not laid their dearest in the grave.*

This is only one instance of the new tragic strain which now forced its entrance into Beddoes' poetry and was to recur again and again until he himself was at last ready to enter the 'loved one's home'. Some of his most beautiful poetry was written at Würzburg. The quantity is minute, but the quality beyond prize.

At Würzburg Beddoes completed his medical studies, receiving his degree of M.D. on 10 September 1831. He did not, however, go through the formality of submitting a dissertation, and so his diploma remained unclaimed. As early as the preceding January he had contemplated an early departure from Würzburg. Perhaps his studies for the degree took longer than he had anticipated, but even after the completion of his examinations he did not leave Bavaria, for he had now become absorbed in politics and was taking an active part in the activities of the radical students' organizations. The German *Burschenschaft* was not open to foreigners, and the case of Beddoes seems to be unique, but in 1831 he was actually accepted as a member of the *Germania* association of the *Burschenschaft*. The circumstances of Würzburg were peculiar and that may to some extent explain an otherwise astounding fact. Whereas in all other German universities the *Burschenschaft* kept strictly aloof from other political societies, at Würzburg they joined forces with the radical party which here worked for the same ideals as they, and on the other hand academic citizenship seems to have been regarded as constituting a right as good as any to take a part in public affairs. Beddoes soon came to play a prominent one. From the autumn of 1831 until the following May he published articles, though anonymous, in the *Bayerisches Volksblatt* on Polish, French, and English politics, and he soon became known as a public speaker. We can follow his activities in some detail, for as a democratic Englishman he was an asset to the radical movement and was given a great deal of publicity in the press, and on the other side the Bavarian government agents were on the watch and furnished reports concerning his movements.

One secret report tells us about a meeting of representatives of the university students and members of *Der Grüne Bund* at the public-house of one Sebald in Reubeltsgasse, where violent speeches were made by several *Burschenschafter* and it was decided to work together for the annihilation of the Russo-Prussian colossus and the overthrow of all German princes except one, under whom the small states were to be united into one constitutional *Reich*. It appears as if Beddoes had been the most important person present, for he spoke several times and was honoured with a presentation of cigars by the 'greenshirts'. More public was the occasion of a banquet given in honour of General Rybinsky, one of the heroes of the Polish war of liberation, and full reports appeared in the radical press. Beddoes was more fully reported than other speakers, perhaps because as a foreigner he was considered the least vulnerable. After many a candid word had been spoken and toasts had been called in freedom's cause, the national anthem was played and sung. Its notes had hardly ceased resounding through the hall, when Beddoes rose and spoke directly to the heart of all. He spoke of Freedom, recalling how its progress had been thwarted during the last few years, but with the assurance that it lived in the hearts of men and would emerge victorious. It was a word, he said, which makes human language divine and contains the promise of a happy future for an enslaved mankind. In a magnificent image, identifying the scythe of time with the emblem of the Polish Guard, he saw the victorious vision of Saturn commanding their army in triumphant war, and at last, apostrophizing the universe's soul, he sounded the appeal for Freedom.

About two months later Beddoes again made a noted public appearance at the anniversary of the Bavarian constitution, celebrated at Gaibach on 27 May 1832. On no previous occasion had popular feeling run so high, and but for the moderation of the leader of the radicals a political separation from Bavaria would have been effected. Again Beddoes spoke last of all. Again he was complimented in the press for his liberal opinions, fluent delivery, and classical metaphors which both on this and previous occasions had gained for him a warm reception and excited admiration for his rhetorical talents. In excuse for speaking on such an occasion Beddoes had referred to the irrepressible feeling that stirred him as the son of a free country present at such a celebration. Forgetting that the festival took place in the grounds of the Count von Schönborn, he depicted the aristocracy as creatures lacking all soul, whereas the reformers, we understand, were such as partook of emanations of the demiurge. He spoke in fiery metaphors of political freedom and of the happiness of the free citizen, foreseeing a home being prepared for such freedom also in beautiful Bavaria. In his mind's eye he visualized how on that very day, only a few years hence, a Herodotus would at that same column where he was speaking tell the history of the victory of German freedom, an Æschylus recite the tragedy of the overthrow of the tyrants, and an Aristophanes hold up the old aristocracy to ridicule.

Beddoes was now received in the very bosom of the subversive movement, a club named the *Freie Reichsstadt*. Again, this is an almost unbelievable achievement for a foreigner, but the facts are not to be doubted. Since the club was a kind of society order on Masonic lines, every *Reichsstädter* had his own *nom de guerre*, and Beddoes was duly identified by the secret police under the name '*des Königsmörders*' Oliver Cromwell, or more familiarly 'Nol'. At this stage, however, the government also saw itself forced to take counter-measures unless its authority were to be thoroughly undermined, and one of its first moves was to get rid of Beddoes. A government decree of 10 July 1832 ordered him to leave Würzburg within three days and Bavaria within a week, because he had made a most violent speech at Gaibach. It could not be permitted, the government maintained, for foreigners to abuse the hospitality of the country by meddling with public affairs in order to subvert the régime. The description of his person appended to the expulsion document enables us to visualize him as he appeared to the agents of government, a grotesque figure enough, pouring out his metaphysics in broken German.

'Height 5′ 7″, hair light-brown, forehead high, eyebrows fair, eyes dark, nose fairly long and pointed, mouth big, chin rather prominent, face oval, complexion pale, build slight, neglected clothing, light-grey coat, white breeches, and either in English fashion or as German hero of Hambach one boot black, the other red, and on one of them a gold or gilt spur, speaks bad German, fair moustache, bad teeth.'

The strange colour scheme was that of the *Burschenschaft*, adopted as a symbol of a pan-German union, and worn in the manner described because badges had been forbidden.

Notice of the deportation order was given to Beddoes on 15 July in the morning. Determined, however, 'to oppose every possible measure to the arbitrary illegality' of the King of Bavaria, Beddoes in his capacity of an academic citizen appealed to the Rector of the university. A special meeting of the senate was immediately summoned, and on 17 July a letter of protest was addressed to the King. The government reply, dated on 21 July, naturally refused to admit the interpretation by the university of the common law of the country so as to exempt academic citizens from its application. Beddoes in the meanwhile had addressed a letter to the British minister in Munich, although this did not reach its destination till 22 July, whereas according to the terms of the deportation order he should have left on the 18th. Apart from a sympathetic answer it does not seem to have effected anything, nor is it known what happened to his remonstrance sent to the Bavarian ministry for the interior.

In the meanwhile his friends were getting anxious, and while waiting for the ruling of the Government decided to secure Beddoes' prolonged stay at Würzburg by somewhat unusual means. One of his creditors, probably genuine, watchmaker Böschl, who was an active radical, ingeniously requested the City Commissary that he should deprive Beddoes of his passport lest he should leave Würzburg without paying his debts. But the authorities were not so easily beguiled. The City Commissary refused, and decided that Beddoes must leave on 21 July. Böschl then brought a summons, and his debtor was duly arrested. So far all seemed well. Yet even his desire by all possible means to oppose 'the absurdity of the King of Bavaria' could not, it seems, overcome Beddoes' distaste for the regional gaol, where, presumably, he was treated no better than common thieves and murderers, and so the next scene of this farce opens with Böschl wanting to withdraw his suit. This, however, the law would not allow, and on 21 June at twelve noon, when he was to have left Würzburg, Beddoes was still in prison. But he had never been an easy lodger and seldom stayed long at the same boarding-house, and prison seems to have palled upon him. He decided to offer Böschl security, the watchmaker consequently applied for the release of his prisoner, and Beddoes left that day.

His exit was triumphal. Numerous friends bade him farewell, and some of them, in three chaises, accompanied him on his way as far as Rohrbrunn. Among these were city magistrates, officials of all the political clubs and societies, the actors in the scene at Sebald's public-house, and others, but against each one of them, as far as the information provided by the Bavarian archives goes, a special charge was to be brought in their indictment on the ground that they 'had accompanied Dr. Beddoes when he left Würzburg'. The radical papers, on the other hand, abused the government for the arbitrary deportation of a person, 'liked by everybody', whose only crime had been the spending of 5,000 guilders a year in a city, apparently not used to such extravagance, and whose benevolence had been proved on numerous occasions. He was also stated to have many sincere friends in Würzburg.

Fortunately, several of these were able to join him at Zürich, where he betook himself after a short stay at Strassbourg. The new university recruited both its professors and many of its undergraduates from the refugees that came pouring across the frontier. One of the first to matriculate as student was Beddoes, one of the first professors to be appointed was his friend Johann Lucas Schönlein, whose fame had originally lured him to Würzburg. The German refugees in fact became quite influential in the government of Zürich, although there was always a conservative opposition powerful enough to make their existence precarious from time to time. On the whole, his years at Zürich were to become the happiest, I think, in Beddoes' life. He had plenty of friends, enjoyed a general reputation for wide and solid scientific learning, could indulge in all the freaks of his disposition, had plenty of leisure for study and writing, and near at hand were lakes on which he rowed and hills and mountains which he climbed and over which he strolled sometimes on extensive walking tours.

Foremost among his friends was Schönlein, with whom he made a visit to England in 1835 and returned with him through France. They did not stay long, and the journey was probably improvised when Schönlein was called to Brussels to assist the Queen of the Belgians in child-birth. On their return to Zürich, however, in June a rumour circulated there that Schönlein was going to be appointed Physician in Ordinary to the King of the Belgians, and we have no difficulty in recognizing Beddoes in the English physician, equally conspicuous for eminent learning and grotesque eccentricity of manners, who emphatically denied such degrading conjectures. 'Schönlein,' he said, 'is a man to have a king in attendance on his own person rather than be himself in attendance on a king.' But not so many years later Schönlein actually became physician to the King of Prussia, and the friendship with Beddoes was then gradually to cool. It seems probable from the parallel case of Keller, the lawyer and virtual dictator of the Zürich Regeneration but later professor at Berlin and trusted adviser of the king, that what amused the free republic among the Alps did not go down so well in Berlin, and the freaks which from all accounts were embarrassing enough at Zürich probably proved intolerable in the Prussian capital.

Through Schönlein Beddoes must have known all the medical professors of Zürich, and in July 1835 the medical faculty informed the Board of Education that it had come to their knowledge that Dr. Beddoes was willing to lecture in the university, particularly on comparative anatomy, and was prepared to pay all expenses connected with his course. As the faculty considered this proposal wholly advantageous to the university, they unanimously recommended it. The Board, however, required further information which Keller undertook to gather privately. Nothing came of it, the most probable reason being that it was found against the statutes to appoint a 'professor' who had neither published anything nor held another university appointment. This is another of the regrettable failures of Beddoes' life, for he needed now, I think, the steadying influence of a regular job on which to concentrate his universal and erratic genius. And it seems as if the university wanted another professor of comparative anatomy, for when the German doctor-poet Georg Büchner arrived in Zürich exactly fifteen months later, he almost immediately lectured as 'privatdozent' and the intention seems to have been to create a chair in comparative anatomy for him. Even less fortunate than Beddoes, he died only four months later, but it seems more than likely that Beddoes met him, for Schönlein was only one among several common acquaintances, another worthy of especial mention being the poet Herwegh.[1]

If Keller's influence was not sufficient to carry Beddoes' nomination through the Board of Education, which was to thwart his wishes on even more important issues, it was nevertheless enough to secure Beddoes' continued residence at Zürich when late in 1835 all politically active refugees were arrested or expelled. Beddoes undoubtedly enjoyed an established reputation for political radicalism, and it does not seem unlikely that this was what turned the Board of Education against his appointment, although the reason

[1] On the other hand, I find it difficult to see the likeness, suggested by Mr. E. Sackville West, between the warm philanthropist Büchner and an intellectual revolutionary like Beddoes or between the thoroughly human *Wozzec* and the speculative *Death's Jest-Book*. (See the *New Statesman*, 10 May 1947, p. 333.)

given was purely formal. This would explain why Beddoes could state to Kelsall that he had

'narrowly escaped becoming professor of comparative Anatomy in the University of Zürich... by means of a timely quarrel, in which I engaged, more solito, with several members of the government'.

To Revell Phillips he seems to have mentioned only that 'a very reasonable regulation' prevented his appointment, unless Phillips himself suppressed further details. On the other hand, Beddoes was not expelled as, in spite of Keller, he probably would have been if political activities could have been proved against him. But he had been careful not formally to join any of the secret societies working on Swiss soil for the liberation of Germany from all her petty princes. At any rate I could not find his name in any of the authentic lists of members preserved in the Swiss archives. German spies, however, in their secret reports did not hesitate to mention him as a member of the *Handwerkerverein*, a widespread organization of students and working men who carried on the aims and principles of the Würzburg *Reichsstadt*. As a secret society it arranged meetings unobtrusively in the open air or at country inns, and since Beddoes was in the habit of stopping on his tours to drink beer and talk politics to the people in the inns he passed, it is not impossible that he fell in with them more than once, and he may even have had an unofficial connexion with them. I do not think that he wrote any political articles or pamphlets during his first years at Zürich, although it seems likely that he did so later.

Beddoes' oddities impressed themselves on people at Zürich very strongly. An acquaintance of his, Ignaz Thomas Scherr, Inspector of Schools in the canton of Zürich, has a passage about him in his memoirs published in 1840. He describes him as 'a young man of very comprehensive scientific knowledge', who possessed means in excess of the cost of living at Zürich, and who was, moreover, an incarnation of all the eccentricities of the English, which, even when less pronounced, so forcibly strike the foreigner. For instance, he greatly enjoyed teasing the plodding keepers of the Zürich coffee-houses, and made them victims of curious practical jokes. Unfortunately Scherr gives no concrete examples. Even the highest in the land did not escape merciless ridicule, and Beddoes loved embarrassing them with a 'behaviour à la Falstaff'. Scherr and the Zürich press together help us in reconstructing one such episode. Beddoes had, we are told, made the acquaintance of an exceptionally stout representative of German manhood and it seems as if he had immediately seized the opportunity of making him ridiculous. For several months Beddoes fed this German Chesterton, in bulk if not in talents, Dr. Schmidt, on the strongest of diets in order to make him look the part. He then rented the local theatre for a performance of *Henry IV* in order to show off his prodigy in the part of Falstaff. Beddoes himself took the part of Hotspur and must have enjoyed railing against the futile art of poetry, as indeed Bourne in his novel makes 'Derwent' do. For the part of Lady Percy he engaged the prima donna of the theatre, Mme Birch-Pfeiffer. Most of the other actors also belonged to the regular company, and we are assured that Beddoes rewarded them most liberally and entertained them royally. The performance was to take place on 20 January 1838, and invitations were sent out in advance. As a hoax it was given out that no radicals were to be given tickets. Yet it appears they were to be had for the asking at the bookshop of one of Beddoes' friends, Julius Blaich. Only when a member of the government, who I think must have been Keller, in a dictatorial voice asked for five tickets in Beddoes' name, it so happened that the poet heard him from the inner shop where he was talking to Blaich, and he then quickly slipped round the corner of the house, so that when 'the Dictator' was just repeating his demand to Blaich himself, Beddoes could impudently shout over his shoulder: 'I have never seen this person before; he shan't have a ticket.' But Keller was at the performance all the same in the company of another distinguished common friend, David Ulrich, the Public Prosecutor, who had been Keller's right hand in drafting the new constitution of Zürich.

The performance was to commence at six in the evening, and the doors were opened at five. The auditorium was crowded—there was room for 800 people—and the mixture of the classes was complete. Whether Beddoes himself had gone into the seating arrangements or no, they turned out in his spirit right enough, for we are told that the highest in the land were in the most shocking manner made to rub shoulders with the proletariat and that the number of radicals of the lower classes was conspicuous. The two parts of *Henry IV* were given in the German version of one play, and in the intervals the Zürich undergraduate choir sang in the orchestra. According to the *Volksbote*, representing Beddoes' own view, Dr. Schmidt played to perfection the part for which nature had destined him, but the Inspector of Schools in his *Memoirs* maintained that he had not grasped one whit of Falstaff's humour, and while complaining that 'eight yards of uneven ground is threescore and ten miles afoot with me', he leapt about the stage with the agility of a professional dancer. According to the same source Hotspur pronounced his German with a pure English accent, but for a first appearance his acting was acceptable enough. The audience at any rate were pleased, and at the last curtain the shouts for Beddoes were clamorously repeated, but he had it given out that he had already left the theatre. Thus did he earn his place in the history of Shakespearian production,[1] and deservedly, because the performances of Shakespeare were certainly encouraged by his example and others were soon to follow on the Zürich stage.

Of a very different nature is a later incident, which happens to be known to us. Returned from an invigorating walking tour in the summer, Beddoes found a well-known and popular, though perhaps slightly ageing singer from the Vienna Opera still in command of public favour, after several months of uninterrupted success. So Beddoes in his idoloclastic manner devised a scheme to undermine her popularity. On 7 December 1838 a hoaxing article appeared in one of the Zürich newspapers, giving full particulars of the formation of a booing society under the leadership of 'the well-known Dr. Beddoes'. As soon as the membership should reach ninety, the popular prima donna was to be greeted with a storm of whistling and booing instead of the wonted enthusiastic applause. The members were already said to number sixty-five. Another organization, the same source informs us, had already been formed for the protection of their idol, and at the first sign of a demonstration the disturbers were to be removed. The law courts were said to have provided tons of paper in anticipation of litigation on a gigantic scale, and Beddoes' friend Ulrich, the Public Prosecutor, was hinted at as destined to be more than usually astute in the eyes of his admirers. Nor did other friends of the poet escape unscathed, and I should be much surprised to learn that Beddoes did not write the

---

[1] See *The New Cambridge Shakespeare*, 1, *Henry IV*, p. xl, and the *Times Literary Supplement*, 24 August 1946, p. 402. I cannot help underlining that this is the performance so grievously misrepresented by the late Sir Edmund Gosse as having taken place in 1848 with Degen in the part of Hotspur and, lamentably unsuccessful, causing Beddoes to commit suicide at Basle.

article himself or at least in collaboration with the editor.

In the congenial surroundings of Zürich and Switzerland and in 'the pleasant translunary moods' into which he rowed and walked himself, there blossomed once more the flowers of poetry. By 1837 he had accumulated enough material to contemplate the publication of a volume of prose and poetry, *The Ivory Gate*, including of course the inevitable *Death's Jest-Book*. Nothing came of the publication. The prose-tales, alas! have perished. The lyrics are among his finest and, almost without exception, among the pearls of English poetry, some gay, some burlesque, some not a little vulgar, others beautifully melancholy, and some sad and sorrowful beyond description. A great many went into *Death's Jest-Book* which Beddoes now started revising in earnest. Necessarily this was a futile task, because the poet was now a different man who ought to have been doing other things, and some of the proposed revisions were too radical ever to be incorporated in the play. Yet there it was and could 'not be helped', and Beddoes had to try and do his best for it. At moments *The Last Man* played again in his imagination, under the influence, it seems, of *Ixion in Heaven*, but as long as *Death's Jest-Book* remained unprinted he had to return to it and rewrite and revise. At this period it really appears how 'infinitely regrettable', in Robert Browning's words, was the refusal of his friends to forward it to the press in 1829. Beddoes still had it in him to do something great, as the new first act to his still-born play was to show, but he was thwarted by the skeleton in his cupboard which he had to take out to be aired and dusted whenever the mood came and creative power was his.

Nor can it be said that his continued German residence was good for him as an English poet. He had started thinking and writing in German, and I have a distinct feeling that English phrasing became increasingly difficult for him. If he had lived in contact with English intellectual life, continued his interchange of ideas with Kelsall and Bourne, developed his relations with Darley and Mrs. Shelley, even with Procter, personally known the young Tennyson and Browning, or Hood and Praed even, what a poet he might have been! In his isolation there was no incitement to write, and what he felt was his great work remained unpublished. So, inevitably in the circumstances, he took to writing in German. We have Degen's evidence that once when there was a paper war among the professors he wrote verses on it so witty and learned that even the academic fathers had to consult their dictionaries. Some of his German poems survive in the Zürich press, and one witticism of exceptional vigour, a poem on the Strauss feud, was printed as a pamphlet over his own signature and quoted by several historians of the downfall of the liberal government of the Zürich Regeneration.

The occasion was one of bitter dissension between the local parties, the beginning of a mortal struggle, which was to end in the revolution of 6 September 1839. It is odd to think that such excitement should have been caused by the question of a university appointment, but this was actually what brought matters to a head, even if it was in itself no more than a sign of wider differences. Since 1836 the Radicals had been pressing for the appointment of D. F. Strauss, the author of *Das Leben Jesu*, to a theological chair in the University, but the faculty had been twice thwarted by the Board of Education. In the autumn of 1838 the Radicals took the offensive again and scored a temporary success when Strauss was actually appointed in January 1839. In the meanwhile, however, the whole nation had come to take part in the feud and become sharply divided into two camps. The protests against Strauss's appointment were so loud and numerous that

lix

on 18 March the government gave way and pensioned off Dr. Strauss before he had time to occupy his chair. The Radicals now moved the abolition of the University. Although not seriously intended, this gave Schönlein an excuse for resigning in favour of a professorship at Berlin. He was prevailed upon to stay for the time being, and the students honoured him with a torch parade. All these matters are reflected in Beddoes' satire, which was immediately and repeatedly quoted in the press. But there was no concealing the fact that the elections were going against the government, and for Beddoes the happy days at Zürich were drawing to a close.

An amusing episode during the summer offers a sidelight on the party alignment as far as it affected Beddoes himself. On 13 July he applied to the Commissioner of Police for a residence permit. He was then informed that this could only be granted if he fulfilled the necessary formalities of submitting a birth certificate or a caution of 800 francs, a very considerable sum. Beddoes, we are told, at first seemed willing to pay the caution, but then changed his mind and maintained that the police ought to be satisfied with his 'diplomatic' passport (possibly a diplomatic visa is intended), otherwise he should be forced to complain to the British Ambassador that British passports were not respected in Zürich. He then called on Burgomaster Hess, protesting against the treatment he had received at the hands of the police. The Burgomaster investigated the case, but found that no treaty, similar to those concluded with France and Sardinia regulating the residence of their nationals in the Canton, existed where England was concerned, and Beddoes would have to pay his caution or remove elsewhere. By 17 August, however, the caution was still unpaid, and Beddoes received notice that failure to pay it within fifteen days would result in an order for his expulsion. At the same time the police were instructed to take such measures as were usual in the case of the deportation of foreigners. But on 29 August the Excutive, of which Beddoes' friend Ulrich was the chief, reported that all the necessary formalities had not been observed by the Town Council, and they did not see their way to deport Beddoes until that was done. The next meeting of the Council did not take place until 19 October, when it was decided to reprimand the Executive and to issue an order for Beddoes' immediate expulsion. Inquiries were further to be made within ten days to ascertain whether the order had been executed. The police consequently made their appearance at Beddoes' lodgings at 1 Rosengasse on 27 October and were received by Beddoes, who, to the confusion of these ministers of justice, produced a certificate of matriculation in the University. Academic citizenship was something which even the Town Council and Burgomaster Hess had to respect, and on 29 October the order for Beddoes' deportation was cancelled and his membership card in the University restored to him. He had learned his lesson at Würzburg, and the University Registers confirm his second matriculation on 4 September 1839. For nearly two months he had been laughing in his sleeve at the angry efforts of the city dignitaries to reduce an independent Englishman to obedience of the letter of the law. But long before the matter was thus settled, the liberal government had been overthrown, Ulrich was in exile with Keller at Baden in the neighbouring canton of Aargau, whereas Burgomaster Hess was confirmed in his position as a member of the new government.

At the revolution on 6 September 1839 most of Beddoes' friends had been compelled to flee, and although normal conditions were soon restored at Zürich, Beddoes' existence cannot have been as free from anxiety as when he enjoyed the protection of some of the most powerful members of the government. He stayed on until 9 April 1840, when, by all accounts, he had suddenly to flee the country. The circumstances are mysterious. There was nothing in the general conditions to necessitate such desperate action. Unless he was acting on a sudden impulse, perhaps even under a misapprehension, the only conclusion seems to be that he had been guilty of some exceptionally violent attack on the government or felt himself under grave suspicion and sought safety before arrest—a fate which indeed did overtake other foreign political agitators at that very time. From this unhappy moment Beddoes was to be 'for ever wandering', unable to settle down for more than one or two years at the utmost in the same place.

At last he returned to England for more than a short visit. On Monday, 15 June, he gave a lecture at the Polytechnic Institution, Regent Street, on 'The History, Past and Present, and the Hopes of Future Dramatic Poetry of the Caucasian Race in Europe'. Very few people went, but among the audience was probably Procter and certainly Emmeline King, the poet's cousin. Seeing the rows of empty benches Beddoes suggested cancelling the lecture, but the gallant few insisted on hearing him. He showed signs of age, we are told. Nobody present had seen him for twelve or fifteen years, and he on his part had been through harrowing experiences and more than once lost all that seemed to make life worth living. His lecture was 'a magnificent piece of writing', but he read it without animation. What it contained we do not know, although it seems likely that *The Ivory Gate*, which was to have contained 'critical and cacochymical remarks on the European literature, in specie the hapless drama of our day', had to give up its buried treasure in order to entertain a handful of the poet's acquaintances in a London lecture hall.

He was probably not a little isolated in London. Procter was married to a wife who 'cordially detested' Beddoes; Bourne was far away in Newfoundland; he did not see Kelsall. English institutions, or I think rather English society as it was then constituted, apparently seemed to him more detestable than ever. It seems as if English people, when they do react against their surroundings, react more strongly than other nations. However that may be, after so many years of vagabondage on the Continent Beddoes could no longer adapt himself to English ways, and his family connexions were all too grand for him now. So he set out for the Continent again and left 'Cantland' for Berlin early in September.

What attracted him there was a new liberal régime which raised high hopes among the radicals, and even more, I suspect, the presence of friends of former days in Würzburg and Zürich, foremost among them Schönlein. We know little of his life there. His habits probably remained much the same as at Zürich. He attended lectures at the University from 1 November 1840 to 8 March 1842. His name occurs in the address-book as Doctor of Medicine, but we do not know whether he practised as a physician. For a time he was joined by his cousin William Minton Beddoes, who now studied medicine in his turn, and the poet was able to give him good and kindly advice concerning his studies. He seems to have been familiar with all the medical schools in the German-speaking world and known most of the professors personally or by reputation. It would seem, however, as if he had found the climate trying after so many winters spent in Switzerland, and after a visit to London in the summer of 1842 he spent the winter and following spring at Baden in Aargau, seeking a cure for rheumatism.

In July 1843 he was in Zürich, where he was to spend a whole year in his old rooms in Rennweg. Here by force of habit Melpomene visited him again, and I think it must have been during this year that he wrote out the new First Act to *Death's Jest-Book* in a new manuscript book. He wrote poems in German too for the Zürich press, all political, all radical and anti-catholic. His English poems were few and fragmentary but all dictated by emotional necessity. In August 1844 he was back at Baden for a two months' stay, before proceeding to Giessen, where he had hoped to study under Liebig, the greatest chemist of the day. Unfortunately there was no room for Beddoes, and so he went on his way to Frankfort where he had friends in the theatre, and where after a short visit to Berlin in December he was to return. Perhaps through his connexions with the theatre Beddoes here made the acquaintance of Konrad Degen, who for the rest of his life was to remain his best friend. Eight years younger than Beddoes, Degen had as a mere child been apprenticed to his step-father, who was a baker. The boy, however, had shown a decided inclination for the stage and, after trying his hand at amateur acting, had joined a travelling company in 1837. His performances led to engagements at Mainz, Wiesbaden, and Bremen, but they were all brief, and he was soon forced to return to his step-father's profession. Only six years after the poet's death did he finally devote himself to the stage as a regular member of the Frankfort company.

Beddoes seems to have spent the summer in Switzerland. Possibly Degen was with him. Baden still remained his headquarters, and there he stored his wardrobe and books. He was there from September till December 1845, staying at the Lion Hotel, and on one occasion managed to disturb the peace of Baden by the noise proceeding from his room, for which he was fined eight francs. In January 1846 he was back at Frankfort and stayed there until the end of July, when he went to pay a visit to England which turned out to be his final one. Perhaps Beddoes himself had some presentiment of this, for he made a point of visiting all his remaining friends. Bourne, his Pembroke fellow-collegiate, was dead. Andrew Phillips, Revell's brother who acted for him in Shropshire, receiving the rents from his farms for him, thus became the first on the list. From Shiffnall he announced his impending arrival to his family and to Kelsall. Yet it seems to have caused no little sensation when he made his appearance at Cheney Longville riding astride a donkey and, apparently, none too sober. But then he did not like 'the society of fine ladies or to dine with three footmen at my back'. I doubt whether it had been his intention to winter in England. It seems more likely that the ailments of an English winter which assail those who are not used to it overtook Beddoes before he had time to get away. His prolonged stay at Cheney Longville was little to his liking, and for six months he remained shut up in his room reading, smoking, and drinking, little to the liking of his hosts. At length he proceeded to William Minton Beddoes at Birkenhead, 'one of the most abominable places this side of Tartarus,' awaiting warmer weather to travel again. In April he visited Kelsall at Fareham and paid him a short call again at the beginning of June before sailing for the Continent. There were few ties now between the former friends, for the poetry that had fascinated Kelsall more than twenty years earlier had ceased to interest its author. He was occupied with graver matters and appeared to Kelsall almost exclusively concerned with his own inner visions. If I am right in thinking that Kelsall on this occasion produced one of Beddoes' early, long-forgotten note-books for the poet to write in it a souvenir of his stay, we can see, if we did not know it otherwise, what were the visions that so occupied him.

Sweet and sweet is their poisoned note,
The little snakes of silver throat,
In mossy sculls that nest and lie,
Ever singing 'die, oh! die.'

The lifelong student was contemplating how to attain the very well of truth. Zoë King, who saw him at Bristol, was 'shocked' at his appearance and thought 'he looked as if he could not live long'.

In London he stayed with Revell Phillips at the Middle Temple, and considering how little these two had met and that the firm friendship between them was a direct result of the impression formed by Phillips of Beddoes' character in his correspondence, it is a remarkable tribute to the poet's moral integrity. There was no more upright man than Phillips, and nobody expressed a greater respect for Beddoes or a higher opinion of his character. He did not see the Procters very often, for he was shy of company. He came when he thought he would find them alone, but if he suspected they had guests he stayed away. One such occasion has become notorious. He had been asked to dinner and afterwards to the theatre. He did not turn up for dinner, but on approaching Drury Lane the Procters found Beddoes arrested by the police for attempting to set the theatre on fire by means of holding a burning five-pound note against a chair. Procter, according to Gosse, had little difficulty in persuading the authorities that such methods were likely to be more injurious to the pocket of the alleged incendiary than to the fabric of the house, but there can be little doubt that this was a genuine demonstration on Beddoes' part against 'the hapless drama of our day', and if his and Isbrand's friend Lord Alcohol supported him in his contention, this makes his gesture none the less significant.

Early in July 1847 Beddoes was back at Frankfort.

Degen was to tell Zoë King in after-years that on one occasion when he returned after an absence he came into the shop and acted a scene with great spirit and then sat down, his eyes beaming. The two friends may have gone for a short tour to Switzerland in the early autumn. Beddoes habitually travelled stick in hand, but with no luggage whatsoever. He liked the common people and talked to them at the inns along the road, and everywhere he was listened to with respect and attention. One morning they arrived at Zürich early, before people were up, and Degen saw somebody open a window and call to another to come and 'look at Herr Beddoes'. He was entirely at home in Switzerland.

At Frankfort Beddoes pursued his scientific experiments and one day, while dissecting, cut his finger and for six months suffered from the effects of blood-poisoning. One almost wonders whether the accident was genuine. As usual when he was ill, he cut himself off from all company, except Degen, who came to see him at least twice a week. But Gosse's insinuation that he lived with Degen is absolutely without foundation. Whatever his friendships, they were not of a nature to convince Beddoes of anything except 'the absurdity and unsatisfactory nature of human life'. His friendship for Reich had not been sufficient to deter him from trying to commit suicide at Göttingen, nor was his deep and genuine attachment to Degen of a nature to make him wish to prolong his existence now. His philosophy, so far from being that of an inverted Don Giovanni, successful in love-making, is on the contrary that of a man whose inmost heart is with the dead, whose soul is in eternity. I am afraid the 'single and sinfully virtuous' of his letter to Kelsall, 9 March 1837, has to be taken literally and applies not only to the happiest period of his life, but to his last melancholy years of wandering as well.

During his illness Beddoes wrote many letters to his friend which were unfortunately not preserved. He was growing thin and worn, and he let his beard grow. In Degen's eyes he looked like Shakespeare. He taught his friend English and invariably made amusing comments on his mistakes in his written exercises, pointed but always kind. Degen's seemingly filial devotion to Beddoes was undiminished when after more than ten years he spoke to Zoë King, and that conversation, as recorded by her, is the only source for our knowledge of their relationship. It is possible, however, that Beddoes had spoken to Revell Phillips of his hopeless longings, for whereas Kelsall was utterly perturbed by the news of his death having in fact been suicidal, Phillips had been long prepared for such a solution, adding that he thought 'it probable that he had a love disappointment'.

On 6 May 1848 Beddoes applied for a residence permit at Frankfort for six months, and it looks as if it had been his intention to return. On 3 July, however, he set out for Switzerland and a fortnight later, on 18 July, was taken to the Basle Hospital because he had that morning opened an artery in his left leg with a razor. When years later Zoë King heard this story from a waiter at the Cigogne Hotel she tried to make him say that Beddoes had been drunk at the time. But not at all. He knew perfectly well what he was doing. He successfully kept the story dark and jealously guarded his loneliness during his last months in hospital. Gosse says that Degen came to his bedside, but there is no such evidence, and I think it must be one of Gosse's fanciful interpretations of the scanty material. Beddoes died alone. 'I am food for *what I am good for*—worms...I ought to have been among other things a good poet.'—A good and true poet he had been, but he had long since passed beyond mere worldly ambitions. There was poetry in his soul still.

The Cigogne Hotel, Basle, where, on 18 July 1848, Beddoes cut open an artery in his leg.

(after lithograph by J. M. Benz)

but he sought what he conceived as the source of all poetry.

The irony that is ever on the watch in our lives would so have it that even at his death he was still remembered as the author of *The Brides' Tragedy*, a work of unique promise, some would say only partly fulfilled, Kelsall among them. But as in life he fulfilled his destiny, so in his poetry also he gave permanent expression to the longing in his heart for a love greater than worldly love and a truth deeper than the transitory truth of mortal life.

CRITICAL COMMENTS

CRITICAL COMMENTS

From *The Album*, May 1823. *On Ancient and Modern Tragedy*, p. 28 and note, pp. 28–9

It will be seen that we have confined ourselves to *acted* plays...and at the present moment when so many poems are thrown into dialogue, it would be endless to give specific consideration to each.

We wish to make one exception to this, and to say a few words concerning a very remarkable production of this sort, which has lately appeared, entitled, 'The Bride's [*sic*] Tragedy'. We call it a remarkable performance, from its being the work of a very young man, (he states himself, in his preface, to be a minor,) and as conjoining very striking poetical merits with what we consider the greatest dramatic faults. It is 'brimmed up and running over' with poetry of the wildest imagination and most beautiful fancy—but we have devoted great part of this article to prove that such writing is out of place in a play. The management of the plot is very inartificial and unskilful, as might be expected from so young a writer,—and the dialogue, as we have said, is nearly all entirely inappropriate, as regards the situation of the speaker; but regarded as poetry alone, it is (with the pardonable exception of occasional unsuccessful daring, and, here and there, of a little downright extravagance,) of a degree of originality and beauty which even these most poetical days rarely present... [Quotes *Brides'* *Tragedy*, I, i, 95–133.]

This is the perfection of graceful and poetical fancy. If Mr. Beddoes would write a poem instead of a play, we have no doubt that he would realize all the expectations which this brilliant first performance has excited.

From *The Examiner*, 20 July 1850, pp. 461–3. John Forster, *Death's Jest-Book, or the Fool's Tragedy*

The mere title of this dramatic poem recalls a play by Webster, or Cyril Tourneur, and its contents more vividly remind us of those great writers. But not as an imitation. The author of this extraordinary production is no imitator. He is a man of the most original genius. Lawless and unrestrained are his flights of imagination, his outlines of character careless or extravagant, and a madman's dream not more violent or improbable than his ideas of a story or plot. Yet the book is a masterpiece of poetry—a perfect study of style for a young poet. We will recommend it to the best attention of the rising generation of genius ... It is radiant in almost every page with passion, fancy, or thought, set in a most apposite and exquisite language. We have but to discard, in reading it, the hope of any steady interest of story, or consistent development of character: and we shall find a most surprising succession of beautiful passages, unrivalled in sentiment and pathos, as well as in terseness, dignity, and picturesque vigour of language; in subtlety and power of passion, as well as in delicacy and strength of imagination; and as perfect and various, in modulation of verse, as the airy flights of Fletcher or Marlowe's mighty line ...

The reader will have observed throughout our extracts the invariably happy use of the best phrases; and often we have that employment of words suggesting subtle analogies of feeling and thought, painting at once a picture and a passion, in which Shakespeare is fond of indulging ...

Art thou alone? WHY SO SHOULD BE CREATORS AND DESTROYERS.

The whole range of the Elizabethan drama has not a finer expression than that—nor indeed does any single work of the period, out of Shakespeare, exhibit so many rich and precious bars of golden verse, side by side with such poverty and misery of character and plot ... Nothing can be meaner than the design, nothing grander than the execution ...

We must frankly say, in conclusion, that we are not acquainted with any living author who could have written the *Fool's Tragedy*; and, though the publication is unaccompanied by any hint of authorship, we believe that we are correct in stating it to be a posthumous production of the author of the *Bride's* [*sic*] *Tragedy*, Mr. Thomas Lovell Beddoes. Speaking of the latter production, now more than a quarter of a century ago (Mr. Beddoes was then, we believe, a student at Pembroke College, Oxford, and a minor), the *Edinburgh Review* ventured upon a prediction of future fame and achievement for the writer, which an illchosen and ill-directed subsequent career unhappily interrupted and baffled. But in proof of the noble natural gifts which suggested such anticipation, the production before us remains; and we may judge to what extent a more steady course and regular cultivation would have fertilized a soil, which, neglected and uncared for, has thrown out such a glorious growth of foliage and fruit as this *Fool's Tragedy*.

From *The Examiner*, 27 September 1851, p. 613b. John Forster, *Poems. By the late Thomas Lovell Beddoes, Author of Death's Jest-Book, or the Fool's Tragedy. With a memoir*

... But surely all we have quoted, fragmentary as it is, proclaims a writer of the highest order—magnificent in diction, terse and close in expression, various and beautiful in modulation, displaying imaginative thoughts of the highest reach, and sweeping the chords of passion with a strong and fearless hand. Plenty of defects may be noted—scenes hastily constructed, characters exalted into mere passionate abstractions, motives too sudden, loves and revenges too abundant and intense—but never a want of sincerity, never a borrowed trick, never a gaudy irrelevance, never a superfluous commonplace.

From a *Letter from Robert Browning to T. F. Kelsall*, 22 May 1868. Printed in *The Browning Box, or the Life and Works of Thomas Lovell Beddoes as reflected in letters by his friends and admirers*, Oxford University Press, 1935, pp. 103–5

As I expected, from the moment I began reading the M.S.S. there was nothing for me but to go on and end. I have done so, wishing the matter to read were a year's work rather than a few days': there is not one word I have missed: nor do I find that difficulty in the characters which you speak of. How such a dose of glorious poetry would have affected my brain had I gulped Beddoes for the first time, I hardly know ... On the whole I think you dealt perfectly with Death's Jest Book, in what you with[h]eld: such capital things as Saint Gingo and the Tailor it is a pity to absolutely lose,—but they may be given stripped of the accompanying dialogue. I see what Beddoes wanted to do, and what effect he aimed at in this inter-fusion of the 'comic stuff' which Milton objects to when blent with 'Tragic sadness & gravity'. The 'stuff' here is immeasurably below the general texture: not that it is other than remarkable,—but what a word would *this* be for the poetry of the piece! Had the comic faculty, and one or two others, been developed in the author equally with the tragic power,—what would have the man been? With the imperfect developments I rate some essential to a complete dramatist: such as a[n] insight into and sympathy with characters quite different from his own. I fancy Beddoes, with no more change than is usual with any one man in various circumstances, at once Melveric, Ziba, Wolfram & the rest. He thinks and speaks now as this and now that personage,—in every sense, as he himself likes best,— I never find a new actor speaking his own peculiarities whether Beddoes like them or no. Sibylla, for instance, is thin as her own ghost,—speaking fine things, all the same,—but they stick on her like a fruiterer's contribution of real cherries & strawberries to an invisible wire-tree,—there is no living plant which one can see naturally has produced them,—a hand intervened and gave the skeleton 'non sua poma'. If I dare conjecture about the cause of the defect,—it may have come from Beddoes' predominating desire, in the first stage of his artistry, to deliver himself of what was absorbingly & exclusively interesting to him at the time: had he printed the piece just as it stands, without any delay at all,—he would have at least done justice, in his own mind, to these conceptions of death and life and the intermediate possible state: the exhibition would have been both done and done with: he would have turned his attention to other subjects of thought and feeling, which, whether as congenial to him as the former, were at least new and unexpressed: whereas, he is prevented somehow from venting these, and so goes round and round them, ends in the exclusive occupation of his soul with them,—does not he? What good was got by suppressing the poem, or what harm could have followed the publication even in the worldly way of looking at things? Suppose it had been laughed at, blackguarded in Blackwood, fallen flat from the press? The worse for the world for the quarter of an hour: Beddoes would not have much cared, but probably made a clean breast and begun on something else. It is infinitely regrettable. I incline to think that in a future edition I should give the work (as Byron says 'since it can do us good!') in its integrity: the indifferent readers won't care in any case,—the sympathetic will bear all Mandrake & his wife, out of a scientific love of the precise intention of the author. And how curiously different it proves from that which is announced, and probably believed in, by Beddoes in his letter of verse to Procter: he was to despoil Death of his terrors, strip him of his dart, & so on,—make him the 'fool of the feast': he does exactly the reverse, materializes and intensifies the horror, and frightens one to death at dying—just as they do abroad when on every church wall you see a horrible capering Death flourishing his scythe in your face, for 'a fair warning to a careless world', as the old divines have it ...

Now, as to the extracts which might be made why, you might pick out scenes, passages, lyrics, fine as fine can be: the power of the man is immense & irresistible. I don't know, however, that it is advisable to make such a collection,—because you would leave little indeed behind you in the two volumes. If one 'cheated'—put in all the superlative passages of Death's J.B. for instance,—telling the story so as to give the idea that it would be found,—equally with those passages—worked out in the original,—to what a poem would you be sending people!

From *The Academy*, 15 August 1891, p. 129. By Arthur Symons. Reprinted, slightly revised, in *Figures of Several Centuries*, Constable 1916, pp. 123–27

... Beddoes is always large, impressive; the greatness of his aim gives him a certain claim on respectful consideration. That his talent achieved itself, or ever could have achieved itself, he himself would have been the last to affirm. But he is a monumental failure, more interesting than many facile triumphs.

The one important work which Beddoes actually completed, *Death's Jest-Book*, is nominally a drama in five acts. All the rest of his work, except a few lyrics and occasional poems, is also nominally dramatic. But there never was anything less dramatic in substance than this mass of admirable poetry in dialogue. Beddoes' genius was essentially lyrical: he had imagination, the gift of style, the mastery of rhythm, a strange choiceness and curiosity of phrase. But of really dramatic power he had nothing. He could neither conceive a coherent plot, nor develop a credible situation. He had no grasp on human nature, he had no conception of what character might be in men and women, he had no faculty of expressing emotion convincingly. Constantly you find the most beautiful poetry where it is absolutely inappropriate, but never do you find one of those brief and memorable phrases—words from the heart—for which one would give much beautiful poetry ...

In scenes which aim at being passionate, one sees the same inability to be natural. What we get is always literature; it is never less than that, nor more than that. It is never frank, uncompromising nature. The fact is, that Beddoes wrote from the head, collectively, and without emotion, or without inspiration, save in literature. All Beddoes' characters speak precisely the same language, express the same desires; all in the same way startle us by their ghostly remoteness from flesh and blood. 'Man is tired of being merely human,' Siegfried says, in *Death's Jest-Book*, and Beddoes may be said to have grown tired of humanity before he ever came to understand it.

Looked at from the normal standpoint, Beddoes' idea of the drama was something wildly amateurish. As a practical playwright he would be beneath contempt; as a writer of the regulation poetic drama he cannot be considered successful. But what he aimed at was something peculiar to himself—a sort of spectral dramatic fantasia. He would have admitted his obligations to Webster and Tourneur, to all the *macabre* Elizabethan work; he would have admitted that his foundations were based on literature, not on life; but he would have claimed, and claimed justly, that he had produced, out of many strange elements, something which has a place apart in English poetry. *Death's Jest-Book* is perhaps the most morbid poem in our literature. There is not a page without its sad, grotesque, gay or abhorrent imagery of the tomb ... Not Baudelaire was more amorous of corruption; not Poe was more spellbound by the scent of graveyard earth. So Beddoes has written a new Dance of Death, in poetry; has become the chronicler of the praise and ridicule of Death. 'Tired of being merely human', he has peopled a play with confessed phantoms. It is natural that these eloquent speakers should pass us by with their words, that they should fail to move us by their sorrows or their hates: they are not intended to be human, except, indeed, in the wizard humanity of Death ...

From *The New Quarterly*, Nov. 1907, pp. 65–7. Lytton Strachey, *The Last Elizabethan*. Reprinted in *Books and Characters*, 1922, pp. 244–6

... To the reader, doubtless, his faulty construction is glaring enough; but Beddoes wrote his plays to be acted, as a passage in one of his letters very clearly shows. 'You are, I think,' he writes to Kelsall, 'disinclined to the stage: now I confess that I think this is the highest aim of the dramatist; and should be very desirous to get on it. To look down on it is a piece of impertinence, as long as one chooses to write in the form of a play, and is generally the result of one's own inability to produce anything striking and affecting in that way.' And it is precisely upon the stage that such faults of construction as those which disfigure Beddoes' tragedies matter least. An audience, whose attention is held and delighted by a succession of striking incidents clothed in splendid speech, neither cares nor knows whether the effect of the whole, as a whole, is worthy of the separate parts. It would be foolish, in the present melancholy condition of the art of dramatic declamation, to wish for the public performance of *Death's Jest-Book*; but it is impossible not to hope that the time may come when an adequate representation of that strange and great work may be something more that 'a possibility more thin than air'. Then, and then only, shall we be able to take true measure of Beddoes' genius ...

It would be vain to look, among such spectral imaginings ..., for guidance in practical affairs, or for illuminating views on men and things, or for a philosophy, or, in short, for anything which may be called a 'criticism of life'. If a poet must be a critic of life, Beddoes was certainly no poet. He belongs to the class of writers of which, in English literature, Spenser, Keats, and Milton are the dominant figures—the writers who are great merely because of their art. Sir James Stephen was only telling the truth when he remarked that Milton might have put all that he had to say in *Paradise Lost* into a prose pamphlet of two or three pages. But who cares about what Milton had to say? It is his way of saying it that matters; it is his expression. Take away the expression from the *Satires* of Pope, or from *The Excursion*, and, though you will destroy the poems, you will leave behind a great mass of thought. Take away the expression from *Hyperion*, and you will leave nothing at all. To ask which is the better of the two styles is like asking whether a peach is better than a rose, because, both being beautiful, you can eat the one and not the other. At any rate, Beddoes is among the roses: it is in his expression that his greatness lies. His verse is an instrument of many modulations, of exquisite delicacy, of strange suggestiveness, of amazing power. Playing on it, he can give utterance to the subtlest visions ...

From Edmund Blunden, *Beddoes and his Contemporaries*, *Votive Tablets*, Cobden Sanderson, 1931, pp. 294–6

... Sir Edmund Gosse points out as Beddoes's worst weakness 'his inability to record conversation', and to distinguish his stage figures by the language allotted to them, nor would it be easy to discover in *Death's Jest Book* any weighty exceptions to this just remonstrance. But where is an explanation? Beddoes *could* record conversation—outside *Death's Jest Book*; we turn to his letters and we find one of the most spirited sketches of talk ever made:

'Capital was my first adventure in 1835 at Dover. London Coffee house, old gentleman in coffee room. Waiter, says I, I wish to smoke a cigar, have you a smoking room? *W.* No occasion, Sir, you can smoke here. *I (to O.G.)* Perhaps it may be disagreeable to you, Sir, in which case—— *O.G.* By no means. I'm myself a smoker (laying aside specs. and looking like Cosmogony Jenkins ——) *I.* I have good cigars, will you d.m.t.f. to accept one? *O.G.* Very kind. *I.* Come from Calais? *O.G.* Boulogne. Go to Bristol. *I.* Anche io sono Bristoliano. *O.G.* Know King? *I.* Wife my aunt. *O.G.* Are Y O U? *I.* Son of well-known physician at Clifton. *O.G.* Not of Dr B.? *I.* Same, unworthily, *O.G.* That's curious. Your brother married my niece a fortnight ago. *I.* Happy man! Hear of it now for yᵉ first time. Tories will never be my heirs. *O.G.* O! G——! (reassumes specs and exit.) *I.* I! *exeo.*'

That plainness, and artfulness, and quickness are the antipodes of the lugubrious and long speeches in *Death's Jest Book*—those prodigious passages which recall a description of Coleridge's conversation— 'monopollylogues'. Among these the painstaking reader discovers expressions of the Beddoes that might have been. Here are the enchanting songs ... and here too are startling moments such as when the scientist in Beddoes speaks. Isbrand's soliloquy at the beginning of Act V is perhaps the best known and the most reverberant of these ... If we bring together that evolutionary passage at full length, and another theoretical discernment of which the central image is

> *that Life's a single pilgrim*
> *Fighting unarmed amongst a thousand soldiers,—*

an image wonderfully varied and emphasized in the fragment on 'Windless Pestilence'; if with these we take up the paradox elaborated towards the end of *Death's Jest Book*—'But dead and living, which are which?' and such of the occasional pieces as the quatorzain 'To Perfume' and that 'To Tartar, a Terrier Beauty', we speedily compose a shape of poetic originality more enduring and more inspiring even than the beautiful but ever-uncertain songs. Exploring the tragic wardrobe, Beddoes is seldom at ease; talking straight from his studies and his practice, he becomes concise, and prophetic, and complete. What future generations may choose to read in poetry cannot be foreseen; but what this generation would have been reading is Beddoes, had he left one volume of short poems on the realities with which his days were spent...

THE BRIDES' TRAGEDY

[First published 1822]

THE BRIDES' TRAGEDY

[First published 1822]

·

DRAMATIS PERSONÆ

THE DUKE	MORDRED
LORD ERNEST	HUBERT
HESPERUS, *his Son*	A HUNTSMAN
ORLANDO	BOY, *Page to Orlando*
CLAUDIO	JAILOR

OLIVIA, *Sister to Orlando*
VIOLETTA, *her Companion*
LENORA, *Wife of Mordred*
FLORIBEL, *her Daughter*

Lords, Citizens, Attendants, Guards, &c.

ACT I

SCENE I. *A garden*

HESPERUS *alone*

Now Eve has strewn the sun's wide billowy couch
With rosered feathers moulted from her wing,
Still scanty-sprinkled clouds, like lagging sheep,
Some golden-fleeced, some streaked with delicate pink,
Are creeping up the welkin, and behind   5
The wind, their boisterous shepherd, whistling drives
    them,
From the drear wilderness of night to drink
Antipodean noon. At such a time,
While to wild melody fantastic dreams
Dance their gay morrice in the midmost air,   10
And sleepers' truant fancies fly to join them;

While that winged song, the restless nightingale
Turns her sad heart to music, sweet it is
Unseen on the moss-cushioned sward to lean,
And into some coy ear pour out the soul   15
In sighs and whispers.

Enter FLORIBEL

So late, Floribel?
Nay, since I see that arch smile on thy cheek
Rippling so prettily, I will not chide,
Although the breeze and I have sighed for you
A dreary while, and the veiled Moon's mild eye   20
Has long been seeking for her loveliest nymph.
Come, come, my love, or shall I call you bride?

   Flor. E'en what you will, so that you hold me dear.
   Hesp. Well, both my love and bride; see, here's a
     bower
Of Eglantine with honeysuckles woven,   25
Where not a spark of prying light creeps in,
So closely do the sweets enfold each other.
'Tis Twilight's home; come in, my gentle love,
And talk to me. So! I've a rival here;
What's this that sleeps so sweetly on your neck?   30

   Flor. Jealous so soon, my Hesperus? Look then,
It is a bunch of flowers I pulled for you:
Here's the blue violet, like Pandora's eye,
When first it darkened with immortal life.   34

   Hesp. Sweet as thy lips. Fie on those taper fingers,
Have they been brushing the long grass aside
To drag the daisy from its hiding-place,
Where it shuns light, the Danäe of flowers,
With gold up-hoarded on its virgin lap?   39

   Flor. And here's a treasure that I found by chance,
A lily of the valley; low it lay
Over a mossy mound, withered and weeping
As on a fairy's grave.

   Hesp.   Of all the posy

Give me the rose, though there's a tale of blood
Soiling its name. In elfin annals old   45
'Tis writ, how Zephyr, envious of his love,
(The love he bore to Summer, who since then
Has weeping visited the world;) once found
The baby Perfume cradled in a violet;
('Twas said the beauteous bantling was the child   50
Of a gay bee, that in his wantonness
Toyed with a peabud in a lady's garland;)
The felon winds, confederate with him,
Bound the sweet slumberer with golden chains,
Pulled from the wreathed laburnum, and together   55
Deep cast him in the bosom of a rose,
And fed the fettered wretch with dew and air.
At length his soul, that was a lover's sigh,
Waned from his body, and the guilty blossom   59
His heart's blood stained. The twilight-haunting gnat
His requiem whined, and harebells tolled his knell,
And still the bee in pied velvet dight
With melancholy song from flower to flower
Goes seeking his lost offspring.
    Flor.   Take it then,
In its green sheath. What guess you, Hesperus,   65
I dreamed last night? Indeed, it makes me sad,
And yet I think you love me.
    Hesp.   By the planet
That sheds it tender blue on lovers' sleeps,
Thou art my sweetest, nay, mine only thought:
And when my heart forgets thee, may yon heaven   70
Forget to guard me.
    Flor.   Aye, I knew thou didst;
Yet surely mine's a sad and lonely fate
Thus to be wed to secrecy; I doubt,
E'en while I know my doubts are causeless torments.
Yet I conjure thee, if indeed I hold   75
Some share in thy affections, cast away
The blank and ugly vizor of concealment,

And, if mine homely breeding do not shame thee,
Let thy bride share her noble father's blessing.

Hesp. In truth I will; nay, prithee let me kiss   80
That naughty tear away; I will, by heaven;
For, though austere and old, my sire must gaze
On thy fair innocence with glad forgiveness.
Look up, my love,
See how yon orb, dressed out in all her beams,   85
Puts out the common stars, and sails along
The stately Queen of heaven; so shall thy beauties,
But the rich casket of a noble soul,
Shine on the world and bless it. Tell me now
This frightful vision.

Flor.   You will banter me;   90
But I'm a simple girl, and oftentimes
In solitude am very, very mournful:
And now I think how silly 'twas to weep
At such an harmless thing: well, you shall hear.
'Twas on a fragrant bank I laid me down,   95
Laced o'er and o'er with verdant tendrils, full
Of dark-red strawberries. Anon there came
On the wind's breast a thousand tiny noises,
Like flowers' voices, if they could but speak;
Then slowly did they blend in one sweet strain,   100
Melodiously divine; and buoyed the soul
Upon their undulations. Suddenly,
Methought, a cloud swam swanlike o'er the sky,
And gently kissed the earth, a fleecy nest,
With roses, rifled from the cheek of Morn,   105
Sportively strewn; upon the ethereal couch,
Her fair limbs blending with the enamoured mist,
Lovely above the portraiture of words,
In beauteous languor lay the Queen of Smiles:
In tangled garlands, like a golden haze,   110
Or fay-spun threads of light, her locks were floating,
And in their airy folds slumbered her eyes,
Dark as the nectar-grape that gems the vines

In the bright orchard of the Hesperides.
Within the ivory cradle of her breast   115
Gambolled the urchin god, with saucy hand
Dimpling her cheeks, or sipping eagerly
The rich ambrosia of her melting lips:
Beneath them swarmed a bustling mob of Loves,
Tending the sparrow stud, or with bees' wings   120
Imping their arrows. Here stood one alone
Blowing a pyre of blazing lovers' hearts
With bellows full of absence-caused sighs:
Near him his work-mate mended broken vows   124
With dangerous gold, or strung soft rhymes together
Upon a lady's tress. Some swelled their cheeks,
Like curling rose-leaves, or the red wine's bubbles,
In petulant debate, gallantly tilting
Astride their darts. And one there was alone,
Who with wet downcast eyelids threw aside   130
The remnants of a broken heart, and looked
Into my face and bid me 'ware of love,
Of fickleness, and woe, and mad despair.
    Hesp. Aye, so he said; and did my own dear girl
Deem me a false one for this foolish dream?   135
I wish I could be angry; hide, distrustful,
Those penitent blushes in my breast, while I
Sing you a silly song old nurses use
To hush their crying babes with. Tenderly
'Twill chide you.   140

Song

    Poor old pilgrim Misery,
        Beneath the silent moon he sate,
    A-listening to the screech owl's cry,
        And the cold wind's goblin prate;
    Beside him lay his staff of yew   145
        With withered willow twined,

7

His scant grey hair all wet with dew,
    His cheeks with grief ybrined;
        And his cry it was ever, alack!
            Alack, and woe is me.   150

Anon a wanton imp astray
    His piteous moaning hears,
And from his bosom steals away
    His rosary of tears:
With his plunder fled that urchin elf,   155
    And hid it in your eyes,
Then tell me back the stolen pelf,
    Give up the lawless prize;
        Or your cry shall be ever, alack!
            Alack, and woe is me.   160

Hesp. Not yet asleep?
Flor.   Asleep! No, I could ever,
Heedless of times and seasons list to thee.
But now the chilly breeze is sallying out
Of dismal clouds; and silent midnight walks
Wrapt in her mourning robe. I fear it's time   165
To separate.
    Hesp. So quickly late! oh cruel, spiteful hours,
Why will ye wing your steeds from happiness,
And put a leaden drag upon your wheels   169
When grief hangs round our hearts. Soon will we meet,
And to part never more.
    Flor.   Oh! that dear never,
It will pay all. Good night, and think of me.
    Hesp. Good night, my love; may music-winged sleep
Bind round thy temples with her poppy wreath;
Soft slumbers to thee.   [*Exeunt.* 175

8

SCENE II. *A room in* ORLANDO'S *palace*

CLAUDIO *and* ORLANDO *meeting*

Orl. Thanks for thy speed, good Claudio; is all done
As I have ordered?

Clau.   Could I be unwilling
In the performance of what you command,
I'd say with what regret I led Lord Ernest
Into the prison. My dear lord,   5
He was your father's friend—

Orl.   And he is mine.
You must not think Orlando so forgetful
As to abuse the reverence of age,
An age, like his, of piety and virtue;
'Tis but a fraud of kindness, sportive force.   10

Clau. You joy me much, for now I dare to own
I almost thought it was a cruel deed.

Orl. Nay, you shall hear. The sums he owed my
                                                   father,
Of which his whole estate is scarce a fourth,
Are never to be claimed, if Hesperus,   15
His son, be weddded to Olivia. Now
This Hesperus, you tell me, is a votary,
A too much favoured votary of my goddess,
The Dian of our forests, Floribel;
Therefore I use this show of cruelty,   20
To scare a rival and to gain a brother.

Clau. Now by the patches on the cheek of the moon,
(Is't not a pretty oath?) a good romance;
We'll have't in ballad metre, with a burthen
Of sighs, how one bright glance of a brown damsel, 25
Lit up the tinder of Orlando's heart
In a hot blaze.

Orl.   Enough to kindle up
An altar in my breast. 'Twas but a moment,
And yet I would not sell that grain of time
For thy eternity of heartlessness.   30

Clau. Well, ...onsense from a lover,
Oh, I've been ....d eighteen times
And three qua...............nty yards, two nails,
An inch and ....easure, of sonnets;
Wasted as m.................ould pickle   35
Leviathan, an.................. to set up
Another wind;

   Orl. ....Claudio, I pray thee, leave me,
I relish not this mockery.

   Clau.   Good sir, attend
To my experience. You've no stock as yet
To set up lover: get yourself a pistol   40
Without a touch-hole, or at least remember,
If it be whole, to load it with wet powder;
I've known a popgun well applied, or even
The flying of a cork give reputation
To courage and despair. A gross of garters   45
Warranted rotten will be found convenient.

   Orl. Now you are troublesome.

   Clau.   One precept more,
Purge and drink watergruel, lanthorn jaws
Are interesting; fat men can't write sonnets,
And indigestion turns true love to bile.   50

   Orl. 'Tis best to part. If you desire to serve me,
Persuade the boy to sacrifice his passion;
I'll lead him to Olivia, they were wont
In childhood to be playmates, and some love
May lie beneath the ashes of that friendship,   55
That needs her breath alone to burst and blaze.

                           [*Exeunt.*

SCENE III. *A prison*

Enter Guards leading LORD ERNEST *in chains*

   L. Ern. I pray you do not pity me. I feel
A kind of joy to meet Calamity,

L. Ern.   Blush not, though I name your mistress,
You soon shall wed her.

Hesp.   I will wed the plague.
I would not grudge my life, for that's a thing,
A misery, thou gavest me: but to wed   65
Olivia; there's damnation in the thought.

L. Ern. Come, speak to him, my chains, for ye've a
          voice
To conquer every heart that's not your kin!
Oh! that ye were my son, for then at least
He would be with me. How I loved him once!   70
Aye, when I thought him good; but now—Nay, still
He must be good, and I, I have been harsh,
I feel, I have not prized him at his worth:
And yet I think if Hesperus had erred,
I could have pardoned him, indeed I could.   75

Hesp. We'll live together.

L. Ern.   No, for I shall die;
But that's no matter.

Hesp.   Bring the priest, the bride.
Quick, quick. These fetters have infected him
With slavery's sickness. Yet there is a secret,
'Twixt heaven and me, forbids it. Tell me, father;   80
Were it not best for both to die at once?

L. Ern. Die! Thou hast spoke a word, that makes my
          heart
Grow sick and wither; thou hast palsied me
To death. Live thou to wed some worthier maid;
Know that thy father chose this sad seclusion;   85
(Ye rebel lips, why do you call it sad?)
Should I die soon, think not that sorrow caused it,
But, if you recollect my name, bestow it
Upon your best-loved child, and when you give him
His Grandsire's blessing, add not that he perished   90
A wretched prisoner.

Hesp.   Stop, or I am made
I know not what,—perhaps a villain. Curse me,

Oh if you love me, curse.
    L. Ern.   Aye, thou shalt hear
A father's curse; if fate hath put a moment
Of pain into thy life; a sigh, a word,   95
A dream of woe; be it transferred to mine;
And for thy days; oh! never may a thought
Of others' sorrow, even of old Ernest's,
Darken their calm uninterrupted bliss,
And be thy end—oh! any thing but mine.   100
    Hesp. Guilt, thou art sanctified in such a cause;
Guards; *(they enter)* I am ready. Let me say't so low,
So quickly that it may escape the ear
Of watchful angels; I will do it all.
    L. Ern. There's nought to do; I've learned to love
        this solitude.   105
Farewell, my son. Nay, never heed the fetters;
We can make shift to embrace.
    Hesp.   Lead him to freedom,
And tell your lord I will not, that's I will.
                 [*Exeunt* LORD ERNEST *and guards.*
Here, fellow; put your hand upon my mouth
Till they are out of hearing. Leave me now.   110
No, stay; come near me, nearer yet. Now fix
The close attention of your eyes on mine.
    Guard. My lord!
    Hesp.   See'st thou not death in them?
    Guard. Forbid it, fate.
    Hesp.   Away! ill-omened hound,
I'll be a ghost and play about the graves,   115
For ghosts can never wed.   [*Exit guard.*
There, there they go; my hopes, my youthful hopes,
Like ingrate flatterers. What have I to do
With life? Ye sickly stars, that look with pity
On this cursed head, be kind and tell the lightning 120
To scathe me to a cinder; or if that
Be too much blessing for a child of sin,
But strike me mad, I do not ask for more.

Come from your icy caves, ye howling winds,
Clad in your gloomy panoply of clouds,   125
And call into your cars, as ye pass o'er
The distant quarters of this tortured world,
Every disease of every clime,
Here shall they banquet on a willing victim;
Or with one general ague shake the earth,   130
The pillars of the sky dissolve and burst,
And let the ebon-tiled roof of night
Come tumbling in upon the doomed world:
Deaf are they still: then death is all a fable,
A pious lie to make man lick his chains   135
And look for freedom's dawning through his grate.
Why are we tied unto this wheeling globe,
Still to be racked while traitorous Hope stands by,
And heals the wounds that they may gape again?
Aye to this end the earth is made a ball,   140
Else crawling to the brink despair would plunge
Into the infinite eternal air,
And leave its sorrows and its sins behind.
Since death will not, come sleep, thou kindred power,
Lock up my senses with thy leaden key,   145
And darken every crevice that admits
Light, life, and misery if thou canst, for ever.   [*Exit.*

ACT II

Scene I. *A chamber in* Orlando's *palace*

Enter Orlando *to his Boy asleep*

Orl. Boy! he is asleep;
Oh innocence, how fairly dost thou head
This pure first page of man. Peace to thy slumbers,
Sleep, for thy dreams are 'midst the seraphs' harps,
Thy thoughts beneath the wings of holiness,   5
Thine eyes in Paradise.

15

The day may come, (if haply gentle death
Say not amen to thy short prayer of being,
And lap thee in the bosom of the blest;)
I weep to think on, when the guilty world   10
Shall, like a fiend, be waiting at thy couch,
And call thee up on ev'ry dawn of crime.

    Boy. (*awaking*) Dear master, didst thou call? I will
      not be
A second time so slothful.

    Orl.   Sleep, my boy,
Thy task is light and joyous, to be good.   15

    Boy. Oh! if I must be good, then give me money,
I pray thee, give me some, and you shall find
I'll buy up every tear, and make them scarcer
Than diamonds.

    Orl. Beautiful pity, thou shalt have enough;   20
But you must give me your last song.

    Boy.   Nay, sir;
You're wont to say my rhymes are fit for girls,
And lovesick idiots; I have none you praise
Full of the heat of battle and the chase.

    Orl. Sing what you will, I'll like it.   25

Song

       A ho! A ho!
      Love's horn doth blow,
    And he will out a-hawking go.
  His shafts are light as beauty's sighs,
And bright as midnight's brightest eyes,   30
    And round his starry way
The swan-winged horses of the skies,
With summer's music in their manes,
Curve their fair necks to zephyr's reins,
    And urge their graceful play.   35

A ho! A ho!
  Love's horn doth blow,
    And he will out a-hawking go.
The sparrows flutter round his wrist,
The feathery thieves that Venus kissed   40
    And taught their morning song,
The linnets seek the airy list,
And swallows too, small pets of Spring,
Beat back the gale with swifter wing,
    And dart and wheel along.   45

    A ho! A ho!
    Love's horn doth blow,
      And he will out a-hawking go,
Now woe to every gnat that skips
To filch the fruit of ladies' lips,   50
    His felon blood is shed;
And woe to flies, whose airy ships
On beauty cast their anchoring bite,
And bandit wasp, that naughty wight,
    Whose sting is slaughter-red.   55

Orl. Who is thy poet, boy?
Boy.   I must not tell.
Orl. Then I will chide thee for him. Who first drew
Love as a blindfold imp, an earthen dwarf,
And armed him with blunt darts? His soul was kin
To the rough wind that dwells in the icy north,   60
The dead cold pedant, who thus dared confine
The universe's soul, for that is Love.
'Tis he that acts the nightingale, the thrush,
And all the living musics, he it is
That gives the lute, the harp and tabor speech,   65
That flutters on melodious wings and strikes
The mute and viewless lyres of sunny strings
Borne by the minstrel gales, mimicking vainly
The timid voice, that sent him to my breast,

That voice the wind hath treasured and doth use   70
When he bids roses open and be sweet.

   Boy. Now I could guess.

   Orl.   What, little curious one?

   Boy. The riddle of Orlando's feelings. Come,
You must not frown. I know the lawn, the cot,
Aye, and the leaf-veiled lattice.

   Orl.   I shall task   75
Your busy watchfulness. Bear you this paper,
I would not trust it to a doubtful hand.

   Boy. Unto the wood-nymph? You may think the road
Already footed.

   Orl.   Go, and prosper then.   [*Exeunt.*

SCENE II. *The interior of* MORDRED'S *cottage*

LENORA *and* FLORIBEL

   Flor. My mother, you're too kind, you ought to check
These wayward humours. Oh, I know too well
I'm a poor, foolish, discontented child;
My heart doth sink when Hesperus is gone,
And leaves me nought but fears. Forgive me then,   5
If I have vexed you.

   Len.   Dear and gentle soul,
You ne'er offended me, but when you said
You had offended. When I look on thee,
If there's a thought that moistens in my eye,
Fear that thy husband cannot match such goodness, 10
Is looking out there.

   Flor.   Fears of Hesperus!
That's not my mother's thought, cast it away:
He is the glass of all good qualities,
And what's a little virtue in all others
Looks into him and sees itself a giant;   15

18

He is a nosegay of the sweets of man,
A dictionary of superlatives;
He walks about, a music among discords,
A star in night, a prayer 'midst madmen's curses;
And if mankind, as I do think, were made   20
To bear the fruit of him, and him alone,
It was a glorious destiny.

   Len. He is a goodly man, and yet they say
Strange passions sleep within him. There's Orlando,
A gentle suitor; Floribel, he loved you,   25
He had no father, I have often wished
What it's too late to tell you.

   Flor.   Mother, your Orlando
Is a good gentleman, I wish him well,
But to my husband—We'll not talk of him.
Yet you shall see I can be cool sometimes,   30
When Hesperus deserves it, as he does
Even now for his delay.

   Len.   He's here: I'll leave you,
You shall not quarrel with him for my pleasure [*Exit.*

Enter HESPERUS

   Hesp. Good morrow, Floribel.
   Flor. Fair noon to Hesperus; I knew a youth,   35
In days of yore, would quarrel with the lark,
If with its joyous matins it foreran
His early pipe beneath his mistress' window;
Those days are passed; alas! for gallantry.

   Hesp. Floribel!
   Flor.   Sir, d'ye know the gentleman?   40
Give him my benison and bid him sleep
Another hour, there's one that does not miss him.

   Hesp. Lady, I came to talk of other things,
To tell you all my secrets, must I wait
Until it fits your humour?

   Flor.   As you please: 45
(The worst of three bad suitors, and his name

19

Began with an H.)

 Hesp. Good morrow then, again.

 Flor.   Heaven help you, sir,
And so adieu.

 Hesp. Madam, you spoke; you said it, Floribel: 50
I never thought mine ears a curse before.
Did I not love thee? Say, have I not been
The kindest?

 Flor.   Yes, indeed thou *hast* been. Now
A month is over. What would I not give 54
For those four sevens of days? But I have lived them,
And that's a bliss. You speak as if I'd lost
The little love you gave your poor one then.

 Hesp. And you as if you cared not for the loss.
Oh Floribel, you'll make me curse the chance
That fashioned this sad clay and made it man; 60
It had been happier as the senseless tree
That canopies your sleep. But Hesperus,
He's but the burthen of a scornful song
Of coquetry; beware, that song may end
In a death groan. 65

FLORIBEL (*sings*)

The knight he left the maid,
 That knight of fickleness,
Her's was the blame he said,
 And his the deep distress.

If you are weary of poor Floribel, 70
Pray be not troubled; she can do without thee.
Oh Hesperus, come hither, I must weep;
Say you will love me still, and I'll believe it,
When I forget my folly.

 Hesp.   Dear, I do;
By the bright fountains of those tears I do. 75

 Flor. You don't despise me much? May I look up
And meet no frown?

20

Hesp.   Try to look through my breast,
And see my truth. But, oh! my Floribel,
Take heed how thou dost look unkindly on me;   79
For grey-beards have been kneeling, and with prayers
Trying to pluck thee from my bosom; fairness,
And innocence and duty league against thee.
Then do 't not, sweet, again; for sometimes strange
And horrid thoughts bring whispers to my soul:
They shall not harm thee, girl. I meant indeed,   85
Hard hearted as I was, to have disclosed
A tale of terror; but I'll back again:
Why let the old man die.
    Flor.   Oh no, no, no;
We will let no one die, but cherish them
With love like ours, and they will soon be well: 90
Stay and I'll tell you how to save him.
Hesp.   Thou!
Excellent loveliness,
Thou save him! But I must be gone or else
Those looks will lure a secret from my breast,
That threatens both. I'll home and think of some-
        thing.   95
Meet me to-morrow in the sweet-briar thicket
When twilight fades to evening. I'm in haste.   [*Exit.*
    Flor. My better thoughts go with thee. It is true
He hath too much of human passion in him,
But I will hold him dear, and if again   100
My wicked senses grow so cruel quick
As to suspect his kindness, I'll be sure
My eyes have got false sight, my ears false hearing,
And my whole mind's become a rebel traitress.

Enter ORLANDO'S *Boy.*

    Boy. These for fair Floribel; you are the one   105
I hear my master talk of, surely, lady;
And yet his words are feeble shadowers
Of such pure beauty. Please you read his thoughts.

21

Flor. You hold a courtly language for such years,
But be you ware of compliment akin   110
To falsehood.

                (*reads*) *From the sad-souled Orlando.*
Fie sir; your gifts are dangerous. Look you here,
As I disperse the wicked syllables
Met in this little parliament of words,
And give them to the light and careless winds,   115
So do I bid him tear the thoughts of me
Out of his breast, and hold me as a thing
Further from him than misery.

    Boy. It is ~~urgently~~ done; nay, I must say so,
To hurt the generous blossoms of his love;   120
I am sorry that a hand so beautiful
Can be so fell.

    Flor.   Boy, thou dost not know
The fears that urge me. Had my Hesperus
Seen these or thee, I know not what of ill
Must have befallen us.

    Boy.   Lady, you must not weep;   125
I have a ballad which my master hears
In his sad moods; it has the art to raise
A dimple on the cheek of moody care.
I'll sing it you.

    Flor.   Young one, I almost love thee.

                          [*Kisses him.*

Enter HESPERUS

    Hesp. Why Floribel,—Girl! Painted fickleness!   130
Madam, I'm rude; but Hesperus did not think
He could intrude on—what was Floribel.

    Flor. Nor doth he ever.

    Hesp.   If he does not now,
Be sure he won't again. Oh girl, girl, girl,
Thou'st killed my heart: I thought thee once, good
        fool,   135
I will not tell thee what, thou'lt laugh at me.

Flor. By heaven!

Hesp.   Don't name it: do not be forsworn.
But why should I regard thy words or oaths?

Flor. Hesperus, Hesperus!

Hesp.   Nay, I should be sorry   140
To cheat the longing boy; he fills thine arms
Excellent well, believe it. Urchin, seek me
When that mis-featured butter-print of thine
Is bearded; I will trim thee with a sword.

Flor. Hesperus, thou art mad.

Hesp. Better be mad than treacherous. Aye, 'twas
          well   145
To tear the letters; there might be a husband;
No, he shall be no more.

Flor.   :   But listen to me,
These lips that thou hast kissed,—

Hesp.   I, and a thousand,
Men, boys, and monsters.

Flor.   And these arms thou callest
Beloved and fair—

Hesp.   And fickle and adulterous.   150
Enough of woman: boy, your paramour
Is troublesome, sirrah, milk-blooded imp,
Raise her; she loves your silken limbs; I give you
All that is mine of her.

Flor.   Oh! save me, dearest.

Hesp. She speaks to you, sir. I beseech you both, 155
Go on; don't heed me: oh, I joy to see
Your love-tricks.

Flor.   By the solemn spousal tie,
I charge you, hear me.

Hesp.   Lady, I will tell you,
Though it is needless, what I meant to say,
And leave you then for ever. You remember   160
A loving dupe you entertained some while,
One Hesperus, you must; oh! that you ever
Forgot him. Well, I will be brief. He gave you,

23

And bid you keep it as you would his love,
A little bird, a sweet red-bosomed creature,   165
To toy with in his absence: (then he knew not
You had another playmate for your chamber.)
This bird, it was a creature that I loved,
Yet it did not deceive me; I have thought
There was a spirit in it—never mind;   170
I dreamed I spoke to one, who valued me
And my poor feelings. Unto you I gave it,
And you have lost it; in my way I passed
Its silent wicker house. Now I have spoken,
Perhaps was tedious: but I'm still so foolish,   175
That I will say, good bye.

    Flor.   Oh, stay, my love.

    Hesp. He will, the lovely cub.

    Flor.   Thee, thee I mean.

    Hesp. I am no lover, I. Madam, we're strangers;
And yet I knew some while ago a form
Like thine, as fair, as delicate. Oh heaven!   180
To think of it. But she was innocent,
Innocent, innocent.

    Flor.   The angels know
I am as spotless.

    Hesp.   Go to them; I'm not one;
Perhaps this pap-faced chit may be. Nay, girl,
Wet not thy cheeks: I've seen a player weep.   185
I will not go, for if I do, the flock
Of her warm suitors will be toying here;
Yet I'll not stay; for she will melt and pray
Till I'm a fool again. Strain not your lungs
With laughter when I'm gone. Oh woman, woman.

                                  [*Exit.* 190

    Flor. Poor boy, thou hast undone me; lead me in.

                                    [*Exeunt.*

SCENE III. *An apartment in* ORLANDO'S *palace*

Enter HESPERUS

Hesp. Oh thou sad self, thou wretched half of
        Hesperus,
Thou'rt lost indeed, there's nought of life about thee,
But the one thought, that thou hast saved a father.
Now I do think that if I meet a goodness
In woman's shape, a fair one I'd not ask,   5
But something that would soothe and comfort me,
I could almost love her.

Enter ORLANDO *and* OLIVIA

Orl. My brother Hesperus, our poor home is hon-
        oured
By thy loved father's presence and thine own.
Here is a living welcome, prithee know her,   10
Olivia.
        Hesp. Blessedness you should have said.
A music waits upon her every step,
That my heart leaps to.
        Oliv.   Courtly, sir, and kind.
        Hesp. And fond I would have made it. Oh fair lady,
A smile of thine will give me health again.   15
        Orl. Sister, thou needst no witness to these blushes.
School her, sir, in the arts of compliment,
You'll find her an apt learner.   [*Exit.*
        Oliv. Had I a right to pray to you, I would.
        Hesp. Pray, Lady? Didst thou ever see the goddess
Step from her dignity of stone, or leave   21
The hallowed picture in its tinted stole
And crouch unto her suppliant? Oh no;
If there is aught so poor a thing as I
Can please you with, command it and you bless me. 25
        Oliv. Try, I beseech thee, try not to detest,
Not utterly to detest a silly girl,
Whose only merit is that she'd be thine.

Hesp. Hate thee, thou virtue?

Oliv.   Well, if it must be,
Play the deceiver for a little while;   30
Don't tell me so.

Hesp.   By Truth's white name I'll tell thee,
Olivia, there was once an idle thought
That aped affection in my heart; nay, nay,
Not in my heart; it was a dream or so;
A dream within a dream; a pale, dim warmth;   35
But thou hast dawned like summer on my soul,
Or like a new existence.

Oliv.   'Twere delightful,
If credible; but you are all too gallant.

Hesp. I knew it must be so: you'll not believe me,
But doubt and say 'tis sudden. Do not minute   40
The movements of the soul, for some there are
Of pinion unimpeded, thrice word-swift,
Outsoar the sluggish flesh; and these, Olivia,
Anticipating their death-given powers, can grasp
A century of feeling and of thought;   45
Outlive the old world's age, and be at once
In the present, past, and future; while the body
Lives half a pulse's stroke. To see and love thee
Was but one soul's step.

Oliv.   Then thou canst endure me;
Thou dost not hate the forward maid? My prayer   50
Through many a year has been for that one word;
And I have kept the precious thought of thee,
Hidden almost from myself. But I'll not speak,
For I have told too much, too childishly.

Hesp. Dear, I could weep, but that my brain is dry,
To think upon thee. Me—'Twere well to court   56
The yellow pestilence, or woo the lightning
Unto thy bosom; but to hold me dear—
It is a crime of hell; forget you thought it.

Oliv. 'Tis sweeter than a virtue, I must love thee.   60

Hesp. And love me truly?

   Oliv.   Heaven grant me life
To prove it.
   Hesp. Then thou shalt be mine own; but not till
     death.
We'll let this life burn out, no matter how;
Though every sand be moistened with our tears,   65
And every day be rain-wet in our eyes;
Though thou shouldst wed some hateful avarice,
And I grow hoary with a daubed deceit,
A smiling treachery in woman's form,
Sad to the soul, heart-cankered and forlorn;   70
No matter, all no matter.
Though madness rule our thoughts, despair our hearts,
And misery live with us, and misery talk,
Our guest all day, our bed-fellow all night;
No matter, all no matter.   75
For when our souls are born then will we wed;
Our dust shall mix and grow into one stalk,
Our breaths shall make one perfume in one bud,
Our blushes meet each other in a rose,
Our sweeter voices swell some sky-bird's throat   80
With the same warbling, dwell in some soft pipe,
Or bubble up along some sainted spring's
Musical course, and in the mountain trees
Slumber our deeper tones, by tempests waked:
We will be music, spring, and all fair things   85
The while our spirits make a sweeter union
Than melody and perfume in the air.
Wait then, if thou dost love me.
   Oliv.   Be it so;
You'll let me pray for death, if it will bring
Such joys as these! Though once I thought to live   90
An happy bride; but I must learn new feelings.
   Hesp. New feelings! Aye to watch the lagging clock,
And bless each moment as it parts from thee,
To court the blighting grasp of tardy age,
And search thy forehead for a silver tress   95

As for a most prized jewel.

 Oliv.   I cannot think
Of that cold bed diseases make for us,
That earthy sleep; oh! 'tis a dreadful thing.

 Hesp. The very air,
I thank it, (the same wild and busy air   100
That numbers every syllable I speak,
In the same instant my lips shape its sound
With the first lisps of him, who died before
The world began its story;) steals away
A little from my being,   105
And at each slightest tremor of a leaf
My hearse moves one step nearer. Joy, my love,
We're nearer to our bridal sheets of lead
Than when your brother left us here just now
By twenty minutes' talk.

 Oliv.   It is not good 110
Thus to spurn life, the precious gift of heaven,
And watch the coming light of dissolution
With such a desperate hope. Can we not love
In secret, and be happy in our thoughts,
Till in devotion's train, th' appointed hour 115
Lead us with solemnly rejoicing hearts
Unto our blessed end?

 Hesp.   End! thou sayest.
And do those cherries ripen for the worms,
Those blue enchantments beam to light the tomb?
Was that articulate harmony, (Love uses 120
Because he seems both Love and Innocence
When he sings to it,) that summer of sweet breath
Created but to perish and so make
The deads' home loveliest?

 Oliv. But what's to live without my Hesperus? 125
A life of dying. 'Tis to die each moment
In every several sense. To look despair,
Feel, taste, breathe, eat, be conscious of despair.
No, I'll be nothing rather.

Hesp.   Nothing but mine!
Thou flower of love, I'll wear thee in my bosom;   130
With thee the wrath of man will be no wrath,
Conscience and agony will smile like pleasure,
And sad remembrance lose its gloomy self
In rapturous expectation.
      Oliv.   Let me look on thee;
Pray pardon me, mine eyes are very fools.   135
      Hesp. Jewels of pity, azure stars of beauty
Which lost affection steers by; could I think
To dim your light with sorrow? Pardon me,
And I will serve you ever. Sweet, go in;
Somewhat I have to think on.   [*Exit* OLIVIA.
                           Floribel,   140
I would not have thee cross my path to-night;
There is an indistinct dread purpose forming,
Something, whose depth of wickedness appears
Hideous, incalculable, but inevitable;
Now it draws nearer, and I do not shudder;   145
Avaunt! haunt me no more; I dread it not,
But almost—hence! I must not be alone.   [*Exit.*

      SCENE IV. *A tapestried chamber in the same*

      HESPERUS *discovered in a disturbed slumber*

Hesp. (*starting from his couch*) Who speaks? Who
      whispers there? A light! a light!
I'll search the room, something hath called me thrice,
With a low muttering voice of toadish hisses,
And thrice I slept again. But still it came
Nearer and nearer, plucked my mantle from me,   5
And made mine heart an ear, in which it poured
Its loathed enticing courtship. Ho! a light.

      Enter Attendant with a torch

Thou drowsy snail, thy footsteps are asleep,

29

Hold up the torch.
    Attend.   My lord, you are disturbed.
Have you seen aught?
    Hesp.   I lay upon my bed,   10
And something in the air, out-jetting night,
Converting feeling to intenser vision,
Featured its ghastly self upon my soul
Deeper than sight.
    Attend.   This is Delusion surely;
She's busy with men's thoughts at all night hours,   15
And to the waking subtle apprehension
The darkling chamber's still and sleepy air
Hath breath and motion oft.
    Hesp. Lift up the hangings, mark the doors, the
      corners;
Seest nothing yet? No face of fiendlike mirth   20
More frightful than the fixed and doggish grin
Of a dead madman?
    Attend.   Nought I see, my lord,
Save the long, varied crowd of warlike shapes
Set in the stitched picture.
    Hesp.   Heard ye then?
There was a sound, as though some marble tongue 25
Moved on its rusty hinge, syllabling harshly
The hoarse death-rattle into speech.
    Attend. The wind is high, and through the silent
      rooms
Murmurs his burthen, to an heedless ear
Almost articulate.
    Hesp.   Thou sleepest, fool,   30
A voice has been at my bedside to-night,
Its breath is burning on my forehead still,
Still o'er my brain its accents, wildly sweet,
Hover and fall. Away and dream again.
I'll watch myself.
        [*He takes the torch and turns to the hangings.*
                Exit Attendant.

                    Aye, these are living colours,   35
Those cheeks have worn their youth these hundred
      years,
Those flowers are verdant in their worsted spring
And blooming still;
While she, whose needle limned so cunningly,
Sleeps and dreams not. It is a goodly state,   40
And there is one I wish had ta'en her bed
In the stone dormitory.
                 (Blindfold moth,
Thou shalt not burn thy life; there, I have saved thee,
If thou art grateful, mingle with the air
That feeds the lips of her I thought of once,   45
Choak her, moth, choak her. I could be content,
If she were safe in heaven.)
                    Yon stout dagger
Is fairly fashioned for a blade of stitches,
And shines, methinks, most grimly; well, thou art
An useful tool sometimes, thy tooth works quickly,   50
And if thou gnawest a secret from the heart,
Thou tellest it not again: ha! the feigned steel
Doth blush and steam. There is a snuff of blood.
               [*Grasps his dagger convulsively.*
Who placed this iron aspic in my hand?
Speak! who is at my ear?
              [*He turns, and addresses his shadow.*
             I know thee now,   55
I know the hideous laughter of thy face.
'Tis Malice' eldest imp, the heir of hell,
Red-handed Murther. Slow it whispers me,
Coaxingly with its serpent voice. Well sung,
Syren of Acheron!
             I'll not look on thee;   60
Why does thy frantic weapon dig the air
With such most frightful vehemence? Back, back,
Tell the dark grave I will not give it food.
Back to thy home of night. What! playest thou still?

Then thus I banish thee. Out, treacherous torch,   65
Sure thou wert kindled in infernal floods,
Or thy bright eye would blind at sights like this.

                     [*Dashes the torch on the ground.*
Tempt me no more; I tell thee Floribel
Shall never bleed. I pray thee, guilty word,
Tempt me no more.   [*Wraps himself in his mantle.*

             I'm deaf, my ears are safe,   70
I do not hear thee woo me to the deed;
Thou tellest to one without auricular sense
Olivia's beauties and that bad one's faults.
Oh! bring me thoughts of pity. Come, come, come,
Or I am lost.

         Bad goblin, must I fly thee?   [*Exit.* 75

SCENE V. *A hall in the same*

LORD ERNEST, ORLANDO, CLAUDIO, OLIVIA

L. Ern. Saw ye my son?
   Oliv.   Some hours ago we parted,
And he was strange, though gentle, in his talk.
   Orl. I passed him in the garden, just at twilight;
He stood with eyes wide open, but their sense
Dreamed, in dumb parley with some fancied thing;   5
For his lips moved, and he did walk and gaze,
Now frown most mournfully, now smile most madly,
And weep, and laugh, groan deep and gnash his teeth,
And now stand still with such a countenance,
As does the marble sorrow o'er a tomb.   10
At last he tore his feet, as they were roots,
Up from the earth, and sighed like one o'ercome;
Then with his fingers thrust upon his eyes,
And dashed unclosed away, he seemed to snatch
Some loathly object out of them, and leapt   15
Into the thicket's gloom.
   L. Ern.   Who saw him since?

Clau. In most distempered wildness he hath left
His chamber now.
    L. Ern.   Go seek him, every one,
I do beseech you, 'tis a fearful period
I know too truly. On his nurse's breast   20
Some twenty years ago, he lay and mused
Upon her singing and bright merry lips;
A viewless bolt dropped on her, and she died
Most hideously; close in the infant's face
Looked all the horrors of her bursting eyes;   25
And as the months bring round that black remem-
    brance,
His brain unsettles, bloody thoughts oppress
And call him from his bed. Search all the darkness,
Each one a several way; dear daughter, in.   [*Exeunt.*

SCENE VI. *A suicide's grave*

ORLANDO *and* CLAUDIO

Clau. There is a plague in this night's breath,
    Orlando,
The dews fall black and blistering from yon cloud
Anchored above us; dost thou mark how all
The smokes of heaven avoid it and crowd on
Far from its fatal darkness? Some men say   5
That the great king of evil sends his spirits
In such a winged car, to stir ill minds
Up to an act of death.
    Orl.   We may not think so,
For there's a fascination in bad deeds
Oft pondered o'er, that draws us to endure them,   10
And then commit. Beware of thine own soul,
'Tis but one devil ever tempts a man,
And his name's *Self.* Know'st thou these rankling
    hemlocks?

Clau. I've seen the ugsome reptiles battening on
   them,
While healthy creatures sicken at the sight.   15
   Orl. Five months ago they were an human heart
Beating in Hugo's breast. A parricide
Here sleeps self-slaughtered. 'Twas a thing of grace,
In his early infancy; I've known him oft
Outstep his pathway that he might not crush   20
The least small reptile. But there is a time
When goodness sleeps; it came, and vice was grafted
On his young thoughts, and grew, and flourished there,
Envenomed passions clustered round that prop;
A double fruit they bore; a double fruit of death.   25
   Clau. Enough, Orlando,
The imps of darkness listen, while we tell
A dead man's crimes. Even now I heard a stir
As if the buried turned them in their shrouds
For mere unquiet. Home, it is the time   30
When the hoarse fowl, the carrier-bird of woe,
Brings fevers from the moon, and maddening dreams;
The hour's unholy, and who hath not sent
After the parted sun his orisons,
Falls 'neath the sway of evil.   [*Exeunt.* 35

Enter HESPERUS

   Hesp. Hail, shrine of blood, in double shadows
   veiled,
Where the Tartarian blossoms shed their poison
And load the air with wicked impulses;
Hail, leafless shade, hallowed to sacrilege,
Altar of death! Where is thy deity?   40
With him I come to covenant, and thou,
Dark power, that sittest in the chair of night,
Searching the clouds for tempests with thy brand,
Proxy of Hades; list and be my witness,
And bid your phantoms all, (the while I speak   45
What if they but repeat in sleeping ears,

34

Will strike the hearer dead, and mad his soul;)
Spread wide and black and thick their cloudy wings,
Lest the appalled sky do pale to day.
Eternal people of the lower world, 50
Ye citizens of Hades' capitol,
That by the rivers of remorseful tears
Sit and despair for ever;
Ye negro brothers of the deadly winds,
Ye elder souls of night, ye mighty sins, 55
Sceptred damnations, how may man invoke
Your darkling glories? Teach my eager soul
Fit language for your ears. Ye that have power
O'er births and swoons and deaths, the soul's attend-
    ants,
(Wont to convey her from her human home 60
Beyond existence, to the past or future,
To lead her through the starry blossomed meads
Where the young hours of morning by the lark
With earthly airs are nourished, through the groves
Of silent gloom, beneath whose breathless shades 65
The thousand children of Calamity
Play murtherously with men's hearts:) Oh pause,
Your universal occupations leave,
Lay down awhile the infant miseries,
That to the empty and untenanted clay 70
Ye carry from the country of the unborn;
And grant the summoned soul one moment more
To linger on the threshold of its flesh;
For I would task you.
             Bear this breath of mine,
This inner Hesperus away, and bring 75
Another guest to its deserted home;
The mind of him whose dust is on my feet,
And let his daring spirit inhabit there
But for a passing day.
          'Tis here. A wind
Is rushing through my veins, and I become 80

As a running water.
I see a shadowy image of myself,
Yet not my perfect self, a brother self,
That steps into my bosom. Am I born
Newly, or newly dead? I'll think a little.   85
Have I e'er lived before, or thought or acted?
Why no; it was the morning doze of being,
I slept content with dreams; but now I wake
And find it noon, a time for stirring deeds.
Yes, this is life that trembles in my veins,   90
Yes, this is courage warms my heart's full tide:
Hesperus is a man, a demon-man,
And there's a thing he lives for, shall amaze
The emulous bad powers.
                              Lead me on,
Mysterious guide, companion wickedness;   95
Olivia calls me forward, and to reach her,
What if we tread upon a world of hearts?
Come, ye ill blasts, ye killing visitants
Of sleeping men, wild creatures of the air,
We'll walk together; come, ye beauteous snakes,   100
Ye lovely fanged monsters of the woods,
We'll grovel in the dust and ye shall hiss
Your tunes of murder to me.   [*An ignis fatuus rises.*
                         Lo, she's here
To light our sports, the Hebe of the dead,
Alecto, 'mid her nest of living hair   105
Bearing a star of Tartarus. Lead on.   [*Exit.*

ACT III

SCENE I. *An apartment in* ORLANDO'S *palace*

HESPERUS *seated. Attendants. Enter to them* CLAUDIO

    Clau. The bridegroom's here?
    Attend.   Yonder he sits, my lord,

And since the morn's first hour, without the motion
Even of a nerve, as he were growing marble,
Has sat and watched, the sun blazed in at noon
With light enough to blind an eagle's ken,   5
He felt it not, although his eyeballs glared
Horribly bright: I spoke: he heard me not:
And when I shook his arm slept on in thought;
I pray you try him.

   Clau.   Sir, good Hesperus,
I wait at your desire; we are to end   10
Our match at tennis. Will you walk with me?

   Attend. Your voice is weak as silence to his sense.

Enter ORLANDO

   Orl. My brother, you must join us at the banquet;
We wait your coming long; how's this?

   Attend.   My lord,
Like trance has held him since the dawn of day,   15
He has looked down upon yon wood since then,
Speechless and still.

Enter LORD ERNEST

   L. Ern.   Now health and good be here,
For I have missed my son the livelong day.
Why what an idle loiterer thou art;
By this your vacant sight must ache with gazing   20
Upon that view. Arise, I'd have you with me
To fix upon some posy for the ring
You wed your love with. Death! Some fearful change
Is here. Speak; speak and tell me if he lives.

   Attend. He does, my lord, if breathing is to live,   25
But in all else is like the coffined dead;
Motion and speech he lacks.

   L. Ern.   O heavens, Orlando
Tell me 'tis false.

   Orl.   I would 'twere in my power,
But it doth seem too true.

L. Ern.   Ride like the wind,
Fetch him the aid of medicine. See you not   30
Some vision has come to him in the night,
And stole his eyes and ears and tongue away?

Enter OLIVIA

Oh, you are come in time to see him die;
Look, look, Olivia, look; he knows us not;
My son, if thou dost hear me, speak one word,   35
And I will bless thee.

Orl.   He is dumb indeed.

Oliv. Let me come near him. Dearest Hesperus,
If thou beholdest these poor unbeauteous cheeks,
Which first thy flattering kindness taught to blush;
Or if thou hearest a voice, that's only sweet   40
When it says Hesperus; oh gentle love,
Speak any thing, even that thou hatest Olivia,
And I will thank thee for 't: or if some horror
Has frozen up the fountain of thy words,
Give but a sign.

Clau.   Lady, alas, 'tis vain.   45

Oliv. (*kneeling*) Nay, he shall speak, or I will never move,
But thus turn earth beseeching his dull hand,
And let the grass grow over me. I'll hold
A kind of converse with my raining eyes,
For if he sees not, nor doth hear, he'll know   50
The gentle feel of his Olivia's tears.

Clau. Sweet sir, look on her.

Orl.   Brother.

Oliv.   Husband.

L. Ern.   Son.
Kind heaven, let him hear, though death should call
     him.   [*Pause, a clock strikes.*

Hesp. The hour is come.   [*Exit.*

SCENE II. *A room in* MORDRED'S *cottage*

FLORIBEL *alone*

Flor. And must I wake again? Oh come to me,
Thou that with dew-cold fingers softly closest
The wearied eye; thou sweet, thou gentle power,
Soother of woe, sole friend of the oppressed,
I long to lay me on thy peaceful breast.   5
But once I saw thee, beautiful as moonlight,
Upon a baby's lips, and thou didst kiss them,
Lingering and oft,
(As a wild bee doth kiss a rifled flower,
And clips its waist, and drops a little tear,   10
Remorsefully enamoured of his prey;)
Come so to me, sweet death, and I will wreath thee
An amorous chaplet for thy paly brows;
And on an odoured bank of wan white buds
In thy fair arms   15
I'll lie, and taste thy cool delicious breath,
And sleep, and sleep, and sleep.

Enter LENORA

                              O here, good mother,
We'll talk together.
        Len.   What; of Hesperus?
Methinks he has grown cold.
        Flor.   Oh no; he is
More full of courtship than he ever was;   20
Don't think him cold, dear mother, or I may;
I'm sure he loves me still; I'll go to him,
'Tis nigh the appointed hour.
        Len. My child, it is a chill and gloomy evening,
So go not out. Thy Hesperus will come,   25
And thou wilt live on every word of his
Till thine eyes sparkle. What means this despondence?
        Flor. Dear mother, I will strive to be at ease,
If you desire; but melancholy thoughts

Are poor dissemblers. How I wish we owned   30
The wealth we've lost.

    Len.   Why girl, I never heard
One such regret escape your lips before;
Has not your Hesperus enough?

    Flor.   Too much;
If he were even poorer than ourselves,
I'd almost love him better. For, methinks,   35
It seemed a covetous spirit urged me on,
Craving to be received his bride. I hope
He did not think so; if he does, I'll tell him
I will not share his wealth, but dwell with you.
Oh that he'd come! How each dull moment drags   40
Its lazy wing along when he is absent.
When was he here?

    Len.   Last night.

    Flor.   Last night? Now pr'ythee
Don't jeer me so, I'm sure, not many days;
But all is night when he's not here to light me,
So let it be last night; although that night   45
Had days for hours, yet in Love's book and mine
'Tis but an empty cypher, a black round.
Oh, I've not lived, I've not been Floribel
Since the last mellow echo of his voice
Lent the air music; is 't not a sweet voice?   50
What can you liken to it?

    Len.   Pan's honeycomb
Of many vocal cells.

    Flor.   How dull you are;
There's nought beneath the thunder-choir so grand;
The wood-birds and the waterfalls but mock him.
He said, dear mother, I should be his countess;   55
To-day he'd come to fetch me, but with day
I've laid my expectation in its grave.
Dost think he will deceive me? Silly girl,
Querulous ingrate, why do I torment me?
Sweet mother, comfort.

Len.   Be you sure he'll come   60
With his whole princely train of friends and kindred,
And he will lift thee to his gorgeous car,
And place thee at his side, a happy wife.
    Flor. Fie! you cajole me, like a sulky child,
With gilded cars; but oh! I wish 'twere here.   65
How gloomily the clouds look, and the wind
Rattles among the brown leaves dolefully;
He will be very chill, heap up the fire.
Hush! hark! What's that?
    Len.   Only your dear father
Heavily breathing in his sleep; he'll wake   70
With his sad smile upon his patient face,
Looking so dear in sickness.
    Flor.   But 'twill cure him,
When he knows all and sees my bridegroom with me,
I know it will: and there's the horse's step,
I'll just run out, it is not cold at all.—
    Len.   Go my love,   75
But you must come to ask your father's blessing,
And bring your Hesperus with you.
    Flor.   That I will. [*Exeunt.*

SCENE III. *A wood*

Enter HUBERT *and a Huntsman*

    Hub. No answer to our shouts but mocking echo?
Where are our fellow huntsmen? Why they vanished
Like mist before the sun, and left us here
Lost in the briary mazes.
    Hunts.   Shame on the rogues
For this their treatment. But look upwards, Hubert,   5
See what a mighty storm hangs right above us.
    Hub. The day is in its shroud while yet an infant,
And Night with giant strides stalks o'er the world,
Like a swart Cyclops, on its hideous front

One round, red, thunderswollen eye ablaze.   10

Hunts. Now mercy save the peril-stricken man,
Who 'mongst his shattered canvas sits aghast
On the last sinking plank alone, and sees
The congregated monsters of the deep
For his dead messmates warring all, save one   15
That leers upon him with a ravenous gaze
And whets its iron tusks just at his feet:
Yet little heeds his wide and tearless eye
That, or the thunder of the mountain flood
Which Destiny commissions with his doom;   20
Where the wild waters rush against the sky,
Far o'er the desolate plain, his star of hope
In mockery gleams, while Death is at his side.

                                        [*lightning.*

Hub. That flash hath rent the heavens; this way for
    shelter.

Hunts. Some steps above there stands a noble oak 25
That from the sun roofs ever-during night
With its thickwoven firmament of leaves:
Thither betake we.   [*Exeunt.*

Enter FLORIBEL

Flor. Hence did I seem to hear a human voice,
Yet there is nought, save a low moaning sound,   30
As if the spirits of the earth and air
Were holding sad and ominous discourse.
And much I fear me I have lost my path;
Oh how these brambles tear; here 'twixt the willows;
Ha! something stirs, my silly prattling nurse   35
Says that fierce shaggy wolves inhabit here,
And 'tis in sooth a dread and lonely place;
There, there again; a rustling in the leaves.

Enter HESPERUS

'Tis he at last; why dost thou turn away
And lock thy bosom from my first embrace?   40

I am so tired and frightened; but thou'rt here;
I knew thou wouldst be faithful to thy promise,
And claim me openly. Speak, let me hear thy voice,
Tell me the joyful news.

 Hesp.   Aye, I am come
In all my solemn pomp, Darkness and Fear, 45
And the great Tempest in his midnight car,
The sword of lightning girt across his thigh,
And the whole dæmon brood of night, blind Fog
And withering Blight, all these are my retainers;
How: not one smile for all this bravery? 50
What think you of my minstrels, the hoarse winds,
Thunder, and tuneful Discord? Hark, they play.
Well piped, methinks; somewhat too rough, perhaps.

 Flor. I know you practise on my silliness,
Else I might well be scared. But leave this mirth, 55
Or I must weep.

 Hesp.   'Twill serve to fill the goblets
For our carousal, but we loiter here,
The bridesmaids are without; well-picked thou'lt say,
Wan ghosts of woe-begone, self-slaughtered damsels
In their best winding sheets; start not, I bid them wipe
Their gory bosoms; they'll look wondrous comely; 61
Our link-boy, Will o' the Wisp, is waiting too
To light us to our grave—bridal I mean.

 Flor. Ha! how my veins are chilled—why Hesperus!

 Hesp. What hero of thy dreams art calling, girl? 65
Look in my face—Is 't mortal? Dost thou think
The voice that calls thee is not of a mouth
Long choaked with dust? What though I have assumed
This garb of flesh and with it the affections,
The thoughts and weakness of mortality? 70
'Twas but for thee; and now thou art my bride;
Lift up thine eyes and smile—the bride of Death.

 Flor. Hold, hold. My thoughts are 'wildered. Is my
    fancy
The churlish framer of these fearful words,

Or do I live indeed to such a fate?   75
Oh! no, I recollect; I have not waked
Since Hesperus left me in the twilight bower.

   Hesp. Come, we'll to our chamber,
The cypress shade hangs o'er our stony couch
A goodly canopy; be mad and merry;   80
There'll be a jovial feast among the worms.   [*aside.*
Fiends, strew your fiercest fire about my heart
Or she will melt it.

   Flor.   Oh, that look of fury!
What's this about my eyes? ah! deadly night,
No light, no hope, no help.

   Hesp.   What! Darest thou tremble
Under thy husband's arm, darest think of fear?   86
Dost dread me, me?

   Flor.   I know not what to dread,
Nor what to hope; all's horrible and doubtful;
And coldness creeps—

   Hesp.   She swoons, poor girl, she swoons.
And, treacherous dæmons, ye've allowed a drop   90
To linger in my eyes. Out, out for ever.
I'm fierce again. Now shall I slay the victim
As she lies senseless? ah! she wakes; cheer up,
'Twas but a jest.

   Flor.   A dread and cruel one;
But I'll forgive you, if you will be kind;   95
And yet 'twas frightful.

   Hesp.   Why 'twere most unseemly
For one marked for the grave to laugh too loud.

   Flor. Alas! he raves again. Sweetest, what mean you
By these strange words?

   Hesp.   What mean I? Death and murder,
Darkness and misery. To thy prayers and shrift;   100
Earth gives thee back; thy God hath sent me for thee,
Repent and die.

   Flor.   Oh, if thou willest it, love,
If thou but speak it with thy natural voice,

And smile upon me; I'll not think it pain,
But cheerfully I'll seek me out a grave,   105
And sleep as sweetly as on Hesperus' breast.
He will not smile, he will not listen to me.
Why dost thou thrust thy fingers in thy bosom?
Oh search it, search it; see if there remain
One little remnant of thy former love   110
To dry my tears with.

   Hesp.   Well, speak on; and then,
When thou hast done thy tale, I will but kill thee.
Come tell me all my vows, how they are broken,
Say that my love was feigned, and black deceit,
Pour out thy bitterest, till untamed wrath   115
Melt all his chains off with his fiery breath,
And rush a-hungering out.

   Flor.   Oh piteous heavens!
I see it now, some wild and poisonous creature
Hath wounded him and with contagious fang
Planted this fury in his veins. He hides   120
The mangled fingers, dearest, trust them to me,
I'll suck the madness out of every pore,
So as I drink it boiling from thy wound
Death will be pleasant. Let me have the hand
And I will treat it like another heart.   125

   Hesp. Here 'tis then,   .   [*stabs her.*
Shall I thrust deeper yet?

   Flor.   Quite through my soul,
That all my senses, deadened at the blow,
May never know the giver. Oh, my love,
Some spirit in thy sleep hath stole thy body   130
And filled it to the brim with cruelty;
Farewell! and may no busy deathful tongue
Whisper this horror in thy waking ears,
Lest some dread desperate sorrow urge thy soul
To deeds of wickedness. Whose kiss is that?   135
His lips are ice. Oh my loved Hesperus,
Help!   [*Dies.*

Hesp. What a shriek was that; it flew to heaven,
And hymning angels took it for their own.
Dead art thou, Floribel; fair, painted earth,
And no warm breath shall ever more disport   140
Between those rubious lips: no, they have quaffed
Life to the dregs, and found death at the bottom,
The sugar of the draught. All cold and still;
Her very tresses stiffen in the air.
Look, what a face: had our first mother worn   145
But half such beauty, when the serpent came,
His heart, all malice, would have turned to love;
No hand but this, which I do think was once
Cain, the arch-murtherer's, could have acted it.
And I must hide these sweets, not in my bosom;   150
In the foul earth. She shudders at my grasp;
Just so she laid her head across my bosom
When first—oh villain! which way lies the grave? [*Exit.*

Enter HUBERT *and a Huntsman*

Hub. It is a fearful and tempestuous time,
The concave firmament, the angel's bridge   155
O'er the world's day and night, is visibly
Bowed down and bent beneath its load of thunder,
And through the fiery fissures of the clouds
Glistens the warfare of armed elements,
Bellowing defiance in earth's stunned ear,   160
And setting midnight on the throne of day.
  Hunts. The roar has ceased; the hush of intercalm
Numbs with its leaden finger Echo's lips,
And angry spirits in mid havoc pause,
Premeditating ruin in their silence.   165
  Hub. Hard by should stand a lone and tattered shed,
Where some tired woodsman may by chance be
        stretched,
Watching his scanty food among the coals;
There may we chafe our drenched and chilly limbs.
  Hunts. The forest has more tenants than I knew,   170

46

Look underneath this branch; seest thou not yonder,
Amongst the brushwood and the briary weeds
A man at work?

   Hub.   My life upon 't some miser,
Who in the secret hour creeps to his hoard,
And kneeling at the altar of his love,   175
Worships that yellow devil, gold.

   Hunts.   'Tis buried,
And now he stamps the sod down, that no light
May spy his mistress; with what a doleful look
He marks its grave, and backward walks away,
As if he left his all of sight behind.   180

   Hub. Let us steal towards it; I would have a peep
Upon this hidden jewel.   [*Exeunt*.

Enter HESPERUS

   Hesp. Shall I turn back and try to thrust my soul
In at her lips, and so re-animate
The beauteous casket while this body dies?   185
I cannot—not the universe of breath
Could give those little lips their life again.
I've huddled her into the wormy earth,
And left the guilty dagger at her side.
Dead Innocence! and must unkindly thistles   190
And rank thick hemlock force their bristling roots
Into thy lovely breast? Fool! Is 't not done?
Why stand I tampering 'midst the listening winds?
My fears are lying traitors.   [*Bells at a distance*.
                Wedding bells,
Thanks for your merry voices; ye have waked   195
A sudden hurry round about my heart,
I'll think it joy. Now for my second bride.   [*Exit*.

SCENE IV. *A saloon in* ORLANDO'S *palace*

OLIVIA, VIOLETTA, *Nurse, and Attendants*

Oliv. You keep me long, am I not yet attired,
Have ye not tricked me out enough? In faith
I am so vain to think I need no more.
   Attend. One moment, madam;
This little necklace, like the marriage yoke   5
Pleasantly binding, I must clasp around you.
   Oliv. A pretty toy, and prettily disposed;
I have, I know not why, this livelong day
Wept drops enough to bead a thousand such.
Where's Violetta? Come, look up, my girl,   10
Make thine eyes sparkle, mine are very moist.
   Viol. Shake off this sadness, lady, 'tis not meet
At such a moment; think upon your bridegroom,
How his affections seek thee.
   Oliv.   Gentle maid,
I'll not be sad; yet, little Violet,   15
How long I've worn thy beauty next my heart,
Aye, in my very thoughts, where thou hast shed
Perpetual summer: how long shared thy being:
Like two leaves of a bud, we've grown together,
And needs must bleed at parting.
   Viol.   No, not so;   20
I am thy handmaid still; and when your lord
Is absent, as he will be, at the tourney,
The court, or camp, we'll drive the long hours on
With prattle as of old.
   Oliv.   Thanks, I'll be cheerful;
But joy 's a plant the showers of many sorrows   25
Must water, ere it bloom. Good nurse, your pardon,
You've known me for a froward child before.
   Nurse. Now, on the scanty remnant of my life,
Grief's an ill wedding garment; if you'd put
One of your rosy smiles on, what a grace

48

You'd look and be. Why all these ohs and sobs
Are more like funeral noises.

  Oliv.   'Troth they are,
And 'tis the funeral of that Olivia
You nursed and knew; an hour and she's no more,
No more the mistress of her own resolves,   35
The free partaker of earth's airs and pleasures;
My very love, the poorest gift I have,
(Which, light as 'tis, I thought you all did prize,)
Is not my own. We must be strangers, girls,
Give me your hands and wishes.

  Nurse.   There is one,   40
Old now, and withered, truly we might call it
Yours, and not mine; oft has it brought you food,
Led you, and served you; yet in gladness parts
To make way for a younger and a worthier.

  Oliv. My kind old nurse; nay, now you are forget-
ting   45
Your words of cheer; this hand shall never want
Aid while I live, your service will be needful;
My house would seem a strange and dismal place
Without your pleasant looks.

  Nurse.   Well, my dear child,
I hope you'll give my arms a new Olivia;   50
Blush not; the old will talk.

  Oliv.   Whose hand is this
I know not from my own? Young Violet's.
My beauteous innocence, you must be with me
Oft, as you said: Go to, my nurse forbids
Our weeping.

  Viol.   Don't chide me then, Olivia,   55
I'm a sad fool, but do not chide.

  Oliv.   A gem
For Friendship's crown, each drop. My loving maids,
To each a farewell that I cannot speak;
All have my heart, and well can read its meaning.
Henceforth I'll look upon my maiden years   60

As lovely pastoral pictures; all of you
Shall smile again 'neath Memory's wizard pencil;
The natural beauties that we've marked together
Will look you back again; the books we've loved
Will talk to me of your sweet-worded praises,   65
The air of our old haunts whisper your voices;
Trust me, I'll not forget you.

    Attend.   Dearest lady,
May all the blessings that rain down from heaven
Upon the marriage-bed, descend on yours;
May many children, innocent and fair,   70
With soft embracements throng about your knees,
Domestic pleasures ever turn your hour-glass,
And when the long sleep falls upon your eyes,
Content and holy Peace, the twins of Eden,
Draw round the curtain 'twixt you and the world,   75
And watch beside you all the dreary night.

SCENE V. *A room in* MORDRED'S *cottage*

Enter LENORA *supporting* MORDRED

    Mor. Here let me rest, in my old oaken chair,
My limbs grow faint, and yet, kind, careful nurse,
Your smiles have chased away my pains.

    Len.   Dear husband,
A thousand thanks for those delightful words,
They bid me hope again and warm my heart.   5

    Mor. It renovates the spirit thus to look
With the clear eyes of health and joyousness
Upon the green creation. But I miss
A smile of hope, the copy of Lenora's,
That's wont to light my soul with its rich love;   10
Where is my peach-cheeked girl, my Floribel?

    Len. She will be with us soon; before you woke,
She went to ramble underneath the boughs,
And feed her forest birds; each bower she knows

Of eglantine and hawthorn; now the air   15
Is calm, she will return.

Mor.   I hope she may;
Yet who could injure such a holy thing?
The frenzied tempest's self, had it a will,
Would leave her path secure. My dear Lenora
There is one thing I wish to see accomplished   20
Before I die.

Len. What is it, love? And yet methinks 'twere fit
For me still to defer its execution,
And cheat you into living to that end.

Mor. Long have I prayed to see her beauty growing
Under some worthy husband's firm protection.   25

Len. What if she be already wedded?

Mor.   No,
That cannot be, she would have told unto me
The first emotions of her infant love;
She never had a thought concealed from me,   30
Even her slightest. 'Tis impossible,
And yet you look in earnest; speak, and tell me
You only jest.

Len.   I speak indeed the truth;
Perhaps I was imprudent not to tell you,
But you were very ill, and such the match,   35
You could not disapprove: Young Hesperus—

Mor. Lord Ernest's son!

Len.   The same.

Mor.   I'm satisfied,
My wish is all fulfilled. There's not a man
Beneath the sun more noble; but his father
Was wont to be a stern imperious lord,   40
A scorner of the poor.

Len.   He did not know it.

Mor. He knew it not! That was a sad omission,
Unworthy of a parent, we might rue it.

Len. This night our daughter's bridegroom
Comes, as his own to claim her, and ere this   45

Doubtless has told the love-tale to his father.

Mor. I wish him speedy, he shall find a welcome,
In the poor man's sole wealth, my hearty love.
Hark! There's a step.

    Len.   'Tis Hesperus'; I know it.

Enter the Huntsman

    Mor. Who comes, who is it?

    Len.   One whose visage wears 50
The darkest sadness; such a man I'd choose
For the mute herald of disaster.

    Hunts.   Lady,
Would that my looks could mirror to your soul
The woe, each syllable of which in speaking 54
Tears through my heart. Alas! your lovely daughter—

    Len. What? Speak I pray thee. Has she met with
        aught?

    Mor. Bid me die, or my fears.

Enter HUBERT *with the body of* FLORIBEL

    Hunts.   Here's all that's left
Of nature's rarest work: this lifeless all.
Oh! fall some strange unheard-of punishment
On Hesperus' head.

    Mor.   Hesperus, Hesperus; oh! 60
                [Falls back in his chair.

    Hub. Aye, 'twas his hand that wrought its passage
        here,
And murdered love in its most sacred temple.
    [LENORA takes the body into her lap and sits nursing it.

    Hunts. Alas! he heeds not; he is with his daughter.
Look at this other.

    Hub.   Oh! I cannot bear it;
Leave her, a mother's agony is holy 65
As nature's mysteries.

    Hunts.   We'll to the Duke,
And crush the viper in his nest, before

Report alarm him. Gently, gently tread
And wake not echo in this home of woe.

[*Exeunt* HUBERT *and the Huntsman.*

LENORA *sings in a distracted manner*

Lullaby, lullaby, sweet be thy sleep!   70
   Thou babe of my bosom, thou babe of my love;
Close, close to my heart, dear caresser, you creep,
   And kiss the fond eyelid that watches above.

One touch of those warm lips and then to bed.
Where is my child? I held her in my arms,   75
Her heart was beating in my bosom. Ha!
It is not she that lies upon my breast,
It is not she that whispers in my ear,
It is not she that kisses my salt cheek;
They've stolen her from my couch and left this change-
   ling,   80
Men call Despair—and she it is I suckle.
I know her by her killing lips of snow,
Her watery eyeballs and her tear-swoll'n cheeks.
My Floribel! oh they have ta'en her soul
To make a second spring of it, to keep   85
The jarring spheres in melody. Come, husband,
We'll wander up and down this wintry world,
And if we see a sadder sight than this,
Or hear a tale, though false, of half such horror,
We'll closely hug our bosom-griefs in transport.   90
Why husband! You're asleep—you're deaf—you're
   dead!
I have not eyes enough to weep for both,
But I'll go steal the sleeping world's, and beg
A little dew from every sipping worm
To wet my cheeks with.   [*Exit.*

53

ACT IV

SCENE I. *An apartment in* ORLANDO'S *palace*

HESPERUS *alone*

Hesp. How now? This quaint attire of countenance,
(Well fitted by prim Conscience's old tailor,
Hypocrisy,) sits rarely, and I'm here,
The affable, good bridegroom. Wickedness,
How easy is thy lesson! Now I stand   5
Up to the throat in blood; from Mercy's records
For evermore my guilty name is rased.
But yesterday, oh blessed yesterday,
I was a man;
And now—I start amazed at myself.   10
This hand, aye this it was I gave to Sin,
His grasp hath blasted it; 'twas made for kindness,
For gentle salutation, to deal out
Merciful alms, confirm the staff of age;
To reach the crust to want, the balm to sickness,   15
And balsam wounds, a limb of charity.
Now the wild adder's sting, the lightning's edge,
Are blunt and tame and gentle to it. Psha!
Why then men dread the adder and the flash,
So shall they cringe to me. A step! In haste   20
I've washed, and thought me spotless. Yet I fear
Mine eye is so familiarized with blood,
It doth pass o'er and disregard the stains:
That recks not. Sure I've brushed away those blushes,
And shaken hesitation from my tongue.   25

Enter Attendant

Menial, you're hasty in intruding thus.
Your errand?
    Attend.   Lady Olivia—
    Hesp. Give me thine hand. That name
Makes him my friend who speaks it. Say 't again;

Olivia, oh! how each sweet syllable   30
Trickles along the tongue, an honied drop
Of harmony, Olivia. I'll give all
The yellow wretchedness of human wealth
Unto the subtle artist, who shall teach
A clock to tell the seconds by that word;   35
So shall I drive these frightful thoughts away,
And happiness—Do I look happy, sirrah?
It matters not. Speak on.
   Attend.   My lord, your bride—
   Hesp. Well, sir, it was not I; why lookest thou so?
Beware. Why layest thine hand across thy breast?   40
Is there a wound on't? Say.
   Attend.   A wound, my lord!
I understand not—
   Hesp.   Fool, I know thou dost not.
(If they would find it out, why let them dig
To hell's foundations.) What! Because I fold
Mine arms like any man unhurt, unhurting,   45
Must every slave suppose 'tis to conceal
Some fearful witness of a deed?
   Attend.   I thought not
'Twould anger thee, forgive me.
   Hesp.   Be it so;
It was too warmly said, for, as I trust,
You could not deem your master villain; never.   50
Yet say it were so, I but say suppose,
That I, whose clay is kneaded up with tears,
Had murdered, as you thought, some kindred creature,
Could not I wash the tokens of my guilt
From this outside, and show a hand as clean   55
As he who fingers first the air?
   Attend.   You might,
Till heaven's justice blasted you, be hid:
But leave these strange and ugly arguments;
The very fear would scare me from your side;
So banish them.

Hesp.   Aye, they are strange indeed; 60
But mirth, believe me, mirth. Come, tell me now,
How sits this ring? Death! Are your eyes nailed there?
Ha! Does the ruby cast a sanguine shade
Across the veins?

Attend.   Nought, save the splendid gem,
Amazed my sight; that's all.

Hesp.   My friend, 'tis thine, 65
Too poor a recompense for the good tidings
Your tongue is laden with; now speak them out.

Attend. First let me bless you for your bounty, sir.
I came to call you to the wedding train,
Which waits without; such smiles on such rare faces 70
Mine eyes have never seen: the bride is there,
None but yourself is wanting to perfect
This sum of joy.

Hesp.   Say I'll be there anon;
And, mark me, on thy life forget each word
I just have spoken, blot them utterly 75
Out of thy mind; I can reward a service.
I like thee well, my trusty, pleasant friend;
Nay, pr'ythee go, there is no need of thanks.

         [Exit Attendant.

I'll give that fellow's blab-tongue to the worms,
He's heard too much; 'twere well to call him back, 80
And fasten down his memory with a dagger.
No, I'll not soil my skin again to-day;
Down, Murder, down!
These untamed passions that I keep about me 84
Will thrive on nought save blood; but they must fast,
And wear a specious tameness. My Olivia,
Now my whole soul is thine,—thine and the fiends'.

          [Exit.

SCENE II. *The interior of the* DUKE's *palace*

Enter the DUKE, HUBERT, *and the Huntsman*

Duke. Your tale hath stunned me with its dreadful
    import,
And turned my every faculty to wonder.
  Hub. You cannot doubt, my liege?
    Duke.   Hubert, I'd give
The best part of my power for hope to whisper
A no to my conviction. Devilish villain!   5
  Hub. Sure all good angels looked another way
When this foul deed was done.
    Duke.   All ancient cruelties
Look pale to it and merciful: henceforth
They that would christen human fiends must write
Hesperus, 'stead of Cain; and chiding nurses,   10
To still their peevish babes, shall offer them,
Not to the wolves, but him, the fiercer beast.
  Hub. Oh! my good lord, even now my sight is
    dimmed
With the salt gush that came between my eyes
And that which seared them: on her turfy couch,   15
Like one just lulled into a heavy sleep,
Smiling and calm she lay; the breath
Had not left fluttering up and down her bosom,
That all blood-dabbled and besprent with gore
Still held the guilty steel; the name was on it   20
Of the cursed owner.
    Duke.   Go, trusty Hubert,
Speed to Orlando's palace with my guard,
And drag the murderer here, e'en now I'll judge him;
Be diligent, put wings upon your feet,
Some vengeance will fall on us in the night,   25
If he remain unsentenced.   [*Exeunt.*

SCENE III. *A banqueting hall*

LORD ERNEST, ORLANDO, CLAUDIO, OLIVIA,
VIOLETTA, *Lords, Ladies, and Attendants*

L. Ern. Sit here, my daughter; sit and welcome, all;
You shall not say my Hesperus' nuptial night
Lacks its due orgies.

 Clau.   Look upon the bride,
How blushes open their envermeiled leaves
On her fair features.

 L. Ern.   Sit, I pray you, sirs,   5
We will have deep and jovial carousal;
Put on the smiles of joy, and think of nought
But present pleasure, we've had woes enough;
Bid 'em be merry, daughter.

 Oliv.   Gentlemen,
My father wills me give you all a welcome,   10
And if you love or honour our poor house,
Be glad with us.

 Clau. We thank your courtesy, lady, and obey.

 L. Ern. Where is this dilatory bridegroom still?
He was not wont to lag; what hast thou done   15
To banish him, Olivia?

 Oliv.   Good my lord,
I fear his heart is ill. A veil of gloom
Darkens his cheeks, an anxious watchfulness
Plays in his eyes; and when he clasped my hand
Now in the chapel, though he smiled and whispered 20
Of bliss and love, an ague thrilled his veins,
And starting back he groaned.

 L. Ern.   Go, fetch him hither,
I warrant wine will cure him.

 Attend.   Here he comes.

Enter HESPERUS

 Hesp. (*aside*) What's all this blaze and riot? Oh, a
  banquet.

They should have got me here the seven sins,   25
And all the evil things that haunt the world;
Then what a goodly revel would we hold;
E'en Death, while hastening to the sick man's pillow,
Should pause to listen our unhallowed talk,
And think us all the brood of Pestilence   30
Met in mysterious council.

    Attend.   Sir, your father
Has been enquiring for you, and desires
The comfort of your presence at the table.

    Hesp. The comfort of my presence! Slave, thou
       mockest me.
Why dost thou thrust thy taper in my face?   35
No price is set on't.

    L. Ern.   Hither, Hesperus;
Thou dost not mark this company of kinsmen,
Met to congratulate you, and partake
Your gladness.

    Hesp.   Sirs, I thank you heartily.
(*aside*) A curse upon the gaping saucy rabble;   40
They must stare too.

    L. Ern.   Come, son, and sit beside me;
They say you're ill, my boy.

    Hesp.   They say the truth.

    L. Ern. What is your ailment?

    Hesp.   Life. But here is one
Born to smile misery out of the world:
Look on me, my Olivia.

    Oliv.   Dearest Hesperus   45
Be calmer, I beseech you; all are here
My friends and yours.

    Hesp.   No doubt. They drain our goblets.
A friend! What is 't? A thing shall squeeze your hand,
Caress with fervent love your 'broidered sleeve,
And wring his mouth into a leering lie,   50
While his heart damns thee. One whose love 's as deep
As your gold coffer. Hast a wife? They come;

Buz, buz, lie, lie, the hungry meat-flies come,
'Dear lord, sweet lord, our only gentle lord!'
Aye, thus they sugar o'er the silent dagger,   55
And love, and love, till they've inhelled thy soul.
Oh! when I call for friend, bring honest poison.
Put out the lights, I like the beams o' th' moon;
And tell those revellers to tope in silence.

    L. Ern. You would not overcast our best-meant
      mirth,   60
Bid us sit palled, like mourners at your bridal,
And hide in night our kindly countenances?

    Hesp. Aye, by my grave, I would. There is on earth
One face alone, one heart, that Hesperus needs;
'Twere better all the rest were not. Olivia,   65
I'll tell thee how we'll 'scape these prying eyes;
We'll build a wall between us and the world,
And in some summer wilderness of flowers,
As though but two hearts beat beneath the sun,
Consume our days of love.

    L. Ern.   I pray you, friends,   70
Excuse the wilful boy, his soul is wholly
Wrapt up in admiration of his bride:
We'll have her health; come, fill your goblets round,
The bride, Olivia.

    Clau.   Happiness befall her,
May she ne'er feel a woe; we drink to her. [*Music.* 75

Enter HUBERT

    Hub. Hush, hush; ye ill-timed sounds, let darkness
      come,
And with her funeral trappings hang the walls,
Or twilight lend a weak and fitful gleam,
That you may watch each others' watery cheeks.
Oh! ladies, deck your beauties with salt diamonds,   80
Wail with the midnight wind, and look as sad
As if ye heard the thunder-voice of doom.

    L. Ern. What art thou, fearful man?

Hub.   Woe's harbinger;
I come to bid you to a funeral;
Prepare your eyes, for they must see dire vengeance 85
Fall on the neck of crime.
    Hesp.   Turn out that fellow;
I know him for a crazy marvel-monger,
A long-faced gossip, with his batch of wonders:
And now he'll tell you the most terrible news,
How many owls and ravens screeched last night,   90
Or how some ghost has left his marble tomb
To blab a drunken lie.
    Hub.   I tell a fiend
His guilt is hid no more. Ho! there, the guard:

Enter Guards

That is your prisoner.
    Hesp.   You tread a scorpion:
The first that stirs brings to my sword his heart;   95
Ye plunge into your graves.   [*The Guards seize him.*
                      Ah! Floribel;
Thou draggest my steel away, thou'st frozen me;
Girl, thou art pale.
    L. Ern.   How's this?
Ruffians, where do you bear my boy? Release him,
Or I'll—
    Oliv.   Oh! do not anger them. They're men   100
Who have sucked pity from their mothers' breasts,
They will not close their ears to my petition;
And if they'll loose him, I will pray for them
While speech is mine.
    L. Ern.   Your swords, my friends, your
      swords.
    Hub. Stand back, my lords; let the Duke's prisoner
      pass.   105
    L. Ern. The Duke! what Duke dare seize my
      Hesperus?
My noble friends, my—sheath your coward swords,

And put your eyes upon the ground for fear,
Your Jove, the Duke he said;—hear ye no thunder?
But all the warriors of the universe   110
Shall not cow me: I'll free him; villains, back.

Hub. Oh! good old man; alas! he is a murderer.

L. Ern. A murderer! (*drops his sword.*) This is a
baby's arm.

Oliv. Save him, oh save him! I am very faint.

[ORLANDO, VIOLETTA, *and Attendants, carry her out.*

Hesp. Hence with that voice! So shrieked—I must
not think.   115

Hub. Look to Lord Ernest. The Duke sits in council
Waiting your presence, lords. On, to the palace.

[*Exeunt* CLAUDIO, HUBERT, HESPERUS,
Guards, Lords, *and Ladies.*

Manent LORD ERNEST *and Attendants.*

L. Ern. Where is he? What! Ye traitors, let him pass,
Chained, guarded? By this light—gird on your swords.
My hairs are grey, but yet I've blood enough—   120
Did they not speak of crime? These limbs aren't mine,
But some consumptive girl's.—Aye, it was murder!
I'll see the Duke—support me to the palace. [*Exeunt.*

SCENE IV. *A street before the ducal palace*

Two Guards attending the body of FLORIBEL.
LENORA *hanging over it*

1st Guard. 'Tis time to bear the body to the council,
The criminal is there already.

2nd Guard.   Stay;
'Twere sacrilege to shake yon mourner off,
And she will perish in the wintry night
If unattended: yet this poor dumb witness   5
Is needful at the trial. While she sleeps
With careful hands convey her to the Duke's,
And bid the women tend her.

1st Guard   Soft! She breaks
Her trance, and rises like a new-born thing
Fresh from the realm of spirits.
   2nd Guard.   Hush! She speaks. 10
   Len. I dreamed, and in that visioned agony
'Twas whispered by strange voices, like the deads',
I was the mother of this Floribel,
And still a wanderer upon man's earth;
No, no, I am her ghost, shade of her essence,   15
Thrust into some strange shape of womanhood
Until the tomb is open. What are these?
Good sir, have you a tear to throw away,
A little sigh to spare unto the wind?
I've heard that there are hearts yet in the world,   20
Perhaps you have one.
   1st Guard.   Lady, for your sorrow
It aches most deeply.
   Len.   Prithee, look you here.
Cold, cold; 'tis all in vain: those lustrous eyes
Will never beam again beneath the stars;
Darkened for ever; and those wan, dead lips: 25
They'll put her in the earth and let the world,
The pitiless bad world tread o'er her beauty,
While I—ye airs of heaven, why will ye feed me?
Why, ye officious ministers, bestow
The loathed blessing of a cursed existence?   30
There's many a one now leans upon the cheek
Of his dead spouse, a-listening for her pulse,
And hears no motion but his bursting heart;
Give him my life and bid him wipe his eyes.
Look here, look here,   35
I've heard them call her flower; oh! had she been
The frailest rose that whitens in the blast,
Thus bruised and rifled by a ruffian hand,
I might have kept her living in my tears
A very little while, until I die;   40

And then—now tell me this and I will bless thee,
Where thinkest our spirits go?

    1st Guard.   Madam, I know not;
Some say they hang like music in the air,
Some that they sleep in flowers of Paradise,
Some that they lie ingirt by cloudy curtains;   45
Or 'mong the stars.

    Len.   Oh! not among the stars,
For, if she's there, my sight's so dimmed with tears,
I ne'er shall find her out,
But wander through the sparkling labyrinth
Wearied, alone; oh! say not 'mong the stars.   50
Why do ye move her?

    1st Guard.   We must bear her hence
Unto the Duke.

    Len.   What! Is it not enough
That she is dead?

    1st Guard.   No hand shall offer hurt,
And in short space we'll bring her back again,
Unto your cottage.

    Len.   Thanks! They shall not harm her; 55
Soldier, I will repay this kindness nobly;
Hark you; I'm going far off, to Paradise,
And if your child, or wife, or brother 's there,
I'll bring them to you in your dreams some night.
Farewell; I will go search about for Comfort,   60
Him, that, enrobed in mouldering cerements, sits
At the grey tombstone's head beneath the yew;
Men call him Death, but Comfort is his name. [*Exeunt.*

Enter Two Citizens

    1st Cit. Well met sir, come you from the trial?
    2nd Cit.   Aye;
In wonder that the stones do not come down   65
To crush that monster of all wickedness,
The wretched Hesperus; there he stands

Biting his chains and writhing in his rage
Like a mad tiger.

    1st Cit.   Is he yet condemned?

    2nd Cit. Death is the sentence. .

    1st Cit.   See, the criminal   70
And his old father; what a sight of pity.

Enter HESPERUS *guarded,* ORLANDO, HUBERT, LORD
      ERNEST, *and Mob*

    Hesp. Well, gaping idiots; have ye stared enough;
Have ye yet satisfied your pious minds
By thanking your most bounteous stars ye're not
A prodigy like this? Get home and tell   75
Your wives, and put me in your tales and ballads;
Get home and live.

    L. Ern.   Oh hush my son,
Get some good priest of Charity to draw
Tears of repentance from your soul, and wake
The sleeping virtue.

    Hesp.   Who's this greybeard driveller?   80
Go, find your wits, old fellow, that bald skull
Is full of leaks; hence! look in last night's bowl;
Search all your money-bags: don't come abroad
Again without them; 'tis amiss.

    L. Ern.   Oh Heavens!
Is this the son, o'er whose sleeping smiles   85
Often I bent, and mingling with my prayers
Thanksgivings, blessed the loan of so much virtue.

    Hesp. That's right; weep on, weep on; for thou art he
Who slew his only child, his first-born child.

    Orl. Oh look upon his galling agony,   90
These desperate yearnings of paternal love,
And try to have an heart.

    Hesp.   You're merry, friend;
Troth 'tis a goodly jest: what, dost thou think
These limbs, the strength of nature's armoury,
That but exist to dare, and dare the things   95

That make the blood of bravery turn pale
For very terror, such a minion's work,
The offspring of those dribbling veins? Go to,
Thou'rt a sad idiot.

   L. Ern. Oh! hear him not, thou ever-present Justice,
And close thy watchful eyelid, thou that weighest 101
Th' allotted scale of crime.

   Hesp.   Come hither, age;
I have a whisper for your secrecy;
Consider; who am I?

   L. Ern.   Thou wast my son,
The pulse of my dead heart, light of my eyes,   105
But now—

   Hesp.   Thy son! I would I'd time to laugh.
No, no; attend. The night, that gave me being,
There was unearthly glee upon the winds,
There were strange gambols played beneath the moon,
The madman smiled uncouthly in his sleep,   110
And children shrunk aghast at goblin sights;
Then came a tap against the rattling casement,
Not the owl's wing, or struggle of the blast;
Thy dotardship snored loudly, and meanwhile
An incubus begot me.

   L. Ern.   Lead me home,   115
My eyes are dim; I cannot see the way:
I fain would sleep.   [*Exit with some of the Citizens.*

   Hesp.   Go, some one, tell his nurse
To get him swaddling clothes.

   Orl.   Prodigious wretch!
Rebel to man and heaven! On thee shall fall
The cureless torture of the soul, the woe   120
Hell nurses for the deepest damned.

   Hesp.   'Tis pity
So much good cursing should be thrown away;
Well spit, my reptile! Officers, lead on:
Shall I, in bondage, stand to glut the sight
Of these poor marvel-dealing things? Away,   125

I'll shut them out; the red death on you all.   [*Going.*
Ah! my good fellow, are you of the train
That wait upon Olivia?
   Attend.   I'm her servant.
   Hesp. How fares she?
   Attend.   Very ill; she wastes,
Careless of living.
   Hesp.   Tell her, on my love   130
I charge her live; oh heaven, *she* must not die,
There are enough accusers in the tomb.
Tell her—Shame, shame, they shall not see me weep.
                                   [*Exeunt.*

ACT V

SCENE I. *A room in* MORDRED'S *cottage*

The dead FLORIBEL *laid upon a couch.* LENORA
and Boy

   Len. Why dost thou weep, thou little churl?
   Boy.   Alas!
I need not say.
   Len. Boy, boy; thou'rt wicked; thou wouldst have
    me think
I have no Floribel, but thou shalt see
How I will make her live.
                 It is the morning,   5
And she has risen to tend her favourite flowers,
And wearied with the toil leans o'er her seat
In silent languor. Now I will steal in
Softly: perchance she sleeps. It's plain she hears not,
Or she would leap all-smiling to my arms;   10
I wish dear Mordred were awake to see
How the sweet girl will start and welcome me
At my first speaking: but I'll wait awhile
And save the pleasure. Ah thou pretty silence,

I know thou'rt thinking what a happy cot   15
'Twill be when our loved patient is quite well.
Yes, you shall take him his first walk; he'll lean
Upon that arm and you shall show the plants
New set in the garden, and the grassy path
Down to the church.

        Now I will stand behind her   20
So, she must drop her head upon my bosom
As she looks up. Good-morrow to thee, sweet;
Now for her gentle cry; she's turning round.
No—for she won't seem startled, but pretend
To have heard my coming. Why art thou so slow?   25
Sweet little wag, I know thou'rt not asleep.
Soft! 'Tis the swiftness of my thought outruns
Her proper motions. I've this instant spoken,
The air has scarcely yet ta'en up my words;
May be she hears not. But I did not speak,   30
'Twas only thought, or whispered. Child, good-
    morrow;
Yes, she hears that, but will not stir even yet.
I'll not be frightened for she surely hears,
Though if I had not seen her garments move,
And caught the tiny echo of her breath,   35
'Twere dreadful. Speak, I pray thee, Floribel,
Speak to thy mother; do but whisper 'aye';
Well, well, I will not press her; I am sure
She has the welcome news of some good fortune,
And hoards the telling till her father comes;   40
Perhaps she's found the fruit he coveted
Last night. Ah! she half laughed. I've guessed it then;
Come tell me, I'll be secret. Nay, if you mock me,
I must be very angry till you speak.
Now this is silly; some of those young boys   45
Have dressed the cushions with her clothes in sport.
'Tis very like her. I could make this image
Act all her greetings; she shall bow her head,
'Good morrow mother'; and her smiling face

Falls on my neck.—Oh, heaven, 'tis she indeed!   50
I know it all—don't tell me.

SCENE II. *The interior of a prison*

HESPERUS *alone*

Hesp. Hark! Time's old iron voice already counts
The steps unto the after-world, o'er which
Sleep in her arms hath carried man to-night;
And all it wakes to business or to joy,
Save one; and mingled with its solemn tone   5
I heard the grating gates of hell expand—
Oh! house of agony,
I feel thy scorching flames already near.
Where shall I 'scape? Is there no hiding-place?
Spirit, that guidest the sun, look round this ball,   10
And through the windows of deep ocean's vault;
Is there no nook just big enough for me?
Or when I'm dead, can I not pass my soul
For common air, and shroud me in some cloud?
But then the earth will moulder, clouds evanish;   15
So Hell, I must unto thee, darksome vale;
For dared I hope, I could not wish, Elysium,
There should I meet the frowns of Floribel;
My father would be there: black gulph of anguish,
Thou art far better than such paradise.   20
Why did they teach me there is such a place?
The pang of misery is there; I know
There is a land of bliss, and am not in it;
This, this, outstings your lashes, torturers;
He has no lack of punishment who feels it.   25

Enter Jailor

Oh! speak not for a moment, speak not, sir,
I know thine errand well; so tell it not.
But let me shut mine eyes and think a little

That I am what I was. Aye, there he sits,
My good old sire, with his large eye of love.   30
How well it smiles upon that lovely maid,
A beauteous one, indeed; and yet they say
She died most cruelly. Oh! tell me something,
Drive out these dreams.
    Jail.   Prisoner, prepare for death.   [*Exit.*
    Hesp. Death! Death! What's death? I cannot think.

Enter LENORA

                      Who art thou?   35
    Len. Ha! knowest thou not the wretch thou'st made
      Lenora?
Alone I've found thee, villain.
    Hesp.   Not alone;
Oh! not alone: the world hath burst its ribs,
And let out all the demons in the pit;
Thick; thick they throng: I cannot breathe for them; 40
The hounds of Lucifer are feeding on me,
Yet I endure; Remorse and Conscience too,
Stirring the dying embers of my heart,
Which Passion hath burnt out, like midnight gossips
Sit idly chattering of the injured dread;   45
But thou'rt the last and worst; I hoped to hide
Beneath the turf from thee.
    Len. Thou shalt not leave me; stand and hear my
      curse,
Oh such a curse! I learned it from a voice
That wandered 'mid the damned: it burns my tongue,
Listen, wretch, listen;   51
Thus, thus I curse thee. . . . No I do revoke it,
My pardon be upon you for your deeds;
Though thou didst stab me through my Floribel,
I think thou once didst love her; didst thou not?   55
    Hesp. With my whole soul, as now I worship her.
    Len. Alas! say no, I wish thou'dst break my heart;
Now, pr'ythee do; I'll bless thee for 't again.

Hesp. What! is it stubborn yet? Then thou canst
   teach me
How to bear misery—but I need it not,   60
They've dug my grave.
   Len.   But while you still are living,
What say you to some frolic merriment?
There are two grassy mounds beside the church,
My husband and my daughter; let us go
And sit beside them, and learn silence there;   65
Even with such guests we'll hold our revelry
O'er bitter recollections: there's no anguish,
No fear, no sorrow, no calamity,
In the deathful catalogue of human pains,
But we will jest upon 't, and laugh and sing: 70
Let pitiful wretches whine for consolation,
Thank heaven we despair.

Enter Guards

   Hesp.   See you these men?
They bid me to a strange solemnity.
   Len. Must thou be gone?
   Hesp.   I must, alas! for ever.
Live and be blessed, mother of Floribel.
                    [Exit with Guards.
   Len. Farewell; farewell. They drag him to the
   scaffold,   76
My son, the husband of my Floribel:
They shall not slaughter him upon the block,
And to the cursing multitude hold up
The blackened features which she loved; they shall
   not.   *[Exit.* 80

SCENE III. *An apartment in* ORLANDO'S *palace*

OLIVIA, VIOLETTA, *and Attendants*

Oliv. Sing me that strain, my gentle Violet,
Which erst we used, in sport and mockery
Of grief, beneath the willow shade at eve
To chaunt together; 'twill allay my woes.

Song, by Two Voices

First Voice

Who is the baby, that doth lie   5
Beneath the silken canopy
Of thy blue eye?

Second

It is young Sorrow laid asleep
In the crystal deep.

Both

Let us sing his lullaby,   10
Heigho! a sob and a sigh.

First Voice

What sound is that, so soft, so clear,
Harmonious as a bubbled tear
Bursting, we hear?

Second

It is young Sorrow, slumber breaking,   15
Suddenly awaking.

Both

Let us sing his lullaby,
Heigho! a sob and a sigh.

Oliv. 'Tis well: you must not weep; 'twill spoil your
  voices,
And I shall need them soon.
  Viol.   For what, Olivia?   20
You were not wont to prize our simple skill
Erewhile so highly: what will please you most?
What lay of chivalry, or rural sport,
Or shepherd love, shall we prepare you next?
  Oliv. My dirge: I shall not tax your music else.   25
It must be: wherefore weep?
  Viol.   I cannot help it,
When you converse so mournfully of death;
You must forgive me.
  Oliv.   Death! thou silly girl,
There's no such thing; 'tis but a goblin word,
Which bad men conjure from their reeking sins   30
To haunt their slumbers; 'tis a life indeed.
These bodies are the vile and drossy seeds,
Whence, placed again within their kindred earth,
Springs Immortality, the glorious plant
Branching above the skies. What is there here   35
To shrink from? Though your idle legends tell
How cruelly he treats the prostrate world;
Yet, unto me this shadowy potentate
Comes soft and soothing as an infant's sleep,
And kisses out my being. Violetta,   40
Dost thou regard my wish, perhaps the last?
  Viol. Oh! madam, can you doubt it? We have lived
Together ever since our little feet
Were guided on the path, and thence have shared
Habits and thoughts. Have I in all that time,   45
That long companionship, e'er thwarted thee?
Why dost thou ask me then? Indeed I know not
Thy wishes from my own, but to prefer them.
Then tell me what you will; if its performance
But occupy the portion of a minute,   50
'Twill be a happy one, for which I thank you.

Oliv. Thine hand upon it, I believe thy promise.
When I am gone you must not weep for me,
But bring your books, your paintings, and your
    flowers,
And sit upon my grassy monument   55
In the dewy twilight, when they say souls come
Walking the palpable gross world of man,
And I will waft the sweetest odours o'er you,
I'll shower down acorn-cups of spicy rain
Upon your couch and twine the boughs above;   60
Then, if you sing, I'll take up Echo's part,
And from a far-off bower give back the ends
Of some remembered airy melody;
Then, if you draw, I'll breathe upon the banks
And freshen up the flowers, and send the birds   65
Stammering their madrigals, across your path;
Then, if you read, I'll tune the rivulets,
I'll teach the neighbouring shrubs to fan your temples,
And drive sad thoughts and fevers from your breast;
But if you sleep, I'll watch your truant sense,   70
And meet it in the fairy-land of dreams
With my lap full of blessings; 'twill, methinks,
Be passing pleasant, so don't weep for me.

    Viol. I fear, Olivia, I'm a selfish creature,
These tears drop not for you, but for myself;   75
'Tis not that death will have you, but that I
Shall be a lone lost thing without your love.

    Oliv. My love will spread its wings for ever near you,
Each gentler, nobler, and diviner thought
Will be my prompting.

    Viol.   Well, I'll bear it then,   80
And even persuade myself this intercourse
Of disembodied minds is no conjecture,
No fiction of romance. The summer sun
Will find me on the sod that covers you,
Among the blossoms; I'll try not to cry;   85
And when I hear a rustle in the grass,

Or the soft leaves come kissing my bent arm,
I shall not lay it to the empty air,
But think I know thy utterance in the noises
That answer me, and see thy rosy fingers   90
Dimpling the brooks.

    Oliv.   Thou wilt be cheerful, then?

    Viol. Yes, with this hope,
That when, some silent, melancholy night,
I've sobbed myself to sleep over your picture,
Or some memorial of your former kindness,   95
I shall awaken to ethereal music,
And find myself a spirit with Olivia.   [*A bell tolls.*

    Oliv. Whose summons loads the gale with mournful
       sound?

    Attend. Dear lady?

    Oliv.   I ask who's dead or who's to die:
You need not tell me: I remember now,   100
It was a thought I wished to keep away.
My love, my Hesperus, unto me thou wert
The gentlest and the kindest; sudden madness
Must have inspired this deed; and why do I,
Wife of the dying, tarry in the world?   105
I feel already dissolution's work,
A languor creeps through all my torpid veins,
Support me, maidens.

    Viol.   Come unto your couch;
Sleep will recruit thee.

    Oliv.   Yes; the breathless sleep;
Come and pray round me, as I fade away,   110
My life already oozes from my lips,
And with that bell's last sound I shall expire. [*Exeunt.*

SCENE IV. *The place of execution*

HESPERUS *guarded*, HUBERT, ORLANDO, *Citizens,* &c.

Hesp. Now in the scornful silence of your features
I see my hated self; my friends, I was
The pestilence you think of; but to-night
Angelic ministers have been with me,
And by the holy communings of conscience   5
Wrought a most blessed change; my soul has wept
And lain among the thorns of penitence;
I ask, (and you will not refuse the boon
To one who cannot crave again) forgiveness
For all that in the noontide of my crimes,   10
Against you, even in thought, I have committed.
  Orl. And we rejoice to grant it, and if prayers
In meek sincerity outpoured, avail,
You have them from our hearts.
  Hesp. Thy sister's soul spake in those words,
    Orlando,   15
A wretch's blessing for them. I'm as one
In some lone watch-tower on the deep, awakened
From soothing visions of the home he loves;
Trembling he hears the wrathful billows whoop,
And feels the little chamber of his life   20
Torn from its vale of clouds, and, as it falls,
In his midway to fate, beholds the gleam
Of blazing ships, some swallowed by the waves,
Some, pregnant with mock thunder, tossed abroad,
With mangled carcases, among the winds;   25
And the black, sepulchre of ocean, choaked
With multitudinous dead; then shrinks from pangs,
Unknown but destined. All I know of death
Is, that 'twill come. I have seen many die
Upon the battle field, and watched their lips   30
At the final breath, pausing in doubt to hear
If they were gone. I have marked oftentimes
Their pale eyes fading in the last blue twilight;

But none could speak the burning agony,
None told his feelings. I ne'er dreamed I died,   35
Else might I guess the torture that attends it.
But men unhurt have lost their several senses,
Grown deaf, and blind, and dumb without a pang,
And surely these are members of the soul,
And when they fail, man tastes a partial death: 40
Besides our minds share not corporeal sleep,
But go among the past and future, or perhaps
Inspire another in some waking world,
And there's another death.
I will not fear; why do ye linger, guards?   45
I've flung my doubts away; my blood grows wild.

  Hub. The hour appointed is not yet arrived,
Some moments we must wait; I pray you, patience.

Enter LORD ERNEST *in the dress of a Peasant, followed*
by CLAUDIO

  Clau. My lord, where dost thou hurry?
  L. Ern.   To Despair;
Away! I know thee not. Henceforth I'll live   50
Those bitter days that Providence decrees me
In toil and poverty. Oh son, loved son,
I come to give thee my last tear and blessing;
Thou wilt not curse the old, sad, wretch again?
  Hesp. (*falling upon the ground and covering himself*
          with the loose earth) Oh trample me to dust.
  L. Ern. (*lying down beside him*) My own dear child;
Aye, we will lie thus sweetly in the grave,   56
(The wind will not awake us, nor the rain,)
Thou and thy mother and myself; but I,
Alas! I have some tearful years to come
Without a son to weep along with me.   60
  Hesp. Father, dear father!
And wilt thou pray for me? Oh, no! thou canst not,
Thou must forget or hate me.
  L. Ern.   Sirs, have pity;

Let him not use me thus. Hesperus, Hesperus,
Thou'rt going to thy mother; tell her, son,   65
My heart will soon be broken; so prepare
To have me with you. Bless thee, boy, good night.
                                              [*Exit.*
  Hesp. My father, heaven will curse thee if I bless;
But I shall die the better for this meeting. [*Kneeling.*
Oh, Floribel! fair martyr of my fury,   70
Oh, thou blessed saint! look down and see thy ven-
    geance,
And if thy injured nature still can pity,
Whisper some comfort to my soul. 'Tis done;
I feel an airy kiss upon my cheek;
It is her breath; she hears me; she descends;   75
Her spirit is around me. Now I'll die.

          Enter LENORA

  Len. Where's Hesperus? Not gone? Speak to me
    loud,
I hear not for the beating of my heart.
We're not both dead? Say thou hast 'scaped the heads-
    man,
Nor felt the severing steel fall through thy neck.   80
  Hesp. I stay one moment for the signal here,
The next I am no more.
  Len.   Then we have conquered.
Friend, leave us: I would speak a private word
Unto thy prisoner. Look upon these flowers;
They grew upon the grave of Floribel,   85
And when I pulled them, through their tendrils blew
A sweet soft music, like an angel's voice.
Ah! there's her eye's dear blue; the blushing down
Of her ripe cheek in yonder rose; and there
In that pale bud, the blossom of her brow,   90
Her pitiful round tear; here are all colours
That bloomed the fairest in her heavenly face;
Is 't not her breath?

Hesp. (*smelling them*) It falls upon my soul
Like an unearthly sense.

    Len.   And so it should,
For it is Death thou'st quaffed: 95
I steeped the plants in a magician's potion,*
More deadly than the scum of Pluto's pool,
Or the infernal brewage that goes round
From lip to lip at wizards' mysteries;
One drop of it, poured in a city conduit,   100
Would ravage wider than a year of plague;
It brings death swifter than the lightning shaft.

    Hesp. 'Tis true: I feel it gnawing at my heart,
And my veins boil as though with molten lead.
How shall I thank thee for this last, best gift?   105

    Len. What is it rushes burning through my mouth?
Oh! my heart's melted.—Let me sit awhile.

    Hub. Hear ye the chime? Prisoner we must be gone,
Already should the sentence be performed.

    Hesp. On! I am past your power.

             (*To* LENORA) How farest thou now? 110

    Len. Oh! come with me, and view
These banks of stars, these rainbow-girt pavilions,
These rivulets of music—hark, hark, hark!
And here are winged maidens floating round   114
With smiles and welcomes; this bright beaming seraph
I should remember; is it not—my daughter?   [*Dies.*

    Hesp. I see not those; but the whole earth 's in
        motion;
I cannot stem the billows; now they roll:
And what's this deluge? Ah! Infernal flames!   [*Falls.*

    Hub. Guards, lift him up.   120

    Hesp. The bloody hunters and their dogs! Avaunt—
Tread down these serpents' heads. Come hither,
    Murder;

---

* The reader will recollect Massinger's *Duke of Milan.*

Why dost thou growl at me? Ungrateful hound!
Not know thy master? Tear him off! Help! Mercy!
Down with your fiery fangs!—I'm not dead yet.

[*Dies.*   125

THE END

POEMS
CHIEFLY FROM *OUTIDANA*
[Composed 1823–5]

The Romance of the Lily

. . . . . .

King Balthasar has a tower of gold,
  And rubies pave his hall;   65
 A magic sun of diamond blazes
  Above his palace wall;
  And beaming spheres play round in mazes,
With locks of incense o'er them rolled.
Young Balthasar is the Libyan king, 70
  The lord of wizard sages;
   He hath read the sun, he hath read the moon,
  Heaven's thoughts are on their pages;
   He knows the meaning of night and noon,
And the spell on morning's wing: 75
The ocean he hath studied well,
  Its maddest waves he hath subdued
    Beneath an icy yoke,
     And lashed them till they howled, and
      spoke
   The mysteries of the Titan brood, 80
And all their god forbade them tell.
He hath beheld the storm,
When the phantom of its form
  Leans out of heaven to trace,
   Upon the earth and sea, 85
  And air's cerulean face,
In earthquake, thunder, war, and fire,
And pestilence, and madness dire,
   That mighty woe, futurity.

From the roof of his tower he talks to Jove, 90
As the god enthroned sits above;
Night roosts upon his turret's height,
And the sun is the clasp of its girdle of light;

And the stars upon his terrace dwell,—
But the roots of that tower are fixed in hell.   95
Balthasar's soul is a curse and a sin,
And nothing is human that dwells within,
    But a tender, beauteous love,
      That grows upon his haunted heart,
Like a scented bloom on a madhouse wall;   100
For amid the wrath and roar of all,
      It gathers life with blessed art,
    And calmly blossoms on above.

Bright Sabra, when thy thoughts are seen
    Moving within those azure eyes,   105
Like spirits in a star at e'en;
    And when that little dimple flies,
    As air upon a rosy bush,
To hide behind thy fluttering blush;
When kisses those rich lips unclose,   110
And love's own music from them flows,—
A god might love—a demon does.
    'Tis night upon the sprinkled sky,
      And on their couch of roses
      The king and lady lie,   115
While the tremulous lid of each discloses
    A narrow streak of the living eye;
As when a beetle, afloat in the sun,
On a rocking leaf, has just begun
      To sever the clasp of his outer wing,   120
        So lightly, that you scarce can see
    His little lace pinions' delicate fold,
    And a line of his body of breathing gold,
      Girt with many a panting ring,
Before it quivers, and shuts again,   125
    Like a smothered regret in the breast of men,
      Or a sigh on the lips of chastity.

One bright hand, dawning through her hair,
Bids it be black, itself as fair
   As the cold moon's palest daughter,   130
The last dim star with doubtful ray
Snow-like melting into day,
   Echoed to the eye on water;
Round his neck and on his breast
   The other curls, and bends its bell   135
   Petalled inward as it fell,
Like a tented flower at rest.
   She dreams of him, for rayed joys hover
      In dimples round her timorous lip,
   And she turns to clasp her sleeping lover,   140
Kissing the lid of his tender eye,
And brushing off the dews that lie
      Upon its lash's tip;
And now she stirs no more—
    But the thoughts of her breast are still,   145
    As the song of a frozen rill
   Which winter spreads his dark roof o'er
     In the still and moony hour
      Of that calm entwining sleep,
  From the utmost tombs of earth,   150
  The vision-land of death and birth,
    Came a black, malignant power,
     A spectre of the desert deep:
And it is Plague, the spotted fiend, the drunkard of the
    tomb;   154
Upon her mildewed temples the thunderbolts of doom,
And blight-buds of hell's red fire, like gory wounds in
    bloom,
     Are twisted for a wreath;
And there's a chalice in her hand, whence bloody
    flashes gleam,
While struggling snakes with arrowy tongues twist o'er
    it for a steam,

And its liquor is of Phlegethon, and Ætna's wrathful
    stream,   160
        And icy dews of death.

Like a rapid dream she came,
  And vanished like the flame
    Of a burning ship at sea,
But to his shrinking lips she pressed   165
    The cup of boiling misery,
And he quaffed it in his tortured rest,
    And woke in the pangs of lunacy.
      As a buried soul awaking
        From the cycle of its sleep,   170
Panic-struck and sad doth lie
Beneath its mind's dim canopy,
    And marks the stars of memory breaking
      From 'neath oblivion's ebbing deep,   174
While clouds of doubt bewilder the true sky,—
  So in the hieroglyphic portal
    Of his dreams sate Balthasar,
Awake amidst his slumbering senses,
  And felt as feels man's ghost immortal,
Whom the corpse's earthen fences   180
    From his vast existence bar.
The pestilence was in his breast,
  And boiled and bubbled o'er his brain,
His thoughtless eyes in their unrest
  Would have burst their circling chain,   185
Scattering their fiery venom wide,
  But for the soft endearing rain,
With which the trembler at his side
Fed those gushing orbs of white,   189
As evening feeds the waves with looks of quiet light.
  The tear upon his cheek's fierce flush;
    The cool breath on his brow;
  And the healthy presage of a blush,
  Sketched in faint tints behind his skin;

And the hush of settling thoughts within,   195
    Sabra hath given, and she will need them now.
For, as the echo of a grove
Keeps its dim shadow 'neath some song of love,
    And gives her life away to it in sound,
Soft spreading her wild harmony,   200
Like a tress of smoking censery,
    Or a ring of water round,—
So all the flowery wealth
Of her happiness and health
Untwined from Sabra's strength, and grew   205
    Into the blasted stem of Balthasar's pale life,
And his is the beauty and bliss that flew
    On the wings of her love from his sinking wife.
    The fading wanness of despair
        Was the one colour of her cheek,   210
    And tears upon her bosom fair
        Wrote the woe she dared not speak;
    But life was in her. Yes: it played
        In tremulous and fitful grace,
Like a flame's reflected breath   215
Shivering in the throes of death
        Against the monumental face
Of some sad voiceless marble maid:
And what is a woman to Balthasar,   219
    Whom love has weakened, bowed, and broken?
Upon his forehead's darksome war,
    His lip's curled meaning, yet unspoken,
The lowering of his wrinkled brow,
'Tis graved,—he spurns, he loaths her now.

Along the sea, at night's black noon,   225
    Alone the king and lady float,
    With music in a snowy boat,
That glides in light, an ocean-moon;
    From billow to billow it dances,
    And the spray around it glances,   230

And the mimic rocks and caves
Beneath the mountains of the waves,
Reflect a joyous song
As the merry bark is borne along;
And now it stays its eager sail   235
Within a dark sepulchral vale,
   Amid the living Alps of Ocean,
Round which the crags in tumult rise
And make a fragment of the skies;
   Beneath whose precipice's motion   240
The folded dragons of the deep
Lie with lidless eyes asleep:
   It pauses; and—Is that a shriek
    That agonizes the still air,
    And makes the dead day move and speak   245
From beneath its midnight pall,—
Or the ruined billow's fall?
    The boat is soaring lighter there,
The voice of woman sounds no more—
That night the water-crescent bore   250
Dark Balthasar alone unto the living shore.

    Tears, tears for Sabra; who will weep?
O blossoms, ye have dew,
And grief-dissembling storms might strew
   Thick-dropping woe upon her sleep.   255
  False sea, why dost thou look like sorrow,
   Why is thy cold heart of water?
Or rather, why are tears of thee,
Compassionless, bad sea?
  For not a drop does thy stern spirit borrow,   260
   To mourn o'er beauty's fairest daughter.
Heaven, blue heaven, thou art not kind,
  Or else the sun is not thine eye,
For thou should'st be with weeping blind,
  Not thus forgetful, bright and dry.   265
Oh that I were a plume of snow,

To melt away and die
In a long chain of bubbling harmony!—
My tribute shall be sweet tho' small;
A cup of the vale-lily bloom   270
Filled with white and liquid woe—
Give it to her ocean-pall;
With such deluge-seeds I'll sow
Her mighty elemental tomb,
Until the lamentations grow   275
Into a foaming crop of populous overflow.

Hither like a bird of prey,
Whom red anticipations feed,
Flaming along the fearful day
Revenge's thirsty hour doth fly.   280
Heaven has said a fearful word;
(Which hell's eternal labyrinths heard,
And the wave of time
Shall answer to the depths sublime,
Reflecting it in deed;)   285
'Balthasar the king must die.'
Must die; for all his power is fled,
His spells dissolved, his spirits gone,
And magic cannot ease the bed
Where lies the necromant alone.   290
What thought is gnawing in his heart,
What struggles madly in his brain?
See, the force, the fiery pain
Of silence makes his eyeballs start.
O ease thy bosom, dare to tell—   295
But grey-haired pity speaks in vain;
That bitter shriek, that hopeless yell,
Has given the secret safe to hell.
Like a ruffled nightingale,
Balanced upon dewy wings,   300
Through the palace weeps the tale,
Leaving tears, where'er she sings;

And, around the icy dead
  Maids are winding
Kingly robes of mocking lead,   305
  And with leafy garlands binding
The unresisting careless head:
Gems are flashing, garments wave
Round the bridegroom of the grave.
Hark! A shout of wild surprise,   310
  A burst of terrible amaze!
The lids are moving up his eyes,
  They open, kindle, beam, and gaze—
Grave, thy bars are broken,
  Quenched the flames of pain,   315
Falsely fate hath spoken,
  The dead is born again.
As when the moon and shadows' strife,
  On some rebellious night,
Looks a pale statue into life,   320
  And gives his watching form the action of
    their light,
So stilly strode the awakened one,
And with the voice of stone,
  Which troubled caverns screech,
   Cursing the tempest's maniac might,   325
  He uttered human speech.
'Tremble, living ones, and hear;
By the name of death and fear,
By lightning, earthquake, fire and war,
And him whose snakes and hounds they are, 330
From whose judgment seat I come,
Listen, crouch, be dumb,
My soul is drowned beneath a flood
Of conscience, red with Sabra's blood;
  And from yon blue infinity,   335
   Doomed and tortured I am sent
  To confess the deed and fly;

Wail not for me—yourselves repent:
　　Eternity is punishment;
Listen, crouch, and die.'　　　　　　　　　340
　　With that word his body fell,
As dust upon the storm,
Flashlike darkened was his form;
While through their souls in horror rang
The dragon shout, the thunderous clang　　345
　　Of the closing gates of hell.

Lines

Written in a blank leaf of the *Prometheus Unbound*.

WRITE it in gold—a Spirit of the sun,
An Intellect ablaze with heavenly thoughts,
A Soul with all the dews of pathos shining,
Odorous with love, and sweet to silent woe
With the dark glories of concentrate song,
Was sphered in mortal earth. Angelic sounds
Alive with panting thoughts sunned the dim world.
The bright creations of an human heart
Wrought magic in the bosoms of mankind.
A flooding summer burst on Poetry;
Of which the crowning sun, the night of beauty,
The dancing showers, the birds whose anthems wild
Note after note unbind the enchanted leaves
Of breaking buds, eve, and the flow of dawn,
Were centred and condensed in his one name
As in a providence—and that was SHELLEY.

OXFORD, 1822

Sonnet to Zoë King

LEAF after leaf like a magician's book
Unfolds the Universe, and needs we now,
    Cousin of mine (while the whole world doth look
Our shoulders over with its rocky brow),
    In turn our living story must transact
Upon the surface of its earthen pages;
    Whence the still shade of our most needless act
Shall paint itself with iron syllables
    In the arched sight of unawakened ages;
Therefore 'tis ours, and his who with us dwells
    Beneath the roof of the same starry hour,
Both in his own and in the general mind,
Which is the world, all truth and good to find,
    And finding practise to his end of power.

Feb. 29, 1824

Lines

Written at Geneva; July 16 [1824]

THE hour is starry, and the airs that stray,
Sad wanderers from their golden home of day,
On night's black mountain melt and fade away
In sorrow that is music. Some there be
Make them blue pillows on Geneva's sea,
And sleep upon their best-loved planet's shade:
And every herb is sleeping in the glade;—
They have drunk sunshine and the linnet's song,
Till every leaf's soft sleep is dark and strong.
Or was there ever sound, or can what was
Now be so dead? Although no flowers or grass
Grow from the corpse of a deceased sound,
Somewhat, methinks, should mark the air around
Its dying place and tomb,

92

A gentle music, or a pale perfume:
For hath it not a body and a spirit,
A noise and meaning? and, when one doth hear it
Twice born, twice dying, doubly found and lost,
That second self, that echo, is its ghost.
But even the dead are all asleep this time,
And not a grave shakes with the dreams of crime:—
The earth is full of chambers for the dead,
And every soul is quiet in his bed;
Some who have seen their bodies moulder away,
Antediluvian minds,—most happy they,
Who have no body but the beauteous air,
No body but their minds. Some wretches are
Now lying with the last and only bone
Of their old selves, and that one worm alone
That ate their heart: some, buried just, behold
Their weary flesh, like an used mansion, sold
Unto a stranger, and see enter it
The earthquake winds and waters of the pit,
Or children's spirits in its holes to play.

Dirge

TO-DAY is a thought, a fear is to-morrow,
And yesterday is our sin and our sorrow;
And life is a death,
    Where the body's the tomb,
And the pale sweet breath
    Is buried alive in its hideous gloom.
Then waste no tear,
For we are the dead; the living are here,
In the stealing earth, and the heavy bier.
Death lives but an instant, and is but a sigh,
And his son is unnamed immortality,

Whose being is thine. Dear ghost, so to die
Is to live—and life is a worthless lie.
Then we weep for ourselves, and wish thee good-bye.

Song of a Maid whose Love is Dead

MERRY, merry little Stream,
   Tell me, hast thou seen my dear?
I left him with an azure dream,
   Calmly sleeping on his bier—
     But he has fled!

'I passed him in his churchyard bed—
A yew is sighing o'er his head,
And grass-roots mingle with his hair.'
     What doth he there?
O cruel! can he lie alone?
   Or in the arms of one more dear?
Or hides he in that bower of stone,
   To cause and kiss away my fear?

'He doth not speak, he doth not moan—
Blind, motionless, he lies alone;
But, ere the grave snake fleshed his sting,
This one warm tear he bade me bring
     And lay it at thy feet
     Among the daisies sweet.'

Moonlight whisperer, summer air,
   Songstress of the groves above,
Tell the maiden rose I wear,
   Whether thou hast seen my love.
'This night in heaven I saw him lie,
   Discontented with his bliss;
   And on my lips he left this kiss,
For thee to taste and then to die.'

Sonnet

To Tartar, a Terrier Beauty.

SNOWDROP of dogs, with ear of brownest dye,
Like the last orphan leaf of naked tree
Which shudders in bleak autumn; though by thee,
Of hearing careless and untutored eye,
Not understood articulate speech of men,
Nor marked the artificial mind of books,
—The mortal's voice eternized by the pen,—
Yet hast thou thought and language all unknown
To Babel's scholars; oft intensest looks,
Long scrutiny o'er some dark-veined stone
Dost thou bestow, learning dead mysteries
Of the world's birth-day, oft in eager tone
With quick-tailed fellows bandiest prompt replies,
Solicitudes canine, four-footed amities.

Letter to B. W. Procter, Esq.

From Oxford; May, 1825.

IN every tower that Oxford has is swung,
Quick, loud, or solemn, the monotonous tongue
Which speaks Time's language, the universal one
After the countenance of moon or sun,
Translating their still motions to the earth.   5
I cannot read; the reeling belfry's mirth
Troubles my senses; therefore, Greek, shut up
Your dazzling pages; covered be the cup
Which Homer has beneath his mantle old,
Steamy with boiling life: your petals fold   10
You fat square blossoms of the yet young tree
Of Britain-grafted, flourishing Germany:
Hush! Latin, to your grave: and with the chime
My pen shall turn the minutes into rhyme

And like the dial blacken them. There sits,   15
Or stands, or lounges, or perhaps on bits
Of this rag's daughter, paper, exorcises
With strange black marks and inky wild devices
The witch of words, the echo of great verse
About the chasms of the universe,   20
Ringing and bounding immortality.—
Give him thy bosom, dark Melpomene,
And let him of thy goblet and thine eye
Exhaust the swimming deep insanity.
He hath the soul, oh let it then be fed,   25
Sea after sea, with that which is not read,
Nor wrung by reasoning from a resolute head,
But comes like lightning on a hill-top steeple;
Heaven's spillings on the lofty laurelled people.
Verse to thee, light to thee, wings upraise thee long 30
In the unvacillating soar of song,
Thou star-seed of a man! But do not dare
To tempt thy Apollonian god too far,
Clogging and smoking thy young snake, Renown,
In the strait stony shadows of the town,   35
Lest he grow weak and pine and never be
What he was born, twin to Eternity.
So come, shake London from thy skirts away:
So come, forget not it is England's May.
For Oxford, ho! by moonlight or by sun;   40
Our horses are not hours but rather run
Foot by foot faster than the second-sand,
While the old sunteam like a plough doth stand
Stuck in thick heaven. Here thou at morn shalt see
Spring's dryad-wakening whisper call the tree   45
And move it to green answers; and beneath,
Each side the river which the fishes breathe,
Daisies and grass whose tops were never stirred,
Or dews made tremulous, but by foot of bird.   49
And you shall mark in spring's heaven-tapestried room
Yesterday's knoppe burst by its wild perfume,

Like woman's childhood, to this morning's bloom;
And here a primrose pale beneath a tree,
And here a cowslip longing for its bee,
And violets and lilies every one   55
Grazing in the great pasture of the sun
Beam after beam, visibly, as the grass
Is swallowed by the lazy cows that pass.
Come look, come walk,—and there shall suddenly
Seize you a rapture and a phantasy,   60
High over mountain sweeping, fast and high
Through all the intricacies of the sky,
As fast and far a ship-wrecked hoard of gold
Dives ocean, cutting every billow's fold.
These are the honey-minutes of the year   65
Which make man god, and make a god—Shakespeare.
Come gather them with me. If not, then go,
And with thee all the ghosts of Jonson's toe,
The fighting Tartars and the Carthaginians:
And may your lady-muse's stiff-winged pinions   70
Be naked and impossible to fly,
Like a fat goose pen-plucked for poetry.
A curse upon thy cream to make it sour:
A curse upon thy tea-pot every hour;
Spirits of ice possess it! and thy tea,   75
Changed at its contact, hay and straw leaves be!
A cold and nipping ague on thine urn!
And an invisible canker eat and burn
The mathematic picture near your fire,
Of the grave compass-handed quiet sire!   80
No more.—Be these the visions of your sorrow
When you have read this doggrel through to-morrow,
And then refuse to let our Oxford borrow
You of the smoky-faced Augustan town,
And unpersuaded drop the paper down.   85

Pygmalion

The Cyprian Statuary

THERE stood a city along Cyprus' side
Lavish of palaces, an arched tide
Of unrolled rocks; and where the deities dwelled
Their clustered domes pushed up the noon and swelled
With the emotion of the god within,   5
As doth earth's hemisphere, when showers begin
To tickle the still spirit at its core
Till pastures tremble and the river-shore
Squeezes out buds at every dewy pore;   9
And there were pillars, from some mountain's heart,
Thronging beneath a wide imperial floor
That bent with riches; and there stood apart
A palace oft accompanied by trees
That laid their shadows in the galleries
Under the coming of the endless light,   15
Net-like; who trod the marble night or day,
By moon, or lamp or sunless day-shine white,
Would brush the shaking ghostly leaves away
Which might be tendrils or a knot of wine,
Burst from the depth of a faint window vine,   20
With a bird pecking it—and round the hall
And wandering stair-case, within every wall
Of sea-ward portico, and sleeping chamber,
Whose patient lamp distilled a day of amber,
There stood and sate or made rough steeds their
    throne   25
Immortal generations wrung from stone
Alike too beautiful for life and death
And bodies that a soul of mortal breath
Would be the dross of.
              Such a house as this
Within a garden hard by Salamis,   30
(Cyprus's city-crown and capital
Ere Paphos was, and at whose ocean-wall

Beauty and love's paternal waves do beat
That sprouted Venus:) such a fair retreat
Lonely Pygmalion self inhabited   35
Whose fiery chisel with creation fed
The shipwrecked rocks; who paid the heavens again
Diamonds for ice; who made gods who make men.
Lonely Pygmalion: you might see him go
Along the streets where markets thickest flow   40
Doubling his gown across his thinking breast
And the men fall aside; nor only pressed
Out of his elbows' way but left a place
A sun-room for him that his mind had space   44
And none went near; none in his sweep would venture
For you might feel that he was but the centre
Of an inspired round, the middle spark
Of a great moon setting aside the dark
And cloudy people. As he went along ——
The chambered ladies silenced the half-song   50
And let the wheel unheeded whirl and skim
To get their eyes blest by the sight of him.
So locks were swept from every eye that drew
Sun for the soul through circles violet-blue
Mild brown or passionate black.

                    Still, discontent,   55
Over his sensual kind the sculptor went
Walking his thoughts. Yet Cyprus' girls be fair;
Daybright and evening-soft the maidens are
And witching like the midnight and their pleasure
Silent and deep as midnight's starry treasure.   60
Lovely and young, Pygmalion yet loved none.
His soul was bright and lonely as the sun
Like which he could create—and in its might
There lived another Spirit wild and bright
That came and went; and when it came, its light   65
On these dim earthy things, turn where he will,
Its light, shape, beauty were reflected still.
Daytime and dark it came—like a dim mist

Shelling a god it rolled, and ere he wist
It fell aside, and dawned a shape of grace   70
And an inspired and melancholy face
Whose lips were smile-buds dewy—into him
It rolled like sunlight, till his sight was dim
And it was in his heart and soul again,
Not seen but breathed.

                              There was a grassy plain   75
A pasture of the deer, Olympus' mountain
Was the plain's night, the picture of its fountain;
Unto which unfrequented dell and wood
Unwittingly his solitary mood
Oft drew him. In the water lay   80
A fragment of pale marble, which they say
Slipped from some fissure in the agued moon
Which had caught earth-quake and a deadly swoon
When the sun touched her with his hilly shade.
Weeds grew upon it and the streamlet made   85
A wanton music with its ragged side
And birds had nests there. One still eventide
When they were perched and sleeping passed this man
Startling the air with thoughts which over-ran
The compass of his mind; writing the sand   90
Idly he paused and laid unwitting hand
On the cold stone. How smooth the touch! It felt
Less porous than a lip which kisses melt
And diamond-hard. That night his workmen wrought
With iron under it and it was brought,   95
This dripping quarry while the sky was starry
Home to the weary yearning statuary.
He saw no sky that day, no dark that night
For through the hours his lamp was full of light,
Shadowing the pavement with his busy right;   100
Day after day they saw not in the street
The wondrous artist, some immortal feat
Absorbed him. And yet often in the noon
When the town slept beneath the sweltering June

—The rich within; the poor man on the stair— 105
He stole unseen into the meadow's air
And fed on sight of summer—till the life
Was too abundant in him and so rife
With light creative he went in alone
And poured it warm upon the growing stone. 110
The magic chisel thrust and gashed and swept
Flying and manifold; no cloud e'er wept
So fast, so thick, so light upon the close
Of shapeless green it meant to make a rose—
And as insensibly out of a stick 115
Dead in the winter-time, the dew-drops quick
And the thin sun-beams and the airy shower
Raise and unwrap a many-leaved flower
And then a fruit—So from the barren stock
Of the deer-shading formless valley-rock, 120
This close stone-bud, he, quiet as the air,
Had shaped a lady wonderfully fair.
—Dear to the eyes—a delicate delight
For all her marble symmetry was white
As brow and bosom should be; save some azure 125
Which waited for a loving lip's erasure
Upon her shoulder to be turned to blush.
And she was smooth and full, as if one gush
Of life had washed her, or as if a sleep
Lay on her eyelid easier to sweep 130
Than bee from daisy. Who could help a sigh
At seeing a beauty stand so life-lessly
But that it was too beautiful to die?
Dealer of immortality
Greater than Jove himself, for only he 135
Can such eternize as the grave has ta'en
And open heaven by the gate of pain;
What art thou now, divine Pygmalion?
Divine! gods counting human. Thou hast done
That glory which has undone thee for ever, 140
For thou art weak and tearful and dost shiver

Wintrily sad and thy life's healthy river,
With which thy body once was overflown,
Is dried and sunken to its banks of bone.

He carved it not; nor was the chisel's play 145
That dashed the earthen hindrances away
Driven and diverted by his muscle's sway;
The winged tool as digging out a spell
Followed a magnet, wheresoe'er it fell,
That sucked and led it right—and for the rest 150
The living form with which the stone be blest
Was the loved image stepping from his breast.
And therefore loves he it and therefore stays
About the she-rock's feet, from hour to hour,
Anchored to her by his own heart; the power 155
Of the isle's Venus therefore doth he pray—
'Goddess that made me, save thy son, and save
The man that made thee, goddess, from the grave.
Thou know'st it not; it is a fearful coop
Dark, cold, and horrible—a blinded loop 160
In Pluto's madhouse' green and wormy wall.
O save me from 't; let me not die, like all,
For I am but like one—not yet, not yet,
At least not yet—and why? my eyes are wet
With the thick dregs of immature despair, 165
With bitter blood out of my empty heart,
I breathe not aught but my own sighs for air,
And my life's strongest is a dying start.
No sour grief there is to me unwed,
I could not be more lifeless being dead. 170
Then let me die—Ha did she pity me?
Oh she can never love—did you not see,
How still she bears the music of my moan?
Her heart? Ah touch it.—Fool. I love the stone.
Inspire her, gods—Oft ye have wasted life 175
On the deformed, the hideous and the vile:
Oh grant it my sweet rock—my only wife.
I do not ask it long: a little while—

A year—a day—an hour let it be!
For that I'll give you my eternity—   180
Or let it be a fiend if ye will send
Something yon form to humanize and bend,
Within those limbs, and when the new-poured blood
Flows in such veins the worst must soon be good.
They will not hear.—Thou Jove—or thou, Apollo, 185
Aye—thou—thou know'st—Oh listen to my groan.
'Twas Niobe thou drovest from flesh to stone,
Shew this the hole she broke, and let her follow
That mother's track of steps and eyelid rain
Treading them backwards into life again.   190
Life said I? lives she not? is there not gone
My life into her which I pasture on,
Dead where she is not? Live, thou statue fair,
Live, thou dear marble! or I shall go wild.
I cover thee my sweet, I leave thee there   195
Behind this curtain, my delicious child,
That they may secretly begin to give
My prayer to thee—when I return, oh live!
Oh live—or I live not.'—And so he went,
Leaving the statue in its darksome tent.   200

    Morn after morn sadder the artist came,
His prayer, his disappointment were the same.
But when he gazed she was more near to woman;
There was a fleshy pink—a dimple wrought   204
That trembled—and the cheek was growing human
With the flushed distance of a rising thought
That still crept nearer. Yet no further sign!
And now, Pygmalion, that weak life of thine
Shakes like a dew-drop in a broken rose—
Or incense parting from the altar glows.   210
'Tis the last look and he is mad no more:
By rule and figure he could prove at large
She never can be born, and from the shore
His foot is stretching into Charon's barge.
Upon the pavement ghastly is he lying   215

Cold with the last and stoniest embrace,
Elysium's light illumines all his face,
His eyes have a wild starry grace
Of heaven, into whose depth of depths he 's dying
   A sound, with which the air doth shake   220
Extinguishing the window of moonlight.
A pang of music dropping round delight,
As if sweet music's honiest heart did break.
Such a flash and such a sound the world
Is stung by as if something was unfurled   225
That held great bliss within its inmost curled.
Roof after roof the palace rends asunder,
And then—a sight of joy and placid wonder!—
He lies beside a fountain on the knee
Of the sweet woman-statue, quietly   230
Weeping the tears of his felicity.

DRAMATIC FRAGMENTS

[Composed 1823–5]

Fragments of
THE LAST MAN
and other projected plays [1]

[Composed 1823–5.]

II. Recognition

SOFT! Stand away! those features—Do not stir!
Be breathless if thou canst!... The trembling ray
Of some approaching thought, I know not what,
Gleams on my darkened mind. It will be here
Directly: now I feel it growing, growing,
Like a man's shadow, when the sun floats slowly
Through the white border of a baffled cloud:
And now the pale conception furls and thickens.
'Tis settled. Yes—Beroe!—How dare thy cheek
Be wan and withered as a wrinkling moon
Upon the tumbled waves? Why camest thou here?
I dreamt of thee last night, as thou wert once,
But I shall never dream of thee again.

The Last Man

III. Doubt

WHAT'S this? Did you not see a white convulsion
Run through his cheek and fling his eyelids up?
There's mischief in the paper.

                Mark again
How, with that open palm, he shades his brain
From its broad, sudden meaning. Once I saw
One who had dug for treasure in a corner,

---

[1] The numbers are those of the Oxford edition.

Where he by torchlight saw a trembling man
Burying a chest at night. Just so he stood
With open striving lips and shaking hair;
Alive but in his eyes, and they were fixed
On a smeared, earthy, bleeding corpse—his sister,
There by her murderer crushed into the earth.

IV. A Ruffian

THERE'S a fellow
With twisting root-like hair up to his eyes,
And they are streaked with red and starting out
Under their bristling brows; his crooked tusks
Part, like a hungry wolf's, his cursing mouth;
His head is frontless, and a swinish mane
Grows o'er his shoulders: brown and warty hands,
Like roots, with pointed nails.—He is the man.

VI. A Crocodile

HARD by the lilied Nile I saw
A duskish river-dragon stretched along,
The brown habergeon of his limbs enamelled
With sanguine almandines and rainy pearl:
And on his back there lay a young one sleeping,
No bigger than a mouse; with eyes like beads,
And a small fragment of its speckled egg
Remaining on its harmless, pulpy snout;
A thing to laugh at, as it gaped to catch
The baulking merry flies. In the iron jaws
Of the great devil-beast, like a pale soul
Fluttering in rocky hell, lightsomely flew
A snowy trochilus, with roseate beak
Tearing the hairy leeches from his throat.

VIII. Hard Dying

By heaven and hell, and all the fools between them,
I will not die, nor sleep, nor wink my eyes,
But think myself into a God; old Death
Shall dream he has slain me, and I'll creep behind him,
Thrust off the bony tyrant from his throne
And beat him into dust. Or I will burst
Damnation's iron egg, my tomb, and come
Half damned, ere they make lightning of my soul,
And creep into thy carcase as thou sleepest
Between two crimson fevers. I'll dethrone
The empty skeleton, and be thy death,
A death of grinding madness.—Fear me now:
I am a devil, not a human soul—

The Last Man

IX. 'Bona de Mortuis'

Aye, the good man, kind father, best of friends—
These are the words that grow like grass and nettles
Out of dead men, and speckled hatreds hide
Like toads among them.

XVII. Hymn

And many voices marshalled in one hymn
Wound through the night, whose still, translucent
        moments
Lay on each side their breath; and the hymn passed
Its long, harmonious populace of words
Between the silvery silences, as when

The slaves of Egypt, like a wind between
The head and trunk of a dismembered king
On a strewn plank, with blood and footsteps sealed,
Vallied the unaccustomed sea.

XIX. Concealed Joy

JUST now a beam of joy hung on his eye-lash;
But as I looked, it sunk into his eye,
Like a bruised worm writhing its form of rings
Into a darkening hole.

XXII. Life a Glass Window

LET him lean
Against his life, that glassy interval
'Twixt us and nothing; and upon the ground
Of his own slippery breath, draw hueless dreams,
And gaze on frost-work hopes. Uncourteous Death
Knuckles the pane, and——

XXVIII. Meditation

THE bitter past
And the untasted future I mix up,
Making the present a dream-figured bowl
For the black poison, which is caked and moulded
By the inside of the enchasing thoughts,
Even as I taste it.

XXIX. *Death Sweet*

Is it not sweet to die? for, what is death,
But sighing that we ne'er may sigh again,
Getting a length beyond our tedious selves;
But trampling the last tear from poisonous sorrow,
Spilling our woes, crushing our frozen hopes,
And passing like an incense out of man?
Then, if the body felt, what were its sense,
Turning to daisies gently in the grave,
If not the soul's most delicate delight
When it does filtrate, through the pores of thought,
In love and the enamelled flowers of song?

XXXVII. *A Mountain*

ITS impossible ascent was steep,
As are the million pillars of a shower
Torn, shivered, and dashed hard against the earth,
When Day no longer breathes but through the black
    hours
The ghost of Chaos haunts the ruined sky.

XXXIX. *Defiance*

      STRIKE, I fear thee not.—
Why? Art a god; or has the slimy Styx
Licked thee invulnerable? Does thy soul
Not wear a fleshy shirt, a cloak of skin,
Art not sewn up with veins and pegged together
With bony sticks and hinges? If thou hast a life
And keep'st it in the cupboard of thy body,
In the least corner, the minutest pore,

More secret than the sunshine in a flint,
I'll drag it out and cast it for a sop
To the three-gated throat of Pluto's hound.
So shut your soul's door closer and come on!
Wert thou like the air, the water or the fire,
Invulnerable though pierced, I'd quench thee, dam
    thee
Or breathe thee up.

XLIV. Life's Uncertainty

  A. THE king looks well, red in its proper place
The middle of the cheek, and his eye's round
Black as a bit of night.
    B.   Yet men die suddenly:
One sits upon a strong and rocky life,
Watching a street of many opulent years,
And Hope 's his mason. Well! to-day do this,
And so to-morrow; twenty hollow years
Are stuffed with action:—lo! upon his head
Drops a pin's point of time; tick! quoth the clock,
And the grave snaps him.
    A.   Such things may have been;
The crevice 'twixt two after-dinner minutes,
The crack between a pair of syllables
May sometimes be a grave as deep as 'tis
From noon to midnight in the hoop of time.
But for this man, his life wears ever steel
From which disease drops blunted. If indeed
Death lay in the market-place, or were—but hush!
See you the tremble of that myrtle bough?
Doth no one listen?
    B.   Nothing with a tongue:
The grass is dumb since Midas, and no Æsop
Translates the crow or hog. Within the myrtle

Sits a hen-robin, trembling like a star,
Over her brittle eggs.
    A.   Is it no more?
    B. Nought: let her hatch.

XLVII. *Dream of Dying*

SHIVERING in fever, weak, and parched to sand,
My ears, those entrances of word-dressed thoughts,
My pictured eyes, and my assuring touch,
Fell from me, and my body turned me forth
From its beloved abode: then I was dead;
And in my grave beside my corpse I sat,
In vain attempting to return: meantime
There came the untimely spectres of two babes,
And played in my abandoned body's ruins;
They went away; and, one by one, by snakes
My limbs were swallowed; and, at last, I sat
With only one, blue-eyed, curled round my ribs,
Eating the last remainder of my heart,
And hissing to himself. O sleep, thou fiend!
Thou blackness of the night! how sad and frightful
Are these thy dreams!

L. *Man's Petty Universe contrasted with the True*

SCENE: *the abyss of Space*: AMBROSIUS *and*
CYNTHIA *in the car, returning to the earth*

Amb. O what a deep delight it is to cleave,
Out-darting thought, above all sight and sound,
And sweep the ceiling of the universe,
Thus with our locks! How it does mad the heart,

How dances it along the living veins,
Like hot and steaming wine! How my eyes ache
With gazing on his mighty vacancy!
O Universe of earth and air and ocean,
Which man calls infinite, where art thou now?
Sooner a babe should pierce the marble ear
Of death, and startle his tombed ancestor
'Mid Hell's thick laughter, shrieks, and flamy noises,
With cradle-pulings, than the gathered voice
Of every thunder, ocean, and wild blast,
Find thee, thou atom, in this wilderness!
This boundless emptiness, this waveless sea,
This desart of vacuity, alone
Is great: and thou, for whom the word was made,
Art as the wren's small goblet of a home
Unto the holy vastness of the temple!

The Last Man

LVII. Dianeme's Death-Scene

DIANEME *and female attendants*

Dianeme. Sing on, sing ever, and let sobs arise
Beneath the current of your harmony,
Breaking its silvery stillness into gushes
Of stealing sadness: let tears fall upon it
And burst with such a sound, as when a lute-string   5
Torn by the passion of its melody
Gasps its whole soul of music in one sound,
And dies beneath the waves of its own voice!
Be pale thou mooned midnight, and ye stars
Shed fluttering tremours of inconstant light   10
Upon the moaning billows; timid leaves
O'erwhelm yourselves with shadow, and give out
Your dewy titterings to the air no more!

114

Clouds, clouds, dark, deadly clouds, let not the moon
Look on his grave! It is too light: the day   15
Will rise before I die: how old is evening?

   Attend. The tide of darkness now is at its height.
Yon lily-woven cradle of the hours
Hath floated half her shining voyage, nor yet
Is by the current of the morn opposed.   20

   Dianeme. The hour is coming: I must give my soul
To the same moment on whose precious air
My Casimir soared heavenward, for I know
There are a million chambers of the dead,
And every other minute but the same   25
Would bear me to the one where he is not,
And that were madness. Bring me yon sick lily,—
Yon fevered one.

   Attend.   Choose any other, lady,
For this is broken, odourless, and scorched,
Where Death has graved his curse.

   Dianeme.   Give it to me;   30
I'll weep it full. I have a love for flowers:
Guess you not why? Their roots are in the earth,
And when the dead awake or talk in sleep,
These hear their thoughts and write them on their
      leaves
For heaven to look on: and their dews come down 35
From the deep bosom of the blue, whereon
The spirits linger, sent by them perchance
With blessings to their friends. Besides all night
They are wide-waking, and the ghosts will pause,
And breathe their thoughts upon them. There, poor
      blossom,
My soul bedews thee, and my breast shall be   41
Thy death-bed, and our deaths shall intertwine.
Now, maids, farewell; this is the very echo
Of his expiring time; one snowy cloud
Hangs like an avalanche of frozen light   45
Upon the peak of night's cerulean Alp,

And yon still pine, a bleak anatomy,
Flows like a river on the planet's disk,
With its black, wandering arms. Farewell to all:
There is my hand to weep on.

Now my soul   50

Developes its great beams, and like a cloud
Racked by the mighty winds, at once expands
Into a measureless, immortal growth.
Crescented night, and amethystine stars,
And day, thou god and glory of the heavens,   55
Flow on for ever! Play, ye living spheres,
Through the infinity of azure wafted
On billowy music! Airs immortal, strew
Your tressed beauty on the clouds and seas!
And thou the sum of these, nature of all,   60
Thou providence pervading the whole space
Of measureless creation; thou vast mind,
Whose thoughts these pageantries and seasons are,
Who claspest all in one imagination,
All hail! I too am an eternity;   65
I am an universe. My soul is bent
Into a girdling circle full of days;
And my fears rise through the deep sky of it,
Blossoming into palpitating stars;   69
And suns are launched, and planets wake within me;
The words upon my breath are showery clouds,
Sailing along a summer; Casimir
Is the clear truth of ocean, to look back
The beams of my soft love, the world to turn
Within my blue embrace. I am an heaven,   75
And he my breezes, rays, and harmony;
'Round and around the curvous atmosphere
Of my own real existence I revolve,
Serene and starry with undying love.
I am, I have been, I shall be, O glory!   80
An universe, a god, a living Ever.   [*Dies.*

The Last Man

Fragments of

LOVE'S ARROW POISONED [1]

[Composed 1823–5]

X. Erminia Abbandonata

ERMINIA *and attendant*

Attend. Come lift your head from that sad pillow,
    lady,
Let comfort kiss thee dry. Nay, weep no more:
Oh! sure thy brain has emptied all its tears,
Thy breast outsighed its passion, leaving room
For sleep to pour her sweetness into them,   5
And the cored sleep of sleep, tranquillity,
That opens but one window of the soul,
And with her hand on sorrow's face, does keep her
Dark in her bed and dayless. Quiet now—
Will you take peace?
    Ermin.   Good-night, you must go in: 10
The door of life is shut upon me now;
I'm sepulchred alone. Look in the west;
Mark you the dusty traveller,
That stumbles down the clouds?
    Attend.   I see the sun
Silently dying.
    Ermin.   Weep till your sight is found.   15
I have been one that thought there was a sun,
A joyful heat-maker; and like a child
By a brook's side spooning the sparkles out,
I caught at his reflection in my soul,
And found 'twas water painted with a lie,   20

---

[1] The numbers are those of the Oxford edition.

117

Cold, bitter water; I have cried it out.
Sometimes you may see some one through the clouds
Stepping about the sky,
He robs some mountain of its child, the day,
And lays it at the sea's door: but for that   25
I' the west, 'tis the fat, unwholesome star,
The bald fool-planet, that has men upon it,
And they nickname it 'world'.
And oh! this humpy bastard of the sun,
It was my slave, my dog, and in my lap   30
Laid down its shoulder-load of pleasure every night,
And spun me sunshine to delight my eyes,
Carried my cities, and did make me summer,
And flower-limbed spring, and groves with shady
      souls:
But now the whelp rolls up his woody back,   35
And turns it on me, and so trundles down,
Leaving this bit of rock for me to live on,
And his round shadow to be cold in. Go!
Follow the rabble clinging at his heels,
Get thee a seat among his rags.—Dost know   40
That Momus picked a burnt-out comet up
From Vulcan's floor, and stuck a man upon it;
Then, having laught, he flung the wick away,
And let the insect feed on planet oil:—
What was't? Man and his ball.
      Attend.   O dearest lady!   45
Let not your thoughts find instruments of mirth
So on the shore where reason has been wrecked,
And lay them in your brain along with grief;
For grief and laughter, mingled in the scull,
Oft boil to madness. Did you hear my words?   50
      Ermin. Aye, comfort was among them—that's a
      plaything
For girls, a rattle full of noisy lies
To fright away black thoughts, and let the sun
In on the breast. For madness, though I hold it

Kinder to man's enjoyment than true sense,   55
And I would choose it, if they lay before me
Even as a grape beside an adder's tongue,
To squeeze into my thoughts as in a cup,
Hating the forked and the bitter truth—
I cannot find it. If my brain were capable   60
Of this dear madness, should it not be now
All in a bubble with't? What can make mad,
If not the abandonment of one, whose love
Is more true life than the veins' crimson sap?
Leonigild has cut my heart away,   65
And flung it from him: if I could be so,
Should I not be tempestuously mad?
   Attend. Alas! his cruelty looked like a snake
Upon Medusa's temple.
   Ermin.   Had I been waked
By torchlight in my eyes, and by a voice   70
That said 'your babes are burning, stabbed your hus-
     band—
Room on your bosom for their murderer's kisses!'
Why, that to this were tickling to a stab,
A pin-wound to an hell-jawed, laughing gash.
You saw me spurned by him who was—Oh! was— 75
What was he? not a father, son, or husband—
Lend me a word.
   Attend.   Indeed your love was much;
Your life but an inhabitant of his.
   Ermin. Loved him! 'tis not enough; the angels
     might—
They might think what I mean, but could not speak it.
I dreamt it was the day of judgment once,   81
And that my soul, in fear of hidden sins,
Went with his stolen body on its shoulders,
And stood for him before the judgment-seat—
O that I now were damned as I was then!   85
But that same body, that same best-loved soul

119

Cursed, spurned me yesterday. Should I not rave,
Rave, my girl, rave?
 Attend.   So most women would,
So all would wonder that another did not.
 Ermin. Why now, I rave not, laugh not, think not,
  care not;   90
But it is well; so far, I said, 'twas well.
Next was I not abandoned on the rock,
That I might starve? and then you know I prayed,
And when 'twas done, behold! there comes a boat,
Climbing about the waves; I thought and said,   95
O bless thee, ocean! hither dost thou come,
On the same errand as thy birds returning
Unto their hungry nest; thus has sweet nature
Sown kindness in thy great, and its small, bosom!
And as I spoke, the waves came sporting on,   100
And laid their burthen, like a pillow, here:
Look! it's my brother dead. Should I not rave,
Rave, my girl, rave? What comet-dragon is there,
That makes the air bleed fire with galloping rage,
But should be dove-like in my simile?   105
 Attend. Alas! such things,
Such sudden pluckings by the heart as these,
People the madhouse, and cram up the grave!
 Ermin. Therefore I laugh: methinks, when I do tell it,
That I am supping up a draught of wine.   110
Would you know why there's death, and tears, and
  blood,
And wrenching hearts out by their shrieking roots,
Which are more tender than the mailed quick
Or the wet eyeball? I will tell you this—
But O! be secret as rocks under sea—   115
When the world draws the winter o'er his head,
Capping himself so whitely round his Alp,
Muffling his feet with ice, and beds him so;
Then underneath the coverlid and cloak
He has a poisonous strumpet in his arms,   120

On whom he gets confusion, war, disease,
Prodigies, earthquakes, blights: she's in his blood,
The hell-wombed witch, hagged and hideous nature!
But I'll unwind her.—Nay, I jest, my child:
Leave me; seek something—What is it we want?   125
O true! 'tis food: take this, and try the huts.
    Attend. 'Tis needful truly: I'll procure it quick,
And turn the hour back I go upon.
A little then, goodbye.   [*Exit.*
    Ermin.   Yes, I do see
The wronger, and will cut her from my heart,   130
Pare myself of her utterly. Thou nature,
Living or dead, thou influence or thou ruler,
I invocate the heaven to hear my charge.
Who tied my heart unto Leonigild
With gordian love-knots of its thousand strings, 135
Then tore them all away to bleed and wither?
Was it not nature?
Who quickened next that heart a lovely babe,
And when its little smile had learnt its mother,
When thought was rising in its heavenly eye,   140
Bade the grave jump and snap it? The same nature.
Here lies a brother in my dead embrace,
Loved after, as before, his human life;
For in each other's unborn arms we lay,
Bedfellows in our mother. Who poisoned him,   145
Alone among the horrible sea-waves,
And then—O murderess above fratricide,
To kill the sister with the brother's corpse!—
Sent him a gift to me? Again 'twas nature.
I had a husband: nature widowed me;   150
A child: she kidnapped it to earth a tree;
A brother: him she murdered with her waves;
Me she would madden: therefore I defy,
Curse, and abandon Nature henceforth ever.
And though I cannot creep up to my mother,   155
Or flow back to my father's veins again—

Resex or uncreate me; thus much can I:
I will spunge out the sweetness of my heart,
And suck up horror; Love, woman's thoughts, I'll kill,
And leave their bodies rotting in my mind,   160
Hoping their worms will sting; not man outside,
Yet will I out of hate engender much:
I'll be the father of a world of ghosts
And get the grave with carcase. For the rest,
I will encorpse me in my brother's garments,   165
Pick me a heart out of a devil's side,
And so, my own creator, my own child,
Tread on the womb of nature, unbegotten.
Now then, ye waves, I step on you again,
And into my new self, my life outlived: 170
Come back and kneel, thou world; submit thy side,
And take me on thy neck again, new-made,
Fiend-hearted, woman-corpsed, but man-arrayed.

XI. Humble Beginnings

WHY, Rome was naked once, a bastard smudge,
Tumbled on straw, the den-fellow of whelps,
Fattened on roots, and, when athirst for milk,
He crept beneath and drank the swagging udder
Of Tyber's brave she-wolf; and Heaven's Judea
Was folded in a pannier.

TORRISMOND

An Unfinished Drama

[Composed 1824]

PERSONS REPRESENTED

GENTS

DUKE OF FERRARA
TORRISMOND, *his son*
THE MARQUIS MALASPINA
CYRANO, *his Son*
AMADEUS, *a boon Companion*
GARCIA ⎫
GOMEZ ⎬ *The Duke's Servants*
ORAN ⎭
MELCHIOR ⎫
[GAUDENTIO] ⎬ *Courtiers*

LADIES

VERONICA, *Miss Malaspina*
ELVIRA, *a Toad-eater*
ERMINIA, *Oran's Sister*

SCENE: *Ferrara*

ACT I

SCENE I. *A hall in the palace of Ferrara*

Enter the DUKE, *Courtiers, and attendants*

Duke. Who has met Torrismond, my son, to-night?
Garcia. My lord, he has not crossed me, all the day.
(*To* GOMEZ *aside*) You need not say we saw him pass
  the terrace,

All red and hot with wine. The duke is angry:
Mark how he plucks his robe.

   Duke.   Gomez, nor you?   5
   Gomez. Your Grace in Garcia's answer
Beheld the face of mine. I have not lent him
A word to-day.

   Duke.   Nor you? none of you, sirs?—
No answer! have ye sold yourselves to silence?
Is there not breath, or tongue, or mouth among you, 10
Enough to croak a curse?—Nay: there's no wonder.
Why do I ask? that know you are his curs,
His echo-birds, the mirrors of his tongue.
He has locked up this answer in your throats,
And scratched it on your leaden memories.   15
What do I ask for? well: go on, go on;
Be his sop-oracles, and suck yellow truth
Out of the nipple of his jingling pouch.
But tell me this, dogs, that do wag your tails
Round this dwarf Mercury, this gilded Lie-god,   20
Will you set out and beg with him to-morrow?

   Garcia. Why, my good lord?
   Duke.   Because, my evil slave,
Because unless he can these sunbeams coin,
Or like a bee in metals suck me out
The golden honey from their marly core,   25
He's like to board with the cameleon:
Because I will untie him from my heart
And drop him to the bottom of the world:
Because I'll melt his wings—Enough!

   Garcia.   With pardon,
You are too rough.

   Duke.   Too rough! were I as loud   30
As shaggy Boreas in his bearish mood,
Did I roll wheels of thunder o'er your souls,
And break them into groans,—weep yourselves waves,
And kneel beneath my storming. Worms ye are,

Born in the fat sides of my pouring wealth: 35
Lie there and stir not, or I dash you off.

  Garcia. My lord—

  Duke.   I am no lord, sir, but a father:
My son has stuck sharp injuries in my heart,
And flies to hide in your obscurity.
Cover him not with falsehoods; shield him not;   40
Or, by my father's ashes,—but no matter.
You said I was a duke: I will be one,
Though graves should bark for it. You've heard me
    speak:
Now go not to your beds until my son
(—It is a word that cases not a meaning—)   45
Come from his riots: send him then to me:
And hark! ye fill him not, as ye are wont,
To the lip's brim with oily subterfuges.
I sit this evening in the library.

  An Attend. Lights, lights there for the duke!   50

  Duke. For the duke's soul I would there were a light!
Well; on thy flinty resolution strike,
Benighted man! The sun has laid his hair
Up in that stone, as I have treasured love
In a cold heart; but it begins to boil   55
And if it breaks its casket, will be out.
Find me a book of fables: he, whose world
Grows in his thoughts, methinks, alone is happy.
So now good-night; and do as I have said.

  Garcia. We shall.—Good dreams, your Grace!

  Duke.   Good acts, you mean.   60
He who does ill, awake, and turns to night
For lovely-painted shades,
Is like a satyr grinning in a brook
To find Narcissus' round and downy cheek.

                         [*Exit with attendants.*

  Gomez. I never saw my lord so sad and angry: 65
His blood foamed white with wrath beneath his face,
Rising and falling like a sea-shore wave.

What boils him thus?

    Garcia.   Perhaps some further outrage
Reported of his son; for the young lord,
Whose veins are stretched by passion's hottest wine 70
Tied to no law except his lawless will,
Ranges and riots headlong through the world;
Like a young dragon, on Hesperian berries
Purplely fed, who dashes through the air,
Tossing his wings in gambols of desire,   75
And breaking rain-clouds with his bulging breast.
Thus has he been from boy to youth and manhood,
Reproved, then favoured; threatened, next forgiven;
Renounced, to be embraced: but, till this hour,
Never has indignation like to this,   80
With lightning looks, black thoughts and stony words,
Burst o'er the palace of their love, which stretches
From heart to heart.

    Gomez.   I fear that both will shake;
And that fair union, built by interchange
Of leaning kindnesses, in the recoil   85
May fall between, and leave no bridge for pardon.

    Garcia. The little that we can, then let us strive
To hold them in the lock of amity:
For which our thoughts let us compare within.

                            [Exeunt.

SCENE II. *A banqueting hall*

CYRANO, AMADEUS, TORRISMOND, *and other
gents, drinking*

    Amad. Another health! Fill up the goblets, sirrah!
This wine was pressed from full and rolling grapes
By the white dance of a Circassian princess,
Whose breast had never aught but sunlight touched,
And her own tears: 'tis spicy, cool, and clear   5
As is a magic fount where rainbows grow

Or nymphs by moonlight bathe their tremulous limbs;
And works an intellectual alchemy,
Touching the thoughts to sunshine. Now, to whom—
To what young saint, between whose breathing paps
Love's inspiration lies, shall we devote   11
This last and richest draught: with whose soft name
Shall we wash bright our hearts? Say, Cyrano.

   Cyran. Let Torrismond be sponsor for this bowl.
He sate so still last night, that by plump Cupid,   15
That merry, cherry-lipped, delicious god
Whose name is writ on roses, I must think
He 's paid away his soul in broken sighs,
Glass oaths, and tears of crocodilish coinage,
For one quick finger-kiss. Ask him what name,   20
Made to be written upon hearts and trees
And grace a sonnet, shall be sugar here,
Making the juice steam music.

   Torris.   I beseech you,
Waste not this Araby of words on me:
I'm dull, but not in love.

   Cyran.   Not ancle-deep?   25
What means a leaning head, eyelids ajar,
And lips thick-sown with whispers? Sir, I say,
Before to-morrow you'll be soused in love
To the ear's tip. In truth, it will be so;
Sure as an almanac.

   Torris.   I lay my fate   30
Upon your mercy: e'en tie love-knots in it,
If you've nought else to do. Good Cyrano,
And you, sirs, all pray drink. I fear the fog
Of my most stupid dulness spreads.

   Amad.   We'll drink
One cup—one more liquid delight, my friends;   35
Then for the masquerade at Signor Paulo's.

   Cyran. Aye; dedicated to the sweet To be,
The lady Future of our comrade's love.

A guest. What rhymes unborn are shut within that
    word!

Amad. Thus then I soak my heart's dear roots in
    wine,   40
And the warm drops roll up and down my blood,
Till every tendril of my straying veins
Rings with delight.   [*They drink.*
              And now, my sons of Bacchus,
To the delirious dance! Nay, Torrismond,
You'll come with us at least.

Torris.   To-night, I thank you, 45
It is against my will; indeed I cannot;
I'm vilely out of tune, my thoughts are cracked,
And my words dismal. 'Pray you, pardon me:
Some other night we will like Bacchanals
Shiver the air with laughter and rough songs,   50
And be most jovial madmen.

Amad.   Be it so,
If be it must. We bid you, sir, farewell.

Torris. Good night, good lads.

              [*Exeunt* AMADEUS *and gentlemen.*
              Now go, dear Cyrano;
Let me not keep you by my wayward mood.

Cyran. If it does not offend you, suffer me—   55

Torris. Offend me! No; thou dost not, Cyrano;
I do offend myself. Hadst thou but eyes
To see the spirit toiling in this breast,
How low a wretch should I appear to thee;
How pitifully weak! Now tell me, sir,—   60
I shrink not from the truth, although it stab,
But beg it from your mouth—what think you of me?

Cyran. Of you, my lord?

Torris.   Yes, yes; my words, my manners,
My disposition, will,—how seem they to you?   64

Cyran. Sir, my heart speaks of you as one most kind;
Spirited and yet mild: a man more noble
Breathes not his maker's air.

Torris.   Stay, my good friend;
I did not ask for flattery.
   Cyran.   Nor I answer it;
Saying, that here I shake him by the hand
That has no better in humanity: 70
A fine, free spirit.
   Torris.   You had better say
A whirring, singing, empty wine-bubble,
Like one of these that left us. So I was;
Vain, futile, frivolous: a boy, a butterfly,—
In semblance: but inside, by heaven! a depth   75
Of thoughts most earnest, an unfuelled flame
Of self-devouring love. Cyrano, Cyrano,
I yearn, and thirst, and ache to be beloved,
As I could love, through my eternal soul,
Immutably, immortally, intensely,   80
Immeasurably. Oh! I am not at home
In this December world, with men of ice,
Cold sirs and madams. That I had a heart,
By whose warm throbs of love to set my soul!
I tell thee I have not begun to live,   85
I'm not myself till I've another self
To lock my dearest and most secret thoughts in;
Change petty faults and whispering pardons with;
Sweetly to rule, and Oh! most sweetly serve.
   Cyran. Have you no father,—nor a friend? Yet I, 90
I, Torrismond, am living, and the duke.
   Torris. Forgive me, sir, forgive me: I am foolish;
I've said I know not what, I know not why;
'Tis nothing,—fancies; I'll to bed;—'tis nothing;
Worth but a smile, and then to be forgotten.   95
Good-night: to-morrow I will laugh at this.
   Cyran. I'll say no more but that I hope you will.
                                   [*Exit.*

   Torris. I knew it would be so. He thinks me now
Weak, unintelligible, fanciful,—
A boy shut up in dreams, a shadow-catcher: 100

So let him think. My soul is where he sees not,
Around, above, below. Yes, yes; the curse
Of being for a little world too great,
Demanding more than nature has to give,
And drinking up for ever and in vain   105
The shallow, tasteless, skimmings of their love,
Through this unfathomable fever here.—
A thought of comfort comes this way; its warmth
I feel, although I see it not. How's this?
There's something I half know; yes, I remember,— 110
The feast last night: a dear, ingenuous girl
Poured soft, smooth hope upon my dashing passions,
Until they tossed their billowy selves to sleep.
I'll seek her, try her: in this very garden
Often she walks; thither I'll bear my wishes   115
And may she prove the echo of their craving!   [*Exit.*

SCENE III. *A garden by moonlight*

VERONICA, ELVIRA, *and others*

Veron. Come then, a song; a winding, gentle song,
To lead me into sleep. Let it be low
As zephyr, telling secrets to his rose,
For I would hear the murmuring of my mind;
And more of voice than of that other music   5
That grows around the strings of quivering lutes;
But most of thought; for with my mind I listen,
And when the leaves of sound are shed upon it,
If there's no seed remembrance grows not there.
So life, so death; a song, and then a dream!   10
Begin before another dewdrop fall
From the soft hold of these disturbed flowers,
For sleep is filling up my senses fast,
And from these words I sink.

Song

How many times do I love thee, dear?   15
   Tell me how many thoughts there be
      In the atmosphere
      Of a new-fall'n year,
Whose white and sable hours appear
   The latest flake of Eternity: 20
So many times do I love thee, dear.

How many times do I love again?
   Tell me how many beads there are
      In a silver chain
      Of evening rain,   25
Unravelled from the tumbling main,
   And threading the eye of a yellow star:
So many times do I love again.

Elvira. She sees no longer: leave her then alone,
Encompassed by this round and moony night.   30
A rose-leaf for thy lips, and then good-night:
So life, so death; a song, and then a dream!   [*Exeunt.*

Enter TORRISMOND

Torris. Herself! her very self, slumbering gently!
Sure sleep is turned to beauty in this maid,
And all the rivalry of life and death   35
Makes love upon her placid face. And here,
How threads of blue, wound off yon thorny stars
That grow upon the wall of hollow night,
Flow o'er each sister-circle of her bosom,
Knotting themselves into a clue for kisses   40
Up to her second lip. On that cheek the blush
That ever dawns dares be no common blush,
But the faint ghost of some dishevelled rose
Unfurls its momentary leaves, and bursts

So quick the haunted fairness knows it not.   45
O that this gaze could be eternity!
And yet a moment of her love were more.
Were there infection in the mind's disease,
Inoculation of a thought, even now
Should she, from all the windings of her dream,   50
Drink my impetuous passion, and become
All that I ask. Break from your buds, dear eyes,
And draw me into you.

    Veron. (*awaking*)   Who's there? I dreamt:
As I do love that broad, [smooth-edged] star,
And her young, vandyked moons that climb the night
Round their faint mother, I'd not have had   56
Another eye peeping upon that dream,
For one of them to wear upon my breast;
And I'll not whisper it, for fear these flags
Should chance to be the green posterity   60
Of that eaves-dropping, woman-witted grass,
That robbed the snoring wasps of their least voice,
To teach their feathery gossips of the air
What long and furry ears king Midas sprouted;
And I'll not think of it, for meditation   65
Oft presses from the heart its inmost wish,
And thaws its silence into straying words.

    Torris. (*aside*) I am no man, if this dream were not
      spun
By the very silkworm, that doth make his shop
In Cupid's tender wing-pit, and winds fancies   70
In lovers' corner thoughts, when grandam Prudence
Has swept the hearth of passion, thrown on cinders,
And gone to bed:—and she is not a woman,
If this same secret, buried in her breast,
Haunt not her tongue,—and hark! here comes its
      ghost.   75

    Veron. A fable and a dream! Here, in this garden,
It seemed I was a lily:—

    Torris. (*aside*)   So you are,

But fitter for Arabian paradise,
Or those arched gardens where pale-petalled stars,
With sunlight honeying their dewy cores,   80
Tremble on sinuous, Corinthian necks,—
Where Morn her roses feeds, her violets Night.
 Veron. And to my lily-ship a wooer came,
Sailing upon the curvous air of morn,
(For 'twas a sunny dream, and a May sky   85
The lid of it;) and this imagined suitor,
A glass-winged, tortoise-shell, heart-broken bee,
Was—he you know of, heart. How did he bend
His slender knee, doffing his velvet cap,
And swearing, by the taste of Venus' lip,   90
If I did not accept his airy love,
The truest heart, that ever told the minutes
Within an insect's breast, should shed its life
Around the hilt of his unsheathed sting.
And then this tiny thunderer of flowers,   95
Quite, quite subdued, let down a string of tears,
(Little they were, but full of beeish truth,)
Almost a dewdrop-much, on the fair pages
Of transmigrated me; whereon, O Love!
Thou tamed'st the straightest prude of Flora's
  daughters;   100
For I did pity Torrismond the bee,
And let him, if his life lived in my love,
Have that for courtesy.—
 Torris. (*coming forward*) O lady! then
Will you deny him now? when here he kneels,
And vows by heaven, and by the sacred souls   105
Of all the dead and living, in your pity
His hope is folded, in your soul his love,
And in that love his everlasting life.
 Veron. Out on my tongue, the naughty runaway!
What has he heard? Now, if this man should be   110
Vain, selfish, light, or hearted with a stone,
Or worthless any way, as there are many,

I've given myself, like alms unto an idiot,
To be for nothing squandered.
   Torris.   Lady, speak!
And for my truth, O that my mind were open,   115
My soul expressed and written in a book,
That thou might'st read and know! Believe, believe
   me!
And fear me not, for, if I speak not truth,
May I speak never more, but be struck dumb!
May I be stripped of manhood and made devil,   120
If I mean not as truly unto thee,
Though bold it be, as thou unto thyself!
I will not swear, for thou dost know that easy:
But put me to the proof, say, 'kill thyself';
I will outlabour Hercules in will,   125
And in performance, if that waits on will.
Shall I fight sword-less wih a youthful lion?
Shall I do aught that I may die in doing?
Oh! were it possible for such an angel,
I almost wish thou hadst some impious task,   130
That I might act it and be damned for thee.
But, earned for thee, perdition 's not itself,
Since all that has a taste of thee in it
Is blest and heavenly.
   Veron.   Stop! You frighten me:
I dare not doubt you.
   Torris.   Dare not? Can you so?   135
   Veron. I dare not, for I cannot. I believe you:
It is my duty.
   Torris.   To the dutiful
Their duty is their pleasure. Is it not?
   Veron. 'Twas a rash word; it rather is my fate.
   Torris. It is my fate to love; thou art my fate,   140
So be not adverse.
   Veron.   How can I say further?
I do believe you: less I'll not avow,
And more I cannot.

Torris.   Stay, Veronica!
This very night we both of us may die,
Or one at least: and it is very likely   145
We never meet; or, if we meet, not thus,
But somehow hindered by the time, the place,
The persons. There are many chances else,
That, though no bigger than a sunny mote,
Coming between may our whole future part,   150
With Milo's force tear our existence up,
And turn away the branches of each life,
Even from this hour, on whose star-knotted trunk
We would engraft our union; it may sever us
As utterly as if the world should split   155
Here, as we stand, and all Eternity
Push through the earthquake's lips, and rise between
          us.
Then let us know each other's constancy:
Thou in my mind, and I in thine shall be;
And so disseparable to the edge   160
Of thinnest lightning.
     Veron.   Stay: be answered thus.
If thou art Torrismond, the brain of feather;
If thou art light and empty Torrismond,
The admiration, oath and bottle-god
Of beer-brained tipplers, he whose corky heart,   165
Pierced by a ragged pen of Cupid's wing,
Spins like a vane upon his mother's temple
In every silly sigh—let it play on:
Or pluck it down and stop musk-phials with it.
     Torris. It is not so; I vow, Veronica.   170
     Veron. If you unpeopled the Olympian town
Of all its gods, and shut them in one perjury,
It would not weigh a flue of melting snow
In my opinion. Listen thus much more:
If thou art otherwise than all have held   175
Except myself; if these, which men do think
The workings of thy true concentrate self,

Have been indeed but bubbles raised in sport
By the internal god, who keeps unseen
The fountains of thine undiscovered spirit;   180
If underneath this troubled scum of follies,
Lies what my hopes have guessed:—why, guess thy
    wishes
What it may be unto Veronica?

   Torris. What need of doubts and guesses? make me
    firm;
With fixed assurance prop my withering hopes,   185
Or tear them up at once; give truth for truth.
I know it is the custom to dissemble,
Because men's hearts are shallow, and their nature
So mean, ill-nurtured, selfish, and debased,
They needs must paint and swaddle them in lies,   190
Before the light could bear to look upon them.
But as thou art, thus unalloyed and fresh
From thy divine creation, soul and body,
Tread artifice to dust, and boldly speak
Thine innocent resolve.

   Veron.   Thus then I say: 195
As I believe thee steadfast and sincere,
(And, if it be not so, God pity me!)
I love thee dearly, purely, heartily;
So witness heaven, and our own silent spirits!

   Torris. And by my immortality I swear,   200
With the like honesty, the like to thee,
Thou picture of the heavens!

   Veron.   Hark! some one comes:
Now we must part. Henceforth remember thou,
How in this azure secrecy of night,
And with what vows, we here have dedicated   205
Ourselves, and our eternity of being
Unto each other in our Maker's presence.
Good-night, then, Torrismond.

   Torris.   And such to thee,

As thou to me hast given, fairest fair!
Best good! of thy dear kind most ever dear!   210
                 [*Exeunt severally.*

SCENE IV. *The* DUKE'S *palace*

DUKE, GARCIA, MELCHIOR, GAUDENTIO

Duke. Yes, was it not enough, good Garcia:
Blood spilt in every street by his wild sword;
The reverend citizens pelted with wrongs,
Their rights and toil-won honours blown aside,
Torn off, and trampled 'neath his drunken foot;   5
The very daughters of the awful church
Smeared in their whiteness by his rude attempts;
The law thus made a lie even in my mouth;
Myself a jest for beer-pot orators;
My state dishonoured;—was it not enough   10
To turn a patience made of ten-years' ice,
Into a thunderbolt?
Garcia.   It was too much:
I wonder at your Grace's long endurance.
Did you ne'er chide him?
Duke.   No, never in his life;
He has not that excuse. My eyes and ears   15
Were frozen-closed. Yet was it not enough
That his ill deeds outgrew all name and number,
O'erflowed his years and all men's memories?
Gaudentio, I was mild; I bore upon me   19
This world of wrongs, and smiled. But mark you now,
How he was grateful. Tell them, Melchior.
Melch. Linked, as it is surmised, with Lutherans
And other rebels 'gainst his father's state,
He has not only for their aid obtained
From me, the steward of the dukedom, money,   25
But also robbed, most treacherously robbed,
By night, and like a thief, the public treasury.

Gauden. I'll not believe it; and he is a villain,
Aye, and the very thief that did the thing,
Who brings the accusation.

Duke.   Knave, I think   30
Thou wert my son's accomplice.

Melch.   Nay, my lord,
He says what all would say, and most myself,
But that these facts—

Gauden.   What facts? What witnesses?
Who saw? Who heard? Who knows?

Duke.   Our trusty steward.

Gauden. A Spanish Jew! a godless, heartless exile, 35
Whose ear 's the echo of the whispering world.
Why, if *he* only knows, and saw, and heard,
This Argus-witness with his blood-hound nose
Who keeps a fairy in his upright ear,
Is no more than a black, blind, ugly devil,   40
Nick-named a lie.

Duke.   Be silent, slave, or dead.
I do believe him: Garcia, so dost thou?
All honest men, good Melchior, like thyself—
For that thou art, I think, upon my life—
Believe thee too.

Melch.   It is my humble trust: 45
And in the confidence of honesty
I pray you pardon this good servant's boldness.
(*Aside*) God help the miserable velvet fellow!
It seems he has forgot that little story,
How he debauched my poor, abandoned sister,   50
And broke my family into the grave.
That's odd; for I exceeding well remember it,
Though then a boy.

Duke.   Gaudentio, thou dost hear
Why I forgive thee: but be cautious, sir.

Gauden. Cautious, but honest,—cautious of a
     villain.
                                                      55

Duke. No more! But see where comes the man we
    talk of.

Leave us together.   *[Exeunt Courtiers.*

Enter TORRISMOND

          Torrismond, well met!—

  Torris. Why then well parted, for I'm going to bed.
I'm weary; so, good-night.

    Duke.   Stay; I must speak to you.

  Torris. To-morrow then, good father, and all day. 60
But now no more than the old sleepy word,
And so again, good-night.

    Duke.   Turn, sir, and stay:
I will be brief, as brief as speech can be.—
Seek elsewhere a good night: there is none here.
This is no home for your good nights, bad son,   65
Who hast made evil all my days to come,
Poisoned my age, torn off my beauteous hopes
And fed my grave with them. Oh! thou hast now,
This instant, given my death an hundred sinews,
And drawn him nearer by a thousand hours.   70
But what of that? You'd sow me like a grain,
And from my stalk pick you a ducal crown.
But I will live.

    Torris.   That you may live and prosper
Is every day my prayer, my wish, my comfort.
But what offence has raised these cruel words?   75

    Duke. That I may live, you plot against my life;
That I may prosper, you have cured my fortunes
Of their encrusted jaundice,—you have robbed me.
So, for your prayers and wishes I do thank you,
But for your deeds I wish and pray Heaven's ven-
    geance.   80

    Torris. Is this your own invention, or—O nature!
O love of fathers! could a father hear
His offspring thus accused, and yet believe?
Believe! Could he endure, and not strike dead

The monster of the lie? Sir, here or there,   85
In you or your informers, there's a villain,
A fiend of falsehood: so beware injustice!

Duke. I never was unjust, but when I pardoned
Your bloody sins and ravening appetites,—
For which Heaven pardon me, as I repent it!   90
But I'll not play at battledore with words.
Hear me, young man, in whom I did express
The venom of my nature, thus the son,
Not of my virtuous will, but foul desires,
Not of my life, but of a wicked moment,   95
Not of my soul, but growing from my body,
Like thorns or poison on a wholesome tree,
The rank excrescence of my tumid sins,—
And so I tear thee off: for, Heaven doth know,
All gentler remedies I have applied;   100
But to this head thy rankling vice has swelled,
That if thou dwellest in my bosom longer,
Thou wilt infect my blood, corrode my heart,
And blight my being: therefore, off for ever!

Torris. O mother, thou art happy in thy grave!   105
And there's the hell in which my father lies,
The serpent that hath swallowed him!

Enter GAUDENTIO

Gauden. (*rushing in; to those without*) Away!
Let me come in!... Now, I beseech you, lords,
Put out this anger; lay a night of sleep
Upon its head, and let its pulse of fire   110
Flap to exhaustion. Do not, sir, believe
This reptile falsehood; think it o'er again
And try him by yourself: thus questioning,
Could I, or did I, thus, or such a fault,
In my beginning days? There stands before you   115
The youth and golden top of your existence,
Another life of yours: for, think your morning
Not lost, but given, passed from your hand to his,

The same except in place. Be then to him.
As was the former tenant of your age,   120
When you were in the prologue of your time,
And he lay hid in you unconsciously
Under his life. And thou, my younger master,
Remember there 's a kind of god in him,
And after heaven the next of thy religion.   125
Thy second fears of God, thy first of man,
Are his, who was creation's delegate
And made this world for thee in making thee.

   Duke. A frost upon thy words, intended dog!
Because thy growth has lost its four-legged way   130
And wandered with thee into man's resemblance,
Shalt thou assume his rights? Get to your bed,
Or I'll decant thy pretext of a soul,
And lay thee, worm, where thou shalt multiply.
Sir slave, your gibbet's sown.

   Torris.   Leave him, Gaudentio,
My father and your master are not here;   136
His good is all gone hence, he 's truly dead;
All that belonged to those two heavenly names
Are gone from life with him, and changing cast
This slough behind, which all abandoned sins   140
Creep into and enliven devilishly.

   Duke. What! stand I in thy shadow? or has Momus
Opened a window 'twixt thy heart and mine?
'Tis plated then!

   Torris.   We talk like fighting boys:
Out on't! I repent of my mad tongue.   145
Come, sir; I cannot love you after this,
But we may meet and pass a nodding question—

   Duke. Never! There lies no grain of sand between
My loved and my detested. Wing thee hence,
Or thou dost stand to-morrow on a cobweb   150
Spun o'er the well of clotted Acheron,
Whose hydrophobic entrails stream with fire;
And may this intervening earth be snow,

And my step burn like the mid coal of Ætna,
Plunging me, through it all, into the core   155
Where in their graves the dead are shut like seeds,
If I do not—O but he *is* my son!
If I do not forgive thee then—but hence!
Gaudentio, hence with him, for in my eyes
He does look demons.—   160

 Melch. (*to* TORRISMOND) Come out with me and
  leave him:
You will be cool, to-morrow.
 Torris.   That I shall;
Cool as an ice-drop in a dead man's eye,
For winter is the season of the tomb,
And that's my country now.
 Duke.   Away with him!   165
I will not hear.—Where did I leave my book?
Or was it music?—Take the beggar out.
Is there no supper yet?—O my good Melchior!
I'm an eternal gap of misery.
Let 's talk of something else.   170
 Torris. O father, father! must I have no father,
To think how I shall please, to pray for him,
To spread his virtues out before my thought,
And set my soul in order after them?
To dream, and talk of in my dreaming sleep?   175
If I have children, and they question me
Of him who was to me as I to them;
Who taught me love and sports and childish lore;
Placed smiles where tears had been; who bent his talk
That it might enter my low apprehension,   180
And laughed when words were lost.—O father, father!
Must I give up the first word that my tongue,
The only one my heart has ever spoken?
Then take speech, thought, and knowledge quite away;
Tear all my life out of the universe,   185
Take off my youth, unwrap me of my years,
And hunt me up the dark and broken past

Into my mother's womb: there unbeget me;
For 'till I'm in thy veins and unbegun,
Or to the food returned which made the blood   190
That did make me, no possible lie can ever
Unroot my feet of thee. Canst thou make nothing?
Then do it here, for I would rather be
At home nowhere, than here nowhere at home.

   Duke. Why ask'st thou me? Hast thou no deeds to
      undo,   195
No virtues to rebuy, no sins to loose?
Catch from the wind those sighs that thou hast caused;
Out of large ocean pick the very tears,
And set them in their cabinets again.
Renew thyself, and then will I remember   200
How thou camest thus. Thou art all vices now
Of thine own getting. My son Torrismond
Did sow himself under a heap of crime,
And thou art grown from him: die to the root,
So I may know thee as his grave at least.—   205
Now, Melchior, we'll away.

   Melch.   Not yet, my lord:
I wait upon this gentleman.

   Duke.   Is 't so?
Why then begone! Good morrow to you, sirs.
Farewell! and be that word a road to death
Uncrossed by any other! Not a word!   [*Exit.* 210

   Melch. Will you not stay?

               He 's gone: and follow not:
There's not a speck of flesh upon his heart!
What shall we do?

   Torris.   What shall we do?—why, all.
How many things, sir, do men live to do?
The mighty labour is to die: we'll do't,—   215
But we'll drive in a chariot to our graves,
Wheel'd with big thunder, o'er the heads of men.

                       [*Exeunt.*

THE SECOND BROTHER

A Tragedy

[Composed 1824–5]

[*PERSONS REPRESENTED*]

MARCELLO } *Brothers of the*   VARINI }
ORAZIO   } *Duke of Ferrara* MICHELE } *Nobles*
EZRIL, *a Jew*   BATTISTA }
MELCHIOR

VALERIA, *Varini's Daughter*   ARMIDA
    and Orazio's Wife   ROSAURA
HEBE   [*A Female Attendant*]
   [*Gentlemen, Ladies, Guards, and Attendants*]

SCENE: *Ferrara*

ACT I

SCENE I. *A street*

MICHELE *and* BATTISTA *meeting*: MARCELLO
at the side

Mich. Fair shine this evening's stars upon your
    pleasures,
Battista Sorbi!
   Batt.   Sir, well met to-night:
Methinks our path is one.
   Mich.   And all Ferrara's.
There's not a candle lit to-night at home;
And for the cups,—they'll be less wet with wine   5
Than is the inmost grain of all this earth
With the now-falling dew. None sit indoors,
Except the babe and his forgotten grandsire

144

And such as, out of life, each side do lie
Against the shutter of the grave or womb.   10
The rest that build up the great hill of life,
From the crutch-riding boy to his sweet mother,
The deer-eyed girl, and the brown fellow of war
To the grey head and grandest sire of all
That 's half in heaven,—all these are forth to-night;   15
And there they throng upon both sides the water,
Which, guessing at its hidden banks, flows on,
A water-river 'twixt two tides of flesh—
And still the streets pour on, each drop a man;
You'd think the deluge was turned upside down,   20
And flesh was drowning water.

   Batt.   And where go they?
To the feast, the wine, the lady-footed dance,—
Where you, and I, and every citizen
That has a feathered and a jewelled cap,
And youthful curls to hang beside it brownly,—   25
To the Duke's brother, Lord Orazio's palace.

   Marc. (*aside*) Orazio! what of him?

   Mich.   Aye, that's a man
After the heart of Bacchus! By my life,
There is no mortal stuff that foots the earth
Able to wear the shape of man, like him,   30
And fill it with the carriage of a god.
We're but the tools and scaffolding of men,
The lines, the sketch, and he the very thing:
And if we share the name of manhood with him,
So in the woods the tattered, wool-hung briar,   35
And the base, bowing poplar, the winds' slave,
Are trees—and so 's the great and kingly oak,
Within whose branches like a soul does dwell
The sun's bold eagle:—as the villain fox,
The weazel, and the sneaking cur are beasts,   40
While he, whose wine is in a giant's heart,
The royal lion, has no bigger name.
Let men be trees, why then he is the oak;

Let men be beasts, he is their lion-master;
Let them be stars, and then he is a sun,   45
A sun whose beams are gold, the night his noon,
His summer-field a marble hall of banquets,
With jasper, onyx, amber-leaved cups
On golden straws for flowers, and, for the dew,
Wine of the richest grape. So let 's not talk   50
And breathe away the time, whose sands are thawed
Into such purple tears, but drink it off.

 Batt. Why, then, away! let 's fit our velvet arms,
And on together.—

 Marc. (*advancing*) Nobles of Ferrara,
My gentle lords, have pity for a man,   55
Whom fortune and the roundness of the world
Have, from his feeble footing on its top,
Flung to deep poverty. When I was born,
They hid my helplessness in purple wraps,
And cradled me within a jewelled crown.   60
But now—O bitter now!—what name of woe,
Beyond the knowledge of the lips of hell,
Is fitted to my poor and withering soul,
And its old, wretched dwelling?

 Batt.   What is this?
Methinks that a præ-adamite skeleton,   65
Burst from the grave in a stolen cloak of flesh,
Ragged and threadbare, from a witch's back,
Who lived an hundred years, would scarcely seem
More miserably old.

 Mich.   A wandering beggar,
Come to Ferrara with the daily lie,   70
That bears him bread. Come on, and heed him not.
The stocks, old sir, grow in our streets.

Enter a gentleman

         How now?
What's your news, sir?

 Gent.   He's coming through this street,

Orazio, wrapt like Bacchus, in the hide
Of a specked panther, with his dancing nymphs,   75
And torches bright and many, as his slaves
Had gathered up the fragments of the sun
That fell just now. Hark! here his music comes.

Enter ORAZIO, *between* HEBE *and* ROSAURA, *attended*

Oraz. Thrice to the moon, and thrice unto the sun,
And thrice unto the lesser stars of night,   80
From tower and hill, by trump and cannon's voice,
Have I proclaimed myself a deity's son:
Not Alexander's father, Ammon old,
But ivied Bacchus do I call my sire.
Hymn it once more.   85

Song

Strew not earth with empty stars,
    Strew it not with roses,
Nor feathers from the crest of Mars,
    Nor summer's idle posies.
'Tis not the primrose-sandalled moon,   90
    Nor cold and silent morn,
Nor he that climbs the dusty noon,
Nor mower war with scythe that drops,
Stuck with helmed and turbaned tops
    Of enemies new shorn.   95

Ye cups, ye lyres, ye trumpets know,
Pour your music, let it flow,
'Tis Bacchus' son who walks below.

Oraz. Now break that kiss, and answer me, my
    Hebe;
Has our great sire a planet in the sky,—   100
One of these lights?
    Hebe.   Not yet, I think, my lord.

Oraz. My lord? my love! I am the Lord of Love;
So call me by my dukedom.—He has not?
We'll make him one, my nymph: when those bright
    eyes
Are closed, and that they shall not be, I swear,   105
'Till I have loved them many thousand hours,—
But when they are, their blue enchanted fire
Cupid shall take upon a torch of heaven,
And light the woody sides of some dim world,
Which shall be Bacchus' godson-star.

    Hebe.   Alas!   110
Their fire is but unsteady, weak and watery,
To guess by your love's wavering.

    Oraz.   Wine in a ruby!
I'll solemnize their beauty in a draught,
Pressed from the summer of an hundred vines.
Look on't, my sweet. Rosaura, this same night   115
I will immortalize those lips of thine,
That make a kiss so spicy. Touch the cup:
Ruby to ruby! Slave, let it be thrown
At midnight from a boat into mid-sea:
Rosaura's kiss shall rest unravished there,   120
While sea and land lie in each other's arms
And curl the world.

    Batt.   Beggar, stand back, I say.
    Marc. No; I will shadow your adored mortal,
And shake my rags at him. Dost fear the plague?
Musk-fingered boy, aside!

    Oraz.   What madman 's this?   125
    Rosau. Keep him away from me!
His hideous raggedness tears the soft sight
Where it is pictured.

    Marc. Your clutch is like the grasping of a wave:
Off from my shoulder!—Now, my velvet fellow,   130
Let 's measure limbs. Well, is your flesh to mine
As gold to lead, or but the common plaister
That wraps up bones? Your skin is not of silk;

Your face not painted with an angel's feather
With tints from morning's lip, but the daubed clay; 135
These veiny pipes hold a dog's lap of blood.
Let us shake hands; I tell thee, brother skeleton,
We're but a pair of puddings for the dinner
Of Lady worm; you served in silks and gems,
I garnished with plain rags. Have I unlocked thee? 140
   Oraz. Insolent beggar!
   Marc.   Prince! but we must shake hands.
Look you, the round earth's sleeping like a serpent
Who drops her dusty tail upon her crown
Just here. Oh, we are like two mountain peaks,
Of two close planets, catching in the air: 145
You, King Olympus, a great pile of summer,
Wearing a crown of gods; I, the vast top
Of the ghosts' deadly world, naked and dark,
With nothing reigning on my desolate head
But one old spirit of a murdered god, 150
Palaced within the corpse of Saturn's father.
Then let's come near and hug. There 's nothing like
    thee
But I thy contrast.—Thou'rt a prince, they say?
   Oraz. That you shall learn. You knaves that wear
    my livery,
Will you permit me still to be defiled 155
By this worm's venom? Tread upon his neck,
And let's walk over him.
   Marc.   Forbear, my lord!
I am a king of that most mighty empire,
That 's built o'er all the earth, upon kings' crowns;
And poverty 's its name; whose every hut 160
Stands on a coronet, or star, or mitre,
The glorious corner-stones.—But you are weary,
And would be playing with a woman's cheek:
Give me a purse then, prince.
   Oraz.   No, not a doit:
The metal, I bestow, shall come in chains. 165

Marc. Well, I can curse. Aye, prince, you have a
    brother—

Oraz. The Duke!—he'll scourge you.

Marc.   Nay, *the second,* sir,
Who, like an envious river, flows between
Your footsteps and Ferrara's throne.

Oraz.   He's gone:
Asia, and Africa, the sea he went on,   170
Have many mouths, and in a dozen years,
(His absence' time,) no tidings or return,
Tell me We are but two.

Marc. If he were in Ferrara—

Oraz.   Stood he before me there,
By you, in you, as like as you're unlike,   175
Straight as you're bowed, young as you are old
And many years nearer him to Death
The falling brilliancy of whose white sword
Your ancient locks so silverly reflect,
I would deny, outswear, and overreach,   180
And pass him with contempt, as I do you.—
Jove! how we waste the stars: set on, my friends.

Batt. But the old ruffian?

Oraz.   Think of him to-morrow.
See, Venus rises in the softening heaven:
Let not your eyes abuse her sacred beams,   185
By looking through their gentleness on ought
But lips and eyes and blushes of dear love.

Song

    Strike, you myrtle-crowned boys,
      Ivied maïdens, strike together:
    Magic lutes are these, whose noise   190
        Our fingers gather,
        Threaded thrice with golden strings
          From Cupid's bow;

And the sounds of its sweet voice
  Not air, but little busy things   195
    Pinioned with the lightest feather
      Of his wings,
    Rising up at every blow
Round the chords, like flies from roses
  Zephyr-touched; so these light minions 200
  Hover round, then shut their pinions,
And drop into the air, that closes
Where music's sweetest sweet reposes.

                    [*Exeunt.*

Marc. Then who hath solitude like mine, that is not
The last survivor of a city's plague,   205
Eating the mess he cooked for his dead father?
Who is alone but I? there 's fellowship
In churchyards and in hell: but I!—no lady's ghost
Did ever cling with such a grasp of love
Unto its soft dear body, as I hung   210
Rooted upon this brother. I went forth
Joyfully, as the soul of one who closes
His pillowed eyes beside an unseen murderer,
And like its horrible return was mine,
To find the heart, wherein I breathed and beat, 215
Cold, gashed, and dead. Let me forget to love,
And take a heart of venom: let me make
A staircase of the frightened breasts of men,
And climb into a lonely happiness!
And thou, who only art alone as I,   220
Great solitary god of that one sun,
I charge thee by the likeness of our state,
Undo these human veins that tie me close
To other men, and let your servant griefs
Unmilk me of my mother, and pour in   225
Salt scorn and steaming hate!

           Enter EZRIL

Ezr.   How now, my lord?

Marc. Much better, my kind Jew. They've weeded out

A troublesome wild plant that grew upon me,
My heart: I've trampled it to dust, and wept it
Wetter than Nilus' side. Out of the sun!   230
And let him bake it to a winged snake.
—Well, you've been shouldered from the palace steps,
And spurned as I—No matter.

Ezr.   Nay, my lord!
Come with me: lay aside these squalid wrappings:
Prepare that honoured head to fit a crown,   235
For 'twill be empty of your brother soon.

Marc. What starry chance has dropped out of the skies?

What's this? Oh! now if it should but be so,
I'll build a bridge to heaven. Tell me, good Jew;
Excellent Ezril, speak.

Ezr.   At your command   240
I sought the ducal palace, and, when there,
Found all the wild-eyed servants in the courts
Running about on some dismaying errand,
In the wild manner of a market crowd,
Waked from the sunny dozing at their stalls   245
By one who cries 'the city is on fire';
Just so they crossed, and turned, and came again.
I asked of an old man, what this might mean;
And he, yet grappling with the great disaster
As if he would have killed it, like a fable,   250
By unbelief, coldly as if he spoke
Of something gone a century before,
Told me, the Duke in hunting had been thrown
And lay on his last bed.

Marc.   Ha! well! what next?
You are the cup-bearer of richest joy.—   255
But it was a report, a lie.—Have done—
I read it on your lip.

Ezr.   It was too true.
I went to his bedside, and there made trial
Of my best skill in physic, with the zeal
Due to my sovereign.

Marc.   Impious, meddling fool!   260
To thrust yourself 'twixt heaven and its victim!

Ezr. My lord, I think you would not have said so
In the sad chamber of the writhing man.
He lay in a red fever's quenchless flames,
Burning to dust: despairing of my skill,   265
I sat myself beside his heart, and spoke
Of his next brother. When he heard of you,
He bade be summoned all his counsellors,
To witness his bequeathing his dominion
Wholly to you.

Marc.   Why did you let me wait?   270
Come, let's be quick: he keeps beneath his pillow
A kingdom, which they'll steal if we're too late.
We must o'ertake his death.   *[Exeunt.*

SCENE II. *Banqueting Hall*

Enter ORAZIO, BATTISTA, HEBE, ARMIDA, *&c. &c.*

Music. Song

Will you sleep these dark hours, maiden,
    Beneath the vine that rested
Its slender boughs, so purply-laden,
    All the day around that elm
      In the mead, nightingale-nested,   5
    Which yon dark hill wears for an helm,
      Pasture-robed and forest-crested?
There the night of lovely hue
Peeps the fearful branches through,
And ends in those two eyes of blue.   10

ORAZIO *and* ARMIDA *come forward*

153

    Armid. What! wrap a frown in myrtle, and look sad
Beneath the shadow of an ivy wreath?
This should not be, my lord.
    Oraz.   Armida dear,
I'm weary of their laughter's empty din.
Methinks, these fellows with their ready jests   15
Are like to tedious bells, that ring alike
Marriage or death. I would we were alone—
Asleep, Armida.
    Armid.   They will soon be gone:
One half-hour more—
    Oraz.   No, it could not be so:
I think and think—Sweet, did you like the feast?   20
    Armid. Methought, 'twas gay enough.
    Oraz.   Now, I did not.
'Twas dull: all men spoke slow and emptily.
Strange things were said by accident. Their tongues
Uttered wrong words: one fellow drank my death,
Meaning my health; another called for poison,   25
Instead of wine; and, as they spoke together,
Voices were heard, most loud, which no man owned:
There were more shadows too than there were men;
And all the air more dark and thick than night
Was heavy, as 'twere made of something more   30
Than living breaths.
    Armid.   Nay, you are ill, my lord:
'Tis merely melancholy.
    Oraz.   There were deep hollows
And pauses in their talk; and then, again,
On tale and song and jest and laughter rang,
Like a fiend's gallop. By my ghost, 'tis strange.   35
    Armid. Come, my lord, join your guests; they look with wonder
Upon your lonely mood.
    Oraz.   It is the trick
Of these last livers to unbuild belief:
They'd rob the world of spirit. Then each look,

Aye, every aspect of the earth and sky,   40
Man's thought and hope, are lies.—Well; I'll return,
And look at them again.

MICHELE *advances*

Mich.   You're tired, my lord.
Our visit 's long: break off, good gentlemen:
The hour is late.
    Oraz.   Nay, I beseech you, stay:
My pleasure grows on yours. I'm somewhat dull;   45
But let me not infect you.

Enter Attendant

                    What with you?
    Attend. A lady, in the garment of a nun,
Desires to see you.
    Oraz.   Lead her in: all such
I thank for their fair countenance.

Enter VALERIA

                        Gentle stranger,
Your will with me?
    Valer.   I am the bearer of another's will: 50
A woman, whose unhappy fondness yet
May trouble her lord's memory,—Valeria,—
Yours for a brief, blessed time, who now dwells
In her abandoned being patiently,
But not unsorrowing, sends me.
    Oraz.   My wronged wife!   55
Too purely good for such a man as I am!
If she remembers me, then Heaven does too,
And I am not yet lost. Give me her thoughts,—
Aye, the same words she put into thine ears,
Safe and entire, and I will thank thy lips   60
With my heart's thanks. But tell me how she fares.
    Valer. Well; though the common eye that has a tear,
Would drop it for the paleness of her skin

And the wan shivering of her torch of life;
Though she be faint and weak, yet very well: 65
For not the tincture or the strength of limb
Is a true health, but readiness to die.—
But let her be, or be not.
   Oraz.   Best of ladies!
And if thy virtues did not glut the mind
To the extinction of the eye's desire,   70
Such a delight to see, that one would think
Our looks were thrown away on meaner things,
And given to rest on thee!
   Valer.   These words, my lord,
Are charitable; it is very kind
To think of her sometimes: for, day and night,   75
As they flow in and out of one another,
She sits beside and gazes on their streams,
So filled with the strong memory of you,
That all her outward form is penetrated,
Until the watery portrait is become   80
Not hers, but yours:—and so she is content
To wear her time out.
   Oraz.   Softest peace enwrap her!
Content be still the breathing of her lips!
Be tranquil ever, thou blest life of her!
And that last hour, that hangs 'tween heaven and
    earth,   85
So often travelled by her thoughts and prayers,
Be soft and yielding 'twixt her spirit's wings!
   Valer. Think'st thou, Orazio, that she dies but once?
All round and through the spaces of creation,
No hiding-place of the least air, or earth,   90
Or sea, invisible, untrod, unrained on,
Contains a thing alone. Not e'en the bird,
That can go up the labyrinthine winds
Between its pinions, and pursues the summer,
Not even the great serpent of the billows,   95
Who winds him thrice around this planet's waist,

Is by itself, in joy or suffering.
But she whom you have ta'en, and like a leaven
With your existence kneaded, must be ever
Another—scarce another—self of thine.   100
 Oraz. If she has read her heart aloud to you,
Or you have found it open by some chance,
Tell me, dear lady, is my name among
Her paged secrets? does she, can she love me?—
No, no; that 's mad:—does she remember me?   105
 Valer. She breathes away her weary days and nights
Among cold, hard-eyed men, and hides behind
A quiet face of woe: but there are things—
A song, a face, a picture, or a word—   109
Which, by some semblance, touch her heart to tears.
And music, starting up among the strings
Of a wind-shaken harp, undoes her secrecy,
Rolls back her life to the first starry hour
Whose flower-fed air you used, to speak of love;
And then she longs to throw her bursting breast, 115
And shut out sorrow with Orazio's arms—
Thus—O my husband!
 Oraz.   Sweetest, sweetest woman!
Valeria, thou dost squeeze eternity
Into this drop of joy. O come, come, come!
Let us not speak; give me my wife again!   120
O thou fair creature, full of my own soul!
We'll love, we'll love, like nothing under heaven,
Like nought but Love, the very truest god.
Here 's lip-room on thy cheek: there, shut thine eye,
And let me come, like sleep, and kiss its lid.   125
Again.—What shall I do? I speak all wrong,
And lose a soul-full of delicious thought
By talking—Hush! Let's drink each other up
By silent eyes. Who lives, but thou and I,
My heavenly wife?
 Valer.   Dear Orazio!   130

Oraz. I'll watch thee thus, till I can tell a second
By thy cheek's change. O what a rich delight!
There's something very gentle in thy cheek,
That I have never seen in other women:
And now I know the circle of thine eye,   135
It is a colour like to nothing else
But what it means—that's heaven. This little tress,
Thou'lt give it me to look on and to wear,
But first I'll kiss its shadow on thy brow.
That little, fluttering dimple is too late,   140
If he is for the honey of thy looks:
As sweet a blush, as ever rose did copy,
Budded and opened underneath my lips,
And shed its leaves; and now those fairest cheeks
Are snowed upon them. Let us whisper, sweet,   145
And nothing be between our lips and ears
But our own secret souls.   [*A horn without.*

Valer. Heaven of the blest, they're here!

Oraz.   Who, what, Valeria?
Thou'rt pale and tremblest: what is it?

Valer.   Alas!
A bitter kernel to our taste of joy,   150
Our foolish and forgetful joy. My father!
Destruction, misery—

Enter VARINI *and attendants*

Varin.   Turn out those slaves,—
Burst the closed doors, and occupy the towers.

Oraz. Varini's self! what can his visit bring?

Valer. Look there; he's walking hither like a man,
But is indeed a sea of stormy ruin,   156
Filling and flooding o'er this golden house
From base to pinnacle, swallowing thy lands,
Thy gold, thine all. Embrace me into thee,
Or he'll divide us.

Oraz.   Never! calm thyself.—   160
Now, Count Varini, what's your business here?

If as a guest, though uninvited, welcome!
If not, then say, what else?

 Varin.   A master, spendthrift!
Open those further doors—

 Oraz.   What? in my palace!

 Varin. Thine! what is thine beneath the night or day?
Not e'en that beggar's carcase, for within that 166
The swinish devils of filthy luxury
Do make their stye. No lands, no farms, no houses—
Thanks to thy debts, no gold. Go out! Thou'rt nothing
Besides a grave and a deep hell.

 Valer.   Orazio, 170
Thou hast Valeria: the world may shake thee off,
But thou wilt drop into this breast, this love,
And it shall hold thee.

 Oraz.   What? lost already!
O that curst steward! I have fallen, Valeria,
Deeper than Lucifer, though ne'er so high, 175
Into a place made underneath all things,
So lost and horrible that hell 's its heaven.

 Varin. Thou shalt not have the idiot, though she be
The very fool and sickness of my blood.—
Gentlemen, here are warrants for my act: 180
His debts, bonds, forfeitures, taxes and fines,
O'erbalancing the worth of his estates,
Which I have bought: behold them!—For the girl,
Abandoned, after marriage, by the villain,
I am her father: let her be removed; 185
And, if the justice of my rightful cause
Ally you not, at least do not resist me.

 Mich. What are these writings?

 Batt.   Bills under the Duke's seal,
All true and valid. Poor Orazio! 189

 Oraz. Why, the rogue pities me! I'm down indeed.

 Valer. Help me! Oh! some of you have been beloved,
Some must be married. Will you let me go?

Will you stand frozen there, and see them cut
Two hearts asunder? Then you will,—you do.
Are all men like my father? are all fathers   195
So far away from men? or all their sons
So heartless?—you are women, as I am;
Then pity me, as I would pity you,
And pray for me! Father! ladies! friends!—
But you are tearless as the desert sands.—   200
Orazio, love me! or, if thou wilt not,
Yet I will love thee: that you cannot help.

 Oraz. My best Valeria! never shalt thou leave me,
But with my life. O that I could put on
These feeble arms the proud and tawny strength   205
Of the lion in my heart!

 Varin.   Out with the girl at once!

 Rosaur. Forgive them, sir, we all of us beseech.

 Varin. Lady, among you all she 's but one sire,
And she says *no*.—Away!   209

 Valer. Have pity, my sweet father! my good father!
Have pity, as my gentle mother would,
Were she alive—thy sainted wife! O pardon,
If I do wish you had been rent asunder
Thus dreadfully; for then I had not been;
Not kissed and wept upon my father's hand,   215
And he denied me!—you can make me wretched!—
Be cruel still, but I will never hate you.—
Orazio, I'll tell thee what it is:
The world is dry of love; we've drunk it all
With our two hearts—

 Oraz.   Farewell, Valeria!   220
Take on thy lost dear hand this truest kiss,
Which I have brought thee from my deepest soul.
Farewell, my wife!

 Valer.   They cannot part us long.
What's life? our love is an eternity:
O blessed hope!   [*Exit by force.*

 Oraz.   Now then, sir; speak to me: 225

The rest is sport—like rain against a tower
Unpalsied by the ram. Go on: what 's next?
    Varin. Your palaces are mine, your sheep-specked
        pastures,
Forest and yellow corn-land, grove and desert,
Earth, water, wealth: all, that you yesterday   230
Were mountainously rich and golden with,
I, like an earthquake, in this minute take.
Go, go: I will not pick thee to the bones:
Starve as you will.
    Oraz.   How, sir! am I not wealthy?
Why, if the sun could melt the brazen man   235
That strode o'er Corinth, and whose giant form
Stretched its swart limbs along sea, island, mountain,
While night appeared its shadow,—if *he* could,—
Great, burning Phœbus' self—could melt ought of
        him,
Except the snow-drift on his rugged shoulder,   240
Thou hast destroyed *me*!
    Varin. Thanks to these banquets of Olympus' top
From whence you did o'erturn whole Niles of wine,
And made each day as rainy as that hour
When Perseus was begot, I have destroyed thee,   245
Or thou thyself; for, such a luxury
Would wring the gold out of its rocky shell,
And leave the world all hollow. So, begone;
My lord, and beggar!
    Batt.   Noble, old Varini,
Think, is it fit to crush into the dirt   250
Even the ruins of nobility?
Take comfort, sir.
    Oraz.   Who am I now?
How long is a man dying or being born?
Is 't possible to be a king and beggar
In half a breath? or to begin a minute   255
I' th' west and end it in the furthest east?
O no! I'll not believe you. When I do,
161

My heart will crack to powder.—Can you speak?
Then do: shout something louder than my thoughts,
For I begin to feel.

Enter a Messenger

Mess.   News from the court: 260
The Duke—
    Oraz.   My brother—speak—
Was he not ill, and on a perilous bed?
Speak life and death, thou hast them on thy tongue—
One's mine, the other his:—a look, a word,
A motion—life or death?
    Mess.   The Duke is dead.   265
    All. Then we salute in thee another sovereign.
    Oraz. Me then, who just was shaken into chaos,
Thou hast created! I have flown, somehow,
Upwards a thousand miles: my heart is crowned.
Your hands, good gentlemen; sweet ladies, yours: 270
And what new godson of the bony death,
Of fire, or steel or poison, shall I make
For old Varini?
    Varin.   Your allegiance, sirs,
Wanders: Orazio is a beggar still.
    Batt. Is it not true then that the Duke is dead?   275
    Oraz. Not dead? O slave!
    Varin.   The Duke is dead, my lords;
And on his death-bed did bestow his crown
Upon his second brother, Lord Marcello—
Ours and Ferrara's Duke.
    Oraz.   I'll not believe it:
Marcello is abroad.
    Varin.   His blest return,   280
This providential day, has saved our lives
From thine abhorred sway. Orazio, go:
And though my clemency is half a crime,
I spare your person.
    Oraz.   I'll to the palace.

When we meet next, be blessed if thou dost kiss   285
The dust about my ducal chair.   [*Exit.*

   Varin.   I shall be there,
To cry Long live Marcello! in thine ear.—
Pray pardon me the breaking of this feast,
Ladies,—and so, good night.

   Rosaur. Your wish is echoed by our inmost will: 290
Good night to Count Varini.   [*Exeunt guests.*

   Attend.   My lord—

   Varin. What are they, sirrah?

   Attend.   The palace-keys.
There is a banquet in the inner room:
Shall we remove the plate?

   Varin.   Leave it alone:
Wine in the cups, the spicy meats uncovered,   295
And the round lamps each with a star of flame
Upon their brink; let winds begot on roses,
And grey with incense, rustle through the silk
And velvet curtains: then set all the windows,
The doors and gates, wide open; let the wolves,   300
Foxes, and owls, and snakes, come in and feast;
Let the bats nestle in the golden bowls,
The shaggy brutes stretch on the velvet couches,
The serpent twine him o'er and o'er the harp's
Delicate chords:—to Night, and all its devils,   305
We do abandon this accursed house.   [*Exeunt.*

ACT II

SCENE I. *An apartment in* VARINI'S *palace*

Enter VALERIA *and attendant*

   Val. I cannot rest. This wakeful bosom holds
A gulph of anguish in its little bounds.

   Attend. Will you not sleep, dear lady? you are weary,
And yet thus eager, quick, and silently,

Like one who listens for a midnight sign,   5
You wander up and down from room to room,
With that wide, sightless eye, searching about
For what you know not. Will you not to bed?
   Valer. No, not to-night: my eyes will not be closed,
My heart will not be darkened. Sleep is a traitor: 10
He fills the poor, defenceless eyes with blackness,
That he may let in dreams. I am not well;
My body and my mind are ill-agreed,
And comfortlessly strange; faces and forms
And pictures, friendly to my life-long knowledge,   15
Look new and unacquainted; every voice
Is hollow, every word inexplicable,
And yet they seem to be a guilty riddle;
And every place, though unknown as a desart,
Feels like the spot where a forgotten crime   20
Was done by me in sleep. Night, O be kind!
I do not come to watch thy secret acts,
Or thrust myself on Nature's mysteries
At this forbidden hour: bestow thy dews,
Thy calm, thy quiet sweetness, sacred mother,   25
And let me be at ease!

                      Now, thou kind girl,
Take thy pale cheeks to rest.
   Attend.   I am not weary:
Believe me now, I am not.
   Valer.   But, my child,
Those eyelids, tender as the leaf of spring,
Those cheeks should lay their roseate delicacy   30
Under the kiss of night, the feathery sleep;
For there are some, whose study of the morn
Is ever thy young countenance and hue.
Ah maid! you love.
   Attend.   I'll not deny it, madam.
O that sweet influence of thoughts and looks!   35
That change of being, which, to one who lives,
Is nothing less divine than divine life

To the unmade! Love? Do I love? I walk
Within the brilliance of another's thought,
As in a glory. I was dark before,   40
As Venus' chapel in the black of night:
But there was something holy in the darkness,
Softer and not so thick as other where;
And as rich moonlight may be to the blind,
Unconsciously consoling. Then love came,   45
Like the out-bursting of a trodden star,
And what before was hueless and unseen
Now shows me a divinity like that
Which, raised to life out of the snowy rock,
Surpass'd mankind's creation, and repaid   50
Heaven for Pandora.
    Valer.   Innocently thought,
And worthy of thy youth! I should not say
How thou art like the daisy in Noah's meadow,
On which the foremost drop of rain fell warm
And soft at evening: so the little flower   55
Wrapped up its leaves, and shut the treacherous water
Close to the golden welcome of its breast,
Delighting in the touch of that which led
The shower of oceans, in whose billowy drops
Tritons and lions of the sea were warring,   60
And sometimes ships on fire sunk in the blood
Of their own inmates; others were of ice,
And some had islands rooted in their waves,
Beasts on their rocks, and forest-powdering winds,
And showers tumbling on their tumbling self,   65
And every sea of every ruined star
Was but a drop in the world-melting flood.
    Attend. Lady, you utter dreams.
    Valer.   Let me talk so:
I would o'erwhelm myself with any thoughts;
Aye, hide in madness from the truth. Persuade me   70
To hope that I am not a wretched woman,
Who knows she has an husband by his absence,

Who feels she has a father by his hate,
And wakes and mourns, imprisoned in this house,
The while she should be sleeping, mad, or dead.—   75
Thou canst, and pity on thine eyelid hangs,
Whose dewy silence drops consent—thou wilt!
I've seen thee smile with calm and gradual sweetness,
As none, that were not good, could light their cheeks:—
Thou wilt assist me. Harden not those lips,   80
Those lovely kissings let them not be stone
With a denial!
   Attend.   But your father's anger—
The watchful faith of all the servants—
   Valer.   Fear not:
Lend me thy help. O come—I see thou wilt.—
Husband, I'll lay me on thine aching breast   85
For once and ever.—Haste! for see, the light
Creates for earth its day once more, and lays
The star of morn's foundation in the east.
Come—come—   [*Exeunt.*

SCENE II. *Before the ducal palace*

Guards driving ORAZIO *from the gate*

   Guard. Back! desperate man: you cannot pass—
   Oraz. By heaven, I must and will:—
   Guard.   By the Duke's order,
The gates are locked on all to-day.
   Oraz.   By mine,
By the Duke's brother's order, or his force,
Open at once yon gates. Slave, by my blood,   5
But that I think thou know'st me not, I'd make
That corpse of thine my path. Undo, I say,
The knitting of this rebel house's arms,
And let their iron welcome be around me.
My sword is hungry: do't.
   Guard.   Advance no further: 10

Another step, and all our swords shake hands
Within your breast.
    Oraz.   Insolent worm of earth,
To earth and worms for this!
    Guard.   Strike all, strike strong!
Strike through him right.   [*a fight.*

Enter EZRIL

    Ezr.   Peace, on your lives, you traitors!
What! would you stain the holy throne of justice,   15
The pure and peaceful temple of the law,
The sacred dwelling of Ferrara's soul,
With the foul juices of your drunken veins?
Put up your impious swords.—What's this? Your
    blood of beer?
    Guard. Pardon our hasty and forgetful choler: 20
We but defend our Duke against the outrage
Of this intemperate brawler.
    Oraz. Cut him to shreds, and fling him to the dogs.—
You wait upon the Duke, sir?
    Ezr.   I am one
Of Lord Marcello's followers.
    Oraz.   Pray you then,   25
Speak to your Lord Marcello: let him know
These house-dogs, these his ducal latch-holders
Dare keep the bolt against his brother's knock.
    Ezr. Are you then—?
    Oraz.   I am Lord Orazio.
Be quick!—O nature, what a snail of men!   30
The morn is frosty, sir: I love not waiting. Let in—
    Ezr. Now all the mercy of the heavens forbid
That thou should'st be that rash and wretched neigh-
    bour
Of the Duke's crown, his brother!
    Oraz. Marcello is my brother; I am his;   35
If coming of one mother brother us:
He is the Duke, and I Orazio;

He elder, younger I. If Jove and Neptune,
And the third Pluto, being Saturn's boys,
Lying in Rhea's womb and on her breast,   40
Were therefore brethren, so are he and I,—
Marcello's mother's son, his grandame's grandson,
Marcello's father's babe, his uncle's nephew,
His nephew's uncle, brother of his brother,
Or what you like,—if this same word of brother   45
Sours the sore palate of a royal ear.

    Ezr. Better thou wert the brother of his foe
Than what thou art, a man of the same getting;
As out of the same lump of sunny Nile
Rises a purple-winged butterfly   50
And a cursed serpent crawls.

    Oraz. Heart-withered, pale-scalped grandfather of
    lies!
Age-hidden monster! Tell me what thou meanest,
And then I'll stab thee for thy falsehood.

    Ezr.   Hold him!
Your swords between us!—Now, the Duke condemns
    thee;   55
And by his mother's, and his father's grave,
And by the dead, that lies within this palace,
His brother's sacred corpse, he dreadly swears;
And by the heaven those three loved souls
Dwell and are blest in, twice he dreadly swears: 60
By which dread oath, and hate of all thy crimes,
The Duke condemns thee,—mixing in his sentence,
Sweet mercy, tearful love, and justice stern,—
To banishment for ever from this hour.

    Oraz. O reddest hour of wrath and cruelty!   65
Banished! Why not to death?

    Ezr.   The pious hope
That bitter solitude and suffering thought
Will introduce repentance to thy woes,
And that conduct thee to religious fear
And humbleness: the lark that climbs heaven's stairs

But lives upon the ground:—Go forth, Orazio;   71
Seek not the house or converse of a citizen,
But think thyself outside the walls of life:
If in Ferrara after this decree,
Your darkest, deepest, and most fearful fear   75
Falls on thy shoulder, digs beneath thy feet,
And opens hell for thee. So, pass away!

   Oraz. Stay, for an instant; listen to a word:
O lead me to his throne! Let me but look
Upon the father in my brother's face!   80
Let me but speak to him this kindred voice,
Our boyish thoughts in the familiar words
Of our one bed-room; let me show to him
That picture which contains our double childhood,
Embracing in inexplicable love,   85
Within each other's, in our mother's arms;
Thou'lt see rejoicing, O thou good old man,
The rigour melting through his changed eyes
Off his heart's roots between whose inmost folds
Our love is kept.

   Ezr.   Impossible and vain!   90
Content thee with thy doom, and look for love
Over the sea-wide grave. Let us be gone!

                           [Exit with guards.

   Oraz. Let me write to him—send a message to him—
A word, a touch, a token! old, benevolent man,
Stay with me then to comfort and advise: 95
Leave one of these beside me: throw me not
Alone into despair!—He's gone; they're gone;
They never will come back; ne'er shall I hear
The sweet voice of my kinsmen or my friends:
But here begins the solitude of death.   100
I was—I am; O what a century
Of darkness, rocks, and ghostly tempest opens
Between those thoughts! Within it there are lost
Dearest Valeria, Marcello whose heart came
From the same place as mine, and all mankind;   105

169

Affection, charity, joy: and nothing 's cast
Upon this barren rock of present time,
Except Orazio's wreck! here let it lie.

Enter VARINI *and Attendants*

Varin. Not in the city? Have you asked the guards
At bridge and gate,—the palace sentinels?   110
    Attend. We have—in vain: they have not seen her
      pass.
Varin. And did you say Valeria, my Valeria,
Heaven's love, earth's beauty?
    Oraz. (*starting up*)   Mine eternally!
Let heaven unscabbard each star-hilted lightning, 114
And clench ten thousand hands at once against me,—
Earth shake all graves to one, and rive itself
From Libya to the North! in spite of all
That threatens, I will stun the adulterous gods—
She's mine! Valeria's mine! dash me to death,
From death to the eternal depth of fire,   120
I laugh and triumph on the neck of fate:
For still she's mine for ever! give me her,
Or I will drag thee to a sea-side rock,
That breaks the bottoms of the thunder-clouds
And taking thee by this old, wicked hair,   125
Swing thee into the winds.
    Varin.   I would, wild man,
That I could quench thine eyes' mad thirst with her.
She 's gone, fled, lost. O think not any more,
Let us forget what else is possible,—
Yea hope impossibly! the city streets,   130
The quay, the gardens,—is there yet a place
Within night's skirt unsearched?
    Oraz.   The wood of wolves:—
    Varin. Merciful god! that frightful forest grows
Under that darksome corner of the sky
Where death's scythe hangs: its murder-shading trees
Are hairs upon Hell's brow. Away: away!   136

And never dare to turn on me again
Those eyes, unfilled with—speak to me never,
Until you cry—'Behold Valeria!'
And drop her on my bosom.   140

   Oraz. We'll wind the gordian paths off the trees'
    roots,
Untie the hilly mazes, and seek her
Till we are lost. Help, ho!   [*Exit with attendants.*
   Varin.   Blessings of mine
Feather your speed! and my strong prayers make
    breaches
Through the air before you!

               Now I'll close my eyes,   145
And, seated on this step, await their coming.
Strange and delightful meetings on strange lands
Of dead-esteemed friends have happened oft,
And such a blessed and benevolent chance
Might bring her here unheard; far on the earth   150
She goes with her light feet, still as the sparrow
Over the air, or through the grass its shade.
Behind me would she steal, unknown, until
Her lip fell upon mine. It might be so:
I'll wait awhile, and hope it.   155

Enter VALERIA

   Valer. I know not what it means. None speak to me:
The crowded street, and solid flow of men,
Dissolves before my shadow and is broken.
I pass unnoticed, though they search for me,
As I were in the air and indistinct   160
As crystal in a wave. There lies a man—
Shall I intreat protection and concealment,
And thaw the pity of his wintry head?
—No time: they come like arrows after me:
I must avoid them.   [*Exit.* 165

Enter EZRIL *and servants*

171

Ezr. Pursue, o'ertake, stay, seize that hurrying girl:
Muffle her face and form, and through the bye-ways
Convey her to the palace. Hasten hounds!   [*Exeunt.*

   Varin. Thou magical deceiver, precious Fancy!
Even now, out of this solitude and silence,   170
Seemed—it was thy creation—music flowing,
And a conviction of some unseen presence;
I could have pointed to that empty spot,
And said, there stands the presence of my daughter!
The air seemed shaken by that voice of hers—   175
But 'tis all hushed.

Enter servants

              How now? speak some of you.
What 's here?
   Serv.   A veil and mantle.
   Varin.   Both Valeria's!
Where 's she they should have wrapped?
   Serv.   'Twas all we found.
   Varin. Where?
   Serv.   On the grass this purple cloak was dropped,
Beside the river.
   Varin.   And the veil—which way?   180
Further on shore, or near those deadly waves?
   Serv. The veil, my lord—
   Varin.   'Tis drenched and dropping wet:
Would I were drowned beside her! thou wert white;
And thy limbs' wond'rous victory over snow
Did make the billows curious of their taste.   185
They drank thee up, thou sweet one, cruelly!
Who was in heaven then?

Enter ORAZIO *and servant*

   Oraz.   My love, art dead?
Wilt thou not ope thy lips, lift up thine eyes?
It is the air, the sun—
   Serv.   We've found the corpse.

Oraz. Her corpse! O no! she is Valeria still: 190
She 's scarce done living yet: her ghost 's the youngest!
To-morrow she'll be—Oh what *she* will be?
No she—a corpse, and then—a skeleton!

Varin. Hast looked upon her?

Serv.   Death has marred her features—
So swollen and discoloured their delight,   195
As if he feared that Life should know her sweet one,
And take her back again.

Varin.   If it be so,
I'll see her once: that beauty being gone,
And the familiar tokens altered quite,
She 's strange—a being made by wicked Death,   200
And I'll not mourn her. Lead me to the corpse.

                                   [*Exit with attendants.*

Oraz. Henceforth, thou tender pity of mankind,
Have nought to do with weeping: let war's eyes
Sweat with delight; and tears be ta'en from grief,
And thrown upon the rocky cheek of hate!   205
For mark! that water, the soft heap of drops,
Water, that feigns to come from very heaven
In the round shape of sorrow, that was wont to wash
Sin from the new-born babe, is hard and bloody;
A murderer of youth; cold death to those   210
Whose life approved thy godhead, piteous virtue!

             Enter EZRIL *and guards*

Ezr. Here still, unhappy man? then take the doom
You wooe so obstinately. To the dungeon,
To the deepest chamber of the dayless rock:
Away and down with him!

Oraz.   I care not whither.   215
Thou canst not drag me deeper, wrap me darker,
Or torture me as my own thoughts have done.

                                   [*Exeunt.*

ACT III

Scene I. *A room in the palace*

Enter MARCELLO

    Marc. I have them all at last; swan-necked Obedi-
      ence;
And Power that strides across the muttering people,
Like a tall bridge; and War, the spear-maned dragon:
Such are the potent spirits he commands,
Who sits within the circle of a crown!   5
Methought that love began at woman's eye:
But thou, bright imitation of the sun,
Kindlest the frosty mould around my heart-roots,
And breathing through the branches of my veins,
Makest each azure tendril of them blossom   10
Deep tingling pleasures, musically hinged,
Dropping with starry sparks, goldenly honied,
And smelling sweet with the delights of life.
At length I am Marcello.

Enter EZRIL

    Ezr.   Mighty Duke,
Ferrara's nobles wait on you, to proffer   15
The homage of their coronets.
    Marc.   I shall not see them.
    Ezr. It was the ancient usage of the state
In every age.—
    Marc.   Henceforth, be it forgotten!
I will not let the rabble's daily sight
Be my look's playmate. Say unto them, Ezril,   20
Their sovereigns of foretime were utter men,
False gods, that beat an highway in their thoughts
Before my car; idols of monarchy,
Whose forms they might behold. Now I am come,
Be it enough that they are taught my name,   25
Permitted to adore it, swear and pray

In it and to it: for the rest I wrap
The pillared caverns of my palace round me,
Like to a cloud, and rule invisibly
On the god-shouldering summit of mankind.   . 30
Dismiss them so.
   Ezr.   'Tis dangerous,—
   Marc.   Begone!
Each minute of man's safety he does walk
A bridge no thicker than his frozen breath
O'er a precipitous and craggy danger
Yawning to death!   [*Exit* EZRIL.
              A perilous sea it is,   35
'Twixt this and Jove's throne, whose tumultuous
    waves
Are heaped contending ghosts! There is no passing,
But by those slippery, distant stepping-stones,
Which frozen Odin trod, and Mahomet,
With victories harnessed to his crescent sledge,   40
And building waves of blood upon the shallows,
O'erpassed triumphant: first a pile of thrones
And broken nations, then the knees of men,
From whence, to catch the lowest root of heaven,
We must embrace the winged waist of fame,   45
Or nest within opinion's palmy top
'Till it has mixed its leaves with Atlas' hair,
Quicker to grow than were the men of Cadmus—

           Re-enter EZRIL

   Ezr. They are departing with the unequal pace
Of discontent and wonder.
   Marc.   Send them home   50
To talk it with their wives: sow them with books
Of midnight marvels, witcheries, and visions:
Let the unshaven Nazarite of stars
Unbind his wondrous locks, and grandame's earth-
    quake
Drop its wide jaw; and let the churchyard's sleep   55

Whisper our goblins. When the fools are ripe
And gaping to the kernel, thou shalt steal
And lay the egg of my divinity
In their fermenting sides.—Where is my brother?
The first I'll aim at.   60

    Ezr. 'Mid the poisonous dregs of this deep building,
Two days and their two nights have had his breath
All of one colour to his darkened eyes.
No voice has fed his ears, and little food
His speech-robbed lips.

    Marc.   'Tis well. This is a man   65
Whose state has sunk i' th' middle of his thoughts:
And in their hilly shade, as in a vale,
I'll build my church, making his heart the quarry.
Take him his meal, and place a guard around
The wood below: the rest of my instructions,   70
For we must juggle boldly, shall be whispered
Secretly in my closet.

    Ezr.   Will you not
First cast this ragged and unseemly garb
And hang your sides with purple?

    Marc.   No: these rags
Give my delight a sting. I'll sit in them;   75
And when I've stretched my dukedom through men's souls,
Fix on its shore my chair, and from it bid
Their doubts lie down. Wilt help me?

    Ezr.   Duke, thou art
A fathomless and undiscovered man,
Thinking above the eagle's highest wings,   80
And underneath the world. Go on: command:
And I am thine to do.   [*Exeunt.*

SCENE II. *A dungeon of Cyclopean architecture*

ORAZIO *solus*

Orazio. I'll speak again:
This rocky wall's great silence frightens me,
Like a dead giant's.
Methought I heard a sound; but all is still.
This empty silence is so deadly low,   5
The very stir and winging of my thoughts
Make audible my being; every sense
Aches from its depth with hunger.
The pulse of time is stopped, and night's blind sun
Sheds its black light, the ashes of noon's beams,   10
On this forgotten tower, whose ugly round,
Amid the fluency of brilliant morn,
Hoops in a blot of parenthetic night,
Like ink upon the crystal page of day,
Crossing its joy! But now some lamp awakes,   15
And with the venom of a basilisk's wink
Burns the dark winds. Who comes?

Enter EZRIL

Ezril.   There's food for thee.
Eat heartily; be mirthful with your cup;
Though coarse and scanty.
    Orazio.   I'll not taste of it.
To the dust, to the air with the cursed liquids   20
And poison-kneaded bread.
    Ezril.   Why dost thou this?
    Orazio. I know thee and thy master: honey-lipped,
Viper-tongued villain, that dost bait intents,
As crook'd and murderous as the scorpion's sting,
With mercy's sugared milk, and poisonest   25
The sweetest teat of matron charity!

Enter MARCELLO

Marc. Thou hast her then, in secret and secure?

Ezr. Not firmer or more quietly this body
Holds its existing spirit.

Marc.   Excellent Ezril!
Thanks, thanks: my gratitude is snail-paced slow,   30
So heavy is its burthen. See'st thou yonder?

Ezr. The husband: where his sorrow, strong in error,
Has spurned him down.

Marc.   I'll raise the broken man:
Aye, I will place my foot upon his soul,
And weigh him up. Leave us alone, good Ezril.

                              [*Exit* EZRIL.   35

Lie there: I see the winding, darkening path
Into thine heart, its mouth and its recess,
As clear as if it were a forest's cavern,
Open to my approach. Henceforth be thou
Another habitation of my life,   40
Its temple, its Olympus, next in birth to
And pressing close beneath the unknown cloud
In which it reigns!

                    Ho! sleep'st thou here?
Mak'st thou the branch-dividing, light noon-air
Thy bedroom? Rise! what dost thou on the ground? 45

Oraz. Didst thou say, Rise? I stand. Where am I
    now,
And how?

Marc.   Alive, and in Ferrara.

Oraz. Why, first there is a life, and then a death,
And then a life again, whose roof is death;
So I have heard. 'Tis true: and though I am   50
Beside you, there's a grave divides our beings,
Which is the second gate of birth to me.—
Leave me to weep and groan.

Marc.   What ails thee thus?
Thy nature is o'erturned, thy features all
Forget joy's offices. These sinking eyes,   55
Whose sight is but a secondary service,
The ashy hiding of thy cheeks,—its cause?

178

Oraz. Am I so like to marble in my form,
So wicked at the heart? No; thou art bad:
A charitable man would never ask.   60
And if thou e'er hadst loved, or been once human,
Loved, grieved, or hoped, thou'dst feel what I have
    lost.
My wife is dead! thou know'st not what I mean,
And therefore art accurst. Now let me weep.
    Marc. Thou dost me wrong. Lament! I'd have thee
    do't: 65
The heaviest raining is the briefest shower.
Death is the one condition of our life:
To murmur were unjust; our buried sires
Yielded their seats to us, and we shall give
Our elbow-room of sunshine to our sons.   70
From first to last the traffic must go on;
Still birth for death. Shall we remonstrate then?
Millions have died that we might breathe this day:
The first of all might murmur, but not we.
Grief is unmanly too.
    Oraz.   Because 'tis godlike.   75
I never felt my nature so divine,
As at this saddest hour. Thou'dst have me busy
In all the common usage of this world:
To buy and sell, laugh, jest, and feast, and sleep,
And wake and hunger that I might repeat 'em;   80
Perchance to love, to woo, to wed again.
    Marc. The wonted wheel.
    Oraz.   O how I hate thee for 't!
I've passed through life's best feelings—they are her's;
Humanity 's behind me. Ne'er I'll turn,
But consecrated to this holy grief,   85
Live in her memory: heaven has no more.
    Marc. Yes, *she* is there. Let not thy woes be impious,
Lest ye should never meet; but anchor thee
On the remembrance that thou there wilt meet
Her deepest self, her spirit.   90

Oraz. Thou talk'st to me of spirits and of souls—
What are they? what know I or you of them?
I love no ghost: I loved the fairest woman,
With too much warmth and beauty in her cheek
And gracious limbs, to hold together long.   95
To-day she's cold and breathless, and to-morrow
They'll lay her in the earth; then she will crumble:
Another year no place in all the world,
But this poor heart, will know of her existence.
Can she come back, O can she ever be   100
The same she was last night in my embrace?
No comfort else, no life!

   Marc.   She can.

   Oraz.   What didst thou speak?
Blaspheme not nature: wake not hope to stab it:
O take not comfort's sacred name in vain!
Wilt say it now again?

   Marc.   There is a way,   105
Which, if thy heart's religion could permit—

   Oraz. What's that but she? Do it, what'er it is;
I take the sin to me. Come, what will come—
And what but pain can come?—for that will be
All paradise concentrate in a minute,   110
When she—but she is dead; I saw her corpse;
Upon my soul! thou liest unfathomably:
No god could do it.

   Marc.   I have earned the taunt.
Seven heavens do fold the secret from thine eye:
Be happily incredulous. Perchance   115
It were a cursed and unhallowed rite:
Let's think it all a fiction. So farewell!

   Oraz. Thou dost not go; thou shalt not leave me
       thus:
No; by the power thou speakest of, I do swear
It shall be tried: if unsuccessful, then   120
We shall be what we are.

   Marc.   Not its success

I doubt, but its impiety. O be quick
To fear perdition!

   Oraz.   Can I fear aught further
Than what I feel?

   Marc.   The sting of grief speaks here,
And not the tongue of thought. A month, a year 125
Pass in reflection: after such a time,
If thou demand'st the same, I'll then assist thee.

   Oraz. What? dost thou think I'll live another month
Without her? No. I did not seek this knowledge:
Thou hast created hope, unbidden, in me;   130
Therefore, I charge thee, let it not be killed!
I pray not, I beseech thee not, again;
But I command thee, by my right to bliss,
Which I have lost in trusting thee, to do it,
Without an instant's loss.

   Marc.   Must it be so?   135
To-morrow night in the Cathedral vault
Valeria will be buried: meet me there.

   Oraz. Thou wilt not fail?

   Marc.   I will not, on my life.

   Oraz. Then she is mine again,
All and for ever.

   Marc. (*aside*) As thou shalt be mine.   140

                      [*Exeunt severally.*

ACT IV

SCENE I. *The Campo Santo*

Enter MARCELLO, EZRIL, MELCHIOR, VALERIA

   Valer. Whither, and by what law of man or nature,
Do ye thus lead me? Awe of sacred justice,
Dread of the clenched punishment that follows
The tremulous shoulder of pale, muffled guilt,—

Do they not gaze from every silent bed   5
In this sad place?

 Melch.   Sheathe that nurse's tongue.
There's wooing 'twixt the moon and Death to-night:
This is his cabinet.

 Marc.   'Beseech you, lady.
Break not this still submission and so force us   9
To stir our power from 'ts feigned, complacent sleep.

 Valer. Force! dost thou know me, that thou threat-
  en'st force?

 Melch. Why, thou'rt some wealthy sinner, very like,
Whose gloves are worn with lips of richest princes:—
It recks not here. The unfashionable worm,
Respectless of the crown-illumined brow,   15
The cheek's bewitchment, or the sceptred clench,
With no more eyes than Love, creeps courtier-like,
On his thin belly, to his food—no matter
How [clad or] nicknamed it might strut above,
What age or sex,—it is his dinner-time.   20
—Now with what name, what coronal's shade, wilt
  scare
Our rigour to the wing?

 Valer.   I have a plea,
As dewy-piteous as the gentle ghost's
That sits alone upon a forest-grave,
Thinking of no revenge: I have a mandate,   25
As magical and potent as e'er ran
Silently through a battle's myriad veins,
Undid their fingers from the hanging steel,
And drew them up in prayer: I AM A WOMAN.
O motherly remembered be the name,   30
And with the thought of loves and sisters, sweet
And comforting! therefore be piteous to me.
O let my hand touch yours! I could do more
By its sad tremors than my tongue.

 Melch.   Away!
We own a mood of marble. There 's no earth   35

In any crevice of my well-built spirit,
Whence woman's rain could wake the weedy leaves
Of the eye-poison, pity.
  Marc.   If I were
Another man than this, Nature's cast child,
Renounced by Life and Death of common men, 40
And placed by wrongs upon an island-peak,
Methinks I could relent.
  Melch.   Draw up thyself.
This bearskin, charity, is a great-coat
For ragged, shivering sin: thine Indian hate,
That shivers like the serpent's noontide tongue 45
With poisonous, candid heat, must trample on it.
  Valer. O icy hearts! but no; soft ice doth melt,
And warms contritely;—I renounce the words,
And roll away the tender side of Heaven
To bare its lightnings. I am innocent,— 50
As white as any angel's lily wing;
And if you wrong me, mark! I will not weep,
Nor pray against your souls, nor curse your lives,
Nor let my madness wake all things that are
To roll destruction on you,—but be silent, 55
Secret as happiness to man and God,
And let the judgment ripen silently,
Under your feet and o'er you—mighty, quiet,
Deadly and tedious, as a silent hell.
Now, what ye dare, begin!
  Marc.   Our purpose glides, 60
Calm and remorseless as this human orb,
Whose moon, thou see'st, bestows an equal beam
Upon the odorous gardens we passed by,
And the gaunt lips of this new-opened grave.
Canst thou reproach our want of charity, 65
Beholding this and all the thoughts it lends?
  Melch. 'Tis a fit oracle for such an hour,
And has the caverns of its inspirations,
More true than Delphian, underneath our being.

Let 's speak to it.
    Ezr.   What would'st thou?
    Melch.   It may teach 70
This tremulous lady resignation, sir.
Ho, there! thou maker of this earthen bed;
Thou porter of the gates,
God-father of the dead, art thou below?
Whose grave is this thou digg'st?   75

.   .   .   .   .   .

Fragments of 'The Second Brother' [1]

I

WHO are you?—
What I cannot express with human language,
Nor thou with thought accept. What do you see?—
A wild old creature.—
                         An old man? Know then,
Across the flaming orifice of hell
Passes, as through a magic lamp its glass,
A frozen ocean, in whose midst is graven
The wrizled grey resemblance of a man
Who lived his centuries before the clouds
Had stolen the first drop of the broad flood,
And the reflection of that antique form,
Ruddy and firm when Hell cheers up and blazes,
Pale when it falls, or darkened by the passing
Of fiends between it and the limning fire,
Now at this midnight moment dyes the sight
Of some distrusting youth, and with a voice
Strayed from a sleeper's tongue, seems likest me;
Speaks just as I do—

---

[1] The numbers are those of the Oxford edition.

What do you mean?—
                    That I am Adam-gotten,
A soul and skeleton in a flesh doublet:
What else? Dost think that I could be this shade?

III. *A Lofty Mind*

HIS thoughts are so much higher than his state,
That, like a mountain hanging o'er a hut,
They chill and darken it.

POEMS
Composed 1826–9

Letter to B. W. Procter

From Göttingen; March, 1826.

TO-DAY a truant from the odd old bones
And winds of flesh, which, as tamed rocks and stones
Piled cavernously make his body's dwelling,
Have housed man's soul: there, where time's billows
    swelling
Make a deep ghostly and invisible sea   5
Of melted worlds antediluvially
Upon the sand of ever-crumbling hours,
God-founded, stands the castle, all its towers
With veiny tendrils ivied: this bright day
I leave its chambers and with oars away   10
Seek some enchanted island where to play.
And what do you, that in the enchantment dwell
And should be raving ever, a wild swell
Of passionate life rolling about the world,
Now sun-sucked to the clouds, dashed on the curled 15
Leaf-hidden daisies; an incarnate storm
Letting the sun through on the meadows yellow;
Or anything except that earthy fellow
That wise dog's brother, man? O shame to tell!
Make tea in Circe's cup, boil the cool well,   20
The well Pierian, which no bird dare sip
But nightingales. There let kettles dip
Who write their simpering sonnets to its song,
And walk on Sundays in Parnassus' park:
Take thy example from the sunny lark,   25
Throw off the mantle which conceals the soul,
The many-citied world, and seek thy goal
Straight as a starbeam falls. Creep not nor climb
As they who place their topmost of sublime
On some peak of this planet pitifully;   30
Dart eaglewise with open wings and fly,

Until you meet the gods. Thus counsel I
The men who can, but tremble to be great;
Cursed be the fool who taught to hesitate
And to regret: time lost most bitterly.   35
And thus I write and I dare write to thee,
Fearing that still, as you were wont to do,
You feed and fear some asinine Review.
Let Jaggernaut roll on, and we, whose sires
Blooded his wheels and prayed around his fires,   40
Laugh at the leaden ass in the god's skin.
Example follows precept: I have been
Giving some negro minutes of the night
Freed from the slavery of my ruling spright
Anatomy the grim, to a new story   45
In whose satiric pathos we will glory.
In it Despair has married wildest Mirth
And to their wedding-banquet all the earth
Is bade to bring its enmities and loves
Triumphs and horrors: you shall see the doves   50
Billing with quiet joy and all the while
Their nest 's the scull of some old king of Nile:
But he who fills the cups and makes the jest
Pipes to the dancers, is the fool o' the feast.
Who 's he? I've dug him up and decked him trim   55
And made a mock, a fool, a slave of him
Who was the planet's tyrant: dotard Death:
Man's hate and dread: not with a stoical breath
To meet him like Augustus standing up,
Nor with grave saws to season the cold cup   60
Like the philosopher, nor yet to hail
His coming with a verse or jesting tale
As Adrian did and More: but of his night,
His moony ghostliness and silent might
To rob him, to uncypress him i' the light   65
To unmask all his secrets; make him play
Momus o'er wine by torchlight is the way
To conquer him and kill; and from the day

Spurned, hissed and hooted send him back again
An unmask'd braggart to his bankrupt den.   70
For death is more 'a jest' than Life, you see
Contempt grows quick from familiarity.
I owe this wisdom to Anatomy.—
Your Muse is younger in her soul than mine:
O feed her still on woman's smiles and wine   75
And give the world a tender song once more,
For all the good can love and can adore
What's human, fair and gentle. Few, I know,
Can bear to sit at my board when I show
The wretchedness and folly of man's all   80
And laugh myself right heartily. Your call
Is higher and more human: I will do
Unsociably my part and still be true
To my own soul: but e'er admire you
And own that you have nature's kindest trust   85
Her weak and dear to nourish, that I must.
Then fare, as you deserve it, well, and live
In the calm feelings you to others give.

The Ghosts' Moonshine

I

IT is midnight, my wedded;
　　Let us lie under
The tempest bright, my dreaded,
　　In the warm thunder:
Tremble and weep not! What can you fear?
　　My heart's best wish is thine,—
　　That thou wert white, and bedded
　　On the softest bier,

191

In the ghosts' moonshine.
Is that the wind? No, no;
Only two devils, that blow
Through the murderer's ribs to and fro,
    In the ghosts' moonshine.

II

Who is there, she said afraid, yet
    Stirring and awaking
The poor old dead? His spade, it
    Is only making—
(Tremble and weep not! What do you crave?)
    Where yonder grasses twine,
A pleasant bed, my maid, that
    Children call a grave,
        In the cold moonshine.
    Is that the wind? No, no;
    Only two devils, that blow
Through the murderer's ribs to and fro,
        In the ghosts' moonshine.

III

What dost thou strain above her
    Lovely throat's whiteness?
A silken chain, to cover
    Her bosom's brightness?
Tremble and weep not: what dost thou fear?
    —My blood is spilt like wine,
Thou hast strangled and slain me, lover,
    Thou hast stabbed me, dear,
        In the ghosts' moonshine.
    Is that the wind? No, no;
    Only her goblin doth blow
Through the murderer's ribs to and fro,
        In its own moonshine.

Lines

Written in the album of one who had watched the progress of the American and French revolutions

As an almighty night doth pass away
From an old ruinous city in a desart,
And all its cloudy wrecks sink into day:
While every monstrous shape and ghostly wizard
That dwelled within the cavernous old place,
Grows pale and shrinks and dies in its dismay:
And then the light comes in, and flowery grace
Covers the sand, and man doth come again
And live rejoicing in the new-born plain:
So you have seen great gloomy centuries,
(The shadow of Rome's Death) in which did dwell
The men of Europe, shudder and arise:
So you have seen break up that smoke of Hell,
Like a great superstitious snake, uncurled
From the pale temples of the awakening world.

Written in an Album at Clifton

March, 1828

Long have I racked my brain for rhymes to please,
But vainly, for the time doth frown upon me,
And throw the lights and shadows of reality
Thro' my mind's caverns, melting in its glare
The fairy-like inhabitants of twilight   5
Which I essayed to summon. Even so
It came to pass as I have heard it told,
That once a lady's grace and gentleness
That shed soft beauty over every one
Standing around her, like to spirits summoned   10
That must so wait and gaze, but dared not step
Within the circled halo of the charmer,
Lent to an almost unknown traveller

A book whose leaves were heavy with the music
Of poetry such as she loved to read, 15
For poetry was her life's element
Which she shook from her, lightly breaking up
The current of men's thoughts, wherein this world
Was pictured drearily, into fair dimples,
As doth a curled swan silently roving 20
Thro' the reflection of a haunted palace
Upon a musically enchanted stream.
And on those pages where her eye would dwell
She had permitted the world-wandering stranger
To leave a token of his poor existence: 25
And now enclosed in his quiet chamber,
Holding the magic volume which contained
The charms to raise the memory of the gone
Out of the night that had closed over them,
The Traveller, grateful for so sweet a task, 30
Fain would have spellbound fiction's fairest shapes
And sent them captive to pay homage there.
But all in vain: the truth was restless in him,
And shook his visionary fabrics down,
As one who had been buried long ago 35
And now was called up by a necromancer
To answer dreadful questions; so compelled,
He left the way of fiction and wrote thus:
'Woe unto him whose fate hath thwarted him,
Whose life has been 'mongst such as were not born 40
To cherish in his bosom reverence,
And the calm awe that comforteth the heart
And lulls the yearnings of hope unfulfilled:
Such have I been. And woe again to him
Who in too late an hour presumptuously 45
O'erhears a wish confessing to his soul,
And must dismiss it to his discontent
With scorn and laughter. Woe again to me!
For now I hear even such an anxious voice
Crying in my soul's solitude and bewailing 50

That I had never in my childhood known
The bud of this manifold beauteousness,
And seen each leaf turn on its tender hinge
Until the last few parted scarce and held
Deep in their midst a heaven-reflecting gem;   55
For then I might—oh vain and flattering wish!—
I might have stood, tho' last, among the friends
Where I am now the last among the strangers,
And not have passed away as now I must
Into forgetfulness, into the cold   60
Of the open homeless world without a hope,
Unless it be of pardon for these words:
For what is 't to the moon that every drop
Of flower-held rain reflects and gazes on her!
Her destiny is in the starry heavens,   65
Theirs here upon the ground, and she doth set,
Leaving her shadow no more to delight them,
And cometh ne'er again till they are fled.
So is 't with me. Yet to have seen, tho' seldom,
And to have fed me on that beauty's light,   70
And to have been allowed to trace these thoughts,
Are undeserved favours from my fortune.'——

Such was the import of his lines which many
Would have rejected with a scornful smile,
But if she smiled, smiled pity; she was gentle,   75
Read and forgave and never thought again
On the presumptuous stranger and his lines.
Away! I should have told a better tale.
Forgive, and shut these pages up for ever.

Dedicatory Stanzas

Who findeth comfort in the stars and flowers
Apparelling the earth and evening sky,
That moralize throughout their silent hours,
And woo us heaven-wards till we wish to die;
Oft hath he singled from the soothing quire,
For its calm influence, one of softest charm
To still his bosom's pangs, when they desire
A solace for the world's remorseless harm.
Yet they, since to be beautiful and bless
Is but their way of life, will still remain
Cupbearers to the bee in humbleness,
Or look untouched down through the moony rain,
Living and being worlds in bright content,
Ignorant, not in scorn, of his affection's bent.

So thou, whom I have gazed on, seldom seen,
Perchance forgotten to the very name,
Hast in my thoughts the living glory been,
In beauty various, but in grace the same.
At eventide, if planets were above,
Crowning anew the sea of day bereft,
Swayed by the dewy heaviness of love,
My heart felt pleasure in the track thou'dst left:
And so all sights, all musings, pure and fair,
Touching me, raised thy memory to sight,
As the sea-suns awakes the sun in air,—
If they were not reflections, thou the light.
Therefore bend hitherwards, and let thy mildness
Be glassed in fragments through this storm and wild-
　　　ness.

And pardon, if the sick light of despair
Usurp thy semblance oft, with tearful gleam
Displaying haunted shades of tangled care
In my sad scenes: soon shall a pearly beam,

196

Shed from the forehead of my heaven's queen,—
That front thy hand is pressed on,—bring delight.
Nor frown, nor blame me, if, such charms between,
Spring mockery, or thoughts of dreadest night.
Death's darts are sometimes Love's. So Nature tells,
When laughing waters close o'er drowning men;
When in flowers' honied corners poison dwells;
When Beauty dies; and the unwearied ken,
Of those who seek a cure for long despair,
Will learn. Death hath his dimples everywhere;
Love only on the cheek, which is to me most fair.

DEATH'S JEST-BOOK

[Composed 1825–8; revised 1829–49]

DEATH'S JEST BOOK

or The Fool's Tragedy

IN FIVE ACTS

[EARLY VERSION]

—— δημαγωγεῖ
ἐν τοῖς ἄνω νεκροῖσι,   420
κἀστὶν τὰ πρῶτα τῆς ἐκεῖ μοχθηρίας.

*   *   *

Χωρῶμεν ἐς πολυρρόδους
λειμῶνας ἀνθεμώδεις,   450
τὸν ἡμέτερον τρόπον,
τὸν καλλιχορώτατον,
παίζοντες, ὃν ὄλβιαι
Μοῖραι ξυνάγουσιν.

ΜΟΝΟΙΣ ΓΑΡ ʹΗΜΙΝ ʹΗΛΙΟΣ
ΚΑΙ ΦΕΓΓΟΣ ʹΙΛΑΡΟΝ ʹΕΣΤΙΝ
ʹΟΣΟΙ ΜΕΜΥΗΜΕΘʹ.

Χορὸς Μυστων.
Aristoph. Ranae. Ed. Dindorf Lips. 1824–8.

PERSONS REPRESENTED

MELVERIC, *Duke of Münsterberg*
ADALMAR ⎫
ATHULF ⎬ *his Sons*
WOLFRAM, *a Knight* ⎫
ISBRAND, *the Court-fool* ⎬ *Brothers*
TORWALD, *Governor in the Duke's absence*
MARIO
SIEGFRIED
ZIBA
HOMUNCULUS MANDRAKE, *Zany to a Mountebank*
[BOY]

SIBYLLA   AMALA, *Torwald's Daughter*   KATE

Knights, Arabs, Attendants, Musicians, Priests, Sailors, Conspirators, Gravediggers, Pall-bearers, Guards, Messengers, Ladies, attending on Sibylla and on Amala

The Dance of Death

SCENE: *in the first act at Ancona, and afterwards in Egypt; in the latter acts at the town of Grüssau, residence of the Duke of Münsterberg, in Silesia.*

TIME: *the end of the thirteenth century*

202

ACT I

Scene I. *The Seashore. Ancona*

Enter MANDRAKE *and* KATE

Mandr. Am I a man of gingerbread that you should mould me to your liking, or hath my will a man's nose to follow? To have my way, in spite of your tongue and reason's teeth, tastes better than Hungary wine; and my heart beats in a honey-pot 5 now I reject you and all sober sense: so, I prithee, go back to my master, the Doctor, and tell him he may seek another zany for his booth, a new wise merry Andrew. My jests are cracked, my coxcomb fallen, my bauble confiscated, my cap mediatized. Toll the 10 bell; for Jack Pudding is no more!

Kate. Wilt thou away from *me* then, sweet Mandrake? Wilt thou not marry me?

Mandr. Child, my studies must first be ended. Thou knowest I hunger after wisdom, as the red sea 15 after ghosts; therefore will I travel awhile.

Kate. Whither then, dear Mandrake?

Mandr. Whither should a student in the black arts, an adept, a Rosicrucian? Where is our native land? You heard the herald this morning thrice in- 20 vite all christian folk to follow the brave knight, Sir Wolfram, to the shores of Egypt, and there help to free from bondage his noble fellow in arms, Duke Melveric, whom, on a pilgrimage to the Holy Sepulchre, wild pagans captured. There, Kate, in that 25 Sphynx land they made the roads with the philosopher's stone. There be wise crocodiles whose daughters are more cunning than the witches of Lapland, and fairer than the Lotus of the Nile. There can one chat with mummies in a pyramid, 30 and breakfast on basilisk's eggs. Thither then, Homunculus Mandrake, son of the great Paracelsus; languish no more in the ignorance of these climes, but aboard with alembic and crucible, and weigh anchor for Egypt.   35

Enter ISBRAND

Isbr. Good morrow, brother Vanity! How? soul of a pickle-herring, body of a spagirical toss-pot, doublet of motley, and mantle of pilgrim, how art thou transmuted! Wilt thou desert our brotherhood, fool sublimate? Shall the motley chapter no 40 longer boast thee? Wilt thou forswear the order of the bell, and break thy vows to Momus? Have mercy on Wisdom and relent.

Mandr. Have reverence, I pray thee. To-morrow I know thee not. In truth, I mark our noble faculty 45 is in decay. The world will see its ears in a glass no longer; so we are laid aside and shall soon be forgotten; for why should the feast of asses come but once a year, when all the days are foaled of one mother? O world, world! The gods and fairies left 50 thee, for thou wert too wise; and now, thou Socratic star, thy demon, the great Pan, Folly, is parting from thee. The oracles still talked in their sleep, shall our grandchildren say, till Master Merriman's kingdom was broken up: now is every man his own 55 fool, and the world's cheerless.

Isbr. Farewell, thou great-eared mind: I mark, by thy talk, that thou commencest philosopher, and then thou art only a fellow-servant out of livery. But lo! here come the uninitiated—now avaunt, 60 wise spirit, thou hast no portion in me.

Enter TORWALD, AMALA, WOLFRAM, *Knights and Ladies*

Torw. The turning tide; the sea's wide leafless wind,
Wherein no birds inhabit and few traffic,

Making his cave within your sunny sails;
The eager waves, whose golden, silent kisses   65
Seal an alliance with your bubbling oars;
And our still-working wishes, that impress
Their meaning on the conscience of the world,
And prompt the unready Future,—all invite you
Unto your voyage. And prosperous be the issue,   70
As is the promise, and the purpose good!
Are all the rest aboard?
    Wolfr.   All. 'Tis a train
Of knights whose bosoms pant with one desire,
Bold hearts and ardent all; their high resolve
So rocky and embattled in the flood   75
Of their desire: a flaming ghost-walked sea:
That Fate's decrees against us, shod in iron
With sails of dragon's wings, and manned with
          devils,
Would scarce escape a wreck. All hearts are ready.
    Mandr. All, sir Knight; but the pigs are just go-   80
ing aboard, and poor dear great Mandrake must
be shipped too.
    Wolfr. Who is this fellow that interrupts?
    Isbr. One of the many you have made. Yester-
day he was a fellow of my kindred and served a   85
quacksalver, but now he lusts after the mummy
land whither you are bound. 'Tis a servant of the
rosy cross, a correspondent with the stars; the
dead are his friends, and the secrets of the moon
his knowledge. He will brew you a gallon of gold   90
out of a shilling. But had I been cook to a chame-
leon, I could not sweeten the air to his praise
enough. Suffice it, of his wisdom Solomon knew
less than a bee of petrified flowers, or your butcher
of the Mammoth. We fools send him as ambas-   95
sador to Africa; take him with you, or be yourself
our representative.

Wolfr. Speedily aboard then; and sink us not
with thy understanding.

Mandr. I thank thee, Knight. Twice shalt thou 100
live for this if I bottle eternity.   [*Exit with* KATE.

Torw. These letters, then, are the last trust I give
    you:
Of his two sons, whose love and dread ambition,
Crossing like murderous swords, teach us affright;
And of the uncertain people who incline   105
Daily more to the present influence,
Forgetting all that their sense apprehends not;
I have at large discoursed unto the Duke:
And may you find his spirit strong to bear
The roughness of such tidings.   110

Isbr. (*aside*) May they flatten him till he have no
more brain than a pancake.

Amala.   And forget not
Our duke, with gentle greetings, to remind
Of those who have no sword to draw for him,   115
But whose unarmed love is not less true,
Than theirs who seek him helmed. And so fare-
    well,
They say you serve a lady in those lands,
So we dare offer you no token, knight,
Beside good wishes.

Wolfr.   Thanks, and farewell to both; 120
And so I take my leave

    [*Exeunt* AMALA, TORWALD *and Attendants.*

Isbr. Stay: you have not my blessing yet. With
what jest shall I curse you in earnest? Know you
this garb, and him who wears it, and wherefore it
is worn? A father slain and plundered; our frater- 125
nal bond against the assassin shall so end that thou
savest him whom we should help to damn? O do it,
and I shall learn to laugh the dead out of their
coffins!

Wolfr. Hence with your idle taunts. I must
    away.   130
The wind so fair, the sun so bright, the waves
Caress invitingly into their bosom
My fleet ship's keel, that at her anchor bounds
As doth the greyhound from his leader's hand,
Following his eye beams after the light roe.   135

Isbr. Away then, away! Thus be our fair purpose shipwrecked. Unfurl your sails and let all the
honest finny folk of ocean, and those fair witty
fishes, the mermaid spinsters, follow your luckless
boats with mockery: there 's not a blubber but 140
shall wish he had a voice to yell parricide in your
sails, not a sea-dog but shall howl and hunt you
down after his salt-water fashion when he knows
your errand. What, O! what spirit of our ancestral
enemies would dare to whisper this tale through 145
our father's bones? Thou wilt save him from the
Saracens' chains, who robbed our sire's grey hairs
of a crown, and trod him down a beggar to the
sceptred corpses of our progenitors? Save *him*,
who slew our hopes; bless him who cozened us of 150
our part of this sepulchral planet? Revenge,
Revenge! lend me your torch, that I may by its
bloody light spell the lines of this man's face, and
note how pitiful an ass the philtres of charity and
friendship have made of my poor brother.   155

Wolfr. Should we repent this change? I know
    not why.—
We came disguised into the court, stiff limbed
With desperate intent, and doubly souled
With murder's devil and our own still ghosts.
But must I not relent, finding the heart,   160
For which my dagger hungered, so inclined
In brotherly affection unto me?
O bless the womanish weakness of my soul,
Which came to slay, and leads me now to save!

Isbr. Hate! Hate! Revenge and blood! These are 165
the only words of any language I will teach my
boys. What accursed poison has that Duke, that
snake, with his tongue, his sting, dropped into
thine ear? Thou art no brother of mine more: he
was a fellow whose soul was of that tune which 170
shall awake the dead; aye if you had played it on a
sow-gelder's horn: for thine! if I should make a
trumpet of the devil's antlers, and blow thee
through it, my lady's poodle would be scarce
moved to a hornpipe. O fie on 't! Say when hast 175
thou undergone transfusion, and whose hostile
blood now turns thy life's wheels? Who has poured
Lethe into thy veins to wash thy father out of heart
and brains? Ha! be pale, and smile, and be pro-
digal of thy body's motions, for thou hast no soul 180
more. *That* thy sire placed in thee; and, with the
determination to avenge, thou hast turned it out of
doors. But 'tis well: why lament? Now I have all
the hatred and revenge of the world to myself to
hate and murder him with. 185

Wolfr. Thou speak'st unjustly, what thou rashly
think'st;
But time must soften and convince: now leave me,
If thou hast nothing but reproach for pastime.

Isbr. Be angry then, and we will curse each
other. But if thou goest now to save this man, 190
come not again for fear of me and the paternal
ghost: for when he comes to me in the night, and
cries revenge! my heart forgets that my head hath
a fool's cap on it, and dreams of daggers: come not
again then! 195

Wolfr. Out of my path! In this despised garb
Alone, durst thou have tempted thus my anger,
Dishonour'd brother! While I am away,
Meditate o'er thy servile state, thou groom,
Crown'd and anointed priest of mockery: 200

And mend thee if thou canst.—I am for Egypt [*Exit.*
  Isbr. Contempt then be thy shadow in the day
And point at thee and call thee parricide!
But I will turn my bosom now to thee,
Brutus, thou saint of the avenger's order;   205
Refresh me with thy spirit, or pour in
Thy whole great ghost. Isbrand, thou tragic fool,
Cheer up! Art thou alone? Why, so should be
Creators and destroyers. I'll go brood
And strain my burning and distracted soul   210
Against the naked spirit of the world,
Till some portent 's begotten.   [*Exit.*

SCENE II. *The African Coast: a woody solitude near the
  sea. In the back ground ruins overshadowed by the
  characteristic vegetation of the oriental regions*

  The DUKE *and* SIBYLLA; *the latter sleeping in a tent*

  Duke. Soft sleep enwrap thee: with his balm bedew
Thy young fair limbs, Sibylla: thou didst need
The downy folding of his arms about thee.
And wake not yet, for still the starless night
Of our misfortune holds its hopeless noon.   5
No serpent shall creep o'er the sand to sting thee,
No blossom-trampling lion, no sea-creature,
(For such are now the partners of thy chamber,)
Disturb thy rest: only the birds shall dare
To shake the dewy blossoms that hang o'er thee,   10
And fan thee with their wings. As I watch for thee,
So may the power, that has so far preserved us,
Now in the uttermost, now that I feel
The cold drops on my forehead, and scarce know
Whether Fear shed them there, or the near breath   15
Of our pursuing foes has settled on it,
Stretch its shield o'er us.

Enter ZIBA

               What bring'st, Ziba? Hope?
Else be as dumb as that thou bring'st, Despair.

Ziba. Fruits: as I sat among the boughs and robbed
The sparrows and their brothers of their bread,   20
A horde of armed Saracens rode by,
Each swearing that thy sword should rest ere night
Within his sheath, his weapon in thy breast.

Duke. Speak lower, Ziba, lest the lady wake.
Perhaps she sleeps not, but with half-shut eyes   25
Will hear her fate. The slaves shall need to wash
My sword of Moslem blood before they sheath it.
Which path took they?

Ziba.   Sleeping, or feigning sleep,
She doth well: 'tis trying on a garb
Which she must wear, sooner or later, long: 30
'Tis but a warmer lighter death. The ruffians,
Of whom I spoke, turned towards the cedar forest,
And, as they went in, there rushed forth a lion
And tore their captain down. Long live the lion!
We'll drink his tawny health: he gave us wine.   35
For, while the Moors in their black fear were flying,
I crept up to the fallen wretch, and borrowed
His flask of rubious liquor. May the prophet
Forgive him, as I do, for carrying it!
This for to-day: to-morrow hath gods too,   40
Who'll ripen us fresh berries, and uncage
Another lion on another foe.

Duke. Brave Arab, thanks. But saw'st thou from the
    heights
No christian galley steering for this coast?

Ziba. I looked abroad upon the wide old world,   45
And in the sky and sea, through the same clouds,
The same stars saw I glistening, and nought else.
And as my soul sighed unto the world's soul,
Far in the north a wind blackened the waters,

210

And after that creating breath was still,   50
A dark speck sat on the sky's edge: as watching
Upon the heaven-girt border of my mind
The first faint thought of a great deed arise,
With force and fascination I drew on
The wished sight, and my hope seemed to stamp   55
Its shape upon it. Not yet is it clear
What, or from whom, the vessel.

Duke.   Who so e'er
The ocean wanderers, Heaven give them welcome:
There 's nothing we can fear. Who dare refuse us
Protection from the savage Moslem's rage?   60
But see, the lady stirs. Once more look out,
And thy next news be safety.   [*Exit* ZIBA.
                              Hast thou gathered
Rest and refreshment from thy desart couch,
My fair Sibylla?

Sibyl.   Deeply have I slept.
As one who doth go down unto the springs   65
Of his existence and there bathed, I come
Regenerate up into the world again.
Kindest protector, 'tis to thee I owe
This boon, a greater than my parents gave.
Me, who had never seen this earth, this heaven,   70
The sun, the stars, the flowers, but shut from nature
Within my dungeon birthplace lived in darkness,
Me hast thou freed from the oppressor's power,
And godlike given me this heaven, this earth,
The flowers, the stars, the sun. Methinks it were   75
Ingratitude to thank thee for a gift
So measurelessly great.

Duke.   As yet, sweet lady,
I have deserved but little thanks of thine.
We've not yet broken prison. This wall of waves
Still lies between us and the world of men;   80
That too I hope to climb. Our true Egyptian
Hath brought me news of an approaching ship.

When that hath borne thee to our German shore,
And thou amongst the living tastest life,
And gallants shall have shed around thy beauties   85
A glory of the starry looks of love,
For thee to move in, thank me then.
 Sibyl.   I wish not
To leave this shady quiet way of life.
Why should we seek cruel mankind again?
Nature is kinder far: and every thing   90
That lives around us, with its pious silence,
Gives me delight: the insects, and the birds
That come unto our table, seeking food,
The flowers, upon whose petals Night tells down   94
Her tremulous dews, these are my dearest playmates.
O let us never leave them.
 Duke.   That would be
To rob thy fate of thee. In other countries
Another godliker mankind doth dwell,
Whose works each day adorn and deify
The world their fathers left them. Thither shalt thou,
For among them must be the one thou'rt born for.   101
Durst thou be such a traitress to thy beauty
As to live here unloving and unloved?
 Sibyl. Love I not thee? O, if I feel beside thee
Delight and an unruffled calm, in which   105
My soul doth gather round thee, to reflect
Thy heavenly goodness: if in thy society
I am so full of comfort, that no room
For any other wish, no doubt, remains;
Love I not thee?
 Duke.   Dear maiden, thou art young.   110
Thou must see many, and compare their merits
Ere thou canst choose. Esteem and quiet friendship
Oft bear Love's semblance for awhile.
 Sibyl.   I know it;
Thou shalt hear how. A year and more is past
Since a brave Saxon knight did share my prison;   115

A noble generous man, in whose discourse
I found much pleasure: yet, when he was near me,
There ever was a pain which I perceived
Even in the very sweetness of my comfort:
My heart was never still: and many times,   120
When he had fetched me flowers, I trembled so
That oft they fell as I was taking them
Out of his hand. When I would speak to him
I heard not, and I knew not what I said.
Yet this I thought was Love. O self deceived!   125
For now I can speak all I think to thee
With confidence and ease. What else can that be
Except true love?
    Duke.   The like I bear to thee,
O more than all that thou hast promised me:
For if another being stepped between us,   130
And were he my best friend, I must forget
All vows, and cut his heart away from mine.
    Sibyl. Think not on that: it is impossible.

Enter ZIBA

    Ziba. O my dear lord, we're saved!
    Duke.   How? Speak!
Though every word hath now no meaning more,   135
Since thou hast said 'she 's saved'.
    Ziba. The ship is in the bay, an armed knight
Steps from his boat upon the shore.
    Duke.   Blest hour!
And yet how palely, with what faded lips
Do we salute this unhoped change of fortune!   140
Thou art so silent, lady; and I utter
Shadows of words, like to an ancient ghost,
Arisen out of hoary centuries
Where none can speak his language. I had thought
That I should laugh, and shout, and leap on high: 145
But see! this breath of joy hath damped my soul,
Melted the icy mail, with which despair

Had propp'd my heart, unsealed the springs of weak-
    ness:
And O! how weary, sad and faint I go
To welcome what I prayed for. Thou art quiet;   150
How art thou then, my love?
    Sibyl.   Now Hope and Fear
Stand by me, masked in one another's shapes;
I know not which is which, and, if I did,
I doubt which I should choose.

Enter WOLFRAM *and Knights*

    Wolfr.   Are these thy comrades?
Then, Arab, thy life's work and mine is done.   155
My duke, my fellow knight!
    Duke.   O friend! So call me!
Wolfram, thou comest to us like a god,
Giving life where thou touchest with thy hand.
    Wolfr. Were it mine own, I'd break it here in twain,
And give you each a half.
    Duke.   I will not thank thee,   160
I will not welcome thee, embrace and bless thee;
Nor will I weep in silence. Gratitude,
Friendship, and Joy are beggar'd, and turned forth
Out of my heart for silly hypocrites:
They understand me not; and my soul, dazzled,   165
Stares on the unknown feelings that now crowd it,
Knows none of them, remembers none, counts none,
More than a new-born child in its first hour.
One word, and then we'll speak of this no more:
At parting each of us did tear a leaf   170
Out of a magic roll, and, robbing life
Of the red juice with which she feeds our limbs,
We wrote a mutual bond. Thou dost remember?
    Wolfr. And if a promise binds beyond the grave
My ghost shall not forget it. There I swore   175
That, if I died before thee, I would come

With the first weed that shoots out of my grave,
And bring thee tidings of our other home.

   Duke. That bond hast thou now fulfilled thus; or
rather   180
Unto me lying in my sepulchre
Comest thou, and say'st, 'Arise and live again'.

   Wolfr. And with thee dost thou bring some angel
back.
Look on me, lady.

   Sibyl. (aside)   Pray heaven, she be not
The angel of the death of one of you,
To make the grave and the flowers' roots amends.—
Now turn I to thee, knight. O dared I hope,   186
Thou hast forgotten me!

   Wolfr.   Then were I dead,
And stripped of the human spirit's inheritance,
The immortality, of which thy love
Gave me the first sure proof. Forgotten thee!   190
Aye; if thou be not she, with whom I shared
Few months ago that dungeon, which thy presence
Lit with delight unknown to liberty;
If thou be not Sibylla, she whose semblance
Here keepeth watch upon my heart. Behold it: 195
Morning and night my eyes do feed upon it.
Thou gavest it me one day, when I admired,
And coveted above all stars a dewdrop,
That in the joyous dimple of a flower
Imaged thee tremulously. Since that time   200
Many a secret tear hath done the same,
Which I have shed over this pictured beauty.—
Speak to me then: or art thou, as this toy,
Only the likeness of the maid I loved?
But there 's no seeming such a one. O come!   205
This talking is a pitiful invention:
We'll leave it to the wretched. All my science,
My memory, I'd give for thy sole love,
And keep that ever secret.

Sibyl.   Thou dost move me.   209
With ghost-compelling words thou draw'st me to thee:
O! at thy call I must surrender me,
My lord, my love, my life.
    Duke. (aside)   O souls that dwell
In these three bosoms, keep your footings fast,
For there's a blasting thought stirring among you.
They love each other. Silence! Let them love;   215
And let him be her love. She is a flower,
Growing upon a grave.—Now, gentle lady,
Retire, beseech you, to the tent and rest.
My friend and I have need to use those words
Which are bequeathed unto the miserable.   220
Come hither; you have made me free of them:
Who dare be wretched in the world beside me?
Think now what you have done; and tremble at it.
But I forgive thee, love. Go in and rest thee.
    Sibyl. And he?
    Duke.   Is he not mine?
    Wolfr.   Go in, sweet, fearlessly.   225
I come to thee, before thou 'st time to feel
That I am absent.

         [*Exeunt* SIBYLLA, ZIBA, *and the Knights.*
    Duke. Wolfram, we have been friends.
    Wolfr.   And will be ever.
I know no other way to live.
    Duke.   'Tis pity.
I would you had been one day more at sea.
    Wolfr.   Why so?   230
    Duke. You're troublesome to-day. Have you not
    marked it?
    Wolfr. Alas! that you should say so.
    Duke.   That's all needless.
Those times are past, forgotten. Hear me, knight:
That lady's love is mine. Now you know that,
Do what you dare.
    Wolfr.   The lady! my Sibylla!   235

Oh that I did not love thee for those words,
That I might answer well.

   Duke.   Unless thou yield'st her,—
For thou hast even subdued her to thy arms,
Against her will and reason, wickedly
Torturing her soul with spells and adjurations,— 240
Unless thou giv'st her the free will again
To take her gentle course of being on,
Which flowed towards me with steady love:—O Wol-
    fram,
Thou know'st not how she fed my soul so doing,
Even as the streams an ocean:—Give her me, 245
And we are friends again. But I forget:
Thou lovest her too; a stern, resolved rival;
And passionate, I know. Nay then, speak out:
'Twere better if we argued warmly here,
Till the blood has its way.

   Wolfr.   Unworthy friend! 250
   Duke. Forget that I am so, and many things
Which we've been to each other, and speak out.
I would we had much wine; 'twould bring us sooner
To the right point.

   Wolfr.   Can it be so? O Melveric!
I thought thou wert the very one of all 255
Who shouldst have heard my secret with delight.
I thought thou wert my friend.

   Duke.   All things like these,
Friendship, esteem, sympathy, hope, faith,
We need no more: away with them for ever!
Wilt follow them out of the world? Thou see'st 260
All human things die and decay around us.
'Tis the last day for us; and we stand naked
To let our cause be tried. See'st thou not why?
We love one creature: which of us shall tear her
Out of his soul? I have in all the world 265
Little to comfort me, few that do name me
With titles of affection, and but one

Who came into my soul at its night-time,
As it hung glistening with starry thoughts
Alone over its still eternity,   270
And gave it godhead. Thou art younger far,
More fit to be beloved; when thou appearest
All hearts incline to thee, all prouder spirits
Are troubled unto tears and yearn to love thee.
O, if thou knew'st thy heart-compelling power,   275
Thou wouldst not envy me the only creature
Who holds me dear. If I were such as thou,
I would not be forgetful of our friendship,
But yield to the abandoned his one joy.

    Wolfr. Thou prob'st me to the quick.

                      O, would to heaven,   280
That I had found thee somewhere in a battle,
Alone against the swords of twenty foes!
Then I had rescued thee, and died content,
Ignorant of the treasure I had saved thee.
But now my fate hath made a wisher of me: 285
Oh shame that it is so; and better were it
If she had never been, who is the cause!

    Duke. He is the cause! Oh fall the curse on him,
And may he be no more, who dares the gods
With such a wish! Speak thou no more of love,   290
No more of friendship here: the world is open:
I wish you life and merriment enough
From wealth and wine, and all the dingy glory
Fame doth reward those with, whose love-spurned
    hearts
Hunger for goblin immortality.   295
Live long, grow old, and honour crown thy hairs,
When they are pale and frosty as thy heart.
Away. I have no better blessing for thee.
Wilt thou not leave me?

    Wolfr.   Should I leave thee thus?

    Duke. Why not? Or, 'cause I hate thee perfectly,   300
Must I then tell thee so? Away I pray thee.

Have I not cut all ties betwixt us off?
Why, wert thou my own soul, I'd drive thee from me.
Go, put to sea again.
   Wolfr.   Farewell, then, Duke.
Methinks thy better self indeed hath left thee,   305
And so I follow.   [*Exit.*
   Duke.   Thither? Thither? Traitor
To every virtue. Then Amen is said
Unto thy time of being in this world:
Thou shalt die. Ha! the very word doth double
My strength of life: the resolution leaps   310
Into my heart divinely, as doth Mars
Upon the trembling footboard of his car;
Hurrying into battle wild and panting,
Even as my death-dispensing thought does now.
Ho! Ziba!

Enter ZIBA

            Hush! How still, how full how lightly   315
I move about the place since this resolve,
Like to a murder-charged thunder cloud
Stepping about the starry streets of night,
Breathless and masked,
O'er a still city sleeping by the sea.   320
Ziba, come hither; thou'rt the night I'll hang
My muffled wrath in. Come, I'll give thee business
Shall make thy life still darker, for one light on 't
Must be put out. O let me joy no more,
Till Fate hath kissed my wooing soul's desire   325
Off her death-honied lips, and so set seal
To my decree, in which he 's sepulchred.
Come, Ziba, thou must be my counsellor.   [*Exeunt.*

SCENE III. *The Interior of a tent*

SIBYLLA, WOLFRAM

Wolfr. This is the oft-wished hour, when we together
May walk upon the sea-shore: let us seek
Some greensward overshadowed by the rocks.
Wilt thou come forth? Even now the sun is setting
In the triumphant splendour of the waves.   5
Hear you not how they leap?
    Sibyl.   Nay; we will watch
The sun go down upon a better day:
Look not on him this evening.
    Wolfr.   Then let 's wander
Under the mountain's shade in the deep valley,
And mock the woody echoes with our songs.   10
    Sibyl. That wood is dark, and all the mountain caves
Dreadful and black, and full of howling winds:
Thither we will not wander.
    Wolfr.   Shall we seek
The green and golden meadows, and there pluck   14
Flowers for thy couch, and shake the dew out of them?
    Sibyl. The snake that loves the twilight is come out,
Beautiful, still, and deadly; and the blossoms
Have shed their fairest petals in the storm
Last night; the meadow's full of fear and danger.
    Wolfr. Ah! you will to the rocky fount, and there 20
We'll see the fireflies dancing in the breeze,
And the stars trembling in the trembling water,
And listen to the daring nightingale
Defying the old night with harmony.
    Sibyl. Nor that: but we will rather here remain,   25
And earnestly converse. What said the Duke?
Surely no good.
    Wolfr.   A few unmeaning words,
I have almost forgotten.
    Sibyl.   Tell me truly,
Else I may fear much worse.

Wolfr.   Well: it may be
That he was somewhat angry. 'Tis no matter;   30
He must soon cool and be content.

Enter ZIBA

Ziba.   Hail, knight!
I bring to thee the draught of welcome. Taste it.
The Grecian sun ripened it in the grape,
Which Grecian maidens plucked, and pressed; then
          came
The desert Arab to the palace gate,   35
And took it for his tribute. It is charmed;
And they who drink of such have magic dreams.
     Wolfr. Thanks for thy care. I'll taste it presently:
Right honey for such bees as I.

Enter a Knight

Knight.   Up, brave knight!
Arouse thee, and come forth to help and save.   40
     Wolfr. Here is my sword. Who needs it?
     Sibyl.   Is 't the Duke?
O my dark Fear!
     Knight.   'Tis he. In the wood hunting,
A band of robbers rushed on us.
     Wolfr.   How many?
     Knight. Some twelve to five of us; and in the fight
Which now is at the hottest, my sword failed me.   45
Up then in speed, good Knight: I'll lead the way.
     Wolfr. Sibylla, what deserves he at our hands?
     Sibyl. Assist him; he preserved me.
     Wolfr.   For what end?
     Sibyl. Death's sickle points thy questions. Hesitate
          not,
But hence.

Enter a second Knight

     Wolfr.   Behold another from the field—   50
221

Now thy news?

2nd Knight.　　My fellow soldiers
Bleed and grow faint: fresh robbers pour upon us,
And the Duke stands at bay unhelmed against them.

　　Wolfr. Brave comrade, keep the rogues before thee,
　　　　dancing
At thy sword's point, but a few moments longer;　　55
Then I am with thee. Farewell thou, Sibylla;
He shall not perish thus. Rise up, my men,
To horse with sword and spear, and follow me.
Where is the cup? One draught and then away:
I pledge thee, lady.　　　　　　　*[Takes the goblet.*

　　Ziba. (dashes it to the ground) Out, thou villainous
　　　　liquor!　　　　　　　　　　　　　　60
Ha! it rings well and lies not. 'Tis right metal
For funeral bells.

　　Wolfr.　　　　Rogue, what dost thou?

　　Ziba. Pour thou unto the subterraneous gods
Libations of thy blood: I have shed wine,
Now, will ye not away?

　　Wolfr.　　　　Come hither, slave:　　65
Say, on your life, why did you spill that wine?

　　Ziba. A superstitious fancy: but now hence.
'Twas costly liquor too.

　　Wolfr.　　　　Then finish it.
'Twas well that fortune did reserve for you
These last and thickest drops here at the bottom.　　70

　　Ziba. Drink them? forbid the prophet!

　　Wolfr.　　　　　　Slave, thou diest else.

　　Ziba. Give me the beaker then.—O God, I dare not.
Death is too bitter so: alas! 'tis poisoned.

　　Sibyl. Pernicious caitiff!

　　Wolfr.　　　　Patience, my Sibylla!
I knew it by thy lying eye. Thou'rt pardoned.　　75
But for thy lord, the Saracen deal with him
As he thinks fit. Wolfram can help no murderer.

Sibyl. Mercy! O let me not cry out in vain:
Forgive him yet.

Wolfr.   The crime I have forgiven:
And Heaven, if he 's forgiven there, can save him! 80
O monster! in the moment when my heart
Turned back to him with the old love again,
Then was I marked for slaughter by his hand.
I can forgive him; but no more:—lie still
Thou sworded hand, and thou be steely, heart.   85

Enter a third Knight wounded

3rd Knight. Woe! woe! Duke Melveric is the Arabs'
    captive.

Sibyl. Then Heaven have mercy on him!

Wolfr.   So 'tis best:
He was his passion's prisoner already.

3rd Knight. They bind him to a column in the desert,
And aim their poisoned arrows at his heart.   90

Wolfr. O Melveric, why didst thou so to me?
Sibylla, I despise this savage Duke,
But thus he shall not die. No man in bonds
Can be my enemy. He once was noble:
Up once again, my men, and follow me.   95
I bring him to thee, love, or ne'er return.

Sibyl. A thousand tearful thanks for this. Farewell.
                    [*Exeunt severally.*

SCENE IV. *A Wood*

MANDRAKE *and his boy*

Mandrake. The roots, the toadstools. That 's
right, and the herbs. Now, where be the bones and
the minerals?

Boy. In the other basket. Art thou in good faith,
a witch?   5

Mandr. A poor amateur. 'Tis my hobby. A

philtre, a nativity, the raising up of a paltry devil or
so. I do no more. Mere retail conjuring.

Boy. But what dish will thy black art stew of these
simples?   10

Mandr. With a pound of crocodile's fat we will
concoct a salve, an ointment. Thou hast heard of
being invisible.

Boy. Aye, and now shall I see it? O lend me thy
spectacles.   15

Mandr. This is the secret: it shall be had in bottles
and to prevent imposition all sealed with the ring of
Gyges.

Boy. How shall I believe such things?

Mandr. Doubt at thy peril, boy. This, I tell thee,   20
will make the true ointment. 'Tis no great rarity.
Look for a true friend, a wit who ne'er borrowed
money or stole verses, a woman without envy; there
are legions of such, but they have anointed their
virtues with this pomatum till they disappeared.   25

Boy. Then will I rub my warts with it. But whence
have you the receit?

Mandr. Out of an ancient island where invisible
honest men trade with invisible money. 'Tis made
according to the law of contraries, but serves best 30
against foibles at Court, and there be horned beasts
which use it with great comfort.

Boy. And wilt thou make thyself invisible?

Mandr. Out, out! Who would ever lose sight of
himself? 'Tis scarce possible nowadays. Alas! 'tis a 35
dangerous and wicked butter, and hath so worked
upon priests' humanity, great men's wisdom, and
poet's immortality, that when death hath anointed
us with it, Posterity shall hold all these things for
fables. But away, our business is secret. Hear you 40
no noise? Here come disturbers.   [*Exeunt.*

Enter Arabs with the DUKE

1st Arab. Against this column: there 's an ancient
    beast
Here in the neighbourhood, which to-night will
    thank us
For the ready meal.

           [*They bind the* DUKE *against a column.*
    2nd Arab.   Christian, in thy heaven
Boast that we took thy blood in recompense   45
Of our best comrades.
    1st Arab.   Hast a saint or mistress?
Call on them, for next minute comes the arrow.
    Duke. O Wolfram! now methinks thou lift'st the
    cup.
Strike quickly, Arab.
    1st Arab.   Brothers, aim at him.

       Enter WOLFRAM *and knights*

    Wolfr. Down, murderers, down.
    2nd Arab.   Fly! there are hundreds on us. 50
    Wolfr. Die, ye slaves!
        [*Fight—the Arabs are part slain, part beaten
          off by the knights, who pursue the flying.*
    Wolfr. (*unbinding the* DUKE) Thank heaven, not too
    late! Now you are free.
There is your life again.
    Duke.   Hast thou drunk wine?
Answer me, knight, hast thou drunk wine this even-
    ing?   54
    Wolfr. Nor wine, nor poison. The slave told me all.
O Melveric, if I deserve it of thee,
Now canst thou mix another draught. But all
Be now forgotten and unknown to Heaven.
    Duke. And wilt thou not now kill me?
    Wolfr.   Let us strive
Henceforward with good deeds against each other, 60
We once were friends and may be so again;
No one shall whisper of that deadly thought.

Now we will leave this coast.

Duke.   Aye, we will step
Into a boat and steer away: but whither?
Think'st thou I'll live in the dread consciousness   65
That I have dealt so wickedly and basely,
And been of thee so like a god forgiven?
No: 'tis impossible. . . . By your leave, friend—

> [*Takes a sword from a fallen Arab.*

O what a coward villain must I be
So to exist.

Wolfr.   Be patient but awhile.   70
And all these thoughts will soften.

Duke.   The grave be patient,
That 's yawning in the wood for one of us.
I want no comfort. I am comfortable,
For one of us must perish in this instant.
Fool, would thy virtue shame and crush me down;   75
And make a grateful blushing bond-slave of me?
O no! I dare be wicked still: and murderer
My thought has christened me, such I must remain.
O curse thy meek, forgiving, childish heart,
Which doth insult me with its cowardly virtue;   80
Twice-sentenced, die!   [*Strikes at* WOLFRAM.

Wolfr.   Madman, keep off.

Duke. I pay my thanks in steel.

> [*Fight:* WOLFRAM *falls.*

Wolfr. Murderer! Mayst thou never more repent—
Duke. So then we both are blasted: but thou diest,
Who durst forgive my treachery. Now proclaim me.   85
Thy worldly work is done. I give thee leave.

The Knights re-enter with SIBYLLA *and* ZIBA

Knight. O luckless victory! our leader wounded!
Sibylla. Bleeding to death! and he, whom he so
      saved,
Armed and unhurt. O Wolfram, speak to me.
Let me not think thou'rt dying.

226

Wolfr.   But I am: 90
Slain villainously. Sibylla, had I stayed—
But thou and life are lost; so I'll be silent.

Sibylla. O Melveric why kneelst thou not beside him
And weepst with me? He saved thee.

Duke.   And I've thanked him.
He'll not deny it.

Sibylla.   O that I could avenge thee!   95
Who did this, Wolfram?

Wolfr.   Thou knowest, Melveric;
At the last day reply thou to that question,
When such an Angel puts it: I'll not answer
Or then, or now.   [*Dies.*

Duke.   Then the tale is out.
He 's dead. Oh heaven, what a word for me!   100

Knight. Accursed be he that did it.

Duke   He is cursed,
And from this moment shut up in a hell
Far from all earthly things.

Sibylla.   He is dead then;
Then all is dead. Speak to me never more
A word of love, pleasure or happiness.   105
My world lies with him.

Knight.   All that liveth here,
Kneel down beside the body of this knight,
And swear revenge against his murderer.

Duke. With all my heart. Methinks I'm of the dead,
And yet 'tis right so. Pray all in silence.   110

(*They kneel. The curtain falls*)

ACT II

Scene I. *A room in a tavern in Ancona*

ISBRAND *and other Guests drinking*, KATE *waiting on them*

Isbr. Another flask, Kate. Thou knowest how fishy I am in my liquid delights. Dryness is akin to barrenness, and of barrenness comes nakedness and bareness, and these are melancholy, being the parables of human extremity, and of the uttermost 5 of death and a pig's tail: therefore, good Kate, 'tis the duty of a wise man to thirst and the part of a good woman to wet his lips.

Kate. Master Isbrand, the wine is sweet, but a sweet seducer. You have had three flasks, and 10 there is morality in all trades.

Isbr. You say true—I had forgot. There have you the morality. (*Gives her money*) Will you have history for it? Then think of that great King in Lydia, Croesus, whom they would have set on fire, 15 but the lucky dog had seen the sun through the bottom of too many glasses, so he was too wet and went out. Will you have divinity for it? There's Bacchus, in his time a clever travelling God and an arch-Tosspot. Wilt have law? Behold my 20 Cudgel. Poetry? Then bring the fourth bottle.

Kate. 'Tis true you are not what you might be, but withal, a wellspoken customer, and the action of your right hand is too irresistible for us poor weak ones, so there's your new flask. 25

Isbr. Gramercy, Hostess. This is the mystery of humanity, drank I not wine I were a tailor tomorrow; next day a dog, and in a week I should have less life than a witch's broomstick. Drinking hath been my education and my path of life. Small 30 beer was my toothless infancy, the days of my

childhood I passed in stout, porter comforted my
years of Love, but my beard growing I took to
sack, and now I quench the aspiration of my soul
in these good wines of Hungary. And for these my 35
merits, I hold my place at Court.—Now your
health, mistress, and your lover's, my late col-
league. Where is he now?

Kate. The silly fellow! He would go to sea with
Sir Wolfram, and of that ship we have heard 40
nothing as yet.

A Guest. A sail has been seen this morning, and
he who keeps the tower said that it was the
Knight's vessel.

Isbr. How? Then she must be in port ere this: 45
first down with the wine, then down to the water.

Enter Sailors and HOMUNCULUS
MANDRAKE'S *Boy*

1st Sailor. Now we're in Christendom, my lads,
we'll get drunk once more. A curse on their
watery superstition! those Turkish dogs do but
lap the Nile. Now who would drink water that's 50
made only to be sailed on?

2nd Sailor. Therefore wine, hostess, ale and
brandy. My legs hate walking on this stupid dead
earth. I'm born to roll through life, and if the
world won't under me tumble and toss, why, I 55
must e'en suck up a sort of marine motion out of
the can.

Isbr. Good morrow, lusty comrades. Are you
just come in?

1st Sailor. Aye, at last the winds have brought 60
our good ship, the Baris,* ashore.

Isbr. The Baris that sailed in the Spring for
Ægypt? What do you bring with you?

---

* The name of Charon's boat according to Orpheus, Diod.
Sic. I. 96.

1st Sailor. A rare cargo. We have on board one
whose body is invisible, another whose soul is in 65
heaven's keeping, and a third, poor lady, whose
life and love are shipwrecked.

Isbr. Now first, your dead. They are my best
acquaintance and my dearest gossips: your departed, who is he?   70

Boy. O mistress, let me speak, else the invisible
man will be here before you know that you are not
able to see him.

Kate. O 'tis my Mandrake's boy. Now say who
has the world lost sight of and where is thy master? 75

Boy. It is even he I would tell of: in Ægypt
we plundered ichneumons of their marrow, and
knocked the yolks out of crocodile's eggs, with
which, and all manner of mummy, he made a
liniment of invisibility, and with it he swore he 80
could anoint men out of sight.

Isbr. Praised be the secrets of alchemy that can
thus embody that subtlety which shall subdue the
flesh and all its wickedness in an ounce of hog's
lard. But is not this ointment called the fat of the 85
land, with which those who are smeared do hide
the hideousness of their souls so often? But go on,
boy, I am but a commentator on this world: to the
text again.

Boy. Now Mandrake had churned his bewitch- 90
ing butter, potted it, and all was well: but last
night in the storm, the waves rolled, and the ship
rolled in them, and in the middle of dreams, fell
the pot of balsam on the man's scull who made it,
broke it to pieces, and bathed him from head to 95
foot, and so ran he about dripping with the oil of
invisibility and tears for his lost body—but here
he comes: see him not.

Kate. Now will we teach thee to leave a poor

woman who loves thee to temptation and the earn- 100
ing of her bread, thou rosicrucian fellow!

Enter MANDRAKE

Isbr. Agreed! A game at blind man's buff.
Therefore, friends, weep no more for he is gone.

Mandrake. I daresay that's my funeral sermon;
—does he praise me poor dear man?—and there's 105
Kate, she weeps buckets I warrant ye.

Isbr. But weep not so, sweet Kate; 'tis true you
have lost a peerless simpleton: such flawless folly
is a rich jewel in the ring of wedlock: but add no
vain tears to the waves which roll over him. 110

Mandrake. Sweetheart Kate, and friends all: I
am not dead nor gone, where are your eyes? I am
here.

Kate. O mercy! there is haunting here; did you
not hear his voice? 115

Boy. Aye, so spake Master, but he is departed,
and here is no one.

Mandrake. Good folks don't pretend any more
that you don't see me. O Lord, I am half frightened already into the belief that I am vanished. 120
Reasonable folks! I stand here in the corner, by
the rack of plates.

Kate. There again! This is impudent haunting in
the daytime in a reputable house. Run and fetch
Holy Water. Alas! that my poor husband's ghost 125
should not know that he is dead! but he was ever
absent.

Isbr. Nay, don't be frightened, hostess: 'tis a jest
of mine; I have ventriloquized a little and mocked
your dear fellow's voice. Now mark you I do it 130
again and abuse you as if I were a ghost against my
will.

Mandrake. But Isbrand, and gentle people, can't
you see me really, not a twinkling of me? Nor my

231

face in the pewter plates? Ah, then I must be lost. 135
But I will be seen soon and heard and felt, rogues
and hypocrites, and you shall weep for it—or I am
not Mandrake.

Isbr. Is it not natural, comrades?

Kate. Very good, but leave it, I pray you, or I 140
shall think I hear him, which is impossible, and
fall a-crying which were a waste of tears here
where there are so few to see me, and no white
kerchief to hold my tears.

Isbr. Then I will please thee, and be no more a 145
skeleton's prompter; but good mimic as I am you
shall hear a better some night, if you live after the
fashion of this world; he is called conscience and
doth prattle with the voices of the dead through
the speaking trumpet of the winds. Beware of him. 150

Mandrake. Well, let me be viewless then, I am
still palpable, so let me cut arguments from the
ash-tree, and convince the incredulous by the aching of their shoulders that they are short-sighted.

                    [*Strikes among the others.*

Sailor. Help! help! the house is falling in.   155

Kate. Does it hail? or can you ventriloquize a
cudgelling, acquaintance?

Boy. Murder, murder! here is the ghost of a
game at single-stick, methinks I begin to see.

Isbr. Be patient: 'tis only electricity.—Knock 160
again.

                    [*They fall on* MANDRAKE

Confess, thou invisible one, is it possible for
Christian eye to see thee?

Kate. (*striking him*) Art thou material, villain-
spectre? Wilt thou not let us mourn for my poor 165
bridegroom, undisturbed?

Boy. If thou wilt have a voice, take this o' thy
chaps.

Mandrake. O gentle people! I confess. I will be
invisible if you will leave off seeing where to put 170
your blows in;—immaterial to keep my bones
whole, and inaudible if you will hear my petition.
I am no Mandrake, I am nothing.

Isbr. Nay, then thou hast gotten no blows, and
that were pity: see, I strike no longer thee—I strike 175
nothing.

Mandrake. Enough! I am a poor invisible man,
and will leave off haunting—But tremble, if I ever
come to sight again.

[*Runs out, the rest after him.*

SCENE II. *The interior of a church at Ancona.
The* DUKE, *in the garb of a pilgrim,* SIBYLLA *and
Knights, assembled round the corpse of Wol-
fram which is lying on a bier.*

Dirge

> If thou wilt ease thine heart
> Of love and all its smart,
> > Then sleep, dear, sleep;
> And not a sorrow
> > Hang any tear on your eyelashes;   5
> > > Lie still and deep,
> > Sad soul, until the sea-wave washes
> The rim o' th' sun to-morrow,
> > > In eastern sky.

> But wilt thou cure thy heart   10
> Of love and all its smart,
> > Then die, dear, die;
> 'Tis deeper, sweeter,
> > Than on a rose bank to lie dreaming
> > With folded eye;   15

233

And then alone, amid the beaming
   Of love's stars, thou'lt meet her
      In eastern sky.

  Knight. These rites completed, say your further
    pleasure.
  Duke. To horse and homewards in all haste: my
    business   20
Urges each hour. This body bury here,
With all due honours. I myself will build
A monument, whereon, in after times,
Those of his blood shall read his valiant deeds,
And see the image of the bodily nature   25
He was a man in. Scarcely dare I, lady,
Mock you with any word of consolation:
But soothing care, and silence o'er that sorrow,
Which thine own tears alone dare tell to thee
Or offer comfort for; and in all matters   30
What thy will best desires, I promise thee.
Wilt thou hence with us?
  Sibyl.   Whither you will lead me.
My will lies there, my hope, and all my life
Which was in this world. Bring me to a nunnery:
There shall I soonest learn the way to heaven.   35
Farewell, my love,—I will not say to thee
Pale corpse,—we do not part for many days.
A little sleep, a little waking more,
And then we are together out of life.
  Duke. Cover the coffin up. This cold, calm stare 40
Upon familiar features is most dreadful:
Methinks too the expression of the face
Is changed, since all was settled gently there,
And threatens now. But I have sworn to speak
And think of that no more, which has been done.—45
Now then into the bustle of the world!
We'll rub our cares smooth there.

Knight.   This gate, my lord;
There stand the horses.

Duke.   Then we're mounted straight.
But, pri'thee, friend, forget not that the Duke   49
Is still in prison: I am a poor pilgrim.   [*Exeunt*.

Enter MANDRAKE

Mandr. Refuge at last: Here then I am at home:
I could weep, or rather I could think that I wept,
for it appears to be but too true that I have given
up the body. Well, what is, is, and what is not, is
not; and I am not what I was—for I am what I was   55
not; I am no more I, for I am no more: I am no
matter, being out of all trouble, and nobody at all,
but poor Mandrake's pure essence. And how came
I to this pass? Marry, I must either have been very
sound asleep when I died, or else I died by mistake   60
for I am sure I never intended it: or else this being
dead is a quite insignificant habit when one's used
to it: 'tis much easier than being alive, now I think
on it: only think of the trouble one has to keep up
life. One must breathe, and pass round the blood   65
and digest and let hair, and nails, and bone and
flesh grow.—Who comes? I dare for the sake of
my skin haunt no longer.   [*Exit*.

Enter ISBRAND *and* SIEGFRIED *attended*

Isbr. Dead and gone! a scurvy burthen to this
ballad of life. There lies he, Siegfried; my brother,   70
and I am not moved; dead, and I weep not. And
why not, Siegfried?

Siegfr. 'Tis well that you are reconciled to his
lot and your own.

Isbr. Reconciled! A word out of a love tale,   75
that's not in my language. No, no. I am patient
and still and laborious, a good contented man;
peaceable as an ass chewing a thistle; and my

thistle is revenge. I do but whisper it now: but
hereafter I will thunder the word, and I shall shoot 80
up gigantic out of this pismire shape, and hurl the
bolt of that revenge.

Siegfr. To the purpose: the priests return to
complete the burial.

Isbr. Right: we are men of business here. Away 85
with the body, gently and silently; it must be
buried in my duke's chapel in Silesia: why, hereafter. (*The body is borne out by attendants.*) That
way, fellows: the hearse stands at the corner of the
square: but reverently, 'tis my brother you carry.   90

Siegfr. But the priests will discover the robbery.

Re-enter MANDRAKE

Mandr. Welcome, fellows: tell me if ye hear,
whether ye be living, or young goblins. For there
is many a fellow with broad shoulders and a
goodly paunch who looks and behaves as if he 95
were alive, although in soul and spirit he be three
times more dead than salt fish in Lent. I, for my
part, am a sort of amateur goblin.

Isbr. The very fellow for us.—What, darest thou
haunt again? Down, Sir, on your bier, and be 100
buried as it beseems thee.

Mandr. Shall I submit to be a body again? No, I
am above being buried. I am but a young angel, as
yet unfledged, but bye and bye I shall try a flight.

Isbr. Lie down, lie down, vampire! or you die.   105

Mandr. Superfluous fellow, will ye be guilty of
tautology, and kill a dead man?

Isbr. Down then, on the bier, and be still.

[*They throw* MANDRAKE *down on the bier and
cover him with the pall.*

Isbr. Cover thy face up if thou wilt have a good
bust; and when thou comest to the churchyard, 110
thou mayst run if thou must needs give death the

slip: but dead thou art, and to be buried is thy
vocation. So submit.

Enter the Priests and bearers

Siegfr. A substitute in time.

Isbr. Here come the priests: now, move not, 115
fellow, belie not thy destiny.—But one more farewell, Fathers; he was my brother. (*Goes to the
bier, and whispers to* MANDRAKE.) Lie quiet, and
be buried, thou ape of the dead! If thou art deceased, it is thy duty; if thou art not, speak and I 120
will despatch thee: I hold a dagger to thy heart till
thou art in the grave. Art dead?

Mandr. I am, I am; I have been so all my life:
bury me in peace.

[*He is borne out, the Priests following.*

Isbr. Away, we must be doing in Münsterberg: 125
the Governor is there, and those two Duke's sons
who shall perish for his sake. I bury my brother
there: he is an earthquake-seed, and will whisper
revenge to earth, and I to heaven; and though we
whisper now, thunder shall speak the word here- 130
after: and it shall be the thunder of the wheels of a
war-chariot in which I shall triumph like Jupiter
in my fool's cap, to fetch the Duke and his sons to
Hell, and then my bells will ring merrily, and I
shall jest more merrily than now: for I shall be 135
Death the Court-fool.—Come, Siegfried.

[*Exeunt.*

MANDRAKE *runs across the stage, crying*

Mandr. Who'll run a race with a ghost? Now,
Musicians, strike up Death's Hornpipe, for I
dance alone through the world like a Jack o'
Lanthorn.   [*Exit.* 140

SCENE III. *A hall in the ducal castle of Münsterberg in the town of Grüssau in Silesia*

TORWALD, ADALMAR, ATHULF, ISBRAND, SIEG-
FRIED; *the* DUKE, *disguised as a pilgrim;*
AMALA; *and other ladies and knights; conversing
in various groups*

Athulf. A fair and bright assembly: never strode
Old arched Grüssau over such a tide
Of helmed chivalry, as when to-day
Our tourney guests swept, leaping billow-like,
Its palace-banked streets. Knights shut in steel,   5
Whose shields, like water, glassed the soul-eyed
        maidens,
That softly did attend their armed tread,
Flower-cinctured on the temples, whence gushed
        down
A full libation of star-numbered tresses,
Hallowing the neck unto love's silent kiss,   10
Veiling its innocent white: and then came squires,
And those who bore war's silken tapestries,
And chequered heralds: 'twas a human river,
Brimful and beating as if the great god,
Who lay beneath it, would arise. So swings   15
Time's sea, which Age snows into and encreases,
When from the rocky side of the dim future,
Leaps into it a mighty destiny,
Whose being to endow great souls have been
Centuries hoarded, and the world meanwhile   20
Sate like a beggar upon Heaven's threshold,
Muttering its wrongs.
    Siegfr.   My sprightly Athulf,
Is it possible that you can waste the day,
Which throws these pillared shades among such
        beauties,
In lonely thought?
    Athulf.   Why I have left my cup,   25

A lady's lips, dropping with endless kisses,
Because your minstrels hushed their harps. Why did
    they?
This music, which they tickle from the strings,
Is excellent for drowning ears that gape,
When one has need of whispers.

    Siegfr.   The old governor 30
Would have it so: his morning nap being o'er,
He'd no more need of music, but is moving
Straight to the lists.

    Athulf.   A curse on that mock war!
How it will shake and sour the blood, that now
Is quiet in the men! And there 's my brother, 35
Whose sword 's his pleasure. A mere savage man,
Made for the monstrous times, but left out then,
Born by mistake with us.

    Adalm. (*to* ISBRAND)   Be sure 'tis heavy.
One lance of mine a wolf shut his jaws on
But cracked it not, you'll see his bite upon it: 40
It lies among the hunting weapons.

    Isbr.   Aye,
With it I saw you once scratch out of life
A blotted Moor.

    Adalm.   The same; it poises well,
And falls right heavy: find it.   [*Exit* ISBRAND.

    Siegfr.   For the tilt,
My brave lord Adalmar?

    Athulf.   What need of asking? 45
You know the man is sore upon a couch
But upright, on his bloody-hoofed steed
Galloping o'er the ruins of his foes,
Whose earthquake he hath been, there will he shout,
Laugh, run his tongue along his trembling lip, 50
And swear his heart tastes honey.

    Siegfr.   Nay, thou'rt harsh;
He was the axe of Mars; but, Troy being felled,
Peace trims her bower with him.

Athulf.   Aye, in her hand
He 's iron still.

   Adalm.   I care not, brother Athulf,
Whether you're right or wrong: 'tis very certain,   55
Thank God for it, I am not Peace's lap-dog,
But Battle's shaggy whelp. Perhaps, even soon,
Good friend of Bacchus and the rose, you'll feel
Your budding wall of dalliance shake behind you,
And need my spear to prop it.

   Athulf.   Come the time!   60
You'll see that in our veins runs brotherhood.

   A Lady. Is Siegfried here? At last! I've sought for
     you
By every harp and every lady's shoulder,
Not ever thinking you could breathe the air
That ducal cub of Münsterberg makes frightful   65
With his loud talk.

   Siegfr.   Happy in my error,
If thus to be corrected.

Re-enter ISBRAND

   Isbr.   The lance, my lord:
A delicate tool to breathe a heathen's vein with.

   The Lady. What, Isbrand, thou a soldier? Fie
     upon thee!
Is this a weapon for a fool?   70

   Isbr. Madam, I pray thee pardon us. The fair
have wrested the tongue from us, and we must give
our speeches a sting of some metal—steel or gold.
And I beseech thee, lady, call me fool no longer:
I grow old, and in old age you know what men   75
become. We are at court, and there it were sin to
call a thing by its right name: therefore call me a
fool no longer, for my wisdom is on the wane, and
I am almost as sententious as the governor.

   The Lady. Excellent: wilt thou become court-   80
confessor?

Isbr. Aye, if thou wilt begin with thy secrets,
lady. But my fair mistress, and you, noble
brethren, I pray you gather around me. I will
now speak a word in earnest, and hereafter jest 85
with you no more: for I lay down my profession
of folly. Why should I wear bells to ring the
changes of your follies on? Doth the besonneted
moon wear bells, she that is the parasite and zany
of the stars, and your queen, ye apes of madness? 90
As I live I grow ashamed of the duality of my legs,
for they and the apparel, forked or furbelowed,
upon them constitute humanity; the brain no
longer; and I wish I were an honest fellow of four
shins when I look into the note-book of your 95
absurdities. I will abdicate.

The Lady. Brave! but how dispose of your domi-
nions, most magnanimous zany?

Isbr. My heirs at law are manifold. Yonder
minister shall have my jacket; he needs many col- 100
ours for his deeds. You shall inherit my mantle;
for your sins, (be it whispered,) chatter with the
teeth for cold; and charity, which should be their
greatcoat, you have not in the heart.

The Lady. Gramercy: but may I not beg your 105
coxcomb for a friend?

Isbr. The brothers have an equal claim to that
crest: they may tilt for it. But now for my crown.
O cap and bells, ye eternal emblems, hieroglyphics of man's supreme right in nature; O ye, 110
that only fall on the deserving, while oak, palm,
laurel, and bay rankle on *their* foreheads, whose
deserts are oft more payable at the other extremity: who shall be honoured with you? Come
candidates, the cap and bells are empty.   115

The Lady. Those you should send to England,
for the bad poets and the critics who praise them.

Isbr. Albeit worthy, those merry men cannot

this once obtain the prize. I will yield Death the
crown of folly. He hath no hair, and in this   120
weather might catch cold and die: besides he has
killed the best knight I knew, Sir Wolfram, and
so is doubly deserving. Let him wear the cap, let
him toll the bells; he shall be our new court-fool:
and, when the world is old and dead, the thin wit   125
shall find the angel's record of man's works and
deeds, and write with a lipless grin on the innocent
first page for a title, 'Here begins Death's Jest-
book'.—There, you have my testament: henceforth speak solemnly to me, and you shall have a   130
measured answer from me, who have relapsed into
courtly wisdom.

 The Lady. Come, Siegfried, let us leave this wild
  odd jester.
Some of us in a corner wait your music,
Your news, and stories. My lord Adalmar,   135
You must be very weary all this time,
The rest are so delighted. Come along, [*To* SIEGFRIED.
Or else his answer stuns me.
 Adalm.   Joyous creature!
Whose life's first leaf is hardly yet uncurled.
 Athulf. Use your trade's language; were I journey-
  man   140
To Mars, the glorious butcher, I would say
She 's sleek, and sacrificial flowers would look well
On her white front.
 Adalm.   Now, brother, can you think,
Stern as I am above, that in my depth
There is no cleft wherein such thoughts are hived   145
As from dear looks and words come back to me,
Storing that honey, love. O! love I do,
Through every atom of my being.
 Athulf.   Aye,
So do we young ones all. In winter time
This god of butterflies, this Cupid sleeps,   150

As they do in their cases; but May comes;
With it the bee and he: each spring of mine
He sends me a new arrow, thank the boy.
A week ago he shot me for this year;
The shaft is in my stomach, and so large   155
I scarce have room for dinner.

   Adalm.   Shall I believe thee,
Or judge mortality by this stout sample
I screw my mail o'er? Well, it may be so;
You are an adept in these chamber passions,
And have a heart that 's Cupid's arrow cushion   160
Worn out with use. I never knew before
The meaning of this love. But one has taught me,
It is a heaven wandering among men,
The spirit of gone Eden haunting earth.   164
Life's joys, death's pangs are viewless from its bosom,
Which they who keep are gods; there 's no paradise,
There is no heaven, no angels, no blessed spirits
No souls, or they have no eternity,
If this be not a part of them.

   Athulf.   This in a Court!
Such sort of love might Hercules have felt   170
Warm from the Hydra fight, when he had fattened
On a fresh-slain Bucentaur, roasted whole,
The heart of his pot-belly, till it ticked
Like a cathedral clock. But in good faith
Is this the very truth? Then I have found   175
My fellow fool. For I am wounded too
E'en to the quick and inmost, Adalmar.
So fair a creature! of such sweets compact
As nature stints elsewhere; which you may find
Under the tender eyelid of a serpent,   180
Or in the gurge of a kiss-coloured rose,
By drops and sparks: but when she moves, you see,
Like water from a crystal overfilled,
Fresh beauty tremble out of her and lave
Her fair sides to the ground. Of other women,   185

(And we have beauteous in this court of ours,)
I can remember whether nature touched
Their eye with brown or azure, where a vein
Runs o'er a sleeping eyelid, like some streak
In a young blossom; every grace count up,   190
Here the round turn and crevice of the arm,
There the tress-bunches, or the slender hand
Seen between harpstrings gathering music from them:
But when she leaves me I know nothing more,
(Like one from whose awakening temples rolls   195
The cloudy vision of a god away)
Than that she was divine.

    Adalm. Fie sir, these are the spiced sighs of a heart,
That bubbles under wine; utter rhyme-gilding,
Beneath man's sober use. What do you speak of?   200

    Athulf. A woman most divine, and that I love
As you dare never.

    Adalm.   Boy, a truce with talk.
Such words are sacred, placed within man's reach
To be used seldom, solemnly, when speaking
Of what both God and man might overhear   205
You unabashed.

    Athulf.   Of what? What is more worthy
Than the delight of youth, being so rare,
Precious, short-lived, and irrecoverable?

    Adalm. When you do mention that adored land,
Which gives you life, pride, and security,   210
And holy rights of freedom; or in the praise
Of those great virtues and heroic men,
That glorify the earth and give it beams,
Then to be lifted by the like devotion
Would not disgrace God's angels.

    Athulf.   Well, sir, laud,   215
Worship, and swear by them, your native country
And virtues past; a phantom and a corpse:
Such airy stuff may please you. My desires
Are hot and hungry; they will have their fill

Of living dalliance, gazes, and lip-touches,   220
Or swallow up their lord. No more rebuking:
Peace be between us. For why are we brothers,
Being the creatures of two different gods,
But that we may not be each other's murderers?

    Adalm. So be it then! But mark me,   225
I spoke not from a cold unnatural spirit,
Barren of tenderness. I feel and know
Of woman's dignity: how it doth merit
Our total being, has all mine this moment:
But they should share with us our level lives: 230
Moments there are, and one is now at hand,
Too high for them. When all the world is stirred
By some preluding whisper of that trumpet,
Which shall awake the dead, to do great things,
Then the sublimity of my affection,   235
The very height of my beloved, shows me
How far above her 's glory. When you've earned
This knowledge, tell me: I will say, you love
As a man should.   [*He retires.*

    Athulf.   But this is somewhat true.
I almost think that I could feel the same   240
For her. For *her*? By heavens, 'tis Amala,
Amala only, that he so can love.
There? by her side? in conference! at smiles!
Then I am born to be a fratricide.
I feel as I were killing him. Tush, tush;   245
A phantom of my passion! But, if true—
What? What, my heart? A strangely-quiet thought,
That will not be pronounced, doth answer me.

  TORWALD *comes forward, attended by the company*

    Torw. Break up! The day 's of age. Knights to the
      lists,
And ladies to look on. We'll break some lances   250
Before 'tis evening. To your sports, I pray;
I follow quickly.   [*He is left alone with the* DUKE.

Pilgrim, now your news:
Whence come you?

Duke.   Straightway from the holy land
Whose sanctity such floods of human blood,
Unnatural rain for it, will soon wash out.   255

Torw. You saw our Duke?

Duke.   I did: but Melveric
Is strangely altered. When we saw him leap,
Shut up in iron, on his burning steed
From Grüssau's threshold, he had fifty years   259
Upon his head, and bore them straight and upright,
Through dance, and feast, and knightly tournament.

Torw. How is he not the same? 'Tis but three years
And a fourth's quarter past. What is the change?
A silvering of the hair? a deeper wrinkle
On cheek and forehead?

Duke.   I do not think you'd know him,
Stood he where I do. No. I saw him lying   266
Beside a fountain on a battle-evening:
The sun was setting over the heaped plain;
And to my musing fancy his front's furrows,
With light between them, seemed the grated shadows
Thrown by the ribs of that field's giant, Death;   271
'Twixt which the finger of the hour did write
'This is the grave's'.

Torw.   How? Looked he sorrowful?
Knows he the dukedom's state?

Duke. (*giving letters to* TORWALD) Ask these. He's
heard
The tidings that afflict the souls of fathers;   275
How these two sons of his unfilially
Have vaulted to the saddle of the people,
And charge against him. How he gained the news,
You must know best: what countermine he digs,
Those letters tell your eyes. He bade me say,   280
His dukedom is his body, and, he forth,
That may be sleeping, but the touch of wrong,

246

The murderer's barefoot tread will bring him back
Out of his Eastern visions, ere this earth
Has swung the city's length.
    Torw.   I read as much: 285
He bids me not to move; no eye to open,
But to sit still and doze, and warm my feet
At their eruption. This security
Is most unlike him. I remember oft,
When the thin harvests shed their withered grain, 290
And empty poverty yelped sour-mouthed at him,
How he would cloud his majesty of form
With priestly hangings, or the tattered garb
Of the step-seated beggar, and go round
To catch the tavern talk and the street ballad,   295
Until he knew the very nick of time,
When his heart's arrow would be on the string;
And, seizing Treason by the arm, would pour
Death back upon him.
    Duke.   He is wary still,
And has a snake's eye under every leaf.   300
Your business is obedience unto him,
Who is your natal star; and mine to worm,
Leaf after leaf, into the secret volume
Of their designs. Already has our slave,
The grape juice, left the side-door of the youngest 305
Open to me. You think him innocent.
Fire flashes from him; whether it be such
As treason would consult by, or the coals
Love boils his veins on, shall through this small crevice,
In which the vine has thrust his cunning tendril,   310
Be looked and listened for.
    Torw.   Can I believe it?
Did not I know him and his spirit's course,
Well as the shape and colour of the sun,
And when it sets and rises? Is this he?
No: 'tis the shadow of this pilgrim false,   315
Who stands up in his height of villainy,

Shadowy as a hill, and throws his hues
Of contradiction to the heavenly light,
The stronger as it shines upon him most.   319
Ho! pilgrim, I have weighed and found thee villain.
Are thy knees used to kneeling? It may chance
That thou must change the altar for the block:
Prove thou'rt his messenger,
    Duke.   Pause! I am stuffed
With an o'erwhelming spirit: press not thou,
Or I shall burst asunder, and let through   325
The deluging presence of thy duke. Prepare:
He 's near at hand.
    Torw.   Forbid it, Providence!
He steps on a plot's spring, whose teeth encircle
The throne and city.
    Duke. (*disrobing*) Fear not. On he comes,
Still as a star robed in eclipse, until   330
The earthy shadow slips away. Who rises?
I'm changing: now who am I?
    Torw.   Melveric!
Münsterberg, as I live and love thee!
    Duke.   Hush!
Is there not danger?
    Torw.   Aye: we walk on ice
Over the mouth of Hell: an inch beneath us,   335
Dragon Rebellion lies ready to wake.
Ha! there behold him.

Enter ADALMAR

    Adalm. Lord Governor, our games are waiting for
        you.
Will you come with me? Base and muffled stranger,
What dost thou here? Away.
    Duke.   Prince Adalmar,   340
Where shall you see me? I will come again,
This or the next world. Thou, who carriest
The seeds of a new world, may'st understand me.

Look for me ever. There 's no crack without me
In earth and all around it. Governor,   345
Let all things happen, as they will. Farewell:
Tremble for no one.

    Adalm.   Hence! the begging monk
Prates emptily.

    Duke.   Believe him.

    Torw.   Well, lead on;
Wert thou a king, I'd not obey thee more.

                        [Exit with ADALMAR.

    Duke. Rebellion, treason, parricidal daggers!   350
This is the bark of the court dogs, that come
Welcoming home their master. My sons too,
Even my sons! O not sons, but contracts,
Between my lust and a destroying fiend,
Written in my dearest blood, whose date run out, 355
They are become death warrants, Parricide,
And murder of the heart that loved and nourished.
Be merry, ye rich fiends! Piety 's dead,
And left the world a legacy to you.
Under the green-sod are your coffins packed,   360
So thick they break each other. The day 's come
When scarce a lover, for his maiden's hair,
Can pluck a stalk whose rose draws not its hue
Out of a hate-killed heart. Nature 's polluted,
There 's man in every secret corner of her,   365
Doing damned wicked deeds. Thou art old, world,
A hoary atheistic murderous star:
I wish that thou would'st die, or could'st be slain,
Hell-hearted bastard of the sun.
O that the twenty coming years were over!   370
Then should I be at rest, where ruined arches
Shut out the troublesome unghostly day;
And idlers might be sitting on my tomb,
Telling how I did die. How shall I die?
Fighting my sons for power; or of dotage,   375
Sleeping in purple pressed from filial veins;

And let my epitaph be, 'Here lies he,
Who murdered his two children?' Hence cursed
    thought!
I will enquire the purpose of their plot:
There may be good in it, and, if there be,   380
I'll be a traitor too.   [*Exit.*

SCENE IV. *A retired gallery in the ducal castle*

Enter ISBRAND *and* SIEGFRIED

   Isbr. Now see you how this dragon-egg of ours
Swells with its ripening plot? Methinks I hear
Snaky rebellion turning restless in it,
And with its horny jaws scraping away
The shell that hides it. All is ready now: 5
I hold the latch-string of a new world's wicket;
One pull—and it rolls in. Bid all our friends
Meet in that ruinous churchyard once again,
By moonrise; until then I'll hide myself;
For these sweet thoughts rise dimpling to my lips, 10
And break the dark stagnation of my features,
Like sugar melting in a glass of poison.
To-morrow, Siegfried, shalt thou see me sitting
One of the drivers of this racing earth
With Grüssau's reins between my fingers. Ha!   15
Never since Hell laughed at the church, blood-drunken
From rack and wheel, has there been joy so mad
As that which stings my marrow now.
   Siegfr.   Good cause,
The sun-glance of a coming crown to heat you,
And give your thoughts gay colours in the steam   20
Of a fermenting brain.
   Isbr.   Not that alone.
A sceptre is smooth handling, it is true,
And one grows fat and jolly in a chair
That has a kingdom crouching under it,

With one's name on its collar, like a dog   25
To fetch and carry. But the heart I have
Is a strange little snake. He drinks not wine
When he'd be drunk, but poison: he doth fatten
On bitter hate, not love. And oh, that duke!
My life is hate of him; and when I tread   30
His neck into the grave, I shall, methinks,
Fall into ashes with the mighty joy,
Or be transformed into a winged star:
That will be all eternal heaven distilled
Down to one thick rich minute. This sounds madly, 35
But I am mad when I remember him:
Siegfried, you know not why.

   Siegfr.   I never knew
That you had quarrelled.

   Isbr.   True: but did you not see
My brother's corpse? There was a wound on 't Sieg-
   fried;
He died not gently, nor in a ripe age;   40
And I'll be sworn it was the duke that did it,
Else he had not remained in that far land,
And sent his knights to us again.

   Siegfr.   I thought
He was the duke's close friend.

   Isbr.   Close as his blood:
A double-bodied soul they did appear,   45
Rather than fellow hearts.

   Siegfr.   I've heard it told
That they did swear and write in their best blood,
And her's they loved the most, that who died first
Should, on death's holidays, revisit him
Who still dwelt in the flesh.

   Isbr.   O that such bond   50
Would move the jailor of the grave to open
Life's gate again unto my buried brother
But half an hour! Were I buried, like him,
There in the very garrets of the grave,

But six feet under earth (that 's the grave's sky),   55
I'd jump up into life. But he 's a quiet ghost;
He walks not in the churchyard after dew,
But gets to his grave betimes, burning no glow-worms,
Sees that his bones are right, and stints his worms
Most miserly. If you were murdered, Siegfried,   60
As he was by this duke, should it be so?

    Siegfr. Here speaks again your passion: what know
      we
Of Death's commandments to his subject-spirits,
Who are as yet the body's citizens?
What seas unnavigable, what wild forests,   65
What castles, and what ramparts there may hedge
His icy frontier?

    Isbr.   Tower and roll what may,
There have been goblins bold who have stolen pass-
      ports,
Or sailed the sea, or leaped the wall, or flung
The drawbridge down, and travelled back again.   70
So would my soul have done. But let it be.
At doomsday's dawning shall the ducal cut-throat
Wake by a tomb-fellow he little dreamt of.
Methinks, I see them rising with mixed bones,
A pair of patchwork angels.

    Siegfr.   What does this mean?   75

    Isbr. A pretty piece of kidnapping, that 's all.
When Melveric's heart's heart, his new-wed wife,
Upon the bed whereon she bore these sons,
Died, as a blossom does whose inmost fruit
Tears it in twain, and in its stead remains   80
A bitter poison-berry: when she died,
What her soul left was by her husband laid
In the marriage grave, whereto he doth consign
Himself being dead.

    Siegfr.   Like a true loving mate.
Is not her tomb 'mid the cathedral ruins,   85
Where we to-night assemble?

Isbr.   Say not her's:
A changeling lies there. By black night came I,
And, while a man might change two goblets' liquors,
I laid the lips of their two graves together,
And poured my brother into hers; while she,   90
Being the lightest, floated and ran over.
Now lies the murdered where the loved should be;
And Melveric the dead shall dream of heaven,
Embracing his damnation. There 's revenge.   94
But hush! here comes one of my dogs, the princes;—
To work with you.   [*Exit* SIEGFRIED.
                    Now for another shape;
For Isbrand is the handle of the chisels
Which Fate, the turner of men's lives, doth use
Upon the wheeling world.

                    Enter ATHULF

                        There is a passion
Lighting his cheek, as red as brother's hate: 100
If it be so, these pillars shall go down,
Shivering each other, and their ruins be
My step into a princedom. Doth he speak?
    Athulf. Then all the minutes of my life to come
Are sands of a great desart, into which   105
I'm banished broken-hearted. Amala,
I must think thee a lovely-faced murderess,
With eyes as dark and poisonous as nightshade;
Yet no, not so; if thou hadst murdered me,
It had been charitable. Thou hast slain   110
The love of thee, that lived in my soul's palace
And made it holy: now 'tis desolate,
And devils of abandonment will haunt it,
And call in Sins to come, and drink with them
Out of my heart. But now farewell, my love;   115
For thy rare sake I would have been a man
One story under God. Gone, gone art thou.
Great and voluptuous Sin now seize upon me,

Thou paramour of Hell's fire-crowned king,
That showedst the tremulous fairness of thy bosom
In heaven, and so didst ravish the best angels.   121
Come, pour thy spirit all about my soul,
And let a glory of thy bright desires
Play round about my temples. So may I
Be thy knight and Hell's saint for evermore.   125
Kiss me with fire: I'm thine.

   Isbr.   Doth it run so?
A bold beginning we must keep him up to 't.

   Athulf. Isbrand!

   Isbr.   My prince.

   Athulf.   Come to me. Thou'rt a man
I must know more of. There is something in thee,
The deeper one doth venture in thy being,   130
That drags us on and down. What dost thou lead to?
Art thou a current to some unknown sea
Islanded richly, full of syren songs
And unknown bliss? Art thou the snaky opening
Of a dark cavern, where one may converse   135
With night's dear spirits? If thou'rt one of these,
Let me descend thee.

   Isbr.   You put questions to me
In an Egyptian or old magic tongue,
Which I can ill interpret.

   Athulf.   Passion's hieroglyphics;
Painted upon the minutes by mad thoughts,   140
Dungeoned in misery. Isbrand, answer me;
Art honest, or a man of many deeds
And many faces to them? Thou'rt a plotter,
A politician. Say, if there should come
A fellow, with his being just abandoned   145
By old desires and hopes, who would do much—
And who doth much upon this grave-paved star,
In doing, must sin much—would quick and straight,

254

Sword-straight and poison-quick, have done with
    doing;
Would you befriend him?

   Isbr.   I can lend an arm   150
To good bold purpose. But you know me not,
And I will not be known before my hour.
Why come you here wishing to raise the devil,
And ask me how? Where are your sacrifices?
Eye-water is not his libation, prayers   155
Reach him not through earth's chinks. Bold deeds and
    thoughts,
What men call crimes, are his loved litany;
And from all such good angels keep us! Now sir,
What makes you fretful?

   Athulf.   I have lost that hope,
For which alone I lived. Henceforth my days   160
Are purposeless; there is no reason further
Why I should be, or should let others be;
No motive more for virtue, for forbearance,
Or anything that's good. The hourly need,
And the base bodily cravings, must be now   165
The aim of this deserted human engine.
Good may be in this world, but not for me;
Gentle and noble hearts, but not for me;
And happiness, and heroism, and glory,
And love, but none for me. Let me then wander   170
Amid their banquets, funerals, and weddings,
Like one whose living spirit is Death's Angel.

   Isbr. What? You have lost your love and so turned
    sour?
And who has ta'en your chair in Amala's heaven?

   Athulf. My brother, my Cain; Adalmar.

   Isbr.   I'll help thee, prince: 175
When will they marry?

   Athulf. I could not wish him in my rage to die
Sooner: one night I'd give him to dream hells.
To-morrow, Isbrand.

Isbr.   Sudden, by my life.
But, out of the black interval, we'll cast   180
Something upon the moment of their joy,
Which, should it fail to blot, shall so deform it,
That they must write it further down in time.

   Athulf. Let it be crossed with red.

   Isbr.   Trust but to me:
I'll get you bliss. But I am of a sort   185
Not given to affections. Sire and mother
And sister I had never, and so feel not
Why sin 'gainst them should count so doubly wicked,
This side o' th' sun. If you would wound your foe,
Get swords that pierce the mind: a bodily slice   190
Is cured by surgeon's butter: let true hate
Leap the flesh wall, or fling his fiery deeds
Into the soul. So he can marry, Athulf,
And then—

   Athulf.   Peace, wicked-hearted slave!
Darest thou tempt me? I called on thee for service, 195
But thou wouldst set me at a hellish work,
To cut my own damnation out of Lust:
Thou'ldst sell me to the fiend. Thou and thy master,
That sooty beast the devil, shall be my dogs,
My curs to kick and beat when I would have you.   200
I will not bow, nor follow at his bidding,
For his hell-throne. No: I will have a god
To serve my purpose; Hatred be his name;
But 'tis a god, divine in wickedness,
Whom I will worship.   [*Exit.* 205

   Isbr. Then go where Pride and Madness carry thee:
And let that feasted fatness pine and shrink,
Till thy ghost 's pinched in the tight love-lean body.
I see his life, as in a map of rivers,
Through shallows, over rocks, breaking its way,   210
Until it meet his brother's, and with that
Wrestle and tumble o'er a perilous rock,
Bare as Death's shoulder: one of them is lost,

And a dark haunted flood creeps deadly on
Into the wailing Styx. Poor Amala!   215
A thorny rose thy life is, plucked in the dew,
And pitilessly woven with these snakes
Into a garland for the King of the grave.   [*Exit.*

ACT III

SCENE I. *An apartment in the ducal castle*

The DUKE *and* TORWALD

Duke. Let them be married: give to Adalmar
The sweet society of woman's soul,
As we impregnate damask swords with odour
Pressed from young flowers' bosoms, so to sweeten
And purify war's lightning. For the other,   5
Who catches love by eyes, the court has stars,
That will take up in his tempestuous bosom
The shining place she leaves.
    Torw.   It shall be done:
The bell, that will ring merrily for their bridal,
Has but few hours to score first.
    Duke.   Good. I have seen too 10
Our ripe rebellion's ringleaders. They meet
By moonrise; with them I: to-night will be
Fiends' jubilee, with heaven's spy among them.
What else was 't that you asked?
    Torw. The melancholy lady you brought with you?
    Duke. Torwald, I fear her's is a broken heart.   16
When first I met her in the Egyptian prison,
She was the rosy morning of a woman;
Beauty was rising, but the starry grace
Of a calm childhood might be seen in her.   20
But since the death of Wolfram, who fell there,
Heaven and one single soul only know how,
I have not dared to look upon her sorrow.

Torw. Methinks she 's too unearthly beautiful.
Old as I am, I cannot look at her,   25
And hear her voice, that touches the heart's core,
Without a dread that she will fade each instant.
There 's too much heaven in her: oft it rises,
And, pouring out about the lovely earth,
Almost dissolves it. She is tender too;   30
And melancholy is the sweet pale smile,
With which she gently doth reproach her fortune.
    Duke. What ladies tend her?
    Torw.   My Amala; she will not often see
One of the others.
    Duke.   Too much solitude
Maintains her in this grief. I will look to 't   35
Hereafter; for the present I've enough.
We must not meet again before to-morrow.
    Torw. I may have something to report...
    Duke. Ho! Ziba.

Enter ZIBA

    Ziba.   Lord of my life!
    Duke. I bought this man of Afric from an Arab,   40
Under the shadow of a pyramid,
For many jewels. He hath skill in language;
And knowledge is in him root, flower, and fruit,
A palm with winged imagination in it,
Whose roots stretch even underneath the grave,   45
And on them hangs a lamp of magic science
In his soul's deepest mine, where folded thoughts
Lie sleeping on the tombs of magi dead:
So said his master when he parted with him.
I know him skilful, faithful; take him with you;   50
He 's fit for many services.
    Torw.   I'll try him:
Wilt thou be faithful, Moor?
    Ziba.   As soul to body.

258

Torw. Then follow me. Farewell, my noble pilgrim.
                                                    [*Exit.*

Duke. It was a fascination, near to madness,
Which held me subjugated to that maiden.   55
Why do I now so coldly speak of her,
When there is nought between us? O! there is,
A deed as black as the old towers of Hell.
But hence! thou torturing weakness of remorse;
'Tis time when I am dead to think on that: 60
Yet my sun shines; so courage, heart, cheer up:
Who should be merrier than a secret villain?   [*Exit.*

SCENE II. *Another room in the same*

SIBYLLA *and* AMALA

Sibyl. I would I were a fairy, Amala,
Or knew some of those winged wizard women,
Then I could bring you a more precious gift.
'Tis a wild graceful flower, whose name I know not;
Call it Sibylla's love, while it doth live;   5
And let it die that you may contradict it,
And say my love doth not, so bears no fruit.
Take it. I wish that happiness may ever
Flow through your days as sweetly and as still,
As did the beauty and the life to this   10
Out of its roots.
   Amala.   Thanks, my kind Sibylla:
To-morrow I will wear it at my wedding,
Since that must be.
   Sibyl.   Art thou then discontented?
I thought the choice was thine, and Adalmar
A noble warrior worthy of his fortune.   15
   Amala. O yes: brave, honourable is my bridegroom,
But somewhat cold perhaps. If his wild brother
Had but more constancy and less insolence
In love, he were a man much to my heart.

But, as it is, I must, I will be happy;   20
And Adalmar deserves that I should love him.
But see how night o'ertakes us. Good rest, dear:
We will no more profane sleep's stillest hour.
  Sibyl. Good night, then.   [*Exeunt.*

SCENE III. *The ruins of a spacious Gothic Cathedral
  and churchyard. On the cloister wall the Dance of
  Death is painted. The sepulchre of the Dukes with
  massy carved folding doors, &c., by moonlight.*

Enter MANDRAKE

  Mandr. After all being dead 's not so uncomfort-
able when one 's got into the knack of it. There's
nothing to do, no taxes to pay, nor any quarrelling
about the score for ale. And yet I begin shrewdly
to suspect that death 's all a take-in: as soon as 5
gentlemen have gained some 70 years of experience
they begin to be weary of the common drudgery of
the world, lay themselves down, hold their breath,
close their eyes and are announced as having
entered into the fictitious condition by means of 10
epitaphs and effigies. But, good living people, don't
you be deceived any more: It is only a cunning invention to avoid paying poor's rates and the reviewers. They live all jollily underground and sneak
about a little in the night air to hear the news and 15
laugh at their poor innocent great-grandchildren,
who take them for goblins, and tremble for fear of
death, which is at best only a ridiculous game at
hide-and-seek. That is my conviction, and I am
quite impartial being in the secret, but I will only 20
keep away from the living till I have met with a few
of these gentle would-be dead, who are shy enough,
and am become initiated into their secrets, and then
I will write to the newspapers, turn King's evidence

and discover the whole import and secret, become 25
more renowned than Columbus, though sure to be
opposed by the doctors and undertakers whose invention the whole most extravagant idea seems to
be. Ah! some living folks.—Well, I must keep up
the joke a little longer, and keep away from them: 30
here are good quarters for the like of me, there I'll
sleep to-night.   [*Goes into the sepulchre.*

Enter ISBRAND *and* SIEGFRIED

Isbr. Not here? That wolf-howled, witch-prayed,
     owl-sung fool,
Fat mother moon hath brought the cats their light
A whole thief's hour, and yet they are not met.   35
I thought the bread and milky thick-spread lies,
With which I plied them, would have drawn to head
The state's bad humours quickly.
Siegfr.   They delay
Until the twilight strollers are gone home.
Isbr. That may be. This is a sweet place methinks: 40
These arches and their caves, now double-nighted
With heaven's and that creeping darkness, ivy,
Delight me strangely. Ruined churches oft,
As this, are crime's chief haunt, as ruined angels
Straight become fiends. This tomb too tickleth me   45
With its wild-rose branches. Dost remember, Siegfried,
About the buried Duchess? In this cradle
I changed the new dead: here the murdered lies.
Siegfr. Are we so near? A frightful theft!
Isbr.   Fright! idiot!—
Peace; there 's a footstep on the pavement.

Enter the DUKE

                        Welcome! 50
I thank you, wanderer, for coming first,
They of the town lag still.

Duke.   The enterprise,
And you its head, much please me.

Isbr.   You are courteous.

Duke. Better: I'm honest. But your ways and words
Are so familiar to my memory,   55
That I could almost think we had been friends
Since our now riper and declining lives
Undid their outer leaves.

Isbr.   I can remember
No earlier meeting. What need of it? Methinks
We agree well enough: especially   60
And you have brought bad tidings of the Duke.

Duke.   If I had time,
And less disturbed thoughts, I'd search my memory
For what thou'rt like. Now we have other matters
To talk about.

Isbr.   And, thank the stingy star-shine,
I see the shades of others of our council.   65

Enter ADALMAR *and other civil and military
conspirators*

Though late met, well met, friends. Where stay the
          rest?
For we're still few here.

Adalm.   They are contented
With all the steps proposed, and keep their chambers
Aloof from the suspecting crowd of eyes,
Which day doth feed with sights for nightly gossip,   70
Until your hour strikes.

Isbr.   That 's well to keep at home,
And hide, as doth Heaven's wrath, till the last minute.
Little 's to say. We fall as gently on them,
As the first drops of Noah's world-washing shower
Upon the birds' wings and the leaves. Give each   75
A copy of this paper: it contains
A quick receipt to make a new creation
In our old dukedom. Here stands he who framed it.

Adalm. The unknown pilgrim! You have warrant,
    Isbrand,   79
For trusting him?
   Isbr.   I have.
   Adalm.   Enough. How are the citizens?
You feasted them these three days.
   Isbr.   And have them by the heart for 't.
'Neath Grüssau's tiles sleep none, whose deepest
    bosom
My fathom hath not measured; none, whose thoughts
I have not made a map of. In the depth
And labyrinthine home of the still soul,   85
Where the seen thing is imaged, and the whisper
Joints the expecting spirit, my spies, which are
Suspicion's creeping words, have stolen in,
And, with their eyed feelers, touched and sounded
The little hiding holes of cunning thought,   90
And each dark crack in which a reptile purpose
Hangs in its chrysalis unripe for birth.
All of each heart I know.
   Duke.   O perilous boast!
Fathom the wavy caverns of all stars,
Know every side of every sand in earth,   95
And hold in little all the lore of man,
As a dew's drop doth miniature the sun:
But never hope to learn the alphabet,
In which the hieroglyphic human soul
More changeably is painted than the rainbow   100
Upon the cloudy pages of a shower,
Whose thunderous hinges a wild wind doth turn.
Know all of each! when each doth shift his thought
More often in a minute, than the air
Dust on a summer path.
   Isbr.   Liquors can lay them: 105
Grape-juice or vein-juice.
   Duke.   Yet there may be one,
Whose misty mind's perspective still lies hid.

Isbr. Ha! stranger, where?

Duke. A quiet, listening, flesh-concealed soul.

Isbr. Are the ghosts eavesdropping? None, that do
    live,   110
Listen besides ourselves.

A struggle behind: SIEGFRIED *brings* MARIO *forward*

                Who 's there?

Siegfr.   A fellow,
Who crouched behind the bush, dipping his ears
Into the stream of your discourse.

Isbr.   Come forward.

Mario. Then lead me. Were it noon, I could not find
    him
Whose voice commands me: in these callous hands 115
There is as much perception for the light,
As in the depth of my poor dayless eyes.

Isbr.   Thy hand then.

Mario. Art thou leader here?

Isbr.   Perchance.

Mario. Then listen, as I listened unto you,
And let my life and story end together,   120
If it seem good to you. A Roman am I;
A Roman in unroman times: I've slept
At midnight in our Capitolian ruins,
And breathed the ghost of our great ancient world,
Which there doth walk: and among glorious visions,
That the unquiet tombs sent forth to me,   126
Learned I the love of Freedom. Scipio saw I
Washing the stains of Carthage from his sword,
And his freed poet, playing on his lyre
A melody men's souls replied unto: 130
Oak-bound and laurelled heads, each man a country;
And in the midst, like a sun o'er the sea
(Each helm in the crowd gilt by a ray from him),
Bald Julius sitting lonely in his car,
Within the circle of whose laurel wreath   135

All spirits of the earth and sea were spell-bound.
Down with him to the grave! Down with the god!
Stab, Cassius; Brutus, through him; through him, all!
Dead.—As he fell there was a tearing sigh:
Earth stood on him; her roots were in his heart;   140
They fell together. Caesar and his world
Lie in the Capitol; and Jove lies there,
With all the gods of Rome and of Olympus;
Corpses: and does the eagle batten on them?
No; she is flown: the owl sits in her nest;   145
The toge is cut for cowls; and falsehood dozes
In the chair of freedom, triple-crowned beast,
King Cerberus. Thence I have come in time
To see one grave for foul oppression dug,
Though I may share it.

    Isbr.   Nay: thou'rt a bold heart. 150
Welcome among us.

    Mario.   I was guided hither
By one in white, garlanded like a bride,
Divinely beautiful, leading me softly;
And she doth place my hand in thine, once more
Bidding me guard her honour amongst men;   155
And so I will, with death to him that soils it:
For she is Liberty.

    Adalm.   In her name we take thee;
And for her sake welcome thee brotherly.
At the right time thou comest to us, dark man,
Like an eventful unexpected night,   160
Which finishes a row of plotting days,
Fulfilling their designs.

    Isbr.   Now, then, my fellows,
No more; but to our unsuspected homes.
Good night to all who rest; hope to the watchful. 164
Stranger, with me. (*To* MARIO) [*Exeunt: manet* DUKE.

    Duke. I'm old and desolate. O were I dead
With thee, my wife! Oft have I lain by night
Upon thy grave, and burned with the mad wish

To raise thee up to life. Thank God, whom then
I might have thought not pitiful, for lending   170
No ear to such a prayer. Far better were I
Thy grave-fellow, than thou alive with me,
Amid the fears and perils of the time.

Enter ZIBA

Who's in the dark there?
   Ziba.   One of the dark's colour:
Ziba, thy slave.
   Duke.   Come at a wish, my Arab.   175
Is Torwald's house asleep yet?
   Ziba.   No: his lights still burn.
   Duke. Go; fetch a lantern and some working
      fellows
With spade and pickaxe. Let not Torwald come.
In good speed do it.   [*Exit* ZIBA.
            That alone is left me:
I will abandon this ungrateful country,
And leave my dukedom's earth behind me; all,   180
Save the small urn that holds my dead beloved:
That relic will I save from my wrecked princedom;
Beside it live and die.

Enter TORWALD, ZIBA, *and gravediggers*

          Torwald with them!
Old friend, I hoped you were in pleasant sleep: 185
'Tis a late walking hour.
   Torw.   I came to learn
Whether the slave spoke true. This haunted hour,
What would you with the earth? Dig you for treasure?
   Duke. Aye, I do dig for treasure. To the vault:
Lift up the kneeling marble woman there,   190
And delve down to the coffin. Aye, for treasure:
The very dross of such a soul and body
Shall stay no longer in this land of hate.
I'll covetously rake the ashes up

Of this my love-consumed incense star,   195
And in a golden urn, over whose sides
An unborn life of sculpture shall be poured,
They shall stand ever on my chamber altar.
I am not Heaven's rebel; think 't not of me;
Nor that I'd trouble her sepulchral sleep   200
For a light end. Religiously I come
To change the bed of my beloved lady,
That what remains below of us may join,
Like its immortal.

Torw.   There is no ill here: 204
And yet this breaking through the walls, that sever
The quick and cold, led never yet to good.

Ziba. Our work is done: betwixt the charmed moon-
      shine
And the coffin lies nought but a nettle's shade,
That shakes its head at the deed.

Duke. Let the men go.   [*Exeunt gravediggers.*
                    Now Death, thou shadowy miser,
I am thy robber; be not merciful,   211
But take me in requital. There she is then;
I cannot hold my tears, thinking how altered.
O thoughts, ye fleeting, unsubstantial things,
Thou formless, viewless, and unsettled memory!   215
How dare ye yet survive that gracious image,
Sculptured about the essence whence ye rose?
That words of hers should ever dwell in me,
Who is as if she never had been born   219
To all earth's millions, save this one! Nay, prithee,
Let no one comfort me. I'll mourn awhile
Over her memory.

Torw.   Let the past be past,
And Lethe freeze unwept on over it.
What is, be patient with; and, with what shall be,
Silence the body-bursting spirit's yearnings.   225
Thou say'st that, when she died, that day was spilt
All beauty flesh could hold; that day went down

An oversouled creation. The time comes
When thou shalt find again thy blessed love,
Pure from all earth, and with the usury   230
Of her heaven-hoarded charms.
    Duke.   Is this the silence
That I commanded? Fool, thou say'st a lesson
Out of some philosophic pedant's book.
I loved no desolate soul: she was a woman,
Whose spirit I knew only through those limbs,   235
Those tender members thou dost dare despise;
By whose exhaustless beauty, infinite love,
Trackless expression only, I did learn
That there was aught yet viewless and eternal;   239
Since they could come from such alone. Where is she?
Where shall I ever see her as she was?
With the sweet smile, she smiled only on me;
With those eyes full of thoughts, none else could see?
Where shall I meet that brow and lip with mine?
Hence with thy shadows! But her warm fair body, 245
Where 's that? There, mouldered to the dust. Old man
If thou dost dare to mock my ears again
With thy ridiculous, ghostly consolation,
I'll send thee to the blessings thou dost speak of.
    Torw. For Heaven's and her sake restrain this
        passion.   250
    Duke. She died. But Death is old and half worn out:
Are there no chinks in 't? Could she not come to me?
Ghosts have been seen, but never in a dream,
After she'd sighed her last, was she the blessing
Of these desiring eyes. All, save my soul,   255
And that but for her sake, were his who knew
The spell of Endor, and could raise her up.
    Torw. Another time that thought were impious.
Unreasonable longings, such as these,
Fit not your age and reason. In sorrow's rage   260
Thou dost demand and bargain for a dream,
Which children smile at in their tales.

Ziba.   Smile ignorance!
But, sure as men have died, strong necromancy
Hath set the clock of time and nature back;   264
And made Earth's rooty, ruinous, grave-piled caverns
Throb with the pangs of birth. Aye, were I ever
Where the accused innocent did pray
The dead, whose murder he was falsely charged with,
To rise and speak him free, I would essay
My sires' sepulchral magic.

Duke.   Slave, thou tempt'st me
To lay my sword's point to thy throat, and say   271
'Do it or die thyself'.

Torw.   Prithee, come in.
To cherish hopes like these is either madness,
Or a sure cause of it. Come in and sleep:
To-morrow we'll talk further.

Duke.   Go in thou.   275
Sleep blinds no eyes of mine, till I have proved
This slave's temptation.

Torw.   Then I leave you to him.
Good night again.   [*Exit* TORWALD.

Duke.   Good night, and quiet slumbers.
Now then, thou juggling African, thou shadow,
Think'st thou I will not murder thee this night,   280
If thou again dare tantalize my soul
With thy accursed hints, thy lying boasts?
Say, shall I stab thee?

Ziba.   Then thou murder'st truth.
I spoke of what I'd do.

Duke.   You told ghost-lies,
And thought I was a fool because I wept.   285
Now, once more, silence: or to-night I shed
Drops royaller and redder than those tears.

Enter ISBRAND *followed by* SIEGFRIED *with
wine, &c.*

Isbr. Pilgrim, not yet abed? Why, ere you've time

To lay your cloak down, heaven will strip off night,
And show her daily bosom.

   Duke.   Sir, my eyes   290
Never did feel less appetite for sleep:
I and my slave intend to watch till morrow.

   Isbr. Excellent. You're a fellow of my humour
I never sleep o' nights; the black sky likes me,
And the soul's solitude, while half mankind   295
Lies quiet in earth's shade rehearsing death.
Come, let 's be merry, I have sent for wine.
And here it comes. These mossy stones about us
Will serve for stools, although they have been turrets
Which scarce aught touched but sunlight, or the claw
Of the strong-winged eagles, who lived here   301
And fed on battle-bones. Come sit, sir stranger;
Sit too, my devil-coloured one; here 's room
Upon my rock. Fill, Siegfried.

   Siegfr.   Yellow wine,
And rich be sure. How like you it?   305

   Duke. Better ne'er wetted lip.

   Isbr. Then fill again. Come, hast no song to-night,
Siegfried? Nor you, my midnight of a man?
I'm weary of dumb toping.

   Siegfr.   Sing, yourself, Sir.
My songs are staler than the cuckoo's tune: 311
And you, companions?

   Duke.   We are quite unused.

   Isbr. Then you shall have a ballad of my making.

   Siegfr. How? do you rhyme too?

   Isbr. Sometimes, in leisure moments
And a romantic humour; this I made   315
One night a-strewing poison for the rats
In the kitchen corner.

   Duke.   And what 's your tune?

   Isbr. What is the night-bird's tune, wherewith she
        startles
The bee out of his dream and the true lover,

And both in the still moonshine turn and kiss   320
The flowery bosoms where they rest, and murmuring
Sleep smiling and more happily again?
What is the lobster's tune when he is boiled?
I hate your ballads that are made to come
Round like a squirrel's cage, and round again.   325
We nightingales sing boldly from our hearts:
So listen to us.

Song by ISBRAND

Squats on a toad-stool under a tree
    A bodiless childfull of life in the gloom,
Crying with frog voice, 'What shall I be?   330
Poor unborn ghost, for my mother killed me
    Scarcely alive in her wicked womb.
What shall I be? shall I creep to the egg
    That 's cracking asunder yonder by Nile,
        And with eighteen toes,   335
        And a snuff-taking nose,
    Make an Egyptian crocodile?
Sing, "Catch a mummy by the leg
    And crunch him with an upper jaw,
        Wagging tail and clenching claw;   340
        Take a bill-full from my craw,
        Neighbour raven, caw, O caw,
        Grunt, my crocky, pretty maw!"

'Swine, shall I be one? 'Tis a dear dog;
    But for a smile, and kiss, and pout,   345
    I much prefer *your* black-lipped snout,
        Little, gruntless, fairy hog,
        Godson of the hawthorn hedge.
    For, when Ringwood snuffs me out,
        And 'gins my tender paunch to grapple,   350
    Sing, " 'Twixt your ancles visage wedge,
        And roll up like an apple."

271

'Serpent Lucifer, how do you do?
Of your worms and your snakes I'd be one or two
   For in this dear planet of wool and of leather   355
'Tis pleasant to need no shirt, breeches or shoe,
   And have arm, leg, and belly together.
   Then aches your head, or are you lazy?
   Sing, "Round your neck your belly wrap,
   Tail-a-top, and make your cap   360
     Any bee and daisy."

'I'll not be a fool, like the nightingale
Who sits up all midnight without any ale,
   Making a noise with his nose;
Nor a camel, although 'tis a beautiful back;   365
Nor a duck, notwithstanding the music of quack
   And the webby, mud-patting toes.
I'll be a new bird with the head of an ass,
   Two pigs' feet, two men's feet, and two of a hen;
Devil-winged; dragon-bellied; grave-jawed, because
     grass   370
  Is a beard that's soon shaved, and grows seldom
    again
   Before it is summer; so cow all the rest;
   The new Dodo is finished. O! come to my nest.'

   Siegfr. A noble hymn to the belly gods indeed:
Would that Pythagoras heard thee, boy!   375
   Isbr. I fear you flatter: 'tis perhaps a little
Too sweet and tender, but that is the fashion;
Besides my failing is too much sentiment.
Fill the cups up, and pass them round again;
I'm not my nightly self yet. There's creation   380
In these thick yellow drops. By my faith, Siegfried,
A man of meat and water's a thin beast,
But he who sails upon such waves as these
Begins to be a fellow. The old gods
Were only men and wine.

Siegfr.   Here's to their memory. 385
They're dead, poor sinners, all of them but Death,
Who has laughed down Jove's broad, ambrosian brow,
Furrowed with earthquake frowns: and not a ghost
Haunts the gods' town upon Olympus' peak.

Isbr. Methinks that earth and heaven are grown bad
                                                     neighbours,   390
And have blocked up the common door between them.
Five hundred years ago had we sat here
So late and lonely, many a jolly ghost
Would have joined company.

Siegfr.   To trust in story,
In the old times Death was a feverish sleep,   395
In which men walked. The other world was cold
And thinly-peopled, so life's emigrants
Came back to mingle with the crowds of earth:
But now great cities are transplanted thither,
Memphis, and Babylon, and either Thebes,   400
And Priam's towery town with its one beech.
The dead are most and merriest: so be sure
There will be no more haunting, till their towns
Are full to the garret; then they'll shut their gates,
To keep the living out, and perhaps leave   405
A dead or two between both kingdoms.

Duke.   Ziba;
Hear'st thou, phantastic mountebank, what's said?

Ziba. Nay: as I live and shall be one myself,
I can command them hither.

Isbr.   Whom?

Ziba.   Departed spirits.

Duke. He who dares think that words of human
                                                     speech,   410
A chalky ring with monstrous figures in it,
Or smoky flames can draw the distant souls
Of those, whose bones and monuments are dust,
Must shudder at the restless, broken death,
Which he himself in age shall fall into.   415

273

Isbr. Suppose we four had lived in Cyrus' time,
And had our graves under Egyptian grass,
D'you think, at whistling of a necromant,
I'd leave my wine or subterranean love
To know his bidding? Mummies cannot pull   420
The breathing to them, when they'd learn the news.

   Ziba. Perhaps they do, in sleep, in swoons, in fevers:
But your belief's not needed.

          (*To the* DUKE) You remember
The damsel dark at Mecca, whom we saw
Weeping the death of a pale summer flower,   425
Which her spear-slain beloved had tossed to her
Galloping into battle?

   Duke.   Happy one!
Whose eyes could yield a tear to soothe her sorrows.
But what's that to the point?

   Ziba.   As those tears fell,
A magic scholar passed; and, their cause known,   430
Bade her no longer mourn: he called a bird,
And bid it with its bill select a grain
Out of the gloomy deathbed of the blossom.
The feathery bee obeyed; and scraped aside
The sand, and dropped the seed into its grave: 435
And there the old plant lay, still and forgotten,
By its just budding grandsons; but not long:
For soon the floral necromant brought forth
A wheel of amber, (such may Clotho use
When she spins lives,) and as he turned and sung,   440
The mould was cracked and shouldered up: there came
A curved stalk, and then two leaves unfurled,
And slow and straight between them there arose,
Ghostlily still, again the crowned flower.
Is it not easier to raise a man,   445
Whose soul strives upward ever, than a plant,
Whose very life stands halfway on death's road,
Asleep and buried half?

Duke.   This was a cheat:
The herb was born anew out of a seed,
Not raised out of a bony skeleton.   450
What tree is man the seed of?

    Ziba.   Of a ghost;
Of his night-coming, tempest-waved phantom:
And even as there is a round dry grain
In a plant's skeleton, which being buried
Can raise the herb's green body up again;   455
So is there such in man, a seed-shaped bone,
Aldabaron, called by the Hebrews Luz,
Which, being laid into the ground, will bear
After three thousand years the grass of flesh,
The bloody, soul-possessed weed called man.   460

    Isbr. Let's have a trick then in all haste, I prithee.
The world's man-crammed; we want no more of them:
But show me, if you will some four-legged ghost;
Rome's mother, the she-wolf; or the fat goat
From whose dugs Jove sucked godhead; any thing;
Pig, bullock, goose; for they have goblins too,   466
Else ours would have no dinner.

    Ziba.   Were you worthy,
I'd raise a spirit whom your conscience knows;
And he would drag thee down into that world,
Whither thou didst send him.

    Isbr.   Thanks for the offer.
Our wine's out, and these clouds, whose blackest
       wombs   471
Seem swelling with a second centaur-birth,
Threaten plain water. So good night.
                 [*Exit with* SIEGFRIED.

    Duke. Obstinate slave! Now that we are alone,
Durst thou again say life and soul has lifted   475
The dead man from the grave, and sent him walking
Over the earth?

    Ziba.   I say it, and will add
Deed to my word, not oath. Within what tomb

Dwells he, whom you would call?

Duke.   There. But stand off!   480
If you do juggle with her holy bones,
By God I'll murder thee. I don't believe you,
For here next to my heart I wear a bond,
Written in the blood of one who was my friend,
In which he swears that, dying first, he would   485
Borrow some night his body from the ground,
To visit me once more. One day we quarrelled,
Swords hung beside us and we drew: he fell
Yet never has his bond or his revenge
Raised him to my bed-side, haunting his murderer   490
Or keeping blood-sealed promise to his friend.
Does not this prove you lie?

   Ziba.   'Tis not my spell:
Shall I try that with him?

   Duke.   Never on him.
The heavy world press on him, where he lies,
With all her towers and mountains!

   Ziba.   Listen, lord.
Time was when Death was young and pitiful,   495
Though callous now by use; and then there dwelt,
In the thin world above, a beauteous Arab,
Unmated yet and boyish. To his couch
At night, which shone so starry through the boughs,
A pale flower-breathed nymph with dewy hair   500
Would often come, but all her love was silent;
And ne'er by daylight could he gaze upon her,
For ray by ray, as morning came, she paled,
And like a snow of air dissolved i' th' light,
Leaving behind a stalk with lilies hung,   505
Round which her womanish graces had assembled.
So did the early love-time of his youth
Pass with delight: but when, compelled at length,
He left the wilds and woods for riotous camps
And cities full of men, he saw no more,   510
Tho' prayed and wept for, his old bed-time vision,

The pale dissolving maiden. He would wander
Sleepless about the waste benighted fields,
Asking the speechless shadows of his thoughts
'Who shared my couch? Who was my love? Where is
    she?'   515
Thus passing through a grassy burial-ground,
Wherein a new-dug grave gaped wide for food,
'Who was she?' cried he, and the earthy mouth
Did move its nettle-bearded lips together,
And said, ''Twas I—I, Death: behold our child!'   520
The wanderer looked, and on the lap of the pit
A young child slept as at a mother's breast.
He raised it and he reared it. From that infant
My race, the death-begotten, draw their blood: 524
Our prayer for the diseased works more than medicine;
Our blessings oft secure grey hairs and happy
To new-born infants; and, in case of need,
The dead and gone are re-begotten by us,
And motherlessly born to second life.   529
    Duke. I've heard your tale. Now exorcise: but mark!
If thou dost dare to make my heart thy fool,
I'll send thee to thy grave-mouthed grandam, Arab.
    Ziba. Wilt thou submit unmurmuring to all evils,
Which this recall to a forgotten being
May cause to thee and thine?
    Duke.   With all my soul,   535
So I may take the good.
    Ziba.   And art thou ready
To follow, if so be its will, the ghost,
Whom you will re-imbody, to the place
Which it doth now inhabit?
    Duke.   My first wish.
Now to your sorcery: and no more conditions,   540
In hopes I may break off. All ill be mine,
Which shall the world revisit with the being
That lies within.
    Ziba.   Enough. Upon this scroll

Are written words, which read, even in a whisper,
Would in the air create another star;   545
And, more than thunder-tongued storms in the sky,
Make the old world to quake and sweat with fear;
And, as the chilly damps of her death-swoon
Fall and condense, they to the moon reflect
The forms and colours of the pale old dead.   550
Laid there among the bones, and left to burn
With sacred spices, its keen vaporous power
Would draw to life the earliest dead of all,
Swift as the sun doth ravish a dew-drop
Out of a flower. But see, the torch goes out: 555
How shall I light it?

   Duke.   Here 's my useless blood-bond;
These words, that should have waked illumination
Within a corpse's eyes, will make a tinder,
Whose sparks might be of life instead of fire.
Burn it.

   Ziba. An incense for thy senses, god of those,   560
To whom life is as death to us; who were,
Ere our grey ancestors wrote history;
When these our ruined towers were in the rock;
And our great forests, which do feed the sea
With storm-souled fleets, lay in an acorn's cup: 565
When all was seed that now is dust; our minute
Invisibly far future. Send thy spirit
From plant of the air, and from the air and earth,
And from earth's worms, and roots, again to gather
The dispersed being, 'mid whose bones I place   570
The words which, spoken, shall destroy death's king-
     dom,
And which no voice, but thunder, can pronounce.
Marrow fill bone, and vine-like veins run round them,
And flesh, thou grass, mown wert thou long ago—
Now comes the brown dry after-crop. Ho! ghost!   575
There 's thy old heart a-beating, and thy life
Burning on the old hearth. Come home again!

Duke. Hush! Do you hear a noise?

Ziba.   It is the sound
Of the ghost's foot on Jacob's ladder-rungs.   579

Duke. More like the tread upon damp stony steps
Out of a dungeon. Dost thou hear a door
Drop its great bolt and grate upon its hinges?

Ziba. (*aside*) Serpentine Hell! That is thy staircase
          echo,
And thy jaws' groaning. What betides it?

Duke. Thou human murder-time of night,   585
What hast thou done?

Ziba. My task: give me death if the air has not
What was the earth's but now. Ho there! i' th' vault.

A Voice. Who breaks my death?

Ziba. Draw on thy body, take up thy old limbs,   590
And then come forth tomb-born.

Mandr. (*within*) I have drawn on my stockings,
and taken up my old jerkin: but before I go out,
can't you give me some water to shave with? I have
a beard of a week's growth with which I decline   595
appearing before the ladies; and on an occasion
of being raised one would willingly be a little
spruce, master Sorcerer.

Duke. One moment's peace and silence!
Let me remember what a grace she had,   600
Even in her dying hour: her soul set not,
But at its noon Death like a cloud came o'er it,
And now hath passed away. O come to me
Thou dear departed spirit of my wife;
And, surely as I clasp thee once again,   605
Thou shalt not die without me.

Ziba.   Ho! there, Grave,
Is life within thee?

A voice from within. Melveric, prepare.

Mandr. from within. Coming, coming!
This cursed boot!

Duke. Did'st hear that answer? Open, and let in   610

The blessing to my eyes, whose subtle breath
Doth penetrate my heart's quick; let me hear
That dearest name out of those dearest lips.
Who 's there? Who comes?

    Ziba.   Momus of Hell, what 's this?

Enter MANDRAKE *from the Sepulchre*

    Mandr. A poor ghost of one Homunculus Man- 615
drake, Apothecary, often called by the boys in the
street, Monkey Drake, at your service. Excuse my
disorder. And, conjurer, I'll give you a little bit of
advice: the next time don't bait your ghost-trap
with bombast and doggrell, but good beef: we live 620
poorly in the dead line: and so I'll promise you,
you may catch as many ghosts, if they are of one
mind with my stomach, in a night in this churchyard, as rats in a granary. But your commands,
gentlemen.   625

    Duke. Is this thy wretched jest, thou villainous
        fool?
But I will punish thee, by heaven, and thou too
Shalt soon be what thou shouldst have better
        acted.

    Mandr. Excuse me. As you have thought proper
to call me to the living, I shall take the liberty of 630
remaining alive. I am more used to it; and living
was ever my hobby. If you want to speak to
another ghost of longer standing, look into the
old lumber room of a vault again. Some one seems
to be putting himself together there: or advertise 635
for a ghost; for my part, I was always dead against
my will, and shall write an Essay on it to be
dedicated to my black friend here: good night,
gentlemen. I must vanish, for I must go to Egypt
once more to make the salve again: and this time 640
I shall pot it in tin. Old Sir, you must not take it

ill, if I offend you: we dead are odd fish. Good
night, all.   [*Exit.*

 Duke. Thou disappointed cheat! Was this a
  fellow,
Whom thou hadst hired to act a ghostly part?   645
Thou see'st how well he does it. But away!
Or I will teach thee better to rehearse it.

 Ziba. Death is a hypocrite, a white dissembler,
Like all that doth seem good! I am put to shame.
          [*Exit.*

 Duke. Deceived and confounded vain desires!   650
Why laugh I not, and ridicule myself?
Come, I will leave this chilly silent place,
For nothing's to be gained by waiting in it.
'Tis still, and cold, and nothing in the air
But an old grey twilight, or of eve or morn   655
I know not which, dim as futurity,
And sad and hoary as the ghostly past,
Fills up the space. Hush! not a wind is there,
Not a cloud sails over the battlements,
Not a bell tolls the hour. Is there an hour?   660
Or is not all gone by, which here did hive,
Of men and their life's ways? If I could but hear
The ticking of a clock, or some one breathing,
Or e'en a cricket's chirping, or the grating
Of the old gates amidst the marble tombs,   665
I should be sure that this was still the world.
Hark! Hark! Doth nothing stir?
No light, and still no light, besides this ghost
That mocks the dawn, unaltered? Still no sound?
No voice of man? No cry of beast? No rustle   670
Of any moving creature? And sure I feel
That I remain the same: no more round blood-drops
Roll joyously along my pulseless veins:
The air I seem to breathe is still the same:
And the great dreadful thought, that now comes o'er
  me,   675

Must remain ever as it is, unchanged.—
This moment doth endure for evermore;
Eternity hath overshadowed time;
And I alone am left of all that lived,
Pent in this narrow, horrible conviction.   680
Ha! the dead soon will wake! My Agnes, rise;
Rise up, my wife! One look, ere Wolfram comes;
Quick, or it is too late: the murdered hasten:
My best-beloved, come once to my heart...
But ah! who art thou?

The gates of the sepulchre fly open and discover
WOLFRAM

    Wolfr.   Wolfram, murderer,   685
To whose heart thou didst come with horrid purpose.
    Duke. Lie of my eyes, begone! Are thou not dead?
Are not the worms, that ate thy marrow, dead?
What dost thou here, thou wretched goblin fool?
Think'st thou, I fear thee? Thou man-mocking air,
Thou art not truer than a mirror's image,   691
Nor half so lasting. Back again to coffin,
Thou baffled idiot spectre, or haunt cradles:
Or stay, and I'll laugh at thee. Guard thyself,
If thou pretendest life.   695
    Wolfr. Is this thin air, that thrusts thy sword away?
Flesh, bones, and soul, and blood that thou stol'st
    from me,
Upon thy summons, bound by bloody signs,
Here Wolfram stands: what wouldst thou?
    Duke.   What paper else,
But that cursed compact, could have made full Hell
Boil over, and spill thee, thou topmost damned?   701
But down again! I'll see no more of thee.
Hound, to thy kennel! to your coffin, bones!
Ghost, to thy torture!
    Wolfr.   Thou returnest with me;
So make no hurry. I will stay awhile   705

To see how the world goes, feast and be merry,
And then to work again.
   Duke.   Darest thou stand there,
Thou shameless spirit, and assert thyself,
While I defy, and question, and deride thee?
The stars, I see them dying: clearly all   710
The passage of this night remembrance gives me,
And I think coolly: but my brain is mad,
Else why behold I that? Is't possible
Thou'rt true, and worms have vomited thee up
Upon this rind of earth? No; thou shalt vanish.   715
Was it for this I hated thee and killed thee?
I'll have thee dead again, and hounds and eagles
Shall be thy graves, since this old, earthy one
Hath spat thee out for poison.
   Wolfr.   Thou, old man,
Art helpless against me. I shall not harm thee;   720
So lead me home. I am not used to sunlight,
And morn's a-breaking.
   Duke.   Then there is rebellion
Against all kings, even Death. Murder's worn out
And full of holes; I'll never make't the prison,
Of what I hate, again. Come with me, spectre;   725
If thou wilt live against the body's laws,
Thou murderer of Nature, it shall be
A question, which haunts which, while thou dost last.
So come with me.   [*Exeunt.*

ACT IV

Scene I. *An apartment in the Governor's palace*

The Duke *and an attendant*

Duke. Your lord sleeps yet?
   Attend.   An hour ago he rose:

About this time he 's busy with his falcons,
And then he takes his meal.
 Duke.   I'll wait for him. [*Exit Attendant.*
How strange it is that I can live to-day;
Nay look like other men, who have been sleeping 5
On quiet pillows and not dreamt! Methinks
The look of the world 's a lie, a face made up
O'er graves and fiery depths; and nothing 's true
But what is horrible. If man could see
The perils and diseases that he elbows, 10
Each day he walks a mile; which catch at him,
Which fall behind and graze him as he passes;
Then would he know that Life 's a single pilgrim,
Fighting unarmed amongst a thousand soldiers.
It is this infinite invisible 15
Which we must learn to know, and yet to scorn,
And, from the scorn of that, regard the world
As from the edge of a far star. Now then
I feel me in the thickest of the battle;
The arrow-shower pours down, swords hew, mines
  open 20
Their ravenous mouths about me; it rains death
But cheerly I defy the braggart storm,
And set my back against a rock, to fight
Till I am bloodily won.

Enter TORWALD

 Torw.   How? here already?
I'm glad on 't, and to see you look so clear 25
After that idle talk. How did it end?
 Duke. Scarcely as I expected.
 Torw.   Dared he conjure?
But surely you have seen no ghost last night:
You seem to have supped well and slept.
 Duke   We'd wine,
And some wild singing. Of the necromancy 30
We'll speak no more. Ha! Do you see a shadow?

Torw. Aye: and the man who casts it.

Duke. 'Tis true; my eyes are dim and dull with
      watching.

This castle that fell down, and was rebuilt

With the same stones, is the same castle still;   35

And so with him.

Enter WOLFRAM

Torw.   What mean you?

Duke.   Impudent goblin!

Darest thou the daylight? Dar'st be seen of more

Than me, the guilty? Vanish! Though thou'rt there,

I'll not believe I see thee.

Torw.   Who 's the stranger?

You speak as one familiar.

Duke.   Is aught here   40

Besides ourselves? I think not.

Torw.   Yet you gaze

Straight on the man.

Duke.   A villainous friend of mine;

Of whom I must speak well, and still permit him

To follow me.—So thou'rt yet visible,

Thou grave-breaker! If thou wilt haunt me thus,   45

I'll make thee my fool, ghost, my jest and zany.—

'Tis his officious gratitude that pains me:

The carcase owes to me its ruinous life,

(Between whose broken walls and cloven sides

You see the other world's grey spectral light;)   50

Therefore he clings to me so ivily.—

Now, goblin, lie about it.—'Tis in truth

A faithful slave.

Wolfr.   If I had come unsummoned,

If I had burst into your sunny world,

And stolen visibility and birth   55

Against thy prayers, thus shouldst thou speak to me:

But thou hast forced me up, remember that.

I am no fiend, no foe; then let me hear

These stern and tyrannous rebukes no more.
Wilt thou be with the born, that have not died?   60
I vanish: now a short farewell. I fade;
The air doth melt me, and, my form being gone,
I'm all thou see'st not.   [*Exit*.

Duke. Dissolved like snow in water! Be my cloud,
My breath, and fellow soul, I can bear all,   65
As long as thou art viewless to these others.—
Now there are two of us. How stands the bridal?

Torw. This evening 'twill be held.

Duke.   Good; and our plot
Leaps on your pleasure's lap; here comes my gang;
Away with you.   [*Exit* TORWALD.
                    I do begin to feel   70
As if I were a ghost among the men,
As all I loved are; for their affections
Hang on things new, young, and unknown to me:
And that I am is but the obstinate will
Of this my hostile body.   75

Enter ISBRAND, ADALMAR, *and* SIEGFRIED

Isbr. Come, let's be doing: we have talked whole
        nights
Of what an instant, with one flash of action,
Should have performed: you wise and speaking people
Need some one, with a hatchet-stroke, to free
The Pallas of your Jove-like headaches.

Duke.   Patience: 80
Fledging comes after hatching. One day more:
This evening is the wedding of the prince,
And with it feasts and maskings. In mid bowls
And giddy dances let us fall upon them.   84

Siegfr. Well thought: our enemies will be assembled.

Isbr. I like to see Ruin at dinner time,
Firing his cannons with the coals they lit
To boil the flesh-pots on. But what say you
To what concerns you most?   [*To* ADALMAR.

Adalm.   That I am ready
To hang my hopeful crown of happiness   90
Upon the temple of the public good.
  Isbr. Of that no need. Your wedding shall be
        finished;
Or left, like a full goblet yet untasted,
To be drunk up with greater thirst from toil.
I'll wed too when I've time. My honest pilgrim,   95
The melancholy lady, you brought with you,
Looks on me with an eye of much content:
I have sent some rhymed love-letters unto her,
In my best style. D' you think we're well matched?   99
  Adalm. How? The lion to thirst after the bee's dew?
  Isbr. True: I am rough, a surly bellowing storm;
But fallen, never tear did hang more tender
Upon the eyelash of a love-lorn girl,
Or any Frenchman's long, frost-bitten nose,
Than in the rosecup of that lady's life   105
I shall lie trembling. Pilgrim, plead for me
With a tongue love-oiled.
  Duke.   Win her, sir, and wear her.
But you and she are scarcely for one world.
  Isbr. Enough; I'll wed her. Siegfried, come with me;
We'll talk about it in the rainy weather.   110
Pilgrim, anon I find you in the ruins,
Where we had wine last night. [*Exit with* SIEGFRIED.
  Adalm. Would that it all were over, and well over!
Suspicions flash upon me here and there:
But we're in the mid ocean without compass,   115
Winds wild, and billows rolling us away:
Onwards with hope!
  Duke.   Of what? Youth, is it possible
That thou art toiling here for liberty,
And others' welfare, and such virtuous shadows
As philosophic fools and beggars raise   120
Out of the world that's gone? Thou'lt sell thy birth-
        right

For incense praise, less tickling to the sense
Than Esau's pottage steam?

 Adalm.   No, not for these,
Fame's breath and praise, its shadow. 'Tis my manner
To do what 's right and good.

 Duke.   Thou'rt a strange prince.
Why all the world, except some fifty lean ones, 126
Would, in your place and at your ardent years,
Seek the delight that lies in woman's limbs
And mountain-covering grapes. What's to be royal,
Unless you pick those girls, whose cheeks you fancy,
As one would cowslips? And see hills and valleys 131
Mantled in autumn with the snaky plant,
Whose juice is the right madness, the best heaven?
Have men, and beasts, and woods with flowers and
  fruit
From all the earth, one's slaves; bid the worm eat 135
Your next year's purple from the mulberry leaf,
The tiger shed his skin to line your robes,
And men die, thousands in a day, for glory?
Such things should kings bid from their solitude
Upon the top of Man. Justice and Good,   140
All penniless, base, earthy kind of fellows,
So low, one wonders they were not born dogs,
Can do as well, alas!

 Adalm.   There 's cunning in thee.
A year ago this doctrine might have pleased me:
But since, I have remembered in my childhood 145
My teachers told me that I was immortal,
And had within me something like a god;
Now, by believing firmly in that promise,
I do enjoy a part of its fulfilment,
And, antedating my eternity,   150
Act as I were immortal.

 Duke.   Think of *now*.
This Hope and Memory are wild horses, tearing
The precious *now* to pieces. Grasp and use

The breath within you; for you know not, whether
That wind about the trees brings you one more.   155
Thus far yourself. But tell me, hath no other
A right, which you would injure? Is this sceptre,
Which you would stamp to dust and let each varlet
Pick out his grain of power; this great spirit,
This store of mighty men's concentrate souls,   160
Which kept your fathers in gods' breath, and you
Would waste in the wide, smoky, pestilent air
For every dog to snuff in; is this royalty
Your own? O! when you were a boy, young prince,
I would have laid my heart upon your spirit: 165
Now both are broken.

   Adalm.   Father?

   Duke.   Yes, my son:
We'll live to be most proud of those two names.
Go on thy way: I follow and o'erlook.
This pilgrim's shape will hang about and guard thee,
Being but the shadow of my sunniness,   170
Looking in patience through a cloudy time. [*Exeunt.*

SCENE II. *A garden*

SIBYLLA *and* ATHULF

   Athulf. From me no comfort. O you specious
       creatures,
So poisonous to the eye! Go! you sow madness:
And one of you, although I cannot curse her,
Will make my grave a murderer's. I'll do nought;
But rather drink and revel at your bridal.   5
And why not Isbrand? Many such a serpent
Doth lick heaven's dew out of as sweet a flower.
Wed, wed! I'll not prevent it.

   Sibyl.   I beseech thee,
If there be any tie of love between thee
And she who is thy brother's.

Athulf.   Curse the word!   10
And trebly curse the deed that made us brothers!
O that I had been born the man I hate!
Any, at least, but one. Then—sleep my soul;
And walk not in thy sleep to do the act,
Which thou must ever dream of. My fair lady,   15
I would not be the reason of one tear
Upon thy bosom, if the times were other;
If women were not women. When the world
Goes round the other way and doing Cain-like
Passes as merrily as doing Eve-like,   20
Then I'll be pitiful. Let go my hand;
It is a mischievous limb, and may run wild,
Doing the thing its master would not.
Lo! Here comes some holy father to console you.

                                        [*Exit.*

   Sibyl. Then no one hears me. O! the world 's too
          loud,   25
With trade and battle, for my feeble cry
To rouse the living. The invisible
Hears best what is unspoken; and my thoughts
Have long been calling comfort from the grave.

Enter WOLFRAM

   Wolfr. Lady, you called me.
   Sibyl.   I?
   Wolfr.   The word was *Comfort*:
A name by which the master, whose I am,   31
Is named by many wise and many wretched.
Will ye with me to the place where sighs are not;
A shore of blessing, which disease doth beat
Sea-like, and dashes those whom he would wreck   35
Into the arms of Peace? But ah! what say I?
You're young and must be merry in the world;
Have friends to envy, lovers to betray you;
And feed young children with the blood of your heart,
Till they have sucked up strength enough to break it,
                    290

Poor woman! Art thou nothing but the straw   41
Bearing a heavy poison, and, that shed,
Cut down to be stamped on? But thou'rt i' th' blade,
The green and milky sun-deceived grass:
So stand till the scythe comes, take shine and shower,
And the wind fell you gently.
 Sibyl.   Do not go.   46
Speak as at first you did; there was in the words
A mystery and music, which did thaw
The hard old rocky world into a flood,
Whereon a swan-drawn boat seemed at my feet   50
Rocking on its blue billows; and I heard
Harmonies, and breathed odours from an isle,
Whose flowers cast tremulous shadows in the day
Of an immortal sun, and crowd the banks
Whereon immortal human kind doth couch.   55
This I have dreamt before: your speech recalled it.
So speak to soothe me once again.
 Wolfr. (*aside*)   Snake Death,
Sweet as the cowslip's honey is thy whisper:
O let this dove escape thee! I'll not plead,
I will not be thy suitor to this innocent: 60
Open thy craggy jaws; speak, coffin-tongued,
Persuasions through the dancing of the yew-bough
And the crow's nest upon it. (*Aloud*) Lady fair,
Listen not to me, look not on me more.
I have a fascination in my words,   65
A magnet in my look, which drags you downwards,
From hope and life. You set your eyes upon me,
And think I stand upon this earth beside you:
Alas! I am upon a jutting stone,
Which crumbles down the steeps of an abyss;   70
And you, above me far, grow wild and giddy:
Leave me, or you must fall into the deep.
 Sibyl. I leave thee never, nor thou me. O no!
You know not what a heart you spurn away;
How good it might be, if love cherished it;   75

And how deserted 'tis; ah, so deserted,
That I have often wished a ghost would come,
Whose love might haunt it. Turn not thou, the last.
Thou see'st I'm young: how happy might I be!
And yet I only wish these tears I shed   80
Were raining on my grave. If thou'lt not love me,
Then do me the next office; show me only
The shortest path to solitary death.

    Wolfr. You're moved to wildness, maiden. Beg not
      of me.
I can grant nothing good: quiet thyself,   85
And seek heaven's help. Farewell.

    Sibyl.   Wilt thou leave me?
Unpitying, aye unmoved in cheek and heart,
Stern, selfish mortal? Hast thou heard my prayer;
Hast seen me weep; hast seen my limbs to quiver,
Like a storm-shaken tree over its roots?   90
Art thou alive, and canst thou see this wretch,
Without a care?

    Wolfr.   Thou see'st I am unmoved:
Infer the truth.

    Sibyl.   Thy soul indeed is dead.

    Wolfr. My soul, my soul! O that it wore not now
The semblance of a garb it hath cast off ;   95
O that it was disrobed of these mock limbs,
Shed by a rocky birth unnaturally,
Long after their decease and burial!
O woe that I must speak! for she, who hears,
Is marked for no more breathing. There are histories
Of women, nature's bounties, who disdained   101
The mortal love of the embodied man,
And sought the solitude which spirits cast
Around their darksome presence. These have loved,
Wooed, wedded, and brought home their moonstruck
    brides   105
Unto the world-sanded eternity.
Hast faith in such reports?

 Sibyl.   So lonely am I,
That I dare wish to prove them true.
 Wolfr.   Dar'st die?
A grave-deep question. Answer it religiously.
 Sibyl. With him I loved, I dared.
 Wolfr.   With me and for me. 110
I am a ghost. Tremble not; fear not me.
The dead are ever good and innocent,
And love the living. They are cheerful creatures,
And quiet as the sunbeams, and most like,
In grace and patient love and spotless beauty,   115
The new-born of mankind. 'Tis better too
To die, as thou art, young, in the first grace
And full of beauty, and so be remembered
As one chosen from the earth to be an angel;
Not left to droop and wither, and be borne   120
Down by the breath of time. Come then, Sibylla,
For I am Wolfram!
 Sibyl.   Thou art come to fetch me!
It is indeed a proof of boundless love,
That thou hadst need of me even in thy bliss.
I go with thee. O Death! I am thy friend,   125
I struggle not with thee, I love thy state:
Thou canst be sweet and gentle, be so now;
And let me pass praying away into thee,
As twilight still does into starry night.   [*Exeunt.*

 Scene III. *A garden, under the windows of* AMALA'S
      apartment ATHULF

 Athulf. Once more I'll see thee, love, speak to thee,
    hear thee;
And then my soul shall cut itself a door
Out of this planet. I've been wild and heartless,
Laughed at the feasts where Love had never place,
And pledged my light faith to a hundred women,   5

Forgotten all next day. A worthless life,
A life ridiculous! Day after day,
Folly on folly! But I'll not repent.
Remorse and weeping shall not be my virtues:
Let fools do both, and, having had their evil,   10
And tickled their young hearts with the sweet sins
That feather Cupid's shafts, turn timid, weep,
Be penitent. Now the wild banquet 's o'er,
Wine spilt, lights out, I cannot brook the world,
It is so silent. And that poisonous reptile,   15
My past self, is a villain I'll not pardon.
I hate and will have vengeance on my soul:
Satirical Murder, help me... Ha! I am
Devil-inspired: out with you, ye fool's thoughts!
You're young, strong, healthy yet; years may you live:
Why yield to an ill-humoured moment? No!   21
I'll cut his throat across, make her my wife;
Huzza! for a mad life! and be a Duke!
I was born for sin and love it.

                      O thou villain,
Die, die! Have patience with me, heavenly Mercy!   25
Let me but once more look upon that blessing,
Then can I calmly offer up to thee
This crime-haired head.

Enter AMALA *as bride, with a bridesmaid*

                  O beauty, beauty!
Thou shed'st a moony night of quiet through me.
Thanks! now I am resolved.
    Bridesm.   Amala, good night: 30
Thou'rt happy. In these high delightful times,
It does the human heart much good to think
On deepest woe, which may be waiting for us,
Masked even in a marriage-hour.
    Amala.   Thou'rt timid:
'Tis well to trust in a good genius.   35

294

Are not our hearts, in these great pleasures godded,
Let out awhile to their eternity
And made prophetic? The past is pale to me;
But I do see my future plain of life,
Full of rejoicings and of harvest-dances,   40
Clearly, it is so sunny. A year hence
I'll laugh at you for this, until you weep.
Good night, sweet fear.

    Bridesm.   Take this flower from me,
(A white rose, fitting for a wedding-gift,)
And lay it on your pillow. Pray to live   45
So fair and innocently; pray to die,
Leaf after leaf, so softly.   [*Exit.*

    Amala.—Now to my chamber; yet an hour or two,
In which years must be sown.

    Athulf.   Stay, Amala;
An old acquaintance brings a greeting to you,   50
Upon your wedding night.

    Amala. His brother Athulf! What can he do here?
I fear the man.

    Athulf.   Dost love him?

    Amala.   That were cause
Indeed to fear him. Leave me, leave me, sir;
It is too late. We cannot be together   55
For any good.

    Athulf.   This once we can. O Amala,
Had I been in my young days taught the truth,
And brought up with the kindness and affection
Of a good man! I was not myself evil,
But out of youth and ignorance did much wrong.   60
Had I received lessons in thought and nature,
We might have been together, but not thus.
How then? Did you not love me long ago?
More, O much more than him? Yes, Amala,
You would have been mine now. A life with thee,   65
Heavenly delight and virtue ever with us!

I've lost it, trod on it, and spurned it. Woe!
O bitter woe is me!

 Amala.   Athulf, why make me
Rue the inevitable? Prithee leave me.

 Athulf. Thee bye and bye: and all that is not thee. 70
Thee, my all, that I've forfeited I'll leave,
And the world's all, my nothing.

 Amala.   Nay; despond not.
Thou'lt be a merry, happy man some day,
And list to this as to a tale of some one
You had forgotten.

 Athulf.   Now no need of comfort: 75
I'm somehow glad that it did thus fall out.
Then had I lived too softly; in these woes
I can stand up, and show myself a man.
I do not think that I shall live an hour.
Wilt pardon me for that my earlier deeds 80
Have caused to thee of sorrow? Amala,
Pity me, pardon me, bless me in this hour;
In this my death, in this your bridal, hour.
Pity me, sweet.

 Amala. Both thee and me: no more!

 Athulf.   Forgive!

 Amala. With all my soul. God bless thee, my dear
   Athulf. 85

 Athulf. Kiss I thy hand? O much more fervently
Now, in my grief, than heretofore in love.
Farewell, go; look not back again upon me.
In silence go.   [*Exit* AMALA.

    She having left my eyes,
There 's nothing in the world, to look on which 90
I'd live a moment longer. Therefore come,
Thou sacrament of death: Eternity,
I pledge thee thus.   [*He drinks from a vial.*

    How cold and sweet! It seems
As if the earth already began shaking,

To sink beneath me. O ye dead, come near;   95
Why see I you not yet? Come, crowd about me;
Under the arch of this triumphal hour,
Welcome me; I am one of you, and one
That, out of love for you, have forced the doors
Of the stale world.   100

Enter ADALMAR

   Adalm. I'm wearied to the core: where 's Amala?
Ha! Near her chambers! Who?
   Athulf.   Ask that to-morrow
Of the marble, Adalmar. Come hither to me.
We must be friends: I'm dying.
   Adalm.   How?
   Athulf.   The cup,
I've drank myself immortal.
   Adalm.   You are poisoned?   105
   Athulf. I am blessed, Adalmar. I've done 't myself.
'Tis nearly passed, for I begin to hear
Strange but sweet sounds, and the loud rocky dashing
Of waves, where time into Eternity
Falls over ruined worlds. The wind is fair,   110
The boat is in the bay,
And the fair mermaid pilot calls away.
   Adalm. Self poisoned?
   Athulf.   Aye: a philosophic deed.
Go and be happy.
   Adalm.   God! What hast thou done?
   Athulf. Justice upon myself.
   Adalm.   No. Thou hast stolen
The right of the deserving good old man   116
To rest, his cheerful labour being done.
Thou hast been wicked; caused much misery;
Dishonoured maidens; broken fathers' hearts;
Maddened some; made others wicked as thyself;   120
And darest thou die, leaving a world behind thee

That groans of thee to heaven?
    Athulf.   If I thought so—
Terrible would it be: then I've both killed
And damned myself. There 's justice!
    Adalm.   Thou should'st have lived;
Devoting every minute to the work   125
Of useful, penitent amendment: then,
After long years, you might have knelt to Fate,
And ta'en her blow not fearing. Wretch, thou diest not
But goest living into hell.
    Athulf.   It is too true;
I am deserted by those turbulent joys.   130
The fiend hath made me death-drunk. Here I'll lie,
And die most wretchedly, accursed, unpitied
Of all, most hated by myself. O God,
If thou could'st but repeal this fatal hour,
And let me live, how day and night I'd toil   135
For all things to atone! Must I wish vainly?
My brother, is there any way to live?
    Adalm. For thee, alas! in this world there is none.
Think not upon 't.
    Athulf.   Thou liest: there must be:
Thou know'st it, and dost keep it secret from me, 140
Letting me die for hate and jealousy.
O that I had not been so pious a fool,
But killed thee, 'stead of me, and had thy wife!
I should be at the banquet, drinking to her,
Kissing her lip, in her eye smiling...
                                  Peace!   145
Thou see'st I'm growing mad: now leave me here,
Accursed as I am, alone to die.
O birth, O breath, O life!
    Adalm. Wretched, yet not despised, farewell my
        brother.
    Athulf. O Arab, Arab! Thou dost sell true drugs.
Brother, my soul is very weary now: 151
Speak comfortably to me.

Adalm.   From the Arab,
From Ziba, had'st the poison?

    Athulf.   Aye. 'Twas good:
An honest villain is he.

    Adalm.   Hold, sweet brother,
A little longer hold in hope on life;   155
But a few minutes more. I seek the sorcerer,
And he shall cure thee with some wondrous drug.
He can, and shall perform it: rest thee quiet:
Hope or revenge I'll bring thee.   [*Exit.*

    Athulf.   Dare I hope?
O no: methinks it is not so unlovely,   160
This calm unconscious state, this breathless peace,
Which all, but troublesome and riotous man,
Assume without resistance. Here I'll lay me,
And let life fall from off me tranquilly.

Enter singers and musicians led by SIEGFRIED; *they
sing under* AMALA'S *windows*

Song

By female voices

We have bathed, where none have seen us,
   In the lake and in the fountain,   166
     Underneath the charmed statue
Of the timid, bending Venus,
   When the water-nymphs were counting
In the waves the stars of night,   170
     And those maidens started at you,
Your limbs shone through so soft and bright.
     But no secrets dare we tell,
       For thy slaves unlace thee,
        And he, who shall embrace thee,   175
     Waits to try thy beauty's spell.

By male voices

We have crowned thee queen of women,
    Since love's love, the rose, hath kept her
      Court within thy lips and blushes,
And thine eye, in beauty swimming,   180
    Kissing, we rendered up the sceptre,
At whose touch the startled soul
    Like an ocean bounds and gushes,
And spirits bend at thy controul.
    But no secrets dare we tell,   185
      For thy slaves unlace thee,
      And he, who shall embrace thee,
Is at hand, and so farewell.

Athulf. Shame on you! Do you sing their bridal song
Ere I have closed mine eyes? Who 's there among you
That dare to be enamoured of a maid   191
So far above you, ye poor rhyming knaves?
Ha! there begins another.

Song by SIEGFRIED

Maiden, thou sittest alone above,
    Crowned with flowers and like a sprite   195
    Starrily clothed in a garment white:
Thou art the only maiden I love,
    And a soul of fondness to thee I bring,
    Thy glorious beauty homaging,—
    But ah! thou wearest a golden ring.   200

Maiden, thou'st broken no vow to me
    But undone me alone with gentleness,
    Wasting upon me glances that bless:
And knew'st that I never was born for thee.
    No hope, no joy, yet never more   205
    My heart shall murmur; now 'tis o'er,
    I'll bless thee, dying at thy door.

Athulf. Ha! Ha! That fellow moves my spleen;
A disappointed and contented lover.
Methinks he 's above fifty by his voice: 210
If not, he should be whipped about the town,
For vending such tame doctrine in love-verses.
Up to the window, carry off the bride,
And away on horseback, squeaker!

    Siefgr. Peace, thou bold drunken fellow that liest
       there!—
Leave him to sleep his folly out, good fellows.   216
          [*Exit with the musicians, &c.*

    Athulf. Well said: I do deserve it. I lie here
A thousand-fold fool, dying ridiculously
Because I could not have the girl I fancied.
Well, they are wedded; how long now will last   220
Affection or content? Besides 'twere possible
He might have quaffed a like draught. But 'tis done:
Villainous idiot that I am to think on't.
She willed it so. Then, Amala, be fearless:
Wait but a little longer in thy chamber,   225
And he will be with thee whom thou hast chosen:
Or, if it make thee pastime, listen sweet one,
And I will sing to thee, here in the moonlight,
Thy bridal song and my own dirge in one.

Song

    A cypress-bough, and a rose-wreath sweet, 230
    A wedding-robe, and a winding-sheet,
        A bridal-bed and a bier.
      Thine be the kisses, maid,
        And smiling Love's alarms;
      And thou, pale youth, be laid   235
        In the grave's cold arms.
        Each in his own charms,

Death and Hymen both are here;
 So up with scythe and torch,
  And to the old church porch, 240
 While all the bells ring clear:
And rosy, rosy the bed shall bloom,
And earthy, earthy heap up the tomb.

Now tremble dimples on your cheek,
Sweet be your lips to taste and speak, 245
 For he who kisses is near:
For her the bridegroom fair,
 In youthful power and force;
For him the grizard bare,
  Pale knight on a pale horse, 250
 To woo him to a corpse.
  Death and Hymen both are here;
   So up with scythe and torch,
    And to the old church porch,
   While all the bells ring clear: 255
  And rosy, rosy the bed shall bloom,
  And earthy, earthy heap up the tomb.

Athulf. Now we'll lie down and wait for our two
 summoners;
Each patiently at least.

Enter AMALA

    O thou kind girl,
Art thou again there? Come and lay thine hand 260
In mine; and speak again thy soft way to me.
 Amala. Thy voice is fainter, Athulf: why sang'st
 thou?
 Athulf. It was my farewell: now I'll sing no more;
Nor speak a great deal after this. 'Tis well
You weep not. If you had esteemed me much, 265
It were a horrible mistake of mine.
Wilt close my eyes when I am dead, sweet maid?

Amala. O Athulf, thou might'st still have lived.

Athulf.   What boots it,
And thou not mine, not even loving me?
But that makes dying very sad to me.   270
Yet even thy pity is worth much.

Amala.   O no;
I pity not alone, but I am wretched—
Love thee and ever did most fervently,
Still hoping thou would'st turn and merit it.
But now—O God! if life were possible to thee,   275
I'd be thy friend for ever.

Athulf. O thou art full of blessings!
Thou lovest me, Amala: one kiss, but one;
It is not much to grant a dying man.

Amala. I am thy brother's bride, forget not that; 280
And never but to this, thy dying ear,
Had I confessed so much in such an hour.
But this be too forgiven. Now farewell.
'Twere not amiss if I should die to-night:
Athulf, my love, my only love, farewell.   285

Athulf. Yet one more minute. If we meet hereafter,
Wilt thou be mine? I have the right to thee;
And, if thou promise, I will let him live
This life, unenvied, with thee.

Amala.   Athulf, I will:
Our bliss there will be greater for the sorrow   290
We now in parting feel.

Athulf.   I go, to wait thee. [*Exit* AMALA.
Farewell, my bliss! She loves me with her soul,
And I might have enjoyed her, were he fallen.
Ha! ha! and I am dying like a rat,
And he shall drink his wine, twenty years hence,   295
Beside his cherished wife, and speak of me
With a compassionate smile! Come, Madness, come,
For death is loitering still.

Enter ADALMAR *and* ZIBA

Adalm.   An antidote!
Restore him whom thy poisons have laid low,
If thou wilt not sup with thy fellow fiends   300
In hell to-night.
    Ziba.   I pray thee strike me not.
It was his choice; and why should he be breathing
Against his will?
    Athulf.   Ziba, I need not perish.
Now my intents are changed: so, if thou canst,
Dispense me life again.
    Adalm.   Listen to him,   305
And once be a preserver.
    Ziba.   Let him rise.
Why, think you that I'd deal a benefit,
So precious to the noble as is death,
To such a pampered darling of delight
As he that shivers there? O, not for him,   310
Blooms my dark Nightshade, nor doth Hemlock brew
Murder for cups within her cavernous root.
Not for him is the metal blessed to kill,
Nor lets the poppy her leaves fall for him.
To heroes such are sacred. He may live,   315
As long as 'tis the Gout and Dropy's pleasure.
He wished to play at suicide, and swallowed
A draught, that may depress and shake his powers
Until he sleeps awhile; then all is o'er.
And so good night, my princes.   [*Exit.*
    Adalm.   Dost thou hear? 320
    Athulf. Victory! victory! I *do* hear; and Fate hears,
And plays with Life for one of our two souls,
With dice made of death's bones. But shall I do 't?
O Heaven! it is a fearful thing to be so saved!
    Adalm. Now, brother, thou'lt be happy.
    Athulf.   With thy wife! 325
I tell thee, hapless brother, on my soul,
Now that I live, I *will* live; I alone;
And Amala alone shall be my love.

There's no more room for you, since you have chosen
The woman and the power which I covet.   330
Out of thy bridal bed, out of thy throne!
Away to Abel's grave.   [*Stabs* ADALMAR.
   Adalm.   Thou murderous traitor!
I was thy brother.   [*Dies.*
   Athulf. (*After a pause*) How long a time it is since I
       was here!
And yet I know not whether I have slept,   335
Or wandered through a dreary cavernous forest,
Struggling with monsters. 'Tis a quiet place,
And one inviting strangely to deep rest.
I have forgotten something; my whole life
Seems to have vanished from me to this hour.   340
There was a foe whom I should guard against;
Who is he?
   Amala. (*from her window*) Adalmar!
   Athulf. (*in a low voice*) Hush! hush! I come to thee.
Let me but see if he be dead: speak gently,
His jealous ghost still hears.
   Amala.   So, it is over
With that poor troubled heart! O then to-night   345
Leave me alone to weep.
   Athulf.   As thou wilt, lady.
I'm stunned with what has happened. He is dead.
   Amala. O night of sorrow! Bear him from the
      threshold.
None of my servants must know where and why
He sought his grave. Remove him. O poor Athulf,   350
Why did'st thou it? I'll to my bed and mourn. [*Retires.*
   Athulf. Hear'st thou, corpse, how I play thy part?
      Thus had he
Pitied me in fraternal charity,
And I lain there so helpless. But what's this,
That chills my blood and darkens so my eyes?   355
What's going on in my heart and in my brain,
My bones, my life, all over me, all through me?

It cannot last. No longer shall I be
What I am now. Oh! I am changing, changing,
Dreadfully changing! Even here and now   360
A transformation will o'ertake and seize me.
It is God's sentence whispered over me.
I am unsouled, dishumanized, uncreated;
My passions swell and grow like brutes conceived;
My feet are fixing roots, and every limb   365
Is billowy and gigantic, till I seem
A wild old wicked mountain in the sea:
And the abhorred conscience of this murder,
Shall be created and become a Lion
All alone in the darkness of my spirit,   370
And lair him in my caves,
And when I lie tremendous in the billows,
Murderers, and men half ghosts, stricken with mad-
        ness,
Will come to live upon my rugged sides,
Die, and be buried in it. Now it comes;   375
I break, and magnify, and lose my form.
And yet I shall be taken for a man,
And never be discovered till I die.
Terrible, terrible: damned before my time,
In secret! 'Tis a dread, o'erpowering phantom.   380
    [*He lies down by the body, and sleeps: the scene closes.*

SCENE IV. *A large hall in the ducal castle. Through the
    windows in the background appears the illuminated
    city*

Enter ISBRAND *and* SIEGFRIED

Isbr. By my grave, Siegfried, 'tis a wedding-night.
The wish, that I have courted from my boyhood,
Comes blooming, crowned, to my embrace. Methinks,
The spirit of the city is right lovely;
And she will leave her rocky body sleeping   5

To-night, to be my queenly paramour.
Has it gone twelve?

Siegfr.   This half hour. Here I've set
A little clock, that you may mark the time.

Isbr. Its hand divides the hour. Are our guards here,
About the castle?

Siegfr.   You've a thousand swordsmen,   10
Strong and true soldiers, at the stroke of one.

Isbr. One 's a good hour; a ghostly hour. To-night
The ghost of a dead planet shall walk through,
And shake the pillars of this dukedom down.
The princes both are occupied and lodged   15
Far from us: that is well; they will hear little.
Go once more round, to the towers and battlements:
The hour, that strikes, says to our hearts 'Be one';
And, with one motion of a hundred arms,
Be the beacons fired, the alarums rung,   20
And tyrants slain! Be busy.

Siegfr.   I am with them.   [*Exit.*

Isbr. Mine is the hour it strikes; my first of life.
To morrow, with what pity and contempt,
Shall I look back new-born upon myself!

Enter a servant

                                What now?

Servant. The banquet 's ready.

Isbr.   Let it wait awhile: 25
The wedding is not ended. That shall be
No common banquet: none sit there, but souls
That have outlived a lower state of being.
Summon the guests.   [*Exit servant.*
                Some shall have bitter cups,
The honest shall be banished from the board   30
And the knaves duped by a luxurious bait.

Enter the DUKE, TORWALD, *and other guests
and conspirators*

307

Friends, welcome hither in the prince's name,
Who has appointed me his deputy
To-night. Why this is right: while men are here,
They should keep close and warm and thick together,
Many abreast. Our middle life is broad;   36
But birth and death, the turnstiles that admit us
On earth and off it, send us, one by one,
A solitary walk. Lord governor,
Will you not sit?
    Torw.   You are a thrifty liver,   40
Keeping the measure of your time beside you.
    Isbr. Sir, I'm a melancholy, lonely man,
A kind of hermit: and to meditate
Is all my being. One has said, that time
Is a great river running to eternity.   45
Methinks 'tis all one water, and the fragments,
That crumble off our ever-dwindling life,
Dropping into 't, first make the twelve-houred circle,
And that spreads outwards to the great round Ever.
    Torw. You're fanciful.
    Isbr.   A very ballad-maker.   50
We quiet men must think and dream at least.
Who likes a rhyme among us? My lord governor,
'Tis tedious waiting until supper time:
Shall I read some of my new poetry?
One piece at least?
    Torw.   Well; without further preface,   55
If it be brief.
    Isbr.   A fragment, quite unfinished,
Of a new ballad called 'The Median Supper'.
It is about Astyages; and I
Differ in somewhat from Herodotus.
But altering the facts of history,   60
When they are troublesome, good governors
Will hardly visit rigorously. Attention!

'Harpagus, hast thou salt enough,
  Hast thou broth enough to thy kid?
And hath the cook put right good stuff   65
  Under the pasty lid?'

'I've salt enough, Astyages,
  And broth enough in sooth;
And the cook hath mixed the meat and grease
  Most tickling to my tooth.'   70

So spake no wild Red Indian swine,
  Eating a forest rattle-snake:
But Harpagus, that Mede of mine,
  And King Astyages so spake.

'Wilt have some fruit? Wilt have some wine?   75
  Here 's what is soft to chew;
I plucked it from a tree divine,
  More precious never grew.'

Harpagus took the basket up,
  Harpagus brushed the leaves away;   80
But first he filled a brimming cup,
  For his heart was light and gay.

And then he looked, and saw a face,
  Chopped from the shoulders of some one;
And who alone could smile in grace   85
  So sweet? Why, Harpagus, thy son.

'Alas!' quoth the king, 'I've no fork,
  Alas! I've no spoon of relief,
Alas! I've no neck of a stork
  To push down this throttling grief.   90

We've played at kid for child, lost both;
  I'd give you the limbs if I could;
Some lie in your platter of broth:
  Good night, and digestion be good.'

Now Harpagus said not a word,   95
  Did no eye-water spill:
His heart replied, for that had heard;
  And hearts' replies are still.

How do you like it?
  Duke.   Poetry, they say,
Should be the poet's soul; and here, methinks,   100
In every word speaks yours.
  Isbr.   Good. Don't be glad too soon.
Do ye think I've done? Three minutes' patience more.

    A cannibal of his own boy,
      He is a cannibal uncommon;
    And Harpagus, he is my joy,   105
      Because he wept not like a woman.

    From the old supper-giver's poll
      He tore the many-kingdomed mitre;
    To him, who cost him his son's soul,
      He gave it; to the Persian fighter: 110
              And quoth,
    'Old art thou, but a fool in blood:
      If thou hast made me eat my son,
    Cyrus hath ta'en his grandsire's food;
      There 's kid for child, and who has won? 115

    All kingdomless is thy old head,
      In which began the tyrannous fun;
    Thou'rt slave to him, who should be dead:
      There 's kid for child, and who has won?'

                    310

Now let the clock strike, let the clock strike now,   120
And world be altered!
       [The clock strikes one, and the hour is repeated
        from the steeples of the city.
                      Trusty timepiece,
Thou hast struck a mighty hour, and thy work 's done;
For never shalt thou count a meaner one.
                [He dashes it on the ground.
Thus let us break our old life of dull hours,
And hence begin a being, counted not   125
By minutes, but by glories and delights.
           [Steps to a window and throws it open.
Thou steepled city, that dost lie below,
Time doth demand whether thou wilt be free.
Now give thine answer.
      [A trumpet is heard, followed by a peal of
        cannon. Beacons are seen. The stage is lined
        with soldiery.
   Torw.   Traitor, desperate traitor!
Yet betrayed traitor! Make a path for me,   130
Or, by the majesty that thou offendest,
Thou shalt be struck with lightning in thy triumph.

    Isbr. All kingdomless is the old mule,
       In which began the tyrannous fun;
       Thou'rt slave to him, who was thy fool;   135
       There 's Duke for Brother; who has won?

Take the old man away.
   Torw.   I go; but my revenge
Hangs, in its unseen might, godlike around you.
                      [Exit guarded.
   Isbr. To work, my friends, to work! Each man his
     way.
These present instants, cling to them: hold fast;   140
And spring from this one to the next, still upwards.

They're rungs to Jacob's ladder to scale heaven with:
Haste, or 'tis drawn away.   [*Exeunt cœteri.*
                                        O stingy nature,
To make me but one man! Had I but body
For every several measure of thought and will,   145
This night should see me world-crowned.

Enter a messenger

                              What news bring'st thou?
  Messr. Friends of the governor hold the strongest
                tower,
And shoot with death's own arrows.
    Isbr.   Get thee back,
And never let me hear thy voice again,
Unless to say, "'Tis taken'. Hark ye, sirrah;   150
Wood in its walls, lead on its roof, the tower
Cries, 'Burn me!' Go and cut away the drawbridge,
And leave the quiet fire to himself:
He knows his business.   [*Exit messenger.*

Enter ZIBA *armed*

                      What with you?
    Ziba.   I'll answer,
When one of us is undermost.
    Isbr.   Ha! Midnight,   155
Can a slave fight?   [*They fight:* ZIBA *is disarmed.*
                      Now darest thou cry for mercy?
    Ziba. Never. Eternity! Come give me that,
And I will thank thee.
    Isbr.   Something like a man,
And something like a fool. Thou'rt such a reptile,
That I do like thee: pick up thy black life: 160
I would not make my brother King and Fool,
Friend Death, so poor a present. Hence!   [*Exit* ZIBA
                                        They're busy.

'Tis a hot hour, which Murder steals from Love,
To create ghosts in.

Enter SIEGFRIED

Now?

Siegfr. Triumph! They cannot stand another half
  hour.   165
The loyal had all supped and gone to bed:
When our alarums thundered, they could only
Gaze from their frighted windows: and some few
We had in towers and churches to besiege.
But, when one hornet's nest was burnt, the rest   170
Cried quarter, and went home to end their naps.

Isbr. 'Twas good. I knew it was well planned. Return,
And finish all. I'll follow thee, and see
How Mars looks in his night-cap.   [*Exit* SIEGFRIED.
O! it is nothing now to be a man.   175
Adam, thy soul was happy that it wore
The first, new, mortal members. To have felt
The joy of the first year, when the one spirit
Kept house-warming within its fresh-built clay,
I'd be content to be as old a ghost.   180
Thine was the hour to live in. Now we're common,
And man is tired of being no more than human;
And I'll be something better:—not by tearing
This chrysalis of psyche ere its hour,
Will I break through Elysium. There are sometimes,
Even here, the means of being more than men: 186
And I by wine, and women, and the sceptre,
Will be, my own way, heavenly in my clay.
O you small star-mob, had I been one of you,
I would have seized the sky some moonless night,   190
And made myself the sun; whose morrow rising
Shall see me new-created by myself.
Come, come; to rest, my soul. I must sleep off
This old plebeian creature that I am.   [*Exit.*

313

ACT V

Scene I. *An apartment in the ducal castle*

ISBRAND *and* SIEGFRIED

Siegfr. They wait still for you in their council
    chamber,
And clamorously demand the keys of the treasure,
The stores of arms, lists of the troops you've hired,
Reports of your past acts, and your intentions
Towards the new republic.

    Isbr.   They demand!   5
A phrase politer would have pleased me more.
The puppets, whose heart-strings I hold and play
Between my thumb and fingers, this way, that way;
Through whose masks, wrinkled o'er by age and
    passion,
My voice and spirit hath spoken continually;   10
Dare now to ape free will? Well done, Prometheus!
Thou'st pitied Punch and given him a soul,
And all his wooden peers. The tools I've used
To chisel an old heap of stony laws,
The abandoned sepulchre of a dead dukedom,   15
Into the form my spirit loved and longed for;
Now that I've perfected her beauteous shape,
And animated it with half my ghost;
Now that I lead her to our bridal bed,
Dare the mean instruments to lay their plea,   20
Or their demand forsooth, between us? Go;
And tell the fools, (you'll find them pale, and dropping
Cold tears of fear out of their trembling cheek-pores;)
Tell them, for comfort, that I only laughed;
And bid them all to sup with me to-night,   25
When we will call the cup to counsel.
    Siegfr.   Mean you
Openly to assume a kingly power,
Nor rather inch yourself into the throne?

Perhaps—but as you will.

Isbr.   Siegfried, I'm one

That what I will must do, and what I do   30

Do in the nick of time without delay.

To-morrow is the greatest fool I know,

Excepting those that put their trust in him.

In one word hear, what soon they all shall hear:

A king 's a man, and I will be no man   35

Unless I am a king. Why, where 's the difference?

Throne steps divide us: they're soon climbed perhaps:

I have a bit of FIAT in my soul,

And can myself create my little world.

Had I been born a four-legged child, methinks   40

I might have found the steps from dog to man,

And crept into humanity. There be

Those that fall down out of their stage of manhood

Into the story where the four-legged dwell.

But to the conclave with my message quickly: 45

I've yet a deal to do.   [*Exit* SIEGFRIED.

                How I despise

All you mere men of muscle! It was ever

My study to find out a way to godhead,

And on reflection soon I found that first

I was but half created; that a power   50

Was wanting in my soul to be its soul,

And this was mine to make. Therefore I fashioned

A will above my will, that plays upon it,

As the first soul doth use in men and cattle.

There 's lifeless matter; add the power of shaping,   55

And you've the crystal: add again the organs,

Wherewith to subdue sustenance to the form

And manner of one's self, and you've the plant:

Add power of motion, senses, and so forth,

And you've all kind of beasts; suppose a pig: 60

To pig add foresight, reason, and such stuff,

Then you have man. What shall we add to man,

315

To bring him higher? I begin to think
That's a discovery I soon shall make.
Thus I, owing nought to books, but being read   65
In the odd nature of much fish and fowl,
And cabbages and beasts, have I raised myself,
By this comparative philosophy,
Above your shoulders, my sage gentlemen.
Have patience but a little, and keep still,   70
I'll find means, bye and bye, of flying higher. [*Exit*.

SCENE II. *Another apartment*

The DUKE, MARIO, ZIBA, *and Conspirators*.
SIEGFRIED

A Conspirator. (*to* SIEGFRIED) Said he nought else?
    Siegfr.   What else he said was worse.
He is no more Isbrand of yesterday;
But looks and talks as one, who in the night
Hath made a bloody compact with some fiend.
His being is grown greater than it was,   5
And must make room, by cutting off men's lives,
For its shadowy increase.
    Conspir.   O friends, what have we done?
Sold, for a promise, still security,
The mild familiar laws our fathers left;
Uprooted our firm country.
    Ziba.   And now sit,   10
Weeping like babes, among its ruins. Up!
You have been cheated; now turn round upon him.
In this his triumph pull away his throne,
And let him into hell.
    Another Conspir.   But that I heard it
From you, his inmost counsel and next heart,   15
I'd not believe it. Why, the man was open;
We looked on him, and saw your looks reflected;
Your hopes and wishes found an echo in him;

316

He pleased us all, I think. Let 's doubt the worst,
Until we see.
   Duke.   Until you feel and perish.   20
You looked on him, and saw your looks reflected,
Because his soul was in a dark deep well,
And must draw down all others to encrease it:
Your hopes and wishes found an echo in him,
As out of a sepulchral cave, prepared   25
For you and them to sleep in. To be brief,
He is the foe of all; let all be his,
And he must be o'erwhelmed.
   Siegfr.   I throw him off,
Although I feared to say so in his presence,
And think you all will fear. O that we had   30
Our good old noble Duke, to help us here!
   Duke. Of him I have intelligence. The governor,
Whose guards are bribed and awed by these good
     tidings,
Waits us within. There we will speak at large:
And O! may justice, for this once, descend   35
Like lightning-footed vengeance.
   Mario.   It will come;
But when, I know not. Liberty, whose shade
Attends, smiles still in patience, and that smile
Melts tyrants down in time: and, till she bids,
To strike were unavailing.
          [*Exeunt.* ZIBA *and* SIEGFRIED *remain.*
   Ziba.   Let them talk: 40
I mean to do; and will let no one's thoughts,
Or reasonable cooling counsels, mix
In my resolve to weaken it, as little
As shall a drop of rain or pity-water
Adulterate this thick blood-curdling liquor.   45
Siegfried, I'll free you from this thankless master.
   Siegfr. I understand. To-night? Why that is best.
In plottings there is still some creak unstopped,
Some heart unsteeled, some fellow who doth talk

In sleep or in his cups, or tells his tale,   50
Love-drunk, unto his secret-selling mistress.
How shall 't be done though?
    Ziba.   I'm his cup-bearer;
An office that he gave me in derision
And I will execute so cunningly
That he shall have no lips to laugh with, long;   55
Nor spare and spurn me, as he did last night.
Let him beware, who shows a dogged slave
Pity or mercy! For the drug, 'tis good:
There is a little, hairy, green-eyed snake,
Of voice like to the woody nightingale,   60
And ever singing pitifully sweet,
That nestles in the barry bones of death,
And is his dearest pet and playfellow.
The honied froth about that serpent's tongue
Deserves not so his habitation's name,   65
As doth this liquor. That 's the liquor for him.
                                    [*Exeunt.*

SCENE III. *A meadow*

SIBYLLA *and ladies, gathering flowers*

    Sibyl. Enough; the dew falls, and the glow-worm 's
      shining:
Now let us search our baskets for the fairest
Among our flowery booty, and then sort them.
    Lady. The snowdrops are all gone; but here are
      cowslips,
And primroses, upon whose petals maidens,   5
Who love to find a moral in all things,
May read a lesson of pale bashfulness;
And violets, that have taught their young buds white-
      ness,
That blue-eyed ladies' lovers might not tear them
For the old comparison; daisies without number,   10

And buttercups and lilies of the vale.

   Sibyl. Sit then; and we will bind some up with
       rushes,
And wind us garlands. Thus it is with man;
He looks on nature as his supplement,
And still will find out likenesses and tokens   15
Of consanguinity, in the world's graces,
To his own being. So he loves the rose,
For the cheek's sake, whose touch is the most grateful
At night-fall to his lip; and, as the stars rise,
Welcomes the memories of delighting glances,   20
Which go up as an answer o'er his soul.

   Lady. And therefore earth and all its ornaments,
Which are the symbols of humanity
In forms refined, and efforts uncompleted,
All innocent and graceful, temper the heart,   25
Of him who muses and compares them skilfully,
To glad belief and tearful gratitude.
This is the sacred source of poesy.

   Sibyl. While we are young and free from care, we
       think so.
But, when old age or sorrow brings us nearer   30
To spirits and their interests, we see
Few features of mankind in outward nature;
But rather signs inviting us to heaven.
I love flowers too; not for a young girl's reason,
But because these brief visitors to us   35
Rise yearly from the neighbourhood of the dead,
To show us how far fairer and more lovely
Their world is; and return thither again,
Like parting friends that beckon us to follow,
And lead the way silent and smilingly.   40
Fair is the season when they come to us,
Unfolding the delights of that existence
Which is below us: 'tis the time of spirits,
Who with the flowers, and like them, leave their
       graves:

But when the earth is sealed, and none dare come   45
Upwards to cheer us, and man 's left alone,
We have cold, cutting winter. For no bridal,
Excepting with the grave, are flowers fit emblems.
   Lady. And why then do we pluck and wreathe them
     now?
   Sibyl. Because a bridal with the grave is near.   50
You will have need of them to strew a corpse.
Aye, maidens, I am dying; but lament not:
It is to me a wished for change of being.
Yonder behold the evening star arising,
Appearing bright over the mountain-tops;   55
He has just died out of another region,
Perhaps a cloudy one; and so die I;
And the high heaven, serene and light with joy,
Which I pass into, will be my love's soul,
That will encompass me; and I shall tremble,   60
A brilliant star of never-dying delight,
'Mid the ethereal depth of his eternity.
Now lead me homewards: and I'll lay me down,
To sleep not, but to rest: then strew me o'er
With these flowers fresh out of the ghosts' abodes,   65
And they will lead me softly down to them.   [*Exeunt.*

SCENE IV. *The ruined Cathedral, in which a large
covered table with empty chairs is set; the sepulchre,
and the cloisters painted with the* DANCE OF DEATH
*as in Act III, Scene 3. Moonlight. The clock strikes
twelve; on which is heard*

A Song in the air

The moon doth mock and make me crazy,
   And midnight tolls her horrid claim
   On ghostly homage. Fie, for shame!
Deaths, to stand painted there so lazy.

There's nothing but the stars about us,   5
    And they're no tell-tales, but shine quiet:
Come out, and hold a midnight riot,
Where no mortal fool dare flout us:
And, as we rattle in the moonlight pale;
Wanderers shall think 'tis the nightingale.   10

    [The Deaths, and the figures paired with them,
        come out of the walls, and dance fantasti-
        cally to a rattling music, singing; some
        seat themselves at the table and drink and
        with mocking gestures, mask the feast,
        &c.

Song

Mummies and skeletons, out of your stones;
    Every age, every fashion, and figure of Death:
The death of the giant with petrified bones;
    The death of the infant who never drew breath.
Little and gristly, or bony and big,   15
    White and clattering, grassy and yellow;
    Dance and be merry, for Death's a droll fellow.
The emperor and empress, the king and the queen,
    The knight and the abbot, friar fat, friar thin,   20
The gipsy and beggar, are met on the green;
    Where's Death and his sweetheart? We want to
        begin.
In circles, and mazes, and many a figure,
    Through clouds, over chimneys and cornfields
        yellow,
We'll dance and laugh at the red-nosed gravedigger, 25
    Who dreams not that Death is so merry a fellow.

One with a scythe, who has stood sentinel, now sings:

Although my old ear
   Hath neither hammer nor drum,
Methinks I can hear
   Living skeletons come.   30
The cloister re-echoes the call,
   And it frightens the lizard,
And, like an old hen, the wall
   Cries 'cluck! cluck! back to my gizzard;
''Tis warm, though it 's stony,   35
   'My chickens so bony.'
So come let us hide, each with his bride,
For the wicked are coming who have not yet died.
     [The Deaths return to their places in the wall.

Enter ISBRAND, *the* DUKE, SIEGFRIED, MARIO, WOLF-
RAM *as fool, and Conspirators, followed by* ZIBA *and
other Attendants*

  Isbr. You wonder at my banqueting-house perhaps:
But 'tis my fashion, when the sky is clear,   40
To drink my wine out in the open air:
And this our sometime meeting-place is shadowy,
And the wind howleth through the ruins bravely.
Now sit, my gentle guests: and you, dark man,
                     [To WOLFRAM.
Make us as merry as you can, and proudly   45
Bear the new office, which your friend, the pilgrim,
Has begged for you: 'twas my profession once;
Do justice to that cap.
  Duke. Now, having washed our hearts of love and
         sorrow,
And pledged the rosiness of many a cheek,   50
And, with the name of many a lustrous maiden,
Ennobled enough cups; feed, once again,
Our hearing with another merry song.
  Isbr. 'Tis pity that the music of this dukedom,
Under the former government, went wrong,   55
Like all the rest: my ministers shall look to 't.

But sing again, my men.
 Siegfr.   What shall it be,
And of what turn? Shall battle's drum be heard?
The chase's trumpet? Shall the noise of Bacchus
Swell in our cheeks, or lazy, sorrowing love   60
Burthen with sighs our ballad?
 Isbr.   Try the piece,
You sang me yesternight to sleep with best.
It is for such most profitable ends
We crowned folks encourage all the arts.

Song

My goblet's golden lips are dry,   65
 And, as the rose doth pine
 For dew, so doth for wine
  My goblet's cup;
Rain, O! rain, or it will die;
 Rain, fill it up!   70

Arise, and get thee wings to-night,
 Ætna! and let run o'er
 Thy wines, a hill no more,
  But darkly frown
A cloud, where eagles dare not soar,   75
 Dropping rain down.

 Isbr. A very good and thirsty melody:
What say you to it, my court poet?
 Wolfr. Good melody! If this be a good melody,
I have at home, fattening in my stye,   80
A sow that grunts above the nightingale.
Why this will serve for those, who feed their veins
With crust, and cheese of dandelion's milk,
And the pure Rhine. When I am sick o' mornings,
With a horn-spoon tinkling my porridge-pot,   85
'Tis a brave ballad: but in Bacchanal night,

O'er wine, red, black, or purple-bubbling wine,
That takes a man by the brain and whirls him round,
By Bacchus' lip! I like a full-voiced fellow,
A craggy-throated, fat-cheeked trumpeter,   90
A barker, a moon-howler, who could sing
Thus, as I heard the snaky mermaids sing
In Phlegethon, that hydrophobic river,
One May-morning in Hell.

Song

  Old Adam, the carrion crow,   95
    The old crow of Cairo;
  He sat in the shower, and let it flow
    Under his tail and over his crest;
      And through every feather
      Leaked the wet weather;   100
  And the bough swung under his nest;
  For his beak it was heavy with marrow.
    Is that the wind dying? O no;
    It 's only two devils, that blow
      Through a murderer's bones, to and fro,
        In the ghosts' moonshine.   106

  Ho! Eve, my grey carrion wife,
    When we have supped on kings' marrow,
  Where shall we drink and make merry our life?
    Our nest it is queen Cleopatra's scull,   110
      'Tis cloven and cracked,
      And battered and hacked,
  But with tears of blue eyes it is full:
  Let us drink then, my raven of Cairo.
    Is that the wind dying? O no;   115
    It 's only two devils, that blow
      Through a murderer's bones, to and fro,
        In the ghosts' moonshine.

Isbr. Pilgrim, it is with pleasure I acknowledge,
In this your friend, a man of genuine taste: 120
He imitates my style in prose and verse:
And be assured that this deserving man
Shall soon be knighted, when I have invented
The name of my new order; and perhaps
I'll make him minister. I pledge you, Fool: 125
Black! something exquisite.

    Ziba.   Here 's wine of Egypt,
Found in a Memphian cellar, and perchance
Pressed from its fruit to wash Sesostris' throat,
Or sweeten the hot palate of Cambyses.
See how it pours, thick, clear, and odorous.   130

    Isbr. 'Tis full, without a bubble on the top:
Pour him the like. Now give a toast.

  • *Wolfr.*   Excuse me:
I might offend perhaps, being blunt, a stranger,
And rustically speaking rustic thoughts.

    Isbr. That shall not be: give us what toast you will,
We'll empty all our goblets at the word,   136
Without demur.

    Siegfr.   Well, since the stranger 's silent.
I'll give a toast, which, I can warrant you,
Was yet ne'er drunk. There is a bony man,
Through whom the sun shines, when the sun is out:
Or the rain drops, when any clouds are weeping;   141
Or the wind blows, if Æolus will; his name,
And let us drink to his success and sanity;—
But will you truly?

    Isbr.   Truly, as I said.

    Siegfr. Then round with the health of Death, round
    with the health   145
Of Death the bony, Death the great; round, round.
Empty yourselves, all cups, unto the health
Of great King Death!

    Wolfr. Set down the cup, Isbrand, set the cup down.
Drink not, I say.

325

Siegfr.   And what 's the matter now?   150

Isbr. What do you mean, by bidding me not drink?
Answer, I'm thirsty.

Wolfr.   Push aside the boughs:
Let 's see the night, and let the night see us.

Isbr. Will the fool read us astronomic lectures?

Wolfr. Above stars; stars below; round the moon
stars.   155
Isbrand, don't sip the grape-juice.

Isbr.   Must I drink,
Or not, according to a horoscope?
Says Jupiter, no? Then he 's a hypocrite.

Wolfr. Look upwards, how 'tis thick and full, how
sprinkled,
This heaven, with the planets. Now, consider;   160
Which will you have? The sun 's already taken,   •
But you may find an oar in the half moon,
Or drive the comet's dragons; or, if you'd be
Rather a little snug and quiet god,
A one-horse star is standing ready for you.   165
Choose, and then drink.

Isbr.   If you are sane or sober,
What do you mean?

Wolfr.   It is a riddle, sir,
Siegfried, your friend, can solve.

Siegfr.   Some sorry jest.

Wolfr. You'll laugh but palely at its sting, I think.
Hold the dog down; disarm him; grasp his right.   170
My lord, this worthy courtier loved your virtues
To such excess of piety, that he wished
To send you by a bye-path into heaven.
Drink, and you're straight a god—or something else.

A Conspirator. O murderous villain! Kill him where
he sits.   175

Isbr. Be quiet, and secure him. Siegfried, Siegfried;
Why hast thou no more genius in thy villany?
Wilt thou catch kings in cobwebs? Lead him hence:

Chain him to-night in prison, and to-morrow
Put a cord round his neck and hang him up,   180
In the society of the old dog
Who killed my neighbour's sheep.

   Siegfr.   I do thank thee.
In faith, I hoped to have seen grass grow o'er you,
And should have much rejoiced. But, as it is,
I'll willingly die upright in the sun: 185
And I can better spare my life than you.
Good night then, Fool and Duke: you have my curse;
And Hell will have you some day down for hers:
So let us part like friends. My lords, good sleep
This night, the next I hope you'll be as well   190
As I shall. Should there be a lack of rope,
I recommend my bowstring as a strong one.
Once more, farewell: I wish you all, believe me,
Happily old, mad, sick, and dead, and cursed.

                       [Exit guarded.

   Isbr. That gentleman should have applied his talent
To writing new-year's wishes. Another cup!   196

   Wolfr. He has made us dull: so I'll begin a story.
As I was newly dead, and sat beside
My corpse, looking on it, as one who muses
Gazing upon a house he was burnt out of,   200
There came some merry children's ghosts to play
At hide-and-seek in my old body's corners:—

   Isbr. But how came you to die and yet be here?

   Wolfr. Did I say so? Excuse me. I am absent,
And forget always that I'm just now living.   205
But dead and living, which are which? A question
Not easy to be solved. Are you alone,
Men, as you're called, monopolists of life?
Or is all being, living? and *what is*,
With less of toil and trouble, more alive,   210
Than they, who cannot, half a day, exist
Without repairing their flesh mechanism?
Or do you owe your life, not to this body,

But to the sparks of spirit that fly off,
Each instant disengaged and hurrying　　　　　　215
From little particles of flesh that die?
If so, perhaps you are the dead yourselves:
And these ridiculous figures on the wall
Laugh, in their safe existence, at the prejudice,
That you are anything like living beings.　　　　220
But hark! The bell tolls, and a funeral comes.
　　　　　　　[Enter a funeral: ladies bearing a pall.

Dirge

We do lie beneath the grass
　　In the moonlight, in the shade
Of the yew-tree. They that pass
　　Hear us not. We are afraid　　　　　　225
　　　　They would envy our delight,
　　　　In our graves by glow-worm night.
Come follow us, and smile as we;
　　We sail to the rock in the ancient waves,
Where the snow falls by thousands into the sea,　　230
　　And the drowned and the shipwrecked have
　　　　happy graves.　　　　　　　*[Exeunt.*

Duke. What 's this that comes and goes, so shadow-
　　like?
Attendant. They bear the fair Sybilla to her grave.
Duke.　　　　　　　　　　　　She dead!
Darest thou do this, thou grave-begotten man,
Thou son of Death? (*To* WOLFRAM)
Wolfr.　　　　　Sibylla dead already?　　　　235
I wondered how so fair a thing could live:
And, now she is no more, it seems to me
She was too beautiful ever to die!
Isbr. She, who was to have been my wife? Here,
　　fellow;
Take thou this flower to strew upon her grave,　　240

A lily of the valley; it bears bells,
For even the plants, it seems, must have their fool,
So universal is the spirit of folly;
And whisper, to the nettles of her grave,
'King Death hath asses' ears'.   245
   Mario. (*Stabbing* ISBRAND) At length thou art con-
demned to punishment.
Down thou usurper, to the earth and grovel!
The pale form, that has led me up to thee,
Bids me deal this; and, now my task is o'er,
Beckons me hence.   [*Exit.*
   Isbr.   Villain, thou dig'st deep: 250
But think you I will die? No: should I groan,
And close my eyes, be fearful of me still.
'Tis a good jest: I but pretend to die,
That you may speak about me bold and loudly;
Then I come back and punish: or I go   255
To dethrone Pluto. It is wine I spilt,
Not blood, that trickles down.

Enter TORWALD *with soldiers*

   Torw. Long live duke Melveric!
   All. Long live duke Melveric!
   Isbr.   Duke Isbrand, long live he!
Duke Melveric is deposed.
   Torw.   Receive the homage   260
Of your revolted city.
   Duke.   Torwald, thanks.
The usurper has his death-wound.
   Torw.   Then cry, Victory!
And long life to duke Melveric! once more.
   Isbr. I will live longer: when he's dead and buried,
A hundred years hence, or, it may be, more,   265
I shall return and take my dukedom back.
Imagine not I'm weak enough to die.
   Wolfr. Meantime Death sends you back this cap of
office.

At his court you're elected to the post:
Go, and enjoy it.
                    [*Sets the fool's cap on* ISBRAND'S *head.*
  Isbr.   Bye and bye. But let not   270
Duke Melveric think that I part unrevenged:
For I hear in the clouds about me voices,
Singing

> All kingdomless is thy old head,
>   In which began the tyrannous fun;   275
> He fetches thee, who should be dead;
>   There's Duke for Brother! Who has won?

Now Death doth make indeed a fool of me.   [*Dies.*
  Duke. Where are my sons? I have not seen them
    lately.
Go to the bridegroom's lodgings, and to Athulf's, 280
And summon both.   [*Exit attendant.*
  Wolfr.   They will be here; and sooner
Than you would wish. Meanwhile, my noble Duke,
Some friends of mine behind us seem to stir.
They wish, in honour of your restoration,
In memory also of your glorious deeds,   285
To present masque and dance to you. Is't granted?
  Duke. Surely; and they are welcome, for we need
Some merriment amid these sad events.
  Wolfr. You in the wall there then, my thin light
    archers,
Come forth and dance a little: 'tis the season   290
When you may celebrate Death's Harvest-Home.
      [*A dance of Deaths. In the middle of it enter*
          AMALA, *followed by a bier, on which the*
          corpse of Adalmar is borne. The dance
          goes out.
  Duke. What's this? Another mummery?
  Wolfr.   The antimasque,
I think they call it: 'tis satirical.

Amala. My lord, you see the bridal bed that waits
    me.
Your son, my bridegroom, both no more, lies here,
Cold, pale, abandoned in his youthful blood: 296
And I his bride have now no duty further,
But to kneel down, wretched, beside his corpse,
Crying for justice on his murderers.
    Duke. Could my son die, and I not know it sooner?
Why, he is cold and stiff. O! now my crown   301
Is sunk down to the dust, my life is desolate.
Who did this deed?

Enter ATHULF

    Wolfr.   Athulf, answer the call.
    Amala. O no! Suspect not him. He was last night
Gentle, and full of love, to both of us,   305
And could imagine ne'er so foul a deed.
Suspect not him; for so thou mak'st me feel
How terrible it is that he is dead,
Since his next friend's accused of such a murder:
And torture not his ghost, which must be here,   310
Striving in vain to utter one soul-sound,
To speak the guiltless free. Tempt not cruelly
The helplessness of him who is no more,
Nor make him discontented with the state,
Which lets him not assert his brother's innocence. 315
    Duke. (*to* ATHULF) Answer! Thou look'st like one, unto
        whose soul
A secret voice, all day and night, doth whisper,
'Thou art a murderer'. Is it so? Then rather
Speak not. Thou wear'st a dagger at thy side;
Avenge the murdered man, thou art his brother;   320
And never let me hear from mortal lips
That my son was so guilty.
    Athulf.   Amala,
Still loves me; weep some gentle drops for me;
And, when we meet again, fulfil thy promise.

Father, look here!   [*Stabs himself to death.*

    Amala. O Athulf! live one moment to deny it;   326
I ask that, and that only. Lo! old man,
He hath in indignation done the deed.
Since thou could'st think him for an instant guilty,
He held the life, which such a base suspicion   330
Had touched, and the old father who could speak it,
Unworthy of him more: and he did well.
I bade thee give me vengeance for my bridegroom,
And thou hast slain the only one who loved me.
Suspect and kill me too: but there 's no need;   335
For such a one, as I, God never let
Live more than a few hours.

              [*She falls into the arms of her ladies.*

    Duke. Torwald, the crown is yours; I reign no more.
But when, thou spectre, is thy vengeance o'er!

    Wolfr. Melveric, all is finished, which to witness
The spirit of retribution called me hither.   341
Thy sons have perished for like cause, as that
For which thou did'st assassinate thy friend.
Sibylla is before us gone to rest.
Blessing and Peace to all who are departed!   345
But thee, who daredst to call up into life,
And the unholy world's forbidden sunlight,
Out of his grave him who reposed softly,
One of the ghosts doth summon, in like manner,
Thee, still alive, into the world o' th' dead.   350

        [*Exit with the* DUKE *into the sepulchre.*

The curtain falls

Songs and Fragments
from the
REVISIONS OF *DEATH'S JEST-BOOK*
[Composed 1829–49]

FROM ACT I, SCENE I
I. The Spirit of Folly

Mandr.... O world, world, the gods and fairies left you, for thou wert too grave, and now, Socratic star, thy Demon, thy great Pan, Folly, is waning from thy side. The oracles still talked in their sleep, shall our grand-children say, till Master Merryman's Kingdom was broken up; now is every man his own Fool, and Fate for us all. So much for my dying speech and confession as the last Fool, or indeed, the last Man, for he who hath no leaven of the original father Donkey in any corner of him, may be an angel, black, white or piebald: he has lost his title to humanity. And now a ballad to the speech, a rhyme to the reason:

> Folly hath now turned out of door
> Mankind and Fate, who were before
>   Jove's Harlequin and Clown.
> The world 's no stage, no tavern more,
>   Its sign, the Fool 's ta'en down.
> With poppy rain and cypress dew
> Weep all, for all, who laughed for you:
> For goose-grass is no medicine more,
>   But the owl's brown eye 's the sky's new blue.
>   Heigho! Foolscap!

Isbr. Well said and truly. 'Twas no idle joke of Heaven's that Tarquin's fool and Manlius' geese saved Earth's only Rome, and in her freedom, civilized manners, art and science, for all future times, but a hint and token which man has overlooked. Why not an owl or a philosopher? If the good lord of the creation, being a beggar in foolery, will in spite of Destiny ride a cock-horse on Wisdom, why! he must needs gallop to Bedlam. I wash my hands of him. Well, now the Fates are no more humorous, they have been converted by the Knowledge Society tracts, and to make something useful of their cotton, do now with the threads of noble men's destinies knit matrimonial night-caps for old Goody Nature and Gaffer Mankind to play Punch and Judy in. But I grow delirious, and utter grave Truths.

II. Mandrake's Embarkation

ARE all the rest aboard?...

Mandr. All, Sir Knight: the very pigs and capons chuck and grunt their magnanimous resolution to yield up their four-footed and biped ghosts without a squeak against Cook Destiny. To be a sausage in such a cause is superhuman: a flitch, or still more roasted whole, is so enviable that were I not Mandrake I could wish myself a cow or a calf; and that, if possible monstrous: with eight legs and double-headed, to be eaten two-fold on so patriotic an expedition. For my good will's sake now, hold me for a calf, though unworthy, and take me with you.

Wolfr. Who is this saucy fellow that prates between?

Isbr. A living somebody or nobody, a false coin of flesh that may pass at Court as a tolerable counterfeit of humanity, so indeed that all who see but skin-deep might take it for a scurvy human creature. Believe it not. Some one of those malicious Gods who envy Prometheus his puppet show have taught all con-

founded sorts of malcontent beasts, saucy birds and
ambitious shell-fish, and hopping creatures of land and
water, the knack of looking human to the life. How? is
the mystery of the cookery-book. Briskets of veal,
liver and lights, tripe and capon, have been so cunningly smuggled into the featherless two-legged ones
that the real history of the World is Æsop's fable-book
in masquerade. A whole people is stout and surly,
being mostly certain steaks and Barons of beef gone
human: another, after centuries of amphibious diet,
owes to the frog's legs in its wooden shoes the agility
with which it jumps over gentle King Log, and devotes
itself patriotically to the appetite of Emperor Stork,
his follower: aye, it would even blow itself up to be
bull itself. Even you, Sir Knight, are still tolerably like
unto a man, but Sirloin labours hard to shoulder away
thy fine old heart, and a whole herd of sheep bleats in
that merciful resolve of thine to pardon thy foe; but
more of that anon.

III. The Home is One

Torw. What say the Princes?

Isbr. (*Aside*)   They remain, good youths;
They trust in Providence and in their birthright,
And let what lion will, sup on their father.
That is the course of nature.

Sibald. Bid him but send us loving thoughts each
        day;
We will reply: and in this interchange
He must be gainer, for he can love us
Not more than doubly with the selfsame love,
But we two him, each with a separate heart,
Twice for his once.

Wolfr.   For kind farewells

This one short word the time allows,
With which we take our leave.
   Erminia.   We to our homes,
You to the homeless waves; unequal parting.
   Wolfr. The earth may open, and the sea o'erwhelm;
Many the ways, the little home is one;
Thither the courser leads, thither the helm,
And at the gate we meet when all is done.

IV. Blindness of Hatred

   Wolfr. Hence with your dark demands: let 's shape
     our lives
After the merciful lesson of the sun,
That gilds our purpose....
   Isbr..... Revenge, Revenge lend me your torch, that
I may by its bloody fire see the furrows of this man's
countenance, which once were iron, like the bars of
Hell gate, and devilish thoughts peeped through them;
but now is as a cage of very pitiful apes.
   Wolfr. Thou knowest not Melveric, for thou lov'st
     him not.

V. Good for Evil

   Wolfr. Now rather let me think, like thou, my body
     perished:
I will revenge me if I die for him;
And let me be the one, if any must:
He shall know who I was, and who my father.
Like to the moon rebuking a blasphemer,
Such vengeance shall shine out and light his deeds.
I can no other execute, and when
I lose this awe and piety towards nature

And human kind,—O God, if such a curse
Awaits me in the winter of my years,—
Rather diseased poverty or madness,
Which I could bear, I hope, with self-content:
If I should cease to be my mother's child,
Let the sea whelm, the lightning strike me down,
Or give me any grave that earth can spare.

VI. Love and Hatred

Wolfr. O think not, brother, that our father's spirit
Breathes earthly passion more: he is with me
And guides me to the danger of his foe,
Bringing from heaven, his home, pity and pardon.
But should his blood need bloody expiation,
Then let *me* perish. Blind these eyes, my sire,
Palsy my vigorous arm, snow age upon me,
Strike me with lightning down into the deep,
Open me any grave that earth can spare,
Leave me the truth of love, and death is lovely. [*Exit.*

Isbr. O lion-heartedness right asinine!
Such lily-livered meek humanity
Saves not thy duke, good brother; it but shines
Sickly upon his doom, as moonbeams breaking
Upon a murderer's grave-digging spade.
Or fate 's a fool, or I will be his fate.—
What ho! Sir Knight! One word—Now for a face
As innocent and lamblike as the wool
That brings a plague.

Re-enter WOLFRAM

Wolfr.　　　　　What will you more with me?
Isbr. Go, if you must and will; but take with you
At least this letter of the governor's,

Which, in your haste, you dropped. I must be honest,
For so my hate was ever. Go.

Wolfr.   And prosper!   [*Exit.*

Isbr. Now then he plunges right into the waters,
Like a possessed pig of Gallilee.
O Lie, O Lie, O lovely lady Lie.
They told me that thou art the devil's daughter.
Then thou art greater than thy father, Lie;
For while he mopes in Hell, thou queen'st it bravely,
Ruling the earth under the name of Truth,
While she is at the bottom of the well,
Where Joseph left her.

VII. Song from the Ship

To sea, to sea! the calm is o'er;
    The wanton water leaps in sport,
And rattles down the pebbly shore;
    The dolphin wheels, the sea-cows snort.
And unseen Mermaids' pearly song
Comes bubbling up, the weeds among.
    Fling broad the sail, dip deep the oar:
    To sea, to sea! the calm is o'er.

To sea, to sea! our wide-winged bark
    Shall billowy cleave its sunny way,
And with its shadow, fleet and dark,
    Break the caved Tritons' azure ray,
Like mighty eagle soaring light
O'er antelopes on Alpine height.
    The anchor heaves, the ship swings free,
    The sails swell full. To sea, to sea!

Isbr. The idiot merriment of thoughtless men!
How the fish laugh at them, that swim and toy
About the ruined ship, wrecked deep below,
Whose pilot's skeleton, all full of sea weeds,
Leans on his anchor, grinning like their Hope.

FROM ACT I, SCENE II

VIII. *Sleeper's Countenance Contemplated*

'Tis but a warmer lighter death, this shadow of our
 life,
The marble sleep, which seldom lifts not up the eyelid
Till the last trumpet: thus so cloud-like light
To kiss the day's life off from our hushed lips;
And, see, even thus we smile.
 Duke.   There smiles methinks
A cherished dream, that lies upon her lips
As the word love written upon a rose,
With which the story of our youth begins.
Could'st thou but see whose image so delights her!
 Ziba. Her thoughts are far from us in early child-
 hood:
For 'tis our wont to dream of distant friends
And half-forgotten times.
 Duke.   Enough! Is this a time
For talk of air like this? Save up your love tales
And dream-book wisdom for a younger hearer
Upon an idler day.

IX. *A Day of Surpassing Beauty*

THE earth is bright, her forests all are golden;
A cloud of flowers breathes blushing over her,

And, whispering from bud to blossom, opens
The half awaken memory of the song
She heard in childhood from the mystic sun:
A thought that seeks impatiently its word.
There is some secret stirring in the world,
A crown, or cross, for one is born to-day.

X. A Night-Scene

THE lake, like her, heaves gently
Its breast of waves under a heaven of sleep,
And pictures in its soothed transparent being
The depth of worlds o'erhanging: o'er the pillow,
Washed by the overflowing flowery locks,
A silver promise of the moon is breathed:
And the light veil of hieroglyphic clouds
The curious wind rends ever and anon,
Revealing the deep dream of Alpine heights,
Which fill the distance of its wondering spirit,
And on its hectic cheeks the prophecies
Doth fearfully reflect, which flicker up
Out of the sun's grave underneath the world.

XI. A Beautiful Night

How lovely is the heaven of this night,
How deadly still its earth. The forest brute
Has crept into his cave, and laid himself
Where sleep has made him harmless like the lamb;
The horrid snake, his venom now forgot,
Is still and innocent as the honied flower
Under his head:—and man, in whom are met
Leopard and snake,—and all the gentleness

And beauty of the young lamb and the bud,
Has let his ghost out, put his thoughts aside
And lent his senses unto death himself;
Whereby the King and beggar all lie down
On straw or purple-tissue, are but bones
And air, and blood, equal to one another
And to the unborn and buried: so we go
Placing ourselves among the unconceived
And the old ghosts, wantonly, smilingly,
For sleep is fair and warm—

XII. Liberty

Duke.   Liberty!
Thou breakest through our dungeon's wall of waves,
As morning bursts the towery spell of night.
Horse of the desart, thou, coy arrowy creature,
Startest like sunrise up, and from thy mane
Shaking abroad the dews of slumber, boundest
With sparkling hoof along the scattered sands,
The livelong day in liberty and light.

XIII

[*Duke.*] Away, away, thou soarest, happy bird,
With pealing song and hearty clap of wings,
Cheerily rowing through the sea of air
Thy little boat of life high overhead,
Startling the gaze of lofty capricorns
On mountain pinnacle; now glidest thou
Softly to settle on a flowering spray
Gay as May morning, love-thought on the eyelid
Of simple maiden; thence to dart ere long

341

Full of heedless song and caring nought
For the tear shed at parting: When thy day,
Spent so in sunshine, darkens, thou art welcomed
In the warm bosom of thy feathery home
By patient mate; and I must hear thee toying
Until the very thought of liberty
Is in my dreams, a bird whose nest is built—

XIV. First Love Unrecognized

Sibyl. . . . Strange dread of meeting, greater dread of
    parting:
Impatient hoping for another word,
Yet sorrow for it, ere it was quite spoken,
Because farewell was nearer. . . .
I saw his image clearer in his absence
Than near him, for my eyes were strangely troubled;
And never had I dared to talk thus to him.

.   .   .   .

Duke. Yet, my Sibylla, oft first love must perish;
Like the poor snow-drop, boyish love of Spring,
Born pale to die, and strew the path of triumph
Before the imperial glowing of the rose,
Whose passion conquers all.

XV. Anticipation of Wolfram's Coming

Enter a knight

Knight. Hither, Sir Knight—
Duke.   What knight?
Knight.   What knight, but Wolfram?
Duke. Wolfram, *my* knight!

Sibyl.   My day, my Wolfram!
Duke.   Know'st him?
Sibyl. His foot is on my heart; he comes, he comes.

XVI. *Duke's Decision*

Duke. . . . Ha! What 's this thought,
Shapeless and shadowy, that keeps wheeling round,
Like a dumb creature that sees coming danger,
And breaks its heart trying in vain to speak?
I know the moment: 'tis a dreadful one,
Which in the life of every one comes once;
When for the frighted hesitating soul
High heaven and luring sin with promises
Bid and contend: oft the faltering spirit,
O'ercome by the fair fascinating fiend,
Gives her eternal heritance of life
For one caress, for one triumphant crime.—
I will possess thee, maiden. Doubt and care
Be trampled in the dust with the worm conscience!
Farewell then, Wolfram.—

XVII

[*Duke.*] Pitiful villain! that dost long to sin
And dar'st not. Shall I dream my soul is bathing
In his reviving blood, yet lose my right,
My only health, my sole delight on earth,
For fear of shadows on a chapel wall
In some pale painted Hell? By thy beauty,
I will possess thee, maiden.

FROM ACT I, SCENE III

XVIII

SIBYLLA, WOLFRAM, *Knights*

Song

I

In lover's ear a wild voice cried:
    'Sleeper, awake and rise!'
A pale form stood by his bed-side,
    With heavy tears in her sad eyes.
'A beckoning hand, a moaning sound,
A new-dug grave in weedy ground
For her who sleeps in dreams of thee.
Awake! Let not the murder be!'
Unheard the faithful dream did pray,
And sadly sighed itself away.
    'Sleep on,' sung Sleep, 'to-morrow
    'Tis time to know thy sorrow.'
    'Sleep on,' sung Death, 'to-morrow
    From me thy sleep thou'lt borrow.'
    Sleep on, lover, sleep on,
    The tedious dream is gone;
        The bell tolls one.

II

Another hour, another dream:
    'Awake! awake!' it wailed,
'Arise, ere with the moon's last beam
    Her rosy life hath paled.
A hidden light, a muffled tread,
A daggered hand beside the bed
Of her who sleeps and dreams of thee.
Thou wak'st not: let the murder be.'

In vain the faithful dream did pray,
And sadly sighed itself away.
  'Sleep on,' sung Sleep, 'to-morrow
  'Tis time to know thy sorrow.'
  'Sleep on,' sung Death, 'to-morrow
  From me thy sleep thou'lt borrow.'
  Sleep on, lover, sleep on,
  The tedious dream is gone;
      Soon comes the sun.

III

Another hour, another dream:
  A red wound on a snowy breast,
A rude hand stifling the last scream,
  On rosy lips a death-kiss pressed.
Blood on the sheets, blood on the floor,
The murderer stealing through the door.
'Now,' said the voice, with comfort deep,
'She sleeps indeed, and thou may'st sleep.'
The scornful dream then turned away
To the first, weeping cloud of day.
  'Sleep on,' sung Sleep, 'to-morrow
  'Tis time to know thy sorrow.'
  'Sleep on,' sung Death, 'to-morrow
  From me thy sleep thou'lt borrow.'
  Sleep on, lover, sleep on,
  The tedious dream is gone;
      The murder 's done.

Wolfr. Sing me no more such ditties: they are well
For the last gossips, when the snowy wind
Howls in the chimney till the very taper
Trembles with its blue flame, and the bolted gates
Rattle before old winter's palsied hand.
If you will sing, let it be cheerily
Of dallying love. There 's many a one among you

Hath sung, beneath our oak trees to his maiden,
Light bird-like mockeries, fit for love in springtime.
Sing such a one.

Song

I

I love thee and I love thee not,
I love thee, and I'd rather not,
All of thee, and I know not what.
 A flowery eye as tender,
 A swan-like neck as slender,
And on it a brown little spot
 For tears to fall afraid on
 And kisses to be paid on,
Have other maidens too.
 Then why love I, love, none but you?
If I could find the reason why,
Methinks my love would quickly die.

II

Aye, knew I how to hate thee, maid,
I'd hate thee for I knew not what,
Excepting that I'd rather not
 Be thy friend or foeman;
 For thou'rt the only woman,
On whom to think my heart 's afraid;
 For if I would abhor thee,
 The more must I long for thee.
What others force me to,
I turn me from; why not from you?
If I could find the reason why,
My disenchanted love would die.

III

But should'st thou cease my heart to move
  To longings, that I'd rather not,
  And tried I hate, I know not what
    My heart would do for mourning;
    Love I,—it bursts, love scorning.
  O loveliest hate, most hateful love,
    This combat and endeavour
    Is what enslaves me ever.
  I'll neither of the two,
    Or hate or love the love of you.
  And now I've found the reason why,
  I know my love can never die.

XIX. *The Duke Overpowered by Enemies*

AND now like to an ancient vine-bound tower,
Which Heaven looks through, beside a countless sea,
Drunken with storm he totters.

XX. *Mercy*

Wolfr. Sibylla, what deserves he at our hands?
Sibyl. Who, were desert the test, were not deserted
By heavenly judges all, save only Mercy?

XXI. *Human Life: Its Value*

THINK what I plead for: for a life! the gift
Of God alone, whom he who saves 't is likest.
How glorious to live; even in one thought
The wisdom of past times,

And from the luminous minds of many men,
Catch a reflected truth; as in one eye
Light from unnumbered worlds and furthest planets
Of the star-crowned universe is gathered
Into one ray.

XXII. Its Danger

AY, rosy life, smile in thy summer triumph,
The morning shine upon thy pearly crown.
The flattering wind kisses thine opening eyelids
And rocks thee on his bosom, silly babe:
Thou heedst not how the traitor mocks the tear
On the dead leaf he careless puffs away.

FROM ACT I, SCENE IV

XXIII. The New Cecilia

Titmouse. How shall I believe such things?
Mandr. How you can: but believe, or thou shalt be
made an example of like St. Gingulph's relict. List to
her legend and tremble, youth, for 'tis exceeding true,
and by St. Cecilia, most musically melancholy.

Whoever has heard of St. Gingo
    Must know that the gipsy
    He married was tipsy
Every day of her life with old Stingo.

And after the death of St. Gingo
    The wonders he did do
    Th' incredulous widow
Denied with unladylike lingo.

'For St. Gingo a fig's and a feather-end!
  He no more can work wonder
  Than a clyster-pipe thunder
Or I sing a psalm with my nether-end.'

As she said it, her breakfast beginning on
  A tankard of home-brewed inviting ale,
Lo! the part she was sitting and sinning on
  Struck the old hundredth up like a nightingale.

Loud as psophia in an American forest, or
  The mystic Memnonian marble in
  A desart at daybreak, that chorister
  Breathed forth his Æolian warbling.

That creature seraphic and spherical,
Her firmament, kept up its clerical
  Thanksgivings, until she did aged die,
Cooing and praising and chirping alert in
Her petticoats, swung like a curtain
  Let down o'er the tail of a Tragedy.

Therefore, ladies, repent and be sedulous
  In praising your lords, lest, ah! well a day!
Such judgement befall the incredulous
  And your latter ends melt into melody.

XXIV. *The Oviparous Tailor and Anxious Fishermen*

Mandr. . . . Hear you no noise? Here come disturbers.
Titmouse. 'Tis only a hen-ostrich laying eggs like a
    tailor.
Mandr. A tailor! Ignorance, that craft is viviparous.
Titmouse. Are they though? What is goose? And

349

why sit they crosslegged but to hatch. Why, it is written in a Bridgewater Treatise that the genus Tailor,—as man and woman's tailor or man-milliner, tailor military or civil, readymoney tailor, and even he that botcheth in a stall—at a certain age become oviparous, and lay eggs like a cod-fish, which are good poached, and brought to table with spinache, also, in egg-flip.

> Wee, wee tailor,
> Nobody was paler
>   Than wee, wee tailor;
> And nobody was thinner.
> Hast thou mutton-chops for dinner,
> My small-beer sinner,
> My starveling rat,—but haler,—
>   Wee, wee tailor?
>
> Below his starving garret
> Lived an old witch and a parrot,—
>   Wee, wee tailor,—
> Cross, horrid and uncivil,
> For her grandson was the Devil
> Or a chimney-sweeper evil;
> She was sooty too, but paler,—
>   Wee, wee tailor.
>
> Her sooty hen laid stale eggs,
> And then came with his splay legs
>   Wee, wee tailor,
> And stole them all for dinner.
> Then would old witch begin her
> Damnations on the sinner,—
> 'May the thief lay eggs,—but staler;'
>   Wee, wee tailor.

Wee, wee tailor,
Witch watched him like a jailor.
Wee, wee tailor
Did all his little luck spill.
Tho' he swallowed many a muck's pill,
Yet his mouth grew like a duck's bill,
Crowed like a hen,—but maler,—
Wee, wee tailor.

Near him did cursed doom stick,
As he perched upon a broomstick,—
Wee, wee tailor.
It lightened, rained and thundered,
And all the doctors wondered
When he laid above a hundred
Gallinaceous eggs,—but staler,—
Wee, wee tailor.

A hundred eggs laid daily;
No marvel he looked palely,—
Wee, wee tailor.
Witch let folks in to see some
Poach'd tailor's eggs; to please 'em
He must cackle on his besom,
Till Fowl-death did prevail o'er
Wee, wee tailor.   [*Exeunt.*

Enter Fishermen

1st Fisherman. Away to the water, the moon 's cloudy.

2nd Fisherman. Push off quick: there 's something like a murder in the air.

1st Fisherman. Will it thunder to-night?

2nd Fisherman. Ay, gaily. 'Twere a right evening to die in.

1st Fisherman. Of the ailing of availing ale: let thy nose die purple on strong beer, and stout be thy porter to paradise. Death shall not catch me in his gin till the swallow comes again.

2nd Fisherman. My wife died on such a night, we had no money to have her buried, and she was sunk into the sea. When the moon looks up at me from the water, I always think of her last look. O that last look! I shall ne'er forget it.

1st Fisherman. Come away: the robbers are at our heels. Off, I say.   [*They row off singing.*

I

As mad sexton's bell, tolling
For earth's loveliest daughter
Night's dumbness breaks rolling
Ghostlily:
So our boat breaks the water
Witchingly.

II

As her look the dream troubles
Of her tearful-eyed lover,
So our sails in the bubbles
Ghostlily
Are mirrored, and hover
Moonily.

XXV. *The Warning*

Duke....   Now proclaim me.
Let my name burn through all dark history
Over the waves of time, as from a lighthouse,
Warning approach.

Wolfr. I will avenge me, Duke, as never man.

Song from the Waters

As sudden thunder
  Pierces night;
As magic wonder,
  Mad affright
Rives asunder
  Men's delight:
Our ghost, our corpse and we
    Rise to be.

As flies the lizard
  Serpent fell;
As goblin vizard,
  At the spell
Of pale wizard,
  Sinks to hell;
Our life, our laugh, our lay
    Pass away.

As wake the morning
  Trumpets bright;
As snowdrop, scorning
  Winter's might,
Rises warning
  Like a sprite:
The buried, dead, and slain
    Rise again.

XXVI. End of Act I

Sibyl. . . . Who did this, Wolfram?
  Wolfr.   'Tis well done, Sibylla:
So burst the portals of sepulchral night
Before th' immortal rising of the sun.
  Sibyl. Who did this, Melveric?

Duke.   Let him die in quiet.
Hush! there 's a thought upon his lips again.
    Sibyl. Wilt thou die, Wolfram? Can I die for thee?
    Duke. I—I should do it, but for love of thee.
    Wolfr. Love Melveric, if thou canst. For me,
    Sibylla,
I may be lonely in the grave without thee,
For I must die too soon. I have oft thought,
(Thou art so beautiful above all women,)
I might be you; but then 'twas happier still
To be another and admire and love thee.
Now, I must die alone, see thee no more.
Yet, can man die? Ay, as the sun doth set:
The earth it is that falls away from day;
Fixed in the heavens, although unseen by us,
The immortal life and light remains triumphant. [*Dies.*

* * * * * * *

Song from the Waters

    The swallow leaves her nest,
    The soul my weary breast;
    But therefore let the rain
        On my grave
    Fall pure; for why complain?
    Since both will come again
        O'er the wave.

    The wind dead leaves and snow
    Doth hurry to and fro;
    And, once, a day shall break
        O'er the wave,
    When a storm of ghosts shall shake
    The dead, until they wake
        In the grave.

354

FROM ACT II, SCENE II

XXVII. *The Death of Wolfram*

AYE, nobly doffed he his humanity.
The bodily cloud that veiled his majesty
Melted away into the elements
As clouds from off a sunny mountain's pinnacle:
'Twas to die nobly.

XXVIII. *Sibylla at Wolfram's Bier*

[*Sibyl.*] Dead, is he? What's that further than a word,
Hollow as is the armour of a ghost
Whose chinks the moon he haunts doth penetrate.
Belief in death is the fell superstition,
That hath appalled mankind and chained it down,
A slave unto the dismal mystery
Which old opinion dreams beneath the tombstone.
Dead is he, and the grave shall wrap him up?
And this you see is he? And all is ended?
Aye this is cold, that was a glance of him
Out of the depth of his immortal self;
This utterance and token of his being
His spirit hath let fall, and now is gone
To fill up nature and complete her being.
The form, that here is fallen, was the engine,
Which drew a great motion of spiritual power
Out of the world's own soul, and made it play
In visible motion, as the lofty tower
Leads down the animating fire of heaven
To the world's use. That utensil is broken,
Which did appropriate to human functions
A portion of the ghostly element,
And in another sphere the spirit works:

This then is all your Death. Say not he 's dead,—
The word is vile—but that he is henceforth
No more excepted from eternity.

XXIX

[*Sibyl.*]   Yet if I shed a tear,
It is not for his death, but for my life.
Aye, say you that he 's dead? You mean he is
No more excepted from Eternity.
If he were dead I should indeed despair.
Can a man die? Ay, as the sun doth set:
It is the earth that falls away from light;
Fixed in the heavens, although unseen by us,
The immortal life and light remains triumphant.
And therefore you shall never see me wail,
Or drop base waters of an ebbing sorrow;
No wringing hands, no sighings, no despair,
No morning weeds will I betake me to;
But keep my thought of him that is no more,
As secret as great nature keeps his soul,
From all the world; and consecrate my being
To that divinest hope, which none can know of
Who have not laid their dearest in the grave.

XXX. Dirge

Sorrow, lie still and wear
No tears, no sighings, no despair,
No trembling dewy smile of care,
    No mourning weeds,
    Nought that discloses
    A heart that bleeds;

356

But looks contented I will bear,
　　And o'er my cheeks strew roses.
Unto the world I may not weep,
But save my sorrow all, and keep
　　A secret heart, sweet soul, for thee,
　　As the great earth and swelling sea—

XXXI. Isbrand at Wolfram's Bier

YET my eyes are weary, Siegfried; are heavy as if all
the salt water of an ocean pressed against them as
against a broad staring Fish's. Oh Friend, I'd give a
thousand crowns for leave to weep one tear. But I dare
not, not one, and why not, Siegfried? Do you see this?
So should every honest man be: cold, dead, and
leaden-coffined. This was one who would be in friendship constant, and the pole wanders: one who would be
immortal, and the light that shines upon his pale forehead now, through yonder gewgaw window, undulated
from its star hundreds of years ago. That is constancy,
that is life. O moral nature!

FROM ACT II, SCENE IV

XXXII. Wolfram's Translation

[*Isbr.*] By still murderous starlight
When the conniving winds held still their breath
And the impatient stars scarce dared to pant,
While the bewitched moon let the earth's shadow
Like to a lid, sink over her jaundiced eye
Came I, with mattocks of such sturdy spells
That raise the dead quicker than exorcisms
Of necromants, whispering doomsday's cue

And forcing her from earth, placed my dead brother
To play her corpse's part within her coffin.

XXXIII. Ziba's Origin

[*Duke*.] I FOUND him in a buried city I went by
    torchlight through—
I followed once a fleet and mighty serpent
Into a cavern in a mountain's side;
And, wading many lakes, descending gulphs,
At last I reached the ruins of a city,
Built not like ours but of another world,
As if the aged earth had loved in youth
The mightiest city of a perished planet,
And kept the image of it in her heart,
So dream-like, shadowy, and spectral was it.
Nought seemed alive there, and the very dead
Were of another world the skeletons.
The mammoth, ribbed like to an arched cathedral,
Lay there, and ruins of great creatures else
More like a shipwrecked fleet, too great they seemed
For all the life that is to animate:
And vegetable rocks, tall sculptured palms,
Pines grown, not hewn, in stone; and giant ferns,
Whose earthquake-shaken leaves bore graves for nests.

FROM ACT III, SCENE III

XXXIV. Duke Awaiting Resurrection of His Wife

[*Duke*.] . . . A gentle feel.—
She cometh and pours out before her coming
Hopes, soothing as the infancy of light
Which warms the sky of the unrisen moon.

FROM ACT IV, SCENE I
XXXV. The Murderer's Haunted Couch

[*Isbr.*] So buckled tight in scaly resolution,
Let my revenge tread on, and if its footsteps
Be graves, the peering eye of critic doubt,
All dazzled by the bold, reflected day,
May take the jaws of darkness that devour   5
My swift sword's flash, as ravening serpent's famine
Locks up birds' sunny life in black eclipse,
For pity's dewy eyelid closing over
Love's sparkles. I have seen the mottled tigress
Sport with her cubs as tenderly and gay,   10
As lady Venus with her kitten Cupids;
And flowers, my sagest teachers, beautiful
Or they were fools, because death-poisonous:
And lies, methinks, oft brighten woman's lips,
And tears have the right pearly trickle and diamond
    shoot   15
When they bowl down false oaths. World, I will win
    thee;
Therefore I must deceive you, gentle World.
Let Heaven look in upon my flaming wrath
As into Ætna's hell: the sides man sees
I clothe with olives, promising much peace.   20
But what 's this talk? Must I be one of those
That cannot keep a secret from himself?
The worst of confidants, who oft goes mad,
Through bites of conscience, after many years.
I came to see thee, brother: there thou art   25
Even in this suit, from which no blood, save his,
This purple doffed by thy imperial life
Shall wash away. To the amazed foe
I will appear thyself returned, and smite him
Ere he has time to doubt or die of horror.   30
I would I were, thus iron-hooped and sworded,

Thy murderer's dream this night, to cry, Awake!
Awake, Duke Melveric! Duke Murderer!
Wrap thee up quickly in thy winding sheet,
Without ado! The hearse is at the door,   35
The widest gate of Hell is open for thee,
And mighty goblins summon thee to Death.
Come down with me! [*He seizes the sleeping* DUKE].
                              Nay, I will shake thy sleep off,
Until thy soul falls out.

                                   What voice more dreadful
Than one at midnight, blood-choaked, crying murder?
Why, Murder's own! His murder's, and now thine! 41
But cheer up. I will let thy blood flow on
Within its pipes to-night.
    [*Duke*.]   Angel of Death!
Can it be? No, 'tis a grave-digging vision:
The world is somewhere else. Yet even this   45
Methought I dreamt, and now it stands beside me,
Rattling in iron.
    [*Isbr*.]   Aye, the murderer's vision
Is ever so: for at the word, 'I'm murdered',
The gaolers of the dead throw back the grave-stone,
Split the deep ocean, and unclose the mountain,   50
And let the buried pass. I am more real
Than any airy spirit of a dream,
As Death is mightier, stronger, and more faithful
To man, than Life.
    [*Duke*.]   Wolfram!—Nay thy grasp
Is warm, thy bosom heaves, thou breath'st, imposter—
Let iron answer iron, flesh crush flesh;   56
Thou art no spirit, fool.
    [*Isbr*.]   Fool, art thou murderer,
My murderer, Wolfram's? To the blood-stained hand
The grave gives way: to the eye, that saw its victim
Sigh off the ravished soul, th' horrid world of ghosts 60
Is no more viewless; day and night 'tis open,

Gazing on pale and bleeding spectres ever.
Come, seat thee; no vain struggle. Write thou here,
(And with my blood I trace it on thy brain,)
Thy sentence; which by night in types of fire   65
Shall stand before thee, never to be closed,—
By night the voice of blood shall whisper to thee,
Word slowly after word, and ne'er be silent.
Melveric, thy conscience I will sing to sleep
With softest hymnings; thou shalt not despair,   70
But live on and grow older than all men,
To all men's dread: like an old, haunted mountain,
Icy and hoary, shalt thou stand 'mid life;
And midnight tales be told in secret of thee,
As of crime's beacon. Thou shalt see thy son   75
Fall for a woman's love, as thy friend fell,
Beneath the stabs of him, with whom together
He was at one breast suckled. Thou shalt lose
Friends, subjects, crown, strength, health and all
      power,
Even despair; thou shalt not dare to break   80
All men's contempt, thy life, for fear of worse:
Nor shalt thou e'er go mad for misery.
Write on. I leave the voice with thee, that never
Shall cease to read thee, o'er and o'er, thy doom.
It will the rest, the worst of all, repeat   85
Till it be written.

        Thou art doomed: no trumpet
Shall wake the bravery of thy heart to battle;
No song of love, no beam of child's glad eye,
Drown that soft whisper, dazzle from thy sight
Those words indelible.

        Follow him, dearest curse;   90
Be true to him, invisible to others,
As his own soul.   [*Exit.*

361

Duke.　　　　　Hold! mercy!... 'Tis enough...
Curse shoulders curse, as in a bloody river.
I will no more.

Enter TORWALD

Torw. Arise, my lord; the sun is broad and busy,　95
Lighting about the creatures of the day.
Now is our time to work.
　　[*Duke.*]　　　　　Art there again?
Forth, Horror, to thy grave; I'll no more haunting.
　　[*Torw.*] My lord!
　　[*Duke.*]　　　　Ah! Torwald. Ah! methinks I
　　　dreamt—
Of one—Away! Why, stands he there again?　100
What! dare the buried morning? Or is this
The work of necromantic conscience? Ha!
'Tis nothing but a picture. Curtain it.
Strange visions, my good Torwald, are begotten
When sleep o'ershadows waking.—Right, you seek
The instructions: here.
　　[*Torw.*]　　　　Duke Melveric?　106
　　[*Duke.*] I saw him though, I heard his armour ring
And feel even now his gauntlet's numbing grasp.—
You spoke?
　　[*Torw.*]　What read I?
　　[*Duke.*]　　　　Read! 'Tis clear as trumpet's cry:
Despair thou of despair. Thou shalt not die:　110
Life shall despise thee, Death reject thee ever.

XXXVI. *Life a Thousand Graves*

Duke. ...　　　　LUCKLESS man
Avoids the miserable bodkin's point,
And, flinching from the insect's little sting,
In pitiful security keeps watch,

While 'twixt him and that hypocrite the sun,
To which he prays, comes windless pestilence,
Transparent as a glass of poisoned water
Through which the drinker sees his murderer smiling;
She stirs no dust, and makes no grass to nod,
Yet every footstep is a thousand graves,
And every breath of her 's as full of ghosts
As a sunbeam with motes.

XXXVII. *Love is Wiser than Ambition*

[*Amala.*] O give not up the promise of your time
For me: for what? an evanescent woman,
A rose-leaf scarce unfolded ere it falls. Your life
Should be a wood of laurels evergreen;
Seek glory!—
[*Adalmar.*] Glory! To be sung to tuneless harps!
A picture, and a name; to live for death!
Seek glory? Never. The world's gossip, Fame
Is busy in the market-place, the change,
At court or wrangling senate, noting down
Him of the fattest purse, the fabulous crest,
The tongue right honied or most poisonous.
If Glory goes among the bristling spears,
Which war is mowing down; or walks the wave,
When Fate weighs kingdoms in their battle-fleets;
Or watches the still student at his work,
Reading the laws of nature, in the heavens
Or earth's minutest creature; she may find me:
If not, I am contented with oblivion,
As all the other millions. My sweet fair,
One little word of confidence and love,
From lips beloved, thrilleth more my heart

Than brightest trumpet-touch of statued Fame.
My bird of Paradise, tell me some news
Of your own home.—

[*Amala.*]　　　　My home should be your heart:
What shall I tell of that?—

[*Adalmar.*]　　　　Can you not see?
Truly the love that burns before thy image,
As sunny as a burning diamond,
Must shed its light without.

XXXVIII. *A Great Sacrifice*
Self-Compensated

[*Adalmar.*] True I have had much comfort gazing on
　　thee,
Much too perhaps in thinking I might have thee
Nearly myself, a fellow soul to live with.
But, weighing well man's frail and perilous tenure
Of all good in the restless, wavy world,
Ne'er dared I set my soul on any thing
Which but a touch of time can shake to pieces.
Alone in the eternal is my hope.
Took I thee, that intensest joy I have
Would soon grow fainter and at last dissolve
But, if I yield thee, there is something done
Which from the crumbling earth my soul divorces,
And gives it room to be a greater spirit.
There is a greater pang, methinks, in nature
When she takes back the life of a dead world
Than when a new one severs from her depth
Its bright, revolving birth. So I'll not hoard thee,
But let thee part, reluctant, though in hope
That greater happiness will thence arise.

FROM ACT IV, SCENE III
XXXIX. Song by Siegfried

LADY, was it fair of thee
To seem so passing fair to me?
  Not every star to every eye
    Is fair; and why
Art thou another's share?
  Did thine eyes shed brighter glances,
Thine unkissed bosom heave more fair,
· To his than to my fancies?
    But I'll forgive thee still;
    Thou'rt fair without thy will.
    So be: but never know,
    That 'tis the hue of woe.

Lady, was it fair of thee
To be so gentle still to me?
  Not every lip to every eye
    Should let smiles fly.
Why didst thou never frown,
  To frighten from my pillow
Love's head, round which Hope wove a crown,
  And saw not 'twas of willow?
    But I'll forgive thee still
    Thou knew'st not smiles could kill.
    Smile on: but never know,
    I die, nor of what woe.

FROM ACT V, SCENE I
XL. The Slight and Degenerate Nature of Man

PITIFUL post-diluvians! from whose hearts
The print of passions by the tide of hours

Is washed away for ever,
As lions' footmark on the ocean sands;
While we, Adam's coevals, carry in us
The words indelible of buried feelings,
Like the millennial trees, whose hoary barks
Grow o'er the secrets cut into their core.

FROM ACT V, SCENE IV

XLI. *Isbrand Dying*

Isbr....   Can I, that stand
So strong and powerful here, even if I would,
Fall into dust and wind?...
Imagine not that I'm weak enough to perish;
The grave, and all its arts, I do defy.

XLII

Isbr.... I jest and sing, and yet alas! am he,
Who in a wicked masque would play the Devil;
But jealous Lucifer himself appeared,
And bore him—whither? I shall know to-morrow,
For now Death makes indeed a fool of me.

XLIII

ASUNDER, burst asunder Chains or Heart,
And let my ghost go shrieking through the night,
Like a Death-angel lighted on the spire
Of Capitol asleep, bellowing woe.

POEMS

chiefly from 'The Ivory Gate'

[Composed 1829–48]

Doomsday

IF I can raise one ghost, why I will raise
And call up doomsday from behind the east.
Awake then, ghostly doomsday!
Throw up your monuments, ye buried men
That lie in ruined cities of the wastes!   5
Ye battle fields, and woody mountain sides,
Ye lakes and oceans, and ye lava floods
That have o'erwhelmed great cities, now roll back!
And let the sceptred break their pyramids,
An earthquake of the buried shake the domes   10
Of arched cathedrals, and o'erturn the forests,
Until the grassy mounds and sculptured floors,
The monumental statues, hollow rocks,
The paved churchyard, and the flowery mead,
And ocean's billowy sarcophagi,   15
Pass from the bosoms of the rising people
Like clouds! Enough of stars and suns immortal
Have risen in heaven: to-day in earth and sea
Riseth mankind. And first yawn deep
Ye marble palace-floors,   20
And let the uncoffined bones, which ye conceal,
Ascend, and dig their purple murderers up,
Out of their crowned death. Ye catacombs
Open your gates, and overwhelm the sands
With an eruption of the naked millions,   25
Out of old centuries! The buried navies
Shall hear the call, and shoot up from the sea
Whose wrecks shall knock against the hollow moun-
    tains
And wake the swallowed cities in their hearts.
Forgotten armies rattle with their spears   30
Against the rocky walls of their sepulchres:
An earthquake of the buried shakes the pillars

Of the thick-sown cathedrals; guilty forests,
Where bloody spades have dug 'mid nightly storms;
The muddy drowning-places of the babes;   35
The pyramids, and bony hiding-places,—

    .   .   .   .

'Thou rainbow on the tearful lash of doomsday's
    morning star
Rise quick, and let me gaze into that planet deep and
    far,
    As into a loved eye;
Or I must, like the fiery child of the Vesuvian womb,
Burst with my flickering ghost abroad, before the sun
    of doom   41
    Rolls up the spectre sky.'

A lowly mound, at stormy night, sent up this ardent
    prayer
    Out of a murderer's grave, a traitor's nettly bed,
And the deeds of him, more dread than Cain, whose
    wickedness lay there,   45
    All mankind hath heard or read.

    .   .   .   .

'What 's o'clock?'—
'It wants a quarter to twelve,
And to-morrow 's doomsday.'

Song

'Oh doomsday, doomsday come! thou creative morn
Of graves in earth, and under sea, all teeming at the
    horn   51
    Of angels fair and dread.
As thou the ghosts shalt waken, so I, the ghost, wake
    thee;
For thy rising sun and I shall rise together from the sea,
    The eldest of the dead.'   55

    .   .   .   .

'World, wilt thou yield thy spirits up and be convulsed
      and die?
And as I haunt the billowy main, thy ghost shall haunt
      the sky,
    A pale unheeded star,
When doomsday, doomsday, doth dawn at length for
      me.'
So having prayed in moonlight waves, beneath the
      shipwrecked sea   60
    In spectral caverns far,
On moonlight o'er the billowy main an old ghost
      stepped,
    And the winds their satire sung.

The Old Ghost

OVER the water an old ghost strode
  To a churchyard on the shore,
And over him the waters had flowed
  A thousand years or more,
And pale and wan and weary
  Looked never a sprite as he;
For it 's lonely and it 's dreary
  The ghost of a body to be
  That has mouldered away in the sea.

Over the billows the old ghost stepped,
  And the winds in mockery sung;
For the bodiless ghost would fain have wept
  Over the maiden that lay so young
'Mong the thistles and toadstools so hoary.
  And he begged of the waves a tear,
But they shook upwards their moonlight glory,
  And the shark looked on with a sneer
  At his yearning desire and agony.

Dream-Pedlary

I

If there were dreams to sell,
  What would you buy?
Some cost a passing bell;
  Some a light sigh,
That shakes from Life's fresh crown
Only a roseleaf down.
If there were dreams to sell,
Merry and sad to tell,
And the crier rung the bell,
  What would you buy?

II

A cottage lone and still,
  With bowers nigh,
Shadowy, my woes to still,
  Until I die.
Such pearl from Life's fresh crown
Fain would I shake me down.
Were dreams to have at will,
This would best heal my ill,
  This would I buy.

III

But there were dreams to sell,
  Ill didst thou buy;
Life is a dream, they tell,
  Waking, to die.
Dreaming a dream to prize,
Is wishing ghosts to rise;
And, if I had the spell
To call the buried, well,
  Which one would I?

IV

If there are ghosts to raise,
    What shall I call,
Out of hell's murky haze,
    Heaven's blue hall?
Raise my loved longlost boy
To lead me to his joy.
    There are no ghosts to raise;
    Out of death lead no ways;
        Vain is the call.

V

Know'st thou not ghosts to sue?
    No love thou hast.
Else lie, as I will do,
    And breathe thy last.
So out of Life's fresh crown
Fall like a rose-leaf down.
    Thus are the ghosts to woo;
    Thus are all dreams made true,
        Ever to last!

Alpine Spirit's Song

As I passed over the bridge I raised involuntarily my eyes and looked towards the perpendicular central rock of the Tödi towering above his mountainous brothers. At that moment a ray of the unseen sun broke through a slit in the cloudy mass in the sky and touched his snowy scalp. At another time I should have thought it more like inspiration descending on a hoary prophet, but now it reminded me of the last pale smile of my unknown fair. As I yet stood and looked, a song burst from the window of the hotel behind me:

I

'O'er the snow, through the air, to the mountain,
   With the antelope, with the eagle, ho!
   With a bound, with a feathery row,
To the side of the icy fountain,
   Where the gentians blue-belled blow.
Where the storm-sprite, the raindrops counting,
   Cowers under the bright rainbow;
     Like a burst of midnight fire,
     Singing shoots my fleet desire,
     Winged with the wing of love,
     Earth below and stars above.

II

Let me rest on the snow, never pressed
   But by chamois light and by eagle fleet,
   And the hearts of the antelope beat
'Neath the light of the moony cresset,
   Where the wild cloud rests his feet,
And the scented airs caress it
   From the alpine orchis sweet:
     And about the Sandalp lone
     Voices airy breathe a tone,
     Charming with the sense of love,
     Earth below and stars above.

III

Through the night, like a dragon from Pilate
   Out of murky cave, let us cloudy sail
   Over lake, over bowery vale,
As a chime of bells at twilight
   In the downy evening gale,
Passes swimming tremulously light;
   Till we reach yon rocky pale

374

Of the mountain crowning all,
Slumber there by waterfall,
Lonely like a spectre's love,
Earth beneath, and stars above.'

The music of the Sandalp she sang of could not have
come more startlingly to the brain of solitary shepherd
than these sounds to me.

Love-in-Idleness

I

He: 'Shall I be your first love, lady, shall I be your
    first?
Oh! then I'll fall before you down on my velvet knee
And deeply bend my rosy head and press it upon
    thee,
And swear that there is nothing more for which my
    heart doth thirst,
    But a downy kiss and pink
    Between your lips' soft chink.'

II

She: 'Yes, you shall be my first love, boy, and you
    shall be my first,
And I will raise you up again unto my bosom's fold;
And when you kisses many one on lip and cheek
    have told,
I'll let you loose upon the grass, to leave me if you
    durst;
    And so we'll toy away
    The night besides the day.'

III

He: 'But let me be your second love, but let me be your
   second,
 For then I'll tap so gently, dear, upon your window
   pane,
 And creep between the curtains in, where never man
   has lain,
And never leave thy gentle side till the morning star
   hath beckoned,
   Within the silken lace
   Of thy young arms' embrace.'

IV

She: 'Well thou shalt be my second love, yes, gentle
   boy, my second,
 And I will wait at eve for thee within my lonely
   bower,
 And yield unto thy kisses, like a bud to April's
   shower,
From moonset till the tower-clock the hour of dawn
   hath reckoned,
   And lock thee with my arms
   All silent up in charms.'

V

He: 'No, I will be thy third love, lady, aye I will be the
   third,
 And break upon thee, bathing, in woody place alone,
 And catch thee to my saddle and ride o'er stream
   and stone,
And press thee well, and kiss thee well, and never
   speak a word,
   'Till thou hast yielded up
   The margin of love's cup.'

VI

She: 'Then thou shalt not be my first love, boy, nor my
   second, nor my third;
 If thou'rt the first, I'll laugh at thee and pierce thy
   flesh with thorns;
 If the second, from my chamber pelt, with jeering
   laugh and scorns;
And if thou darest be the third, I'll draw my dirk un-
   heard
   And cut thy heart in two,—
   And then die, weeping you.'

Epilogue to Ernest's Story

Sung by NORMAN

HAS no one seen my heart of you?
 My heart has run away;
And if you catch him, ladies, do
 Return him me, I pray.

On earth he is no more, I hear,
 Upon the land or sea;
For the women found the rogue so queer,
 They sent him back to me.

In heaven there is no purchaser
 For such strange ends and odds,
Says a jew who goes to Jupiter
 To buy and sell old gods.

So there's but one place more to search,
 That's not genteel to tell,
Where demonesses go to church:
 So Christians fair, farewell.

Epilogue to Chapter I

EDWARD's *Song*

I

I THINK of thee at daybreak still
  And then thou art my playmate small,
Beside our straw-roofed village rill
  Gathering cowslips tall,
And chasing oft the butterfly
  Which flutters past like treacherous life.
You smile at me and at you I,
  A husband boy and baby wife.

II

I think of thee at noon again,
  And thy meridian beauty high
Falls on my bosom like young rain
  Out of a summer sky:
And I reflect it in the tear
  Which 'neath thy picture drops forlorn,
And then my love is bright and clear
  And manlier than it was at morn.

III

I think of thee by evening's star,
  And softly, melancholy slow,
An eye doth glisten from afar,
  All full of lovely woe.
The air then sighingly doth part
  And, or from Death the cold or Love,
I hear the passing of a dart,
  But hope once more and look above.

IV

I think of thee at black midnight,
　And woe and agony it is
To see thy cheek so deadly white,
　To hear thy grave-worm hiss.
But looking on thy lips is cheer,
　They closed in love, pronouncing love;
And then I tremble, not for fear,
　But in thy breath from heaven above.

Epilogue to Human Woe

By KENELM

I

WHEN we were girl and boy together,
　We tossed about the flowers
　And wreathed the blushing hours
Into a posy green and sweet.
　I sought the youngest, best,
　And never was at rest
Till I had laid them at thy fairy feet.
But the days of childhood they were fleet
　And the blooming sweet-briar breathed weather,
　When we were boy and girl together.

II

Then we were lad and lass together,
　And sought the kiss of night
　Before we felt aright,
Sitting and singing soft and sweet.
　The dearest thought of heart
　With thee 'twas joy to part,

And the greater half was thine, as meet.
Still my eyelid 's dewy, my veins they beat
    At the starry summer-evening weather,
    When we were lad and lass together.

III

And we are man and wife together,
    Although thy breast, once bold
    With song, be closed and cold
Beneath flowers' roots and birds' light feet.
    Yet sit I by thy tomb
    And dissipate the gloom
With songs of loving faith and sorrow sweet.
And fate and darkling grave kind dreams do cheat,
    That, while fair life, young hope, despair and death
    are,
    We're boy and girl and lass and lad and man and
    wife together.

The Tale of the Lover to His Mistress

AFTER the fall of Jupiter came Love one night to
Psyche: it was dark in her cottage and she began to
strike a light. 'Have done,' said he, in a low whispering
tone—in which the hinge of some dreadful dark truth
out of another world seemed to turn. 'Youth, power,
and heaven have passed away from the gods: the curse
of age has changed their shapes:—then seek not to
look on me, Psyche; but if thou art faithful, kiss me,
and we will then go into the darkness for ever.'—'How
art thou changed?' asked she; 'methinks you do but try
me, jestingly, for thou canst only have grown more
beautiful. That thou art more powerful I hear, for the

night air is full of rushing arrows, and many are struck and sigh. Hast thou lost thy wings that were so glorious?'—'Aye, but I am swifter than of old.'—'Thy youth?'—'Aye, but I am stronger: all must fall before me.'—'Thy charms and wiles?'—'Aye, but he whom I have once stricken, is mine for ever and ever.'—'Why should I not see thee then? art thou Love no more?'—'Aye; but not fleeting, earthly: eternal, heavenly Love.' —Just then the moon rose, and Psyche saw beside her a gaunt anatomy, through which the blue o' th' sky shone and the stars twinkled, gold promises beaming through Death, armed with arrows, bearing an hour-glass. He stepped with her to the sea-side, and they sank where Venus rose.

Dirge and Hymeneal

THE Bells rang out suddenly with a merry peal; on one side was a newly opened grave for the devoted head of [one of] the two youthful maidens, on the other the open church door at which the clergyman was waiting to pronounce the happiest blessing of life on the wreathed brow of the other.... So the jester of the Duke and the pet fool of the murdered Sebald were alone in the place. The former sate in the church porch playing with the wedding garlands, the latter with folded arms and vile melancholy under the ancient yew, half in the new-dug grave, and thus they sung:

SEBALD'S FOOL

Woe! woe! this is death's hour
Of spring; behold his flower!
Fair babe of life, to whom
Death and the dreamy tomb

Was nothing yesterday
    And now is all!
The maiden from her play
Beside her lover gay
    The churchyard voices call
        Tolling so slow,
            Woe! woe!

DUKE'S JESTER

Joy! joy! it is love's day;
Strew the young conqueror's way
With summer's glories young
O'er which the birds have sung,
Bright weeds from fairy rings;
    Here, there, away!
Joy, joy, the tree-bird sings,
Joy, joy, a hundred springs'
    Melodies ever say,
        Maiden and boy,
            Joy! joy!

THE FOOL

She cut the roses down
And wreathed her bridal crown.
Death, playful, culled her blossom
And tore her from life's bosom.
Fair maiden or fair ghost—
    Which is thy name?—
Come to the spectral host;
They pity thee the most
    And to the cold world's shame
        Soft cry they, low,
            Woe! woe!

The Two Archers

I

At break of bright May morning,
When triumphing o'er dark
The sun's inspired lark,
All sprites and spectres scorning,
And laughing at all creatures' joys
Who could not hang and dive and poise
In their own web and flood of noise,
Dropped out of his heart's treasure
The sunbeam's path along
Sparks and dews of song,
As if there were no pleasure
But to rise and sing and fly
Winged and all soul into the sky:

II

At break of this May morning
A maiden young and coy
Saw a wild archer boy
Flying around and scorning,
Birdlike, a withered bowman's arts
Who aimed, as he, at roses' hearts.
Each cried 'Come buy our darts,
They are with magic laden
To deify the blood;
An angel in the bud,
Half-closed, is a maiden,
Till opened by such wound she fly
Winged and all soul into the sky.'

III

'You archers of May morning,'
　　Said she, 'if I must choose,
　　Such joy is to peruse
　In the star-light adorning
The urchin's eye, that my desire
Is for his darts, whose breath fans higher
The smitten roses like a fire.'
　　So Love—'twas he—shot smiling
　　His shaft, then flew away;
　　Alas! that morn of May!
　Love fled, there 's no beguiling
　　Repentance, but by hopes to fly
　　Winged and all soul into the sky.

IV

So one December morning,
　　When the bold lark no more
　　Rebuked the ghosts so sore,
　When dews were not adorning
Aught but that maiden's cheek where wide
The blushes spread their leaves, to hide
The broken heart which such supplied;
　　She sought the pair of May-day,
　　And to the old one saith,
　　'Let thy dart, steadfast Death,
　Cure a forsaken lady;
　　Its point is but for those who'd fly
　　Winged and all soul into the sky.'

The Lily of the Valley

WHERE the hare-bells are ringing
 Their peal of sunny flowers,
And a bird of merry soul
 Sings away the birthday hours
 Of the valley-lily low,
 Opening dewily and slow
 Petals dear to young and fair
 For the prophecy they bear
 Of the coming roses—
The free bold bird of merry soul
Amidst his leaves cannot control
 His triumphant love of spring.

Thou bird of joyous soul,
Why can'st thou not control
 Thy triumphant love of spring?
I know that thou dost rally
 Thy spirit proud to sing,
Because to-day is born
 The lily of the valley.
Oh! rather should'st thou mourn;
 For that flower so meek and low,
 Born with its own death-bell,
 Only cometh to foretell
 Unpitying winter's doom,
Who in scorn doth lay it low
 In the tomb.

Vain is all its prayer:
It may flatter, as it will,
 The ungentle hours
 With its ring of toying flowers;
Unrelenting they must kill
 With their scornful breath,

For the very petals fair
　　Which the destined flower uncloses
　　　　In its innocence,
　　　　To plead for its defence,
By the prophecy they bear
　　Of the coming roses,
　　　　Sign the warrant for its death.

Dirge

LET dew the flowers fill;
　　No need of fell despair,
　　Though to the grave you bear
One still of soul—but now too still,
　　Since the still soul fled—
　　　One fair—but now too fair,
The lily being dead.—
For beneath your feet the mound,
And the waves that fleet around,
Have meaning in their grassy and their watery smiles;
And with a thousand sunny wiles
　　Each says, as he reproves,
　　Death's arrow oft is Love's.
Aye, doubt'st thou of the reading there,
　　About all nature's movements seek:
Thou'lt find Death has his dimples every where,
　　Love only on the lovely cheek.

Fragment

As veined petal closes over
　　A dewy spark
　　Ere Eve is dark,
And starry fireflies flit and hover,

Dreams of the Rose
O'er it repose;
So bend thy head, and sleep awhile
In the Moon's visionary smile.

The Rosy Hour

AND in that rosy rosy hour
When bird sung out and scented flower
Came words to me from heaven above:
'Awake, young heart, awake and love.'

The Flowery Alchemist

HIST, oh hist!
My pretty pale young violet,
Thy moony cheek uncover;
Lift that hood of fallen sky,
And my lips once more I'll wet
Against the dew-ball of thine eye.
Hist, oh hist!

So a leafy whisper said
Underneath a sweet-briar shade.
Guess the lady-blossom's lover!
'Twas the flowery Alchymist,
A stinging gay intriguing fellow,
The wildest bee in black and yellow.

Hist, oh hist!
My pretty pale young violet!
Glowworm's lightning blind me

387

When I leave my bud's embrace,
  When I traitorously forget
Thy cerulean baby's grace.
    Hist, oh hist!

The very next night he told the tale
To a little lily of the vale,
  And the poor young violet died of shame.
Oh! fie, thou flowery Alchymist,
  Thou stinging, gay, intriguing fellow,
  Thou wildest bee in black and yellow!

Song of the Stygian Naiades

'WHAT do you think the mermaids of the Styx were
singing as I watched them bathing the other day'—

I

Proserpine may pull her flowers,
  Wet with dew or wet with tears,
  Red with anger, pale with fears;
Is it any fault of ours,
If Pluto be an amorous king
  And come home nightly, laden
Underneath his broad bat-wing
  With a gentle earthly maiden?
Is it so, Wind, is it so?
All that I and you do know
Is that we saw fly and fix
'Mongst the flowers and reeds of Styx,
      Yesterday,
Where the Furies made their hay
For a bed of tiger cubs,
A great fly of Beelzebub's,

The bee of hearts, which mortals name
Cupid, Love, and Fie for shame.

II

Proserpine may weep in rage,
   But ere I and you have done
   Kissing, bathing in the sun,
What I have in yonder cage,
   She shall guess and ask in vain,
Bird or serpent, wild or tame;
   But if Pluto does 't again,
It shall sing out loud his shame.
   What hast caught then? What hast caught?
Nothing but a poet's thought,
   Which so light did fall and fix
   'Mongst the flowers and reeds of Styx,
         Yesterday,
Where the Furies made their hay
For a bed of tiger cubs,
A great fly of Beelzebub's,
The bee of hearts, which mortals name
Cupid, Love, and Fie for shame.

Silenus in Proteus

OH those were happy days, heaped up with wine-skins,
And ivy-wreathed and thyrsus-swinging days,
Swimming like streamy-tressed wanton Bacchantes,
When I was with thee and sat kingly on thee,
My ass of asses. Then quite full of wine—
Morning, eve—and leaning on a fawn,
Still pretty steady, and on t'other side
Some vinous-lipped nymph of Ariadne,
Her bosom a soft cushion for my right:
Half dreaming and half waking, both in bliss,

I sat upon my ass and laughed at Jove
But thou art dead, my dapple, and I too
Shall ride thee soon about the Elysian meadow,
Almost a skeleton as well as thou.
And why, oh dearest, could'st not keep thy legs
That sacred pair, sacred to sacred me?
Was this thy gratitude for pats and fondlings,
To die like any other mortal ass?
Was it for this, oh son of Semele,
I taught thee then, a little tumbling one,
To suck the goatskin oftener than the goat?

Lord Alcohol

'BEFORE we proceed to the solemnity of the corona-
tion,' said Norman who had now recovered some
spirits out of a bottle of Madeira before him (thanks to
the adulterators), after offering his congratulations to
the conqueror—'let me sing you a hymn of triumph,
in which I defend my own opinions on the subject of
this night's discussion....'

Song

I

WHO tames the lion now?
Who smoothes Jove's wrinkles now?
Who is the reckless wight
   That in the horrid middle
Of the deserted night
Doth play upon man's brain,
   As on a wanton fiddle,
The mad and magic strain,
The reeling, tripping sound,
To which the world goes round?
   Sing heigh! ho! diddle!

And then say—
Love, quotha, Love? Nay, nay!
It is a spirit fine
Of ale or ancient wine,
   Lord Alcohol, the drunken fay,
      Lord Alcohol alway!

II

Who maketh pipe-clay man
Think all that nature can?
Who dares the gods to flout,
   Lay fate beneath the table,
And maketh him stammer out
   A thousand monstrous things,
   For history a fable,
   Dish-clouts for kings?
And sends the world along
Singing a ribald song
   Of heigho! Babel?
     Who, I pray—
Love, quotha, Love? Nay, nay!
It is a spirit fine
Of ale or ancient wine,
   Lord Alcohol, the drunken fay,
      Lord Alcohol alway!

An Unfinished Draft

.   .   .   .   .

The snow falls by thousands into the sea;
   A thousand flowers are shedding
     Their leaves all dead and dry;
   A thousand birds are threading
     Their passage through the sky;
   A thousand mourners treading

The tearful churchyard way
In funeral array:
Birds, whither fly ye?—whither, dead, pass ye?
The snow falls by thousands into the sea.

The City of the Sea

FLOWED many a woodbird's voice, and insects played
On wings of diamond o'er the murmuring tide,
So on the billows of thy ocean's heaven,
Dark with the azure weight of midnight hours,
Thy marble shadow like a root of towers
Young city of the sea,—

The Father of the Deep

WHO passed by sea or land
Beheld an ancient monumental man
Aye sitting by coeval ocean's side,
Titanic, upright, with large eyes whose use
Was but to weep to them invisible
And therefore twice dread woes. His watch no man
Had seen begun, nor yet hath seen him end.
Turned towards sunset, wishing for his own,
He there expects the coming of his son,
Eldest of things created save himself,
Over the western billow—

Lament of Thanatos

I WAS to wait, to wait my only time of youth away—
As many a maiden isle far in the sea
From Adam to Columbus did for him
Who was its destined finder—
Silent as a mountain before it falls, or as the world
shall be on doomsday eve,
Keeping the secret of to-morrow's morn,
Still as a summer's noon—

Thanatos to Kenelm

And the Song by THANATOS

'I HAVE no feeling for the monuments of human lab-our,' she would say, 'the wood and the desert are more peopled with my household gods than the city or the cultivated country. Even with the living animals and the prevailing vegetation of the forests in this hemi-sphere, I have little sympathy. I know not the meaning of a daisy, nor what nature has symbolized by the light bird and the butterfly. But the sight of a palm with its lofty stem and tuft of long grassy leaves, high in the blue air, or even such a branch as this' (breaking off a large fern leaf) 'awake in me a feeling, a sort of nostalgy and longing for ages long past. When my ancient sire used to sit with me under the old dragon tree or Dracaena, I was as happy as the ephemeral fly balanced on his wing in the sun, whose setting will be his death-warrant. But why do I speak to you so? You cannot understand me.'—And then she would sing whisperingly to herself:

The mighty thoughts of an old world
Fan, like a dragon's wing unfurled,
  The surface of my yearnings deep;
And solemn shadows then awake,
Like the fish-lizard in the lake,
  Troubling a planet's morning sleep.

My waking is a Titan's dream,
Where a strange sun, long set, doth beam
  Through Montezuma's cypress bough:
Through the fern wilderness forlorn
Glisten the giant harts' great horn
  And serpents vast with helmed brow.

The measureless from caverns rise
With steps of earthquake, thunderous cries,
  And graze upon the lofty wood;
The palmy grove, through which doth gleam
Such antediluvian ocean's stream,
  Haunts shadowy my domestic mood.

Threnody

FAR away,
    As we hear
The song of wild swans winging
    Through the day,
The thought of him, who is no more, comes ringing
    On my ear.

    Gentle fear
    On the breast
Of my memory comes breaking,
    Near and near,
As night winds' murmurous music waking
    Seas at rest.

As the blest
Tearful eye
Sees the sun behind the ocean
Red i' th' west,
Grow pale, and in changing hues and fading motion
Wane and die:

So do I
Wake or dream

Lines Written in Switzerland

WHAT silence drear in England's oaky forest,
Erst merry with the redbreast's ballad song
Or rustic roundelay! No hoof-print on the sward,
Where sometime danced Spenser's equestrian verse
Its mazy measure! Now by pathless brook   5
Gazeth alone the broken-hearted stag,
And sees no tear fall in from pitiful eye
Like kindest Shakespeare's. We, who marked how fell
Young Adonais, sick of vain endeavour
Larklike to live on high in tower of song;   10
And looked still deeper thro' each other's eyes
At every flash of Shelley's dazzling spirit,
Quivering like dagger on the breast of night,
That seemed some hidden natural light reflected
Upon time's scythe, a moment and away: 15
Darkness unfathomable over it.
We, who have seen Mount Rydal's snowy head
Bound round with courtly jingles; list so long
Like old Orion for the break of morn,
Like Homer blind for sound of youthful harp;   20
And, if a wandering music swells the gale,
'Tis some poor solitary heartstring burst.
Well, Britain; let the fiery Frenchman boast

That at the bidding of the charmer moves
Their nation's heart, as ocean 'neath the moon   25
Silvered and soothed. Be proud of Manchester,
Pestiferous Liverpool, Ocean-Avernus,
Where bullying blasphemy, like a slimy lie,
Creeps to the highest church's pinnacle,
And glistening infects the light of heaven.   30
O flattering likeness on a copper coin!
Sit still upon your slave-raised cotton ball,
With upright toasting fork and toothless cat:
The country clown still holds her for a lion.
The voice, the voice! when the affrighted herds   35
Dash heedless to the edge of craggy abysses,
And the amazed circle of scared eagles
Spire to the clouds, amid the gletscher clash
When avalanches fall, nation-alarums—
But clearer, though not loud, a voice is heard   40
Of proclamation or of warning stern.

Yet, if I tread out of the Alpine shade,
And once more weave the web of thoughtful verse,
May no vainglorious motive break my silence;
If I have sate unheard so long, it was in hope   45
That mightier and better might assay
The potent spell to break, which has fair Truth
Banished so drear a while from mouths of song.
Though genius, bearing out of other worlds
New freights of thought from fresh-discovered mines,
Be but reciprocated love of Truth: 51
Witness kind Shakespeare, our recording angel,
Newton, whose thought rebuilt the universe,
And Galileo, broken-hearted seer,
Who, like a moon attracted naturally,   55
Kept circling round the central sun of Truth.
Not in the popular playhouse, or full throng
Of opera-gazers longing for deceit;
Not on the velvet day-bed, novel-strewn,
Or in the interval of pot-and pipe;   60

Not between sermon and the scandalous paper,
May verse like this e'er hope an eye to feed on't.
But if there be, who, having laid the loved
Where they may drop a tear in roses' cups,
With half their hearts inhabit other worlds; 65
If there be any—ah! were there but few—
Who watching the slow lighting up of stars,
Lonely at eve, like seamen sailing near
Some island city where their dearest dwell,
Cannot but guess in sweet imagining— 70
Alas! too sweet, doubtful, and melancholy—
Which light is glittering from their loved one's home:
Such may perchance, with favourable mind,
Follow my thought along its mountainous path.
  Now then to Caucasus, the cavernous.— 75

Fragment of the Same

YET who hath looked into the eye of truth
And seen mankind after the will of nature,
Should live the fair and innocent life of flowers.

The Phantom-Wooer

I

A GHOST, that loved a lady fair,
  Ever in the starry air
    Of midnight at her pillow stood;
And, with a sweetness skies above
The luring words of human love,
  Her soul the phantom wooed.

Sweet and sweet is their poisoned note,
The little snakes of silver throat,
In mossy skulls that nest and lie,
Ever singing 'die, oh! die.'

II

Young soul put off your flesh, and come
With me into the quiet tomb,
   Our bed is lovely, dark, and sweet;
The earth will swing us, as she goes,
Beneath our coverlid of snows,
   And the warm leaden sheet.
Dear and dear is their poisoned note,
The little snakes of silver throat,
In mossy skulls that nest and lie,
Ever singing 'die, oh! die.'

On Himself

Poor bird, that cannot ever
   Dwell high in tower of song:
Whose heart-breaking endeavour
   But palls the lazy throng.

Manuscript für des Nachtwächters Freunde.

———

AntiSt - raussian - ossianisch - oceanischer

Graus - Gruss

an einen

HERRN ANTISTES

von

Struthio Camelus,

gehaltlos – pensionirtem Professor in Zürich, nunmehr
Nachtwächter in Bülach,
Freunde der Religion in Gefahr, Mitgliede aller gelahrten Gesellschaften,
sämmtlicher Orden Inhaber.

———

Parturiunt montes, nascetur Rádicalis-mus.

HOR.

———

Die alte Baubo kommt allein,	*Upon a sowswine, whose farrows were nine.*
Sie reitet auf einem Mutterschwein	*Old Baubo rideth alone*
So EL.re dem, wem Ehre gebührt'	*Honour to her, to whom honour is due*
Frau Baubo vor! und angeführt'	*Old mother Baubo, honour to you!*
Ein tuchtig Schwein und Mutter drauf.	*An able sow, with old Baubo upon her*
Da folgt der ganze Hexenhauf —	*Is worthy of glory, and worthy of honour*
Faust	*Shelley s translation*

———◆———

Herausgegeben von der Gesellschaft für Veredlung
des Abtritt-Papiers.

Ueberall die Liberalen alle wiederhallend knallend fallen ,
Und die orthodoxen Ochsen Theorie - asch-grau [1]) und Bauer - harn - be-
           schauer-Auer-Ochsen grochzend bochsen.
Darum ist es , Herr Antistes , Antichristes wüsten Zwistes
Bald ein Ende : Und ich sende drum behende , ohn' Umstände , in die
           Häuser, und die Läuser-knackend Hände
Der geehrten , lieb - und - werthen längst bekehrten Schrift - Gelehrten
(Die nebst Eulen, und Postg-äulen und Froschk-eulen waren unsers Athens
           Säulen ,) diese ungefeilten Eilen - zeilen.
Kein Kreutz - otter Hottentotter Ott - eid - otter ,
Kein bigotter hugen-ott nota-B'lUnschlitt-gesotten Cotta-stotternd , lotter-
        bübisch , ratten - rotten - fangend - führend , Gott die Schlote fegend ,
        schlotternd Spotter .
Kein Zopf, Nachttopf, klopf d'rauf mein Tropf , grütz - und grenzen-
        los verstopfter , kropfig Goldschmidts kupfer-knopfig , klopfernas-
        hornmännisch , Knopper-kopf.
        Auch kein momento-mori-grinsend Semitory .
        Auch kein winselnd Insel - Pinsel [2]),
        Sondern flotter Paulus Potter [3])
Sollte schildern kühn in Bildern [4]) das Verwildern
Unserer puren Winterthur - und Zürcher Buuren , die nach Uhren , nicht
           Obse - uhren gingen , fuhren ,
Sich richteten , sichteten , und wie die Unterrichteten , aus der Kirche
           flüchteten ,
Bis die Macht die hält in Pacht Zion's Wacht auferwacht, gab nun Acht,
         und sah Küss - statt Mitter - nacht
        Leuchten durch die Geister - schlacht
        Ja , Antistes , Wahrheit ist es ; Hinter - list es
        Leugnet nicht : manches Licht ,
        Das der Bluntschli nicht gezogen ,
Manche schwere Irrlichts - Lehre , und des Schicksals Donner - hagels-
           schwaben - lichtputz - scheere

---

1) Grau, lieber Freund, ist alle Diarrhö — Faust.
2) Ein angelnder Anglikaner.
3) Grosser niederländischer Viehmaler. Sein bestes Stück (in Haag).
die pissende Kuh, erinnert einen an manches verchlichte Hornvieh, welches
mit harnsauren Thränen , wegen der Religion in Gefahr den wilden Sihl
strom vermehrt.
4) In Küh-Bildern. MS. Bodleian Cott. Nr. 666666 Z.

Hat sich auf dem Stuhl gewogen,

Frech und dreist, wo kein Geist [5]), sondern feister Leib, und weiss der
Guck-guck allermeist

Die Nacht [6]) der Papst [7]) und Sie mit Ehren allein gehören:

Denn per se, eine chaise percée

Ist der Stuhl, wo nicht Verkehrtheit, sondern göttliche Gelehrtheit,
und ehrwürdige Elwertheit [8])

Sass nicht demokr-atisch, Attisch, sondern dogm-und Elephanten
akrob-atisch.

Doch, Neumünster hat's vollbracht. Genug getagt!

Es werde finster! hat's gesagt,

Drum Hochschule, gute Nacht [9])

Das unmündige, sündige, in Windeln (Religionsch-Windeln) befindige
Volk sagt mit Populi-Dei-vox,

Fiat Nox!

Und am Berge steht der Ochs [10]).

Nicht der Schweizer Alexander, auch ein Glaubens-salamander, noch
Ferdinand der Stillste-Stander [11]),

---

5) Neuerlich kurirte ein hiesiger grosser Mediciner einen Geister
sehenden Kranken auf überraschende Art, er schickte ihn in den Versamm
lungssaal vom Glaubenscomité, wo er durchaus keinen Geist mehr sehen
konnte. Den Fall werde ich weitläufiger erzählen in der vielg-el-esel-en
Zeitschrift des Ritters von Pommer, Professors an der Alt-Hochschule.

6) Jeder kann sich ein sprechend ähnliches Bildniss von einem Haupt-
Finsterniss-Knacker, wie der Angeredete, leicht verschaffen. Man nimmt
irgend einen gewöhnlichen Stuhl und thut etwas Nacht oder Leib hinzu,
und da hat man einen Nacht- oder Leib-Stuhl fertig.

7) Wegen des bekannten Mythus von der Päpstinn Johanna wird jeder
neu-erwählte Papst auf einem topf-losen Nachtstuhl baararsch sitzend, von
den Cardinälen von unten beschaut. Habetne testes? fragt vox pop. Habet,
sagt violetter Strumpf-Chor. S. P. Q. Turicensis thut das wohl nicht bei der
Bürgermeisterwahl.

8) Der Parrer Elwert war als Gelehrter wohl eher dick als gross; doch
tanzte er blindlings unter den Dogmen-Eiern bei weitem flinker als z. B. E.
S. und ohne allen Anstoss mit den Knieen, wie Melchior.

9) Einige behaupten, die Anstalt bestehe noch; offenbar eine optische
Täuschung. Ein grosser Mediciner übt sich schon auf's Theetrinken für
Berlin ein, spottet darüber, dass der Zürcher-Thee (Université) zu Wasser
geworden sei u. s. w.

10) Ja wohl steht er; bald wird er aber verrecken an einem Antist-
esEl-ende.

11) Warum, fragt man unter allen Ständen, brachte man den Stillstand
nicht auf die Polizei, als er dem Ver-Stande die Fenster einschlug? Ad
vocem bitte ich in diesem meinem verständigen Vers-Tande die Aeusserung
von keiner Nation, ausser der Indig-nation, erblicken zu wollen.

Nicht Gottes Hofnarr, Pfarrer Zeller,
Nicht der fromme Mond - anbeller
Dort in Peter, schreiend Zeter,
Nicht Fraubasen - bebrillte - naseweisen östlichen Tagblätter - Läuse [12],
Nicht die greise Schlangenspeise [13])
Hieb den Knoten stark entzwei,
Sondern deine Sauer - Ei [14]).

Ja. Antistes, Wahrheit ist es:
Darum wend' ich diese Spende ohne Ende,
Reich mit Lobes - Elementen
Der Kreuz - Spinne der Kreuz - Kirche, und dem ✝ Correspondenten,
Nebst den andern Sacramenten.

Blindes Simson - Volk! Den Stempel
Drückt das Schicksal auf dein Leben.
Warst gerufen in den Tempel
Voll des Saft's der geist'gen Reben
Wie der riesig Juden - held;
Deine Stärke sollst du zeigen.
Zieh! die Säulen torkeln, weichen.
Die Gesetzes - Tafel schwankt,
Kracht das Dach, der Boden wankt.
Wissenschaft und Freiheit fällt.
Hier liegt Zürich! liest die' Welt.

Ja, du Volk, die Wahrheit ist es,
Ja auf Ehre, Herr Antistes.

T. L. Beddoes.

---

12) Es ist bekannt, dass quadrupede Esel nicht aufkommen können im Canton, wegen zu starker Concurrenz von Seiten D. Bs. und anderer. Gerold Meyer führt in seiner Statistik nicht einen auf. Wenn der östliche B. sich mit hinlänglich langen Ohren, wie z. B. mit den Past - Ohren in Andelfingen, Schwammendingen oder Stäfa versehen wollte, so könnte er als equus — haud aequus — Asinus allenthalben mit Ehren auftreten, jetzt ist er wenig mehr als ein Maulthier.

13) Nach dem Buche Genesis, Staub. Die Glaubensarmee soll mehr als ein Stäubchen in sich aufgenommen haben. Schade, dass in deren Reihen ein Major, der nicht mehr in auswärtigen Diensten steht, nicht zu finden war: der Major Amica Veritas.

14) Gelegt in's Straussen-nest. Man nennt sie auch Predigt. Ed. Füssli Sudel - ei

---

INDEXES

INDEX OF TITLES

405

INDEX OF FIRST LINES